Geological Survey of Canada
Miscellaneous Report 50

ROCKS AND MINERALS FOR THE COLLECTOR

The Alaska Highway; Dawson Creek, British Columbia to Yukon/Alaska border

Ann P. Sabina

1992

Available in Canada through
authorized bookstore agents and other bookstores

or by mail from

Canada Communication Group - Publishing
Ottawa, Canada K1A 0S9

and from

Geological Survey of Canada offices:

601 Booth Street
Ottawa, Canada K1A 0E8

3303-33rd Street N.W.,
Calgary, Alberta T2L 2A7

100 West Pender Street
Vancouver, B.C. V6B 1R8

A deposit copy of this publication is also available for reference
in public libraries across Canada

Cat. No. M41-8/50E
ISBN 0-660-14420-4

Price subject to change without notice

Author's address
Geological Survey of Canada
601 Booth Street
Ottawa, Ontario
K1A 0E8

Aussi disponible en français

CONTENTS

Maps

Plates

Frontispiece. Washing out gold in the Klondike, 1897. (National Archives of Canada/ C 16459)

Abstract

Occurrences of minerals, rocks and fossils are noted and described from localities along and adjacent to the Alaska Highway from Dawson Creek, British Columbia to the Yukon-Alaska border. Occurrences along roads branching from the Alaska Highway are similarly covered; these include the Klondike, Canol, Haines, Cassiar-Dease Lake, Atlin, and Sixtymile roads, and the Campbell Highway.

Our knowledge of mineral occurrences in the area covered by this booklet, is derived from information gathered by explorers, traders, missionaries, miners, and geologists who, in turn, garnered much of their information from their trusted Indian guides. The first mineral deposits to attract attention were the gold placers that were known to the fur traders and missionaries in the early 1860s. The first streams to be worked were the Liard River (1872), those in the Dease Lake-Cassiar area (1873), and the Big Salmon (1881) and Stewart (1883) rivers. The first utilization of minerals was by the Indians who used native copper of the White River area for weapons and tools, and probably the first building stone used was the basalt in the construction of the Hudson's Bay Company trading post, Fort Selkirk, in 1848. Lode metal exploration has been conducted since 1893 when the gold-antimony deposits in the Wheaton district were investigated. Mining operations commenced in 1899 at the Engineer Mine, and in the early 1900s at Atlin-Ruffner Mine, at the Whitehorse copper deposits, and in the Keno Hill-Galena Hill area. The recently discovered producers are the Anvil, Cantung, Cassiar, Churchill, Clinton Creek, Mount Nansen, and Wellgreen mines.

The mineral and rock collecting localities include road-cuts and rock exposures, lakeshores and river-beds, and active and inactive mines. Rock exposures along roads and rivers yield fossils and some minerals (calcite, barite, fluorite, etc.). Pebbles of jasper, chalcedony, epidote-bearing volcanic rocks, and quartzite are found along lakeshores and stream beds. Gold, copper, platinum, siliceous hematite ("black diamond"), scheelite, and cassiterite occur in stream placers. The various mines yield specimens of asbestos, serpentine, copper minerals, tungsten minerals, and ore minerals of lead, zinc, nickel, silver, and gold.

Minerals and rocks suitable for lapidary purposes include jasper, chalcedony, epidote, quartzite, jade (nephrite), serpentine, rhodonite, zoisite, siliceous hematite, and cassiterite ("Yukon diamond"). Gold nuggets are used in fashioning nugget jewellery.

Résumé

L'auteur note et décrit les manifestations de minéraux, les roches et les fossiles que l'on peut trouver le long de la route de l'Alaska, de Dawson Creek, en Colombie-Britannique, à la frontière Yukon-Alaska. Sont aussi comprises les manifestations qui se trouvent le long des routes qui se joignent à la route de l'Alaska comme les routes Klondike, Canol, Haines, Cassiar-Dease Lake, Atlin et Sixtymile de même que la route Campbell.

Les connaissances que nous avons des gisements minéraux de la région décrite dans cette brochure proviennent de renseignements recueillis par les explorateurs, les commerçants, les missionnaires, les mineurs et les géologues, renseignements qu'ils ont pour la plupart obtenus de guides indiens dignes de confiance. Les premiers gisements qui aient attiré l'attention sont les placers aurifères connus des commerçants de fourrures et des missionnaires dès le début des années 1860. Les premiers cours d'eau à avoir été exploités ont été la rivière Liard (1872), les cours d'eau de la région du lac Dease et de Cassiar (1873) et les rivières Big Salmon (1881) et Stewart (1883). Ce sont les Indiens qui ont d'abord utilisé les minéraux. Ils fabriquaient des armes et des outils avec le cuivre natif de la région de White River et la première pierre de taille à être utilisée a probablement été le basalte qui a servi à la construction en 1848 du fort Selkirk de la Compagnie de la Baie d'Hudson. L'exploration minérale se poursuit depuis 1893, soit depuis le moment où l'on a procédé à l'évaluation des gisements d'or et d'antimoine du district de Wheaton. L'exploitation minière remonte à 1899 (mine Engineer) et au début des années 1900 alors que la mine Atlin-Ruffner exploitait les gisements de cuivre de Whitehorse; d'autres travaux étaient aussi entrepris dans la région de Keno Hill-Galena Hill. Parmi les exploitants d'aujourd'hui, on compte les mines Anvil, Cantung, Cassiar, Churchill, Clinton Creek, Mount Nansen et Welgreen.

Les endroits où l'on peut recueillir des échantillons de minéraux et de roches comprennent des tranchées de route et des affleurements rocheux, les rives des lacs et les lits des rivières, des mines abandonnées et des mines en exploitation. Les affleurements rocheux le long des routes et des rivières renferment des fossiles et quelques minéraux (calcite, barytine, fluorine, etc.). On peut trouver sur les rives des lacs et dans le lit des cours d'eau des cailloux de jaspe et de calcédoine, des roches volcaniques à épidote et du quartzite. On rencontre aussi dans les alluvions de l'or, du cuivre, du platine, de l'hématite siliceuse ("carbonado"), de la scheelite et de la cassitérite. Les diverses mines peuvent donner des échantillons d'amiante, de serpentine, des minerais de cuivre et de tungstène ainsi que des minerais de plomb, de zinc, de nickel, d'argent et d'or.

Parmi les minéraux et les roches qui peuvent servir en joaillerie, on peut trouver du jaspe, de la calcédoine, de l'épidote, du quartzite, du jade (néphrite), de la serpentine, de la rhodosite, de la zoisite, de l'hématite siliceuse et de la cassitérite ("diamant du Yukon"). Les pépites d'or servent aussi à fabriquer des bijoux en forme de pépites.

ROCKS AND MINERALS FOR THE COLLECTOR: THE ALASKA HIGHWAY: DAWSON CREEK, BRITISH COLUMBIA TO YUKON/ALASKA BORDER

INTRODUCTION

This booklet describes mineral, rock and fossil occurrences along and adjacent to the Alaska Highway, and along the main roads branching from it.

Some localities are accessible by automobile, some by 4-wheel drive vehicles only. The condition of roads leading to inactive properties should be checked with local authorities prior to embarking on them. A few localities are accessible by boat or by float-equipped aircraft. Directions to reach each of the occurrences are given in the text, and are designed for use with official road-maps. Locality maps are included where deposits may be difficult to find. Additional detailed information can be obtained from the appropriate topographic and geological maps listed for each locality. These maps are available from the agencies listed on page 101. Unless otherwise stated, all geological maps are published by the Geological Survey of Canada.

Many of the inactive mines have not been operated for several years and entering shafts, tunnels, and other workings is dangerous. Due to safety reasons, collectors are not permitted to visit a few properties; their description is included only as a point of interest to the collector. Some of the occurrences are on private property and are held by claims; the fact that they are listed in this booklet does not imply permission to visit them. Please respect the rights of property owners at all times.

The localities were investigated during the summer of 1971 by the author ably assisted by Frances Gombos. The field investigation was facilitated by information and courtesies received from Dr. D.C. Findlay, Morrisburg, Ontario; from Dr. D.B. Craig, Department of Indian and Northern Affairs, Whitehorse; from Dr. R.G. Garrett, Geological Survey of Canada, Ottawa; from the staff of the Yukon Chamber of Mines, Whitehorse; from the Mining Recorders at Cassiar, Watson Lake, and Whitehorse; and from geologists and mine managers associated with the mines in the area. Information on the Dempster Highway was kindly supplied by Mr. S.P. Baker, Department of Public Works, Whitehorse, and by Mr. S.W. Horrall, Royal Canadian Mounted Police, Ottawa. Mr. C.F. Stevenson of Surveys and Mapping Branch advised on Yukon toponymy. The laboratory identification of minerals was performed by G.J. Pringle and M. Bonardi, Geological Survey of Canada. This assistance is gratefully acknowledged.

A brief geological history

Most of the area traversed by the Alaska Highway is within the Cordilleran Region, a geological province consisting of northwest-trending mountain belts separated by broad valleys and vast plateaux. This region is bordered on the east by the Interior Plains, a fairly flat area extending to the margins of the Canadian Shield; the first 560 km of the Alaska Highway is within this geological region.

In the Cordilleran Region, great thicknesses of sediments were deposited on the existing rocks from late Precambrian to late Mesozoic and early Tertiary times. In the Rocky Mountain

Table 1. Geological history

AGE (millions of years)	ERA	PERIOD	ROCKS FORMED	WHERE TO SEE THEM
	Cenozoic	Quaternary	Gravel, sand, till Volcanic ash	Lakeshores, stream-beds, eskers, moraines Alaska Highway: Whitehorse to White River; Klondike Road
63		Tertiary	Coal deposit Basalt, andesite Sandstone, shale, conglomerate Basalt	Coal River (B.C.) Road to Mount Nansen; Amphitheatre Mountain Slopes of Amphitheatre Mountain Miles Canyon, Whitehorse rapids
	Mesozoic	Cretaceous	Pegmatite Granodiorite, granite Sandstone, shale Basalt, rhyolite, andesite	Seagull Creek topaz occurrence Boundary Ranges; Ruby Ranges; Arctic Caribou Mine Kiskatinaw, Peace, Pine river exposures; Pink Mountain Mount Nansen, Yukon Antimony Mine
		Jurassic	Conglomerate Sandstone, argillite, greywacke	Five Finger Rapids Miners Range
		Triassic	Shale, sandstone, limestone Amygdaloidal basalt Basalt, andesite, volcanic breccia Limestone	Alaska Highway exposure between km 605 and 630 Canyon City area Kluane Ranges, km 1707 to 1759 (Alaska Highway) Whitehorse Copper Mines
240		Permian	Peridotite Argilite, tuff, basic lava	Canalask, Wellgreen mines; Atlin area Kluane Ranges (Burwash to White River)
	Paleozoic	Pennsylvanian	Chert, argilite	Anvil Range
		Mississippian	Sandstone, shale Limestone, argilite	Alaska Highway km 613 (creek exposure) Hills bordering MacDonald Creek; Lower Liard River bridge
		Devonian	Argilite, chert, greenstone Limestone	Cassiar Mine Alaska Highway, km 636, 907, to 916
		Silurian	Limestone Sandstone, limestone	Alaska Highway exposure, km 636.3 Alaska Highway exposure, km 907 to 916
		Ordovician	Shale, chert, limestone Dolomite, limestone, shale	Ogilvie Mountains Richardson Mountains
		Cambrian	Conglomerate Phyllite Limestone	Muncho Lake Faro Mine Cantung Mine
570	Precambrian		Quartzite Argilite Limestone, dolomite, shale	MacDonald Creek area; Alaska Highway km 638 Toad River bridge Mountains on either side of Good Hope Lake

area, these sedimentary rocks (limestone, shale, quartzite) have been folded and faulted, and eroded over a long interval of time (to early Tertiary times) producing the characteristic saw-tooth ridges. In the area west of the Rocky Mountains and of Watson Lake, the sedimentary strata were deformed and intruded by granitic rocks in Mesozoic time producing mountains that were eroded to almost flat surfaces over which lava flows spread during the Tertiary era. The land was subsequently uplifted, then deeply dissected forming mountain ranges and plateaux. The geological activity produced conditions favourable to the formation of the mineral deposits found in the Yukon and adjoining British Columbia.

The Interior Plains region is underlain by flat-lying or gently folded sedimentary rocks deposited during repeated cycles of inundation and sedimentation during the Paleozoic, Mesozoic and Cenozoic eras. These strata contain accumulations of oil and gas.

During the Pleistocene Period, most of the area was over-ridden by great ice sheets that moulded the landscape as we know it today leaving behind accumulations of sand, gravel, clay and till. Other deposits - beach sands, stream detritus, volcanic ash - are of recent times.

The geological history with examples of rocks formed is summarized in Table 1.

How to use this guide

The route is shown in Figure 1; it consists of the British Columbia and Yukon sections of the Alaska Highway, the Klondike Road, and other roads leading from the Alaska Highway.

Information on each locality is systematically listed as follows: km distances (in bold type) with principal mileage points along the highways starting at the beginning of each section; name of locality or deposit; minerals or rocks found in the deposit (shown in capital letters); mode of occurrence; brief notes on the locality with specific features of interest to the collector; location and access; references to other publications indicated by a number and listed at the end of the booklet; references to maps of the National Topographic System (T), and to geological maps (G) of the Geological Survey of Canada, and of the British Columbia Department of Energy, Mines and Petroleum Resources. Unless noted otherwise, geological maps listed are published by the Geological Survey of Canada.

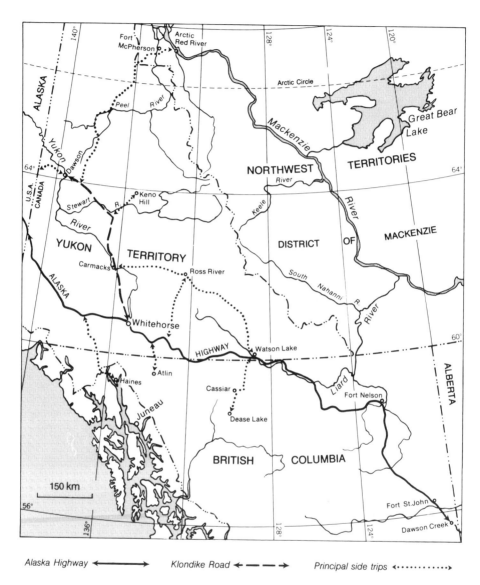

Alaska Highway ◄————►   Klondike Road ◄— — —►   Principal side trips ◄··········►

Figure 1. Map showing collecting route.

THE ALASKA HIGHWAY

km	0	Dawson Creek. Mile "0" of the Alaska Highway (Highway 97) is marked by a commemorative plaque at the east end of the town; the road log commences at this point.
km	1.6	Dawson Creek, at the junction of John Hart Highway.

Kiskatinaw River Occurrences

CHALCEDONY, FOSSILS

In sandstone, in shale

White chalcedony nodules occur in a sandstone layer between shale. The shale above and below the chalcedony layer contains microforaminifera fossils of Upper Cretaceous age.

The occurrence is exposed along the upper part of the steep bank of the Kiskatinaw River at a point 1.6 km north of Arras (sec. 15, tp. 78, rge. 17, w. 6th mer.). The Hart Highway bridges the Kiskatinaw River at Arras, 193 km from Dawson Creek.

Pelecypods occur in Cretaceous shale in the banks of the Kiskatinaw River east of Sunset Prairie (in N.E. 1/4 sec., tp. 79, rge. 18, w. 6th mer.).

To reach the occurrences proceed west along the Hart Highway; at a point 12.9 km west of the bridge at Arras, proceed north toward Sunset Prairie for a distance of 7.6 km to a road leading north 2.9 km to the Kiskatinaw River.

Refs.:   108; 118 p. 63-64; 124 p. 212, 217.

Maps: (T):   93 P/15 Sunset Prairie
             (G):   19-1961 Dawson Creek, British Columbia (1 inch to 4 miles)
                       1000A Northeastern British Columbia (1 inch to 10 miles)

Pine River Occurrences

FOSSILS, GYPSUM, PYRITE

In shale, limestone, mudstone

Pelecypods occur in Cretaceous shale on the north side of the Pine River valley, 3.2 km west of the mouth of Bowlder Creek. Pelecypods and brachiopods occur in limestone and shale exposed by railway cuts and roadcuts on the John Hart Highway at the West Pine bridge, 175 km from its junction with the Alaska Highway. Also reported from the Pine River valley, are ammonites in limestone, and gypsum and pyrite in shale and mudstone.

The John Hart highway parallels the Pine River, and bridges Bowlder Creek at a point 24.9 km west of Chetwynd (formerly Little Prairie), 101 km from the Alaska Highway.

Refs.: <u>65</u> p. 30, 31, 49; <u>91</u> p. 82.

Maps: (T): 93 O/9 Mount Hulcross
93 O/10 Callazon Creek
93 P/12 Commotion Creek
93 O Pine Pass
(G): 1000A Northeastern British Columbia (1 inch to 10 miles)
43-13A Mt. Hulcross - Commotion Creek, British Columbia
(Preliminary map, 1 inch to 1 mile)
Figure 2, Geological map of the Pine Valley area, British Columbia,
Sheets 1, 2 (1 inch to 1 mile, Bull. 52, B.C. Dept. Mines Petrol. Res.)

Plate I

Km 0, The Alaska Highway, in Dawson Creek, British Columbia. (GSC 159516)

km	32.7	Bridge over Kiskatinaw River. Sandstone and shale of Cretaceous age are exposed along the banks of the Kiskatinaw River.
km	41.8	The highway passes over the Kiskatinaw gas field, the first of several gas fields between this point and Fort Nelson.
km	56.3	Bridge over the Peace River at Taylor, a gas processing centre for natural gas from the Fort St. John area gas fields. Sulphur is also produced from the natural gas.

Peace River Valley Occurrences

GYPSUM, FOSSILS, CONCRETIONS

In shale, sandstone

Crystals of gypsum occur along fractures and bedding planes in shale exposed at several locations along the Peace River Valley. Cretaceous fossils, including ammonites and pelecypods, occur in shale at a number of localities along the banks of the Peace and Pine rivers, as indicated on Map 1. Plant fossils have been found in coal in Cretaceous sandstone on the north bank of the Peace River near Bear Flat, 16 km from the Alaska Highway on Highway 29. Concretions containing fossils (ammonites, pelecypods) have been reported from shale along the Peace River below the mouth of Wilder Creek. In the vicinity of Hudson's Hope, ammonites have been reported from Cretaceous shale along the bank of the Peace River upstream from the town and along cliffs of the islands in the Peace River at The Gates, 11 km northeast of Hudson's Hope.

Most of the exposures of the fossil-bearing rocks are along steep river banks. A road to the mouth of the Pine River leads west from the Alaska Highway just south of the Peace River bridge. Fossiliferous rocks are exposed at the mouth of Pine River, at the mouth of Septimus Creek and on the north bank of Pine River, 3 km further west. Access to the other occurrences is given in the succeeding pages.

Refs.:   8 p. 311; 66; 91 p. 91-92; 103 p. 72-74; 122 p. 96; 24 p. 210-213.

Maps: (T): 94 A/2, Fort St. John
                94 A/3 Moberly River
                94 A/4 Hudson Hope
                94 A/6 Bear Flat
                94A Charlie Lake
         (G): 17-1958 Charlie Lake, British Columbia (1 inch to 4 miles)
                1000A Northeastern British Columbia (1 inch to 10 miles)

| km | 58.8 | Junction, road on left leading west 2.6 km to fossil-bearing shale exposures along the Peace River bank. |
| km | 74.4 | Fort St. John, at junction road on left leading south 2.7 km to exposures of fossiliferous shale at a gravel pit. Fossils are also found in the exposures along the north shore of the Peace River opposite the islands east of the mouth of Moberly River (see Map 1). |

		Fort St. John, a Hudson's Bay Company trading post was formerly located on the north side of the river approximately opposite the mouth of the Moberly River. It was established in 1805 by Simon Fraser.
km	**75.1**	Turn-off (right) to Fort St. John business district. Several oil and gas fields are located in the vicinity of this centre. Processing plants for natural gas are located in Fort St. John and at the Boundary Lake Field, 45 km west of Fort St. John.
km	**76.3**	Road on left leads south 8.3 km to Fort St. John Historic Park. Fossiliferous shale is exposed along the Peace River west of the park.
km	**88.2**	Junction, Highway 29 to Hudson's Hope.

Road log to fossil occurrences described on page 7:

km	0	Junction, Alaska Highway and Highway 29; proceed along Highway 29 toward Hudson's Hope.
	14.5	Viewpoint overlooking the Peace River Valley at Bear Flat. Fossils occur in the exposures below the viewpoint. The highway descends to Bear Flat and passes over the Bear Flat gas field.
	62.1	Bridge over Farrell Creek.
	65.0	Bridge over creek. Fossils occur in the exposures up this creek.
	67.9-73.2	Fossils occur in the rock exposures on the north side of the Peace River, and along the to cliffs of the islands in the river. The openings between the islands are known as the Gates or Hells Gates.
	79.0	Hudson's Hope, a former trading post established by Simon Fraser in 1805. Fossils are found in the rocks exposed along the Peace River, 4.8 km south of Hudson's Hope. Highway 29 parallels the river at this point. West of Hudson's Hope, the Peace River flows through the treacherous Peace River Canyon.

Peace River Valley Deposits

GOLD, PLATINUM, COAL

In placers; in sedimentary rocks

Fine gold and platinum were found in a flat, known as Branham Flat, on the north side of the Peace River approximately 48.3 km west of Hudson's Hope. The Peace River Gold Dredging Company tested the deposit in 1923 and the yield was reported to be about 50 cents a cubic yard.

This portion of the Peace River was flooded by the W.A.C. Bennett Dam.

Bituminous coal was formerly mined on the east and west slopes of Portage Mountain which is on the north side of the Peace River Canyon, 19 to 24 km southwest of Hudson's Hope. The coal seams occur in sedimentary strata of Cretaceous age.

Coal was first observed along the walls of Peace River Canyon by the explorer Alexander MacKenzie in 1793. Initial production from the deposit was recorded in the 1920s. With the opening of the Alaska Highway, several mines came into production and the coal was transported by truck to Dawson Creek and Fort St. John. The mines discontinued operations when natural gas replaced coal as a fuel.

Ref.: 91 p. 140-141, 143, 150-151, 154-176.

Maps: (T): 93 O/16 Portage Mountain
       (G): 1000A Northeastern British Columbia (1 inch to 10 miles)

The road log along the Alaska Highway is resumed.

km	88.2	Junction, Highway 29 to Hudson's Hope. From this point to km 233, the Alaska Highway follows the height of land between Cameron River to the west and Blueberry and Beaton rivers to the east; the underlying rocks are sandstone, shale and conglomerate of Cretaceous age.
km	231.8	Sandstone quarry on right; the rock was used in the construction of the Alaska Highway.

Part of 94 A

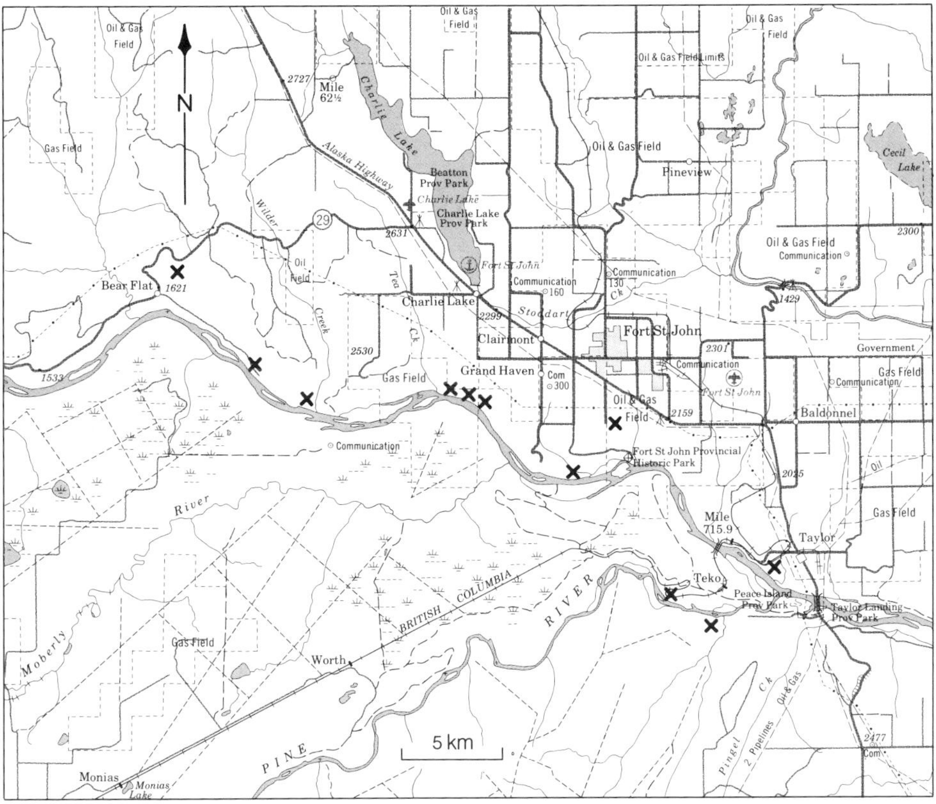

Map 1. Peace River Valley occurrences.

km	236.5	Bridge over Beaton River. Deposits of bog iron occur along the Beaton River at two localities: one is 0.4 km south of the river at a point 3.2 km upstream (west) from the bridge; the other is on the north side of the river 8 km upstream from the bridge (Ref.: 59 p. 20).
km	241	Pink Mountain is visible on left. The mountain is an anticlinal structure outlined by quartzitic sandstone. This rock is more resistant to erosion than the shales of the surrounding area resulting in a relief of 975 m. The summit is at an elevation of 1800 m. The rocks are of Cretaceous age.
		To about **km 322** the Alaska Highway was built along a plateau-like scarp that parallels the mountains to the west and was dissected by streams and rivers (Beatton, Sikanni Chief, Buckinghorse, Prophet rivers). From a distance, these deeply incised valleys have a mesa-like appearance. The scarp is composed of sandstone and shale of Cretaceous age. (Ref.: 59 p. 1-3, 14-15).
km	259.8	Bridge over Sikanni Chief River. Cretaceous sandstone and shale are exposed along the Highway at the bridge. The Alaska Highway begins a gradual ascent from the bridge at an elevation 812 m to 1261 m at the summit of Trutch Mountain at **km 306**, the highest point on the highway.
km	281.9	Bridge over Buckinghorse River.
km	314.9	Viewpoint overlooking Minaker River valley below, and Rocky Mountains in the distance. Road-cut opposite the viewpoint exposes sandstone and shale of Cretaceous age. Rusty brown concretions measuring several cm in diameter and consisting of a mixture of quartz and goethite are common in the shale.
km	332.6	Bridge over Beaver Creek.
km	362	The Highway follows the east side of the Prophet River valley to **km 471**. Prophet River is a preglacial stream (as are the major stream valleys along the Highway) so that the course of the river today is very much as it was before glaciation in Pleistocene time. Outcrops of bedrock consisting of Cretaceous shale and sandstone have been exposed by the river cutting through the thick deposit of glacial material and into the old river bank (Ref.: 59 p. 13).
km	475.5	Junction, road (on right) to Clarke Lake and Yoyo-Kotcho gas fields. Natural gas is produced and processed at Clarke Lake, the largest gas processing plant in British Columbia accounting for approximately one-third of the province's output. A pipeline transporting the gas to southern points joins the pipeline from Fort St. John west of Dawson Creek.
km	477.2	Bridge over Muskwa River. From Trutch Mountain, the Highway has descended to its lowest elevation of 305 m above sea level at this bridge.
km	483	Fort Nelson, originally established as a fur trading post, is now an important centre serving the natural gas industry.
km	522.3	Bridge over Raspberry Creek. In the distance to the right are the Poplar Hills.
km	539	Bridge over Kledo River.

| km | 560 | At about this point the Alaska Highway completes its course through the Interior Plains physiographic region which is underlain by Cretaceous shale and sandstone. For the next 80 km it traverses the Rocky Mountain Foothills belt which is characterized by nearly flat-lying shale and sandstone of Cretaceous age in the eastern part, and folded and faulted sedimentary formations of Triassic and Paleozoic age in the western portion. A number of flat-topped, mesa-like hills – remnants of former land surfaces – are conspicuous topographical features visible from the highway. The most prominant is Steamboat Mountain with an elevation of 1464 m. These mountains are capped by Cretaceous sandstone and conglomerate which resisted the erosion suffered by the more susceptible |

Plate II

Concretions in sandstone, shale beds, **km 315**. (GSC photo 159513)

11

shales which form the lower more rounded mountains and the deep valleys in between. The conglomerate is composed of pebbles of chert, quartz and quartzite (Ref.: 23 p. 3-6, 10).

km	**570**	The Highway begins a semicircular course around Teepee Mountain (on right), a fairly flat-topped hill rising to an elevation of 1310 m.
km	**575.2**	Sandstone exposure on right. This rock is also represented in the lower part of Teepee Mountain.
km	**580**	On right is Steamboat Mountain with its overhanging cliff on the east side. A little farther to the northwest is Table Mountain, another of the plateau-topped hills belonging to the same range as Steamboat and Teepee Mountains and capped by the same resistant rocks. The Alaska Highway parallels Tetsa River for the next 30 km.
km	**581.5**	Bridge over Mill Creek. Just before reaching this bridge, there is a view of Table Mountain featuring, near its eastern face, a large cube-shaped block of conglomerate positioned on one of its corners. The block has separated from the main mass of conglomerate capping the mountain. This separation is due to the erosion of the soft clay shale interbedded with sandstone that underlies the conglomerate. The same weathering process produced cliffs and precipices, and separated blocks extending from Steamboat Mountain to Table Mountain. (Ref.: 123 p. 24-25.)
km	**604.2**	Road-cut on right exposes coal-bearing shale with siltstone and sandstone. The rocks are Cretaceous age.
km	**605.6**	Road-cuts expose Triassic shale, sandstone and limestone. Ammonite and pelecypod fossils have been found in some of the exposures. (Ref.: 91 p. 38; 123 p. 22.)

Plate III

Mesa-like topography, **km 570**. (GSC 159523)

km	611-613	On the south side of Tetsa River fossiliferous limestone and shale are exposed along the river bed. Corals and brachiopods of Carboniferous age occur in the rocks. (Ref.: 109 p. 28-30.)
		At **km 613.8** limy sandstone and shale of Mississippian age are exposed along the valley of a small creek entering Tetsa River. Brachiopods occur in the rock exposed a short distance north of the Highway. (Ref.: 123 p. 20.)
km	616.7	No. 1 bridge over Tetsa River.
km	619.3	No. 2 bridge over Tetsa River.

Tetsa River Ornamental Quartzite Occurrence

In the river beds below the Tetsa River bridges, there are numerous pebbles and boulders of quartzite in various tones of red to maroon and white to cream. Many are banded and attractively patterned. The fine grained specimens take a good polish and are suitable for ornamental purposes. Also occurring in the river beds are boulders of grey limestone containing abundant fossil corals.

km	626.1	Road-cut on right exposes Triassic shale and limestone. Pelecypods and brachiopods occur in the rock.
km	630.6	Bridge over the north fork of Tetsa River. Boulders and pebbles of quartzite similar to those found in Tetsa River at **km 616.7** and **km 619.3** and of coral-bearing limestone occur in the river at the bridge.
		At about **km 629** the Highway begins its 15-km course through the Front Range of the Rocky Mountains. The rocks conspicuously exposed along the slopes and in 1.5 km-long road-cut (**km 635**) are grey limestones of Silurian and Devonian age.
km	631	Summit Lake on left. Summit Pass, the highest point along the Alaska Highway at an elevation of about 1280 m, comprises a 1.6 km section of road between this lake and a smaller one to the west. The peak on right is Mount St. Paul (2129 m) and the one behind Summit Lake is Mount St. George (2263 m). The highest peaks of the northern Rockies are 15 to 25 km to the south with elevations close to 2745 m. This range of mountains is known as the Stone Range.
km	634.6	Hoodoos on wooded slope on right. Erosion of the glacial till along the slope produced these pillars. Terraces of glacial till flank the lower slopes of the mountains to elevations of 213 m above the level of the Highway. Boulders of quartzite similar to those found along Tetsa River occur in the flats between the Highway and the ridges.
km	636.3	The Highway descends through a rock-cut to MacDonald Creek which it parallels for the next 22 km. Limestone of Silurian and Devonian age is exposed in the cut.

km	638.4	Bridge over 107 Creek. The stream bed on right exposes coral reef limestone of Devonian age along with underlying white to yellowish Precambrian quartzite. Nearby cliffs expose limestone containing coarse cleavable masses of white calcite (cleavages up to 20 cm across) and tiny cavities lined with transparent "micro" quartz crystals. Above the falls, erosion of the sedimentary strata has produced deep crevices in the rock.
km	638	The low rounded hills bordering MacDonald Creek are composed predominantly of shale, argillite, chert and sandstone of Devonian and Mississippian age.
km	639	Waterfall in gully on right. White massive barite occurs in a white calcite vein cutting grey limestone. Transparent purple fluorite is associated with the barite. The occurrence is exposed in the bed of the stream and on the left side of the gully about 30 m from the Highway.
km	643.6	Road-cut. White calcite coated with yellow jarosite occurs in the limestone on right.
km	645.0	Junction, road to Churchill Mine.

Plate IV

Hoodoos on mountain slope, **km 635**. Pebbles and boulders of quartzite in foreground. (GSC 159520)

14

Churchill Mine

CHALCOPYRITE, PYRITE, DOLOMITE, QUARTZ CRYSTALS, MALACHITE, ARAGONITE, MICA, AZURITE

In veins cutting sheared slate and calcareous siltstone

Massive chalcopyrite is the ore mineral. It occurs with pyrite in quartz-dolomite veins. Curved rhombohedral and platy crystals of colourless to white dolomite are associated with colourless terminated quartz crystals; tiny tetrahedrons of chalcopyrite were noted on the dolomite crystals. A bright green encrustation of malachite occurs on the vein minerals and on the associated rocks; on and near the malachite, aragonite has formed colourless to white aggregates

Plate V

Eroded clefts in limestone, **km 638**. White quartzite is exposed in the stream-bed, and boulders of quartzite and of limestone (coral reef) are strewn in foreground. (GSC 159519)

15

of microscopic acicular crystals. Massive bluish green mica occurs with massive white quartz. Azurite has also been reported.

The deposit was discovered in about 1945 by Albin Larson of **km 656**, Alaska Highway and staked by him and William Lembke, also of **km 656**, in 1957. It was originally explored by Magnum Consolidated Mining Company Limited, and underground development by an adit was commenced in 1967 by Churchill Copper Corporation Limited. The mine and mill (located 21 km from the mine) came into production in 1970. The ore averaged between 3 and 4 per cent copper. Operations were suspended in 1971 and were resumed for 15 months beginning in January 1974.

The mine is located at the headwaters of Delano Creek, about 4 km southwest of Yehde Lakes and 8.8 km northwest of Mount Roosevelt. A 53 km road connects the mine to the Alaska Highway at km 645. The mill and camp are located near the mouth of Delano Creek on the Racing River, 32 km from the Highway, and from there the road follows Delano Creek. About 24 km almost due south of the camp is Churchill Peak which, at 3202 m, is the highest mountain in the northern Rockies. It is capped by glaciers and ice-fields.

Refs.: 62 p. 21; 131 p. 95-96.

Maps: (T): 94 K/11 Racing River
              94 K Tuchodi Lakes

| km | 660.2 | Bridge over MacDonald Creek. Quartzite, limestone and shale are exposed beneath the bridge. Cavities in massive white quartz cutting the limestone are lined with "micro" crystals of quartz. |

Plate VI

Muncho Lake viewed from the north end with Terminal Range of Rocky Mountains in background. (GSC 159518)

		From here to **km 695** there are numerous exposures of Paleozoic shale and limestone cut by veins of calcite and quartz. The Highway follows the gorge of Toad River (**km 690-km 710**) with the Sentinel Range of the Rocky Mountains on either side. The highest peaks (elevations to 3000 m) of the northern Rockies are in this range, south of the Highway.
km	**673.7**	Bridge over Racing River. The valley of this river forms the boundary between the Sentinel Range and the Stone Range. Both ranges are composed of folded and faulted Paleozoic and Mesozoic sediments and the valley consists of relatively low, gently folded Paleozoic strata.

Toad River Hot Springs

About fifteen small pools fed by hot springs are located 20 m north of the Toad River at a point 2.5 km beyond its junction with the Racing River (13 km east of the Highway).

Access is by boat down the right bank of Racing River, then up the left bank of the Toad River.

Ref.:   91 p. 148.

Map: (T):   94 K/14 Toad Hot Springs

km	**703.9**	Bridge over Toad River. A road-cut on the west side of the bridge exposes argillite cut by veins of coarsely crystalline white dolomite. The rock is of Precambrian age and is associated with quartzite and slate which also form the peaks to the south.
km	**709.9**	Road-cut on right exposes grey limestone cut by veins of white calcite which, on exposed surfaces, has a layer of light brown calcite that fluoresces pale yellow under ultraviolet rays ("long" rays more effective than "short").
		The Highway swings north and follows a valley formed by the upper waters of Toad River, by the river itself, and by Muncho Lake. The Sentinel Range parallels the east side of the road.
km	**725**	Road-cut exposes buff-coloured calcareous sandstone.
km	**734.5**	Muncho Lake on left with the Terminal Range of the Rockies flanking its western shores. The lake, at an elevation of 818 m, is 12 km long and up to 1.5 km wide. Its emerald-green colour contrasts with the red conglomerate exposed along the west shore; beyond it to the west, limestone peaks reach altitudes of about 2165 m. The conglomerate consists of a red shale matrix with boulders of reddish quartzite, and is of early Paleozoic (possibly Cambrian) age. (Ref.: 123 p. 14-15.)
km	**746.9**	Viewpoint; Muncho Lake is viewed from its north end.
km	**775.7**	Exposure on left. White massive calcite occurs in grey limestone that is associated with black cherty rock. Also present are colourless crystals of calcite that fluoresce white when exposed to ultraviolet rays.

km	**790**	Bridge over Washout Creek. The Highway, in resuming a westerly course, leaves the Northern Rockies and follows the bench of Liard River for the next 80 km. This river forms the northern boundary of the Rockies. In the first 30 km (to Smith River), the Highway traverses Liard Plateau, an area of broad rolling valleys separating truncated ridges (to elevations of 1370 m) that extend north from the Rockies. The hills are composed of Paleozoic and Mesozoic sedimentary formations, and thick deposits of glacial silt cover the valleys. The valley of the Liard is heavily timbered and rock exposures along the road are few.
km	**797.7**	Bridge over Lower Liard River. Beneath the bridge, rock exposures include limestone and argillite of Mississippian age. Brachiopods and gastropods have been reported from the argillite, brachiopods and pelecypods from the limestone. (Ref.: <u>78</u> p. 1617; <u>123</u> p. 18.) Nodules of pyrite measuring up to 3 cm in diameter and white fibrous calcite occur in the limestone.
km	**798.9**	Junction, road to Liard River Hot Springs.

Plate VII

Liard River Hot Springs. (GSC 159511)

Liard River Hot Springs

Several mineral springs with temperatures of up to 50°C occur in this part of the Liard Valley now designated as a park area. Deposits of calcareous tufa in the vicinity of the springs are derived from the mineral water which is rich in sulphur and calcium but also contains magnesium, sodium, silicon and strontium. The smaller pool (near the dressing-house) is the hotter one, while the large one (90 m by 45 m) to the north has a temperature of 43°C.

Access is by automobile to the parking lot (about 155 m from the Highway), then by a footpath across a beaver pond to the springs.

This particular spot has been referred to as Tropical Valley where a trapper, Tom Smith, lived and gardened several plots of land. His cabin was replaced by a dressing-house.

Ref.:   123 p. 2, 8, 31-32.

Maps: (T): 94 M/8 Vents River
         (G): 1000A Northeastern British Columbia (1 inch to 10 miles)

km	801	Fluorite occurs in limestone about 11 km north of the Highway. The deposit was explored by Jorex Limited and Conwest Exploration Company in 1971; a truck road connects it to the Alaska Highway at **km 801**. (Ref.: 33 p. 1, 16.)
km	807.3	Bridge over Teeter Creek.
km	815.4	Rock exposure on right. Black coral reef limestone of Silurian age containing coarse cleavable masses of white calcite is exposed.
km	826.9	Bridge over Smith River. This river forms the eastern boundary of the Liard Plain, a drift-covered rolling plateau with low rounded hills and deep valleys; this physiographic province comprises most of the Liard River valley and the Highway is within it to about **km1095**. Sedimentary Paleozoic and Tertiary rocks underlie the drift.

Smith River Occurrence

JAROSITE, GYPSUM, ALUNOGEN, CALCITE

In shale

Secondary minerals have formed along the black shale exposure giving it a rusty appearance. Jarosite occurs as a dull rust-coloured to yellow coating. Associated with it are encrustations of: gypsum, as colourless to white flat microscopic crystals and as silky white flakes; alunogen, as, waxy white botryoidal aggregates; and calcite, as a greyish white powder.

The rock is exposed along the side of a ridge on the southeast side of the bridge over Smith River.

Ref.:   123 p. 8-19.

Maps: (T): 94 M/9 Teeter Creek
         (G): 1000A Northeastern British Columbia (1 inch to 10 miles)
              44-28A (Prelim. map) Alaska Highway, Fort Nelson to Watson Lake, British Columbia and Yukon (1 inch to 8 miles).

Liard River Placers

GOLD

In placers

Placer gold was mined from the bars of the Liard River near the Hudson's Bay Company's former trading post of Fort Halkett located at the mouth of Smith River. It was found in the gravels as far down as 13 km below the mouth of the Coal River.

The discovery of gold here in 1872 by two explorers, McCulloch and Thibert, marked the first time gold had been found in the Cassiar district and led to a prospecting rush that resulted in richer discoveries in the Dease Lake and Cassiar areas. The latter two deposits were worked for several years, but the Liard placers proved to be of little value.

Refs.:   42 p. 84B-85B; 70 p. 39A; 123 p. 27.

Maps: (T):   94 M/9 Teeter Creek
94 M/10 Grant Lake
94 M/11 Lower Kechika
(G):   1000A Northeastern British Columbia (1 inch to 10 miles)
44-28A (Prel. Map) Alaska Highway, Fort Nelson to Watson Lake,
British Columbia and Yukon (1 inch to 8 miles)

km	857.9	Bridge over Coal River. Chunks and masses of dark brown lignite coal and fragments of lignitized wood occur in the river bars beneath the bridge. It is derived from a coal seam along the bank of Coal River and in the bed of the river forming a rapid about 10 km due north of the bridge. The deposit is Tertiary in age. (Ref.: 123 p. 9, 25-26). Coal River joins the Liard River just south of the bridge. During the building of the Highway, the coal was used for fuel.
km	866.4	Turn-off (left) to Whirlpool Canyon camp-site. Tilted shale formation of Paleozoic age is exposed at the rapids of the Liard River at the camp-site.
km	877.1	Road-cut on right (at bend) exposes a banded rock consisting of interbedded light brown siltstone and black shale. White massive quartz with small cavities lined with "micro" quartz crystals and others filled with clay occurs in buff-coloured sandstone that is also exposed in the road-cut.
km	880.1	Bridge over Army Creek.
km	897.8	Bridge over Legull Creek.
km	907.8-916.8	Road-cuts on right expose buff-coloured calcareous sandstone and grey limestone. The rocks are of Silurian and Devonian age. (Ref.: 123 p. 9, 19). Coarsely cleavable white calcite occurs in the limestone at km 916.8.
km	917	Allen's Lookout onto the Liard River valley.
km	945.3	Shale cut by white cleavable calcite is exposed on right.
km	946.3	Bridge over Contact Creek. The creek is so named because it was at this point in 1942 that the northern section of the Highway from Alaska was joined to the southern section beginning at Dawson Creek.

km	974.9	Bridge over Hyland River.
km	997	Lower Post. A Hudson's Bay Company trading post was located here on the Liard River near the mouth of the Dease River. In the 1870s prospectors for gold followed the Dease River route to the placers in the Dease Lake and Cassiar areas.
km	1008.2	Yukon Territory border.
km	1022	Watson Lake, at the junction of Campbell Highway (Highway 4) leading to Ross River.

The Campbell Highway

The highway leads north from Watson Lake leaving the Liard Plain near the Simpson Lake camp ground; it then traverses Yukon Plateau, an undulating upland area dissected by deep river valleys and bordered by the Selwyn Mountains to the north and the Pelly Mountains to the south. The last 65 km of the section to Ross River is within the Tintina Trench which is a broad valley extending about 640 km in a northwesterly direction from near Ross River through Dawson City and into Alaska. The trench is the result of profound faulting and erosion. The highway has been built along the valleys of the Frances, Finlayson, and Pelly rivers and, between Frances Lake and Finlayson Lake, it parallels the east side of the Campbell Range which has peaks reaching elevations up to 1830 m. The valleys are thickly wooded and covered with unconsolidated glacial and alluvial deposits; exposures of rock near the road are few.

Cantung Mine

SCHEELITE, PYROXENE, GARNET, ACTINOLITE, EPIDOTE, TITANITE, AXINITE, TOURMALINE, ANTIGORITE, CHALCOPYRITE, CUBANITE, SPHALERITE, PYRRHOTITE, QUARTZ, CALCITE, MICROCLINE, BIOTITE, CHLORITE, FLUORITE, APATITE, PLAGIOCLASE, BISMUTH

In skarn zone in marble at contact of chert

Scheelite, the ore mineral, occurs in the rock as cream-white, medium to coarse grains distinguished from other white minerals by their white fluorescence under ultraviolet radiation. Associated minerals in the skarn include: dark green pyroxene (diopside-hedenbergite), reddish brown to pink garnet (grossularite-andradite), actinolite, epidote, titanite, axinite, tourmaline, antigorite, chalcopyrite, cubanite, pyrrhotite, quartz and calcite. Quartz veins cutting the skarn contain scheelite, microcline, biotite, chlorite, fluorite, apatite, garnet, actinolite, plagioclase and calcite. Specks of native bismuth have been reported from the vein material.

The deposit was discovered in 1958 by the Mackenzie Syndicate. Prospecting methods included panning and ultraviolet lamp-testing of the outcrops. In 1959, Canada Tungsten Mining Corporation Limited was formed to develop the orebody. Prior to the completion of the all-weather road to Watson Lake in 1962, supplies and equipment were flown in by float- and ski-equipped aircraft and helicopters. A camp was built in the Flat Creek Valley. Mining was conducted by an open pit restricted to the summer months until 1974 when underground operations began. The mill commenced operations in 1962; tungstic oxide (WO_3) and copper were produced. The mine ceased operations in 1986.

21

The mine is located on the northeast side of a mountain range that forms the boundary between Yukon Territory and Northwest Territories; it is within the Logan Mountains at an elevation of about 1677 m and overlooks the Flat River Valley. A 200 km road (Nahanni Range Road) connects it to the Campbell Highway at km 108. It follows the Hyland River valley and the east side of the Logan Mountains crossing the range at Harrison Pass a few km from the townsite of Cantung.

Refs.:   7 p. 28-29; 23 p. 510-513; 121 p. 390-393; 131 p. 74-75.

Maps: (T):   105 H Frances Lake
         (G):   4-1967 Geology vicinity of the Canada Tungsten mine, Yukon Territory
                and District of Mackenzie (1 inch to 800 feet)
                6-1966 Frances Lake, Yukon Territory and District of Mackenzie
                (1 inch to 4 miles)

King Jade Mines

NEPHRITE JADE

In serpentinite

A nephrite deposit found in situ in the Campbell Range of the Pelly Mountains near Frances Lake was staked in 1971 by Roy Sowden and Karl Ebner of Fort St. John. Two locations were staked: at the 1677 m level about 4.8 km due west of km 135 on the Campbell Highway and, at the 1677 m level approximately 11 km due west of the Campbell Highway at km 156. The jade occurs at the contact of a body of serpentine with Paleozoic sediments. Botryoidal jade occurs with the massive nephrite.

Ref.:   78a p. 37-38.
Maps: (T):   105 H/3 Klatsa River
         (G):   6-1966 Frances Lake, Yukon Territory and District of Mackenzie
                (1 inch to 4 miles)

km	1033.9	Bridge over Upper Liard River. Lignite coal occurs on the bank of the Liard River at localities approximately 6 and 10 km downstream from the bridge; it is associated with clay, shale and sandstone. (Ref.: 79 p. 19.)
		The Highway continues along Liard Plain, a relatively flat drift- and gravel-covered area with elevations between 610 and 915 m.
km	1044.1	Junction, Cassiar Road (Highway 37).

Side trip to the Cassiar and Dease Lake areas

km	0	Proceed south from the Alaska Highway onto Cassiar Road. For the first 48 km the road traverses Liard Plain.
km	33.0	Bridge over Blue River. Boulders and pebbles of amygdaloidal basalt occur in the bed of the river beneath the bridge. Some of the vesicles are filled with light greenish yellow transparent olivine.

km	48	The road begins its course through Dease Plateau, an area of low to moderate relief with elevations of up to 1525 m. The underlying rocks are of Paleozoic age. The road has been built along the drift-covered Dease River Valley.
km	64	From about this point southward for several km, the Horseranch Range is visible in the distance to the left. It forms a prominant ridge resembling a giant hogs back and extends in a north-south direction for 48 km. Its peaks reach elevations of up to 2226 m and there are numerous cirques along its flanks. The ridge is underlain by metamorphosed sedimentary rocks of Paleozoic age.
km	84	The road begins its course through the Stikine Range of the rugged Cassiar Mountains. A batholithic intrusion of granitic rocks, believed to have been emplaced in Mesozoic time, forms the backbone of these mountains for many km to the southeast and northwest. As seen from the road, the rocks are exposed above timberline (about 1372 m) in the jagged, saw-tooth peaks reaching elevations of 2287 m from Cassiar southward to within 16 km of Dease Lake. Cirques on the mountain slopes are visible from the road.
km	98	Good Hope Lake on left. The mountains rising from the lake are composed of red and green limestone, shale, slate and siltstone of Proterozoic age. Weathering of these rocks along the mountain slopes produces the attractive muted tones of red, brown and green as seen from the road.
km	104.8	Trail on left to the former Hudson's Bay Company post of McDame at the junction of Dease River and McDame Creek.
km	109.4	1st North Fork bridge. The abandoned settlement of Centreville was located in this area.
km	116.6	Hot Creek bridge.
km	123.6	Snowy (Snow) Creek bridge.
km	123.9	Junction. Cassiar-Stewart Road begins on left; road straight ahead proceeds to the Cassiar Mine (page 24) and to the town of Cassiar, a distance of about 13.5 km. The road log continues along Highway 37.
km	230	Dease Lake on right. The lake is 38 km long, less than 1.5 km wide, and its deepest point at Steamboat Point at the northern end is about 116 m. It is at an elevation of 811 m and it dissects Stikine Plateau – an irregular upland area separating the Cassiar Mountains from the Coast Mountains. The plateau in the Dease Lake area has elevations between 915 and 1220 m with isolated peaks to 1830 m, and it is deeply dissected by Dease Lake, Thibert, and Dease creeks, and by many other streams. Its approximate boundary is Canyon Creek to the north of Dease Lake and Little Eagle River to the west of the lake. The area on the east side and to the west of Dease Lake is underlain by Paleozoic sediments. The Arctic Divide is located about 1.5 km south of Dease Lake: streams on the north side flow to the Arctic Ocean, those on the south side to the Pacific. (Refs.: 53 p. 6-7, 11-18, 21-23, 88-90; 70 p. 44A-46A; 73 p. 77A-79A.)

Cassiar Asbestos Mine

ASBESTOS, JADE, GARNET, MAGNETITE, ANTIGORITE, PICROLITE, TREMOLITE, MAGNESITE, CALCITE, CLINOZOISITE, CHOLORITE, TALC, MICA, PLAGIOCLASE, GALENA, GARNIERITE

In serpentinite

Light greyish green cross-fibre chrysotile asbestos with fibres measuring up to 8 cm long, occurs in a massive serpentine rock intruding argillite, chert, quartzite and greenstone. Nephrite jade, varying from medium greyish green to a fairly bright green, is associated with the serpentine. Small grains of bright green transparent grossular are disseminated through the nephrite; on the polished surface they appear as emerald-green spots in a more subdued green matrix. Some microscopic grains of magnetite occur in the jade. Other minerals associated with the deposit are: antigorite (light green to almost black massive, and dark green platy) and picrolite (greyish

Plate VIII

Cassiar Mine in Cassiar Mountains, 1971. (GSC 159508)

24

green columnar) varieties of serpentine; white tremolite, as fibrous aggregates with fibres several cm long; white columnar masses of magnesite; massive light pink garnet; massive white calcite that fluoresces deep pink when exposed to ultraviolet rays ("long" rays more effective than "short"); light smoky brown prismatic aggregates of clinozoisite; chlorite; green to white foliated talc; mica, and plagioclase feldspar. The ore-bearing massive serpentine contains crystals of antigorite, pseudomorphs after orthopyroxene; they are known as bastite. Fibrous magnetite occurs in a shear zone along with other fibrous minerals such as picrolite and magnesite. Zoisite is associated with tremolite in altered greenstone. Galena and garnierite have also been reported from the deposit.

The asbestos deposit was found as an outcrop between 1830 m and 1952 m on the western flank of McDame Mountain which reaches an elevation of 2074 m. It was staked in 1950 by V.A. Stittler, R.L. Kirk, and H.H. Nelson of Fort Nelson, and R.W. Kirk of Lower Post, and development commenced shortly after by Conwest Exploration Company. In 1951 Cassiar Asbestos Corporation (now Cassiar Mining Corporation) began mining operations. Original mining was done by processing the asbestos fibre that formed a talus along the slope of the mountain in the outcrop area. Subsequent mining has been done by the open pit method. A mill began operations in 1953. The mine was connected to the mill (at an elevation of 1067 m) by a 10 km road and by a 5 km aerial tramway. The fibre was transported by truck to Whitehorse, then by rail to Skagway and finally by boat to warehouses in Vancouver. Another deposit to the southeast of the Cassiar Mine, was developed by adits driven into McDame Mountain. The mine was closed in 1992.

Refs.:   53 p. 123-126; 82 p. A211-A214; 96 p. A207-A212; 99; 107 p. 49-53; 138 p. 35-36.

Maps: (T):   104 P/5 Cassiar
                 104 P McDame
         (G):   1110A McDame, Cassiar District, British Columbia (1 inch to 4 miles)

Snowy Creek Jade Occurrence

JADE, RHODONITE

Jade (nephrite) and rhodonite are recovered from the gravels of Snowy Creek in the vicinity of the Cassiar Road which bridges the creek at km 123.6. (See road log on page 23.) The occurrence has been staked by Mrs. Mary Fentie of Watson Lake. Visitors to the area are reminded that collecting is not permitted where the claims are in good standing.

Maps: (T):   104 P/5 Cassiar
                 104 P McDame
         (G):   1110A McDame, Cassiar District, British Columbia (1 inch to 4 miles)

McDame Creek Jade Occurrence

JADE, RHODONITE, GOLD

In placers

Jade (nephrite), rhodonite and gold are recovered from the gravels of McDame Creek at Centreville. The deposit was staked by Mr. George Zimick and is operated by Centerville Placers Limited of Cassiar.

A road to the camp leads south from the Cassiar Road at the 1st North Fork bridge (km 109.4). (See road log on page 23.)

Maps: (T):   104 P/6 Good Hope Lake
               104 P McDame
        (G):   1110A McDame Cassiar District, British Columbia (1 inch to 4 miles)

Cassiar Gold Occurrences

GOLD

In placers

Placer gold was discovered on McDame Creek in 1874 during a gold rush to the Cassiar district following the discovery of gold on Liard River (1872) and in the richer placers in the Dease Lake area (1873). A nugget valued at $1,300 was found on McDame Creek in 1877; the total production from this stream was about $1,172,000 most of it being obtained prior to 1900 (gold was then worth about $17 an ounce) making this the second most productive stream in the Cassiar-Dease Lake area. Most of the mining was done on the north side of McDame Creek at Centreville and near the mouths of its tributaries; smaller yields were obtained from Hot Creek, Snowy Creek and from Quartzrock (Quartz) Creek. The gold was mined from gravels on benches of pre-glacial channels and from present stream gravels. It is believed to have originated in the gold-quartz veins cutting Paleozoic rocks in the mountains to the north.

In the early days, hand methods of mining were employed and, in about 1900, hydraulic mining was introduced. In 1949, Moccasin Mines Limited used a floating washing plant at its McDame Creek operation between the 1st North Fork and the McDame trail. A road was built from the Alaska Highway to McDame Creek in the winter of 1946-47 by Moccasin Mines Limited and the British Columbia government. Prior to that, access was via the Stikine River from the Pacific Coast to Telegraph Creek, then by truck road to Dease Lake and by boat to McDame Creek. A Hudson's Bay Company trading post was maintained until 1943 at McDame which is located at the mouth of McDame Creek on the Dease River. A paddle-wheel steamer operated briefly in about 1940 along the Dease River between McDame and Lower Post.

Highway 37 bridges 1st North Fork Hot Creek and Snowy Creek (see road log on page 23). The Cassiar Road bridges Quartzrock Creek at a point 5.5 km west of it's junction with Highway 37. The former operations are indicated on G.S.C. Map 1110A.

Refs.:   42 p. 82B-86B; 53 p. 2-3, 110-112; 60 p. 1-2, 12-13; 61 p. 59; 70 p. 33A-44A.

Maps: (T):   104 P/5 Cassiar
               104 P/6 Good Hope Lake
               104 P McDame
        (G):   1110A McDame, Cassiar District, British Columbia (1 inch to 4 miles)

Dease Lake Area Placers

GOLD, PLATINUM, COPPER

In placers

Gold was obtained from the gravels of Dease, Thibert, Mosquito, and Deloire creeks on the west side of Dease Lake, and on Goldpan and Wheaton creeks to the east of the lake. Dease Creek was the most productive in the Cassiar district with a yield of $2,000,000, over half being obtained in the period 1874-75. The gold was mined from high-level benches of old (probably preglacial) channels and from the low beaches of present streams. Early mining methods

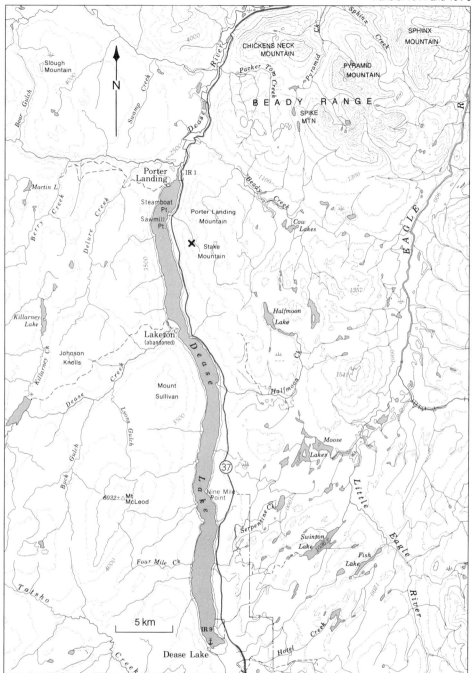

Map 2. Dease Lake area: jade occurrence.

included sluicing, drifting, open-cuts, tunneling and hydraulicking. Platinum was found on Thibert Creek, and native copper on Boulder Gulch (on Thibert Creek). A 396 g gold nugget was found on Depot Creek, a tributary from the south of Canyon Creek. Chromite, ilmenite, magnetite and manganese carbonate have also been reported from the gold placers; serpentine is abundant in some creeks.

This area was explored in the 1830s by the Hudson's Bay Company which set up trading posts on Dease Lake and on the Stikine River. Placer gold was discovered on Stikine River in 1861, and in the Dease Lake area in 1873. The latter was discovered by Henry Thibert who came up from the Red River country in Manitoba, met McCulloch and prospected with him on the Liard, then proceeded via the Dease River to Dease Lake. The Discovery claim is on Thibert Creek, 5 km above its mouth. The Dease Creek placers were discovered in the same year and other discoveries were made shortly after. As a result, the population rapidly rose to 2,000, the settlement of Laketon (on the west side of Dease Lake at the mouth of Dease Creek) came into being, a pack trail from Telegraph Creek to Dease Lake was opened by the British Columbia government, and beef cattle were introduced to the region from the upper Fraser Valley. Production declined steadily after reaching a peak in 1875 in spite of additional discoveries to the east of Dease Lake. Interest in the district was revived in 1897-98 during the rush to the Klondike because two of the overland routes (one from the Pacific via Telegraph Creek, the other from Edmonton via the Finlay River) passed through the area bringing an influx of prospectors. Attention was again renewed when the gold placers of Goldpan Creek were discovered in 1924. Hydraulic mining was applied to former workings, and the Provincial government rebuilt the pack trail from Telegraph Creek into a truck road to assist development. Another discovery was made at Wheaton (Boulder) Creek in 1932 but gold production in the district continued its decline.

The placers were worked at the following locations: Dease Creek, from its mouth on the west side of Dease Lake to Lyons Gulch; Thibert Creek, from its mouth on Dease River (north of Porters Landing) to Berry Creek, and in the mouths of its tributaries – Deloire and Mosquito creeks; Goldpan Creek, near its mouth on Little Eagle River, 15 km east of Dease Lake; and Wheaton Creek, near its mouth on Turnagain River, 56 km east of Dease Lake.

Access to the localities on the west side of Dease Lake is by boat from Dease Lake on the Cassiar-Stewart Road. There are no motor roads to the east of Dease Lake.

Refs.: 42 p. 61B-64B, 80B, 82B; 60 p. 13-14; 61 p. 56-61; 70 p. 33A-36A, 39A-69A; 73 p. 98A-99A; 97 p. 76-77.

Maps: (T): 104 J/9 Little Dease Lake
             104 J/16 Porter Landing
             104 J Dease Lake
             104 I Cry Lake
       (G): 21-1962 Dease Lake, British Columbia (1 inch to 4 miles)
             29-1962 Cry Lake, British Columbia (1 inch to 4 miles)
             2104 Dease Lake area, Cassiar district, British Columbia (1 inch to 2 miles)

Dease Lake-Cry Lake Jade Occurrences

JADE

Nephrite jade was first found in the Dease Lake-Cry Lake area in 1938 when W.J. Storie located jade boulders in Wheaton Creek while placer mining for gold. A boulder estimated to weigh 9t was reported from the stream. Wheaton Creek was soon after staked for jade, as were a number of other localities. The jade is believed to be derived from serpentinite associated with peridotite rocks in the district. Originally, the jade was found only as boulders; later it was

28

found in bedrock at Seywerd Creek near the north end of Dease Lake and in the Provencher Lake area, south of Cry Lake. The host serpentinite rocks occur in a belt extending 50 km southeastward from the south end of Englehead Lake to Kutcho Creek.

Jade has been produced from Wheaton Creek midway between its mouth and its junction with Alice Shea Creek, from King Mountain, Provencher Lake, Provencher Mountains, Letain Lake and from claims near the head of Seywerd Creek which enters the northeast end of Dease Lake at Sawmill Point, 2.4 km south of Porter Landing. Jade boulders have been reported from west of Dease Lake at Thibert and Delure creeks. Claims have been staked at these locations and, before collecting in the area, a check should be made with the Mining Recorder in Victoria to determine the status of the claims; collecting is not permitted in deposits for which the claims are in good standing. Wheaton Creek is located about 60 km (by air) east of the south end of Dease Lake. Access is by air from Dease Lake.

Refs.:   63 p. 119-126; 132 p. 498; 78a p. 31-35.

Maps: (T):   104 I/6 Snowdrift Creek
              104 I/7 Letain Lake
              104 J/16 Porter Landing
        (G):   21-1962 Dease Lake, British Columbia (1 inch to 4 miles)
              29-1962 Cry Lake, British Columbia (1 inch to 4 miles)

The road log along the Alaska Highway is resumed.

| km | 1105.7 | Bridge over Lower Rancheria River. The Highway proceeds westward along the deeply incised valley of the Rancheria River that dissects the rugged Cassiar Mountains. A granitic intrusion emplaced in Mesozoic time constitutes the core of the mountain system, and the granitic exposures can be seen from various points along the Highway. The peaks at this, the (northern) end of the Cassiars reach elevations of nearly 2135 m. |
| km | 1128.9 | Bridge over Boulder Creek (George's Gorge). |

Fiddler Yukon Mine

WOLFRAMITE, QUARTZ CRYSTALS, GALENA, SPHALERITE, CHALCOPYRITE, FLUORITE, SCHEELITE, MICA, MALACHITE, AZURITE, CASSITERITE

In quartz veins cutting crystalline limestone and phyllite

Dark brown blade-like crystal aggregates of wolframite occur in quartz that contains vugs lined with quartz crystals measuring up to 4 cm in diameter. Minerals associated with the wolframite include galena, sphalerite, chalcopyrite, green fluorite, scheelite and greenish mica. Secondary minerals – malachite and azurite – are also present. Tiny crystals of cassiterite have been reported to occur in fractures in quartz.

The deposit was originally staked in 1943 as a tungsten prospect for the Consolidated Mining and Smelting Company of Canada, Limited. The property was acquired by the Yukon Tungsten Corporation Limited in 1951; between 1951 and 1953, the company explored the deposit by trenches and an adit, and installed a mill. There was no production. Native Minerals Limited did further trenching in 1961-62.

The deposit is located at about 1555 m level of a ridge north of Boulder Creek.

Road log from the Alaska Highway at **km 1128.9** (see page 29):

km   0   Proceed north onto a rough road.

           4.3   Bridge over Boulder Creek; after crossing the bridge follow the right fork of the road. This part of the road is very steep and 4-wheel drive is required.

           8.4   Mine.

Refs.:   55 p. 80-82; 79 p. 16-17.

Maps: (T):   105 B/1 Spencer Creek
                  105 B Wolf Lake
         (G):   44-25A Alaska Highway, Watson Lake to Teslin River, British Columbia and Yukon (1 inch to 4 miles)
                  10-1960 Wolf Lake, Yukon Territory (1 inch to 4 miles)

---

km   **1162**   The Great Divide. The rivers on the west side of the divide, including the Morley and Swift rivers, flow westward into the Yukon River system, while the Rancheria River flows eastward into the Mackenzie River system.

km   **1180**   Bridge over Seagull Creek.

Seagull Creek Occurrence

TOPAZ, FLUORITE, COLUMBITE, TOURMALINE

In pegmatite

Transparent crystals of topaz have been found in a pegmatite dyke on the north face of a 1800-m mountain on the east side of Seagull Creek. The crystals obtained varied from colourless, light blue, yellow to reddish; some were of gem quality. Specimens from this locality have been acquired by several museums, including the National Museum of Canada. Associated with the topaz are light green fluorite and crystals of black tourmaline and black columbite. The deposit was a small one and is now thought to be exhausted. It was discovered and staked in about 1960 by the late Jack Shields.

The locality is approximately 7 km north of **km 1180**.

Ref.:   114 p. 570.

Maps: (T):   105 B/3 Seagull Creek
                  105 B Wolf Lake
         (G):   10-1960 Wolf Lake, Yukon Territory (1 inch to 4 miles)

---

km   **1188**   Road-cut exposes shale and argillite traversed by white quartz veinlets. "Micro" crystals of pyrite and white and colourless gypsum occur along fracture surfaces of the rocks. A rusty powdery coating on the rocks is due to ankerite. Graphite has developed along planes in shear zones.

---

km	1209	Swan Lake, formed by the widening of Swift River, is on left. Simpson Peak (2175 m), the highest peak of the northern Cassiars, is to the south of Swan Lake.
km	1220	For the next 65 km the Highway is within the Yukon Plateau, an undulating upland area incised by deep interlocking valleys; the rounded hills reach elevations of up to 1525 m. Precambrian and/or Paleozoic limestone, quartzite, greenstone, gneiss and schist outcrop in the vicinity of the Highway between Smart River and **km 1260**, and for the next 19 km the area is underlain by granitic rocks of Mesozoic age. (Ref.: 79 p. 6, 12.)
km	1292	Bridge over Nisutlin Bay.
km	1294	Teslin (formerly Teslin Post). From here to Johnsons Crossing the Alaska Highway is sandwiched between Teslin Lake on the left and the Big Salmon Range on the right. Teslin Lake is 95 km long, 2.5 to 3.2 km wide and 683 m above sea level. The Big Salmon Range with elevations of about 1980 m is part of the Pelly Mountain system. Extending westward from Teslin Lake is an upland formed of rounded summits visible from the Highway. The valley in which the Highway was built is drift-covered.
km	1308	Teslin Lake; Mackinaw Camp site. Jasper and chalcedony occur as pebbles along the shoreline of Teslin Lake.
km	1345	Junction, Canol Road (Highway 6). This road was constructed in 1944 as a World War II military project by the United States Army to service pumping stations along the pipeline that transported oil from the Normal Wells oil fields to Whitehorse. The road was originally 804 km long but the portion from the Yukon border in the Mackenzie Mountains to Camp Canol on the Mackenzie River opposite Norman Wells has not been maintained for travel; the Yukon portion is maintained for summer travel only, and except for Ross River, there are no facilities along the route.

Side trip along Canol Road to Ross River

km	0	Junction, Canol Road and the Alaska Highway; proceed north along the Canol Road. In the first 45 km of its scenic course, the highway cuts through the Big Salmon Range. Between this range and km 180, the highway traverses an area underlain by Precambrian schists, quartzites, slates, marbles, greywacke, greenstone and andesite; these rocks have, in places, been intruded by granitic rocks of Mesozoic age. The latter form the core of the Big Salmon Range and of the mountains to the west of Quiet Lake. Since the highway was built along the heavily drift-covered valleys of the Nisutlin, Rose, and Lapie rivers, rock exposures adjacent to the road are few.
km	16	Mountain pass at 1232 m. The highway begins its descent to the valley of Nisutlin River which it parallels to Quiet Lake.
km	47	Bridge over Sidney Creek. Placer gold was formerly obtained from the gravels of Iron Creek, a tributary of Sidney Creek, 14 km northwest of the bridge.
km	64	Bridge over Cottonwood Creek. Placer gold was obtained from this creek.

km	96	Campsite at Quiet Lake. This lake is 30 km long and up to 3 km wide. To the west of the lake, peaks of the Salmon Range rise to elevations of over 1830 m.
km	100	Mountain pass at 976 m; the 3 km descent to the Rose River valley begins. Placer gold was found prior to 1935 in Brown Creek, which flows into Sandy Lake, about 9 km west of the highway.
km	127	Cirques are visible on the mountains to the west.
km	129	In the course of the next 27 km, the highway passes over a belt of granitic rocks that form the backbone of the high jagged summits of the Pelly Mountains on either side of the road; the mountain peaks reach elevations of over 2135 m.
km	158	Rose Lake on right. Rose Lake and the Lapie Lakes are kettle-holes or depressions that resulted from the melting of stagnant masses of ice during Pleistocene time. An esker extending from the west side of Rose Lake to the west side of the southernmost of the Lapie Lakes is crossed by the highway at km 158. Other examples of glaciation in the area are terraces of sand, gravel and boulders along the valley walls.
km	161	Mountain pass at an elevation of 1098 m.
km km	162- 167	Lapie Lakes on left.
km	180	Sedimentary rocks (shale, sandstone, limestone and dolomite) of Paleozoic age underlie the area between km 180 and km 206, and form the St. Cyr Range of the Pelly Mountains on either side of the road.
km	185	Barite Mountain on left. Barite was found in veins, 30 cm to 3 m wide, traversing Paleozoic limestone on Barite Mountain, 2 to 3 km west of km 185. The barite is white, coarsely crystalline in some places, and finely granular in others. The occurrence is on the southwest side of a steep ravine between an elevation of 1464 m and the top of the mountain (elevation 1860 m).
km	188	Bridge over Fox Creek. Fox Mountain, the crowning peak of the Pelly Mountains at 2405 m is approximately 24 km west of this point.
km	190	Pyrite and galena occur in a quartz vein that cuts a shear zone in shale. The quartz vein is exposed along the road and along the steep bank of Lapie River on the right side of the road.
km	195	Glaicer Creek. The new mineral *lapieite* was originally found in a glacial erratic located along this creek about 100 m upstream from the highway (Ref. 60a).
km	206	The road descends into a northwest-trending trough-like depression known as the Tintina Trench or Tintina Valley. It is about 640 km long and, where crossed by the Canol Road, 13 km wide. It is the result of profound faulting and differential erosion. The Pelly, Stewart, Klondike and Yukon rivers occupy segments of the valley.
km	221	Pelly River. Placer gold was discovered in the Pelly River in 1882. Only fine gold was obtained and the productive streams were those entering the Pelly from the south between Lapie River (9.6 km west of the Canol Road crossing) and Hoole Canyon (29 km east of the crossing).

Plate IX

Atlin Lake looking south from the village. Pebbles of jasper and of serpentine occur on the beach. (GSC 159507)

km   222   Ross River. This settlement, at the confluence of the Pelly and Ross rivers had its beginnings as a trading post.

Ref.:   <u>75</u> p. 5-7, 11-12, 15, 18, 21-22, 23, 25-26.

Maps: (T):   105 C Teslin
                 105 F Quiet Lake
       (G):   45-21A Canol Road, Teslin River to MacMillan Pass, Yukon
                 (1 inch to 4 miles)
                 1125A Teslin, Yukon Territory, (1 inch to 4 miles)
                 7-1960 Quiet Lake, Yukon Territory (1 inch to 4 miles)

The main road log along the Alaska Highway is resumed

km	1345.9	Johnson's Crossing and bridge over Teslin River. The Highway, having skirted the Pelly Mountain region, returns to the Yukon Plateau which it follows for the duration of its course in the Yukon. Between Teslin Lake and Whitehorse, its route is along heavily drift-covered valleys separating peaks that rise 600 to 900 m above the valley floors.
km	1393	Junction, road to Atlin (Highway 7).

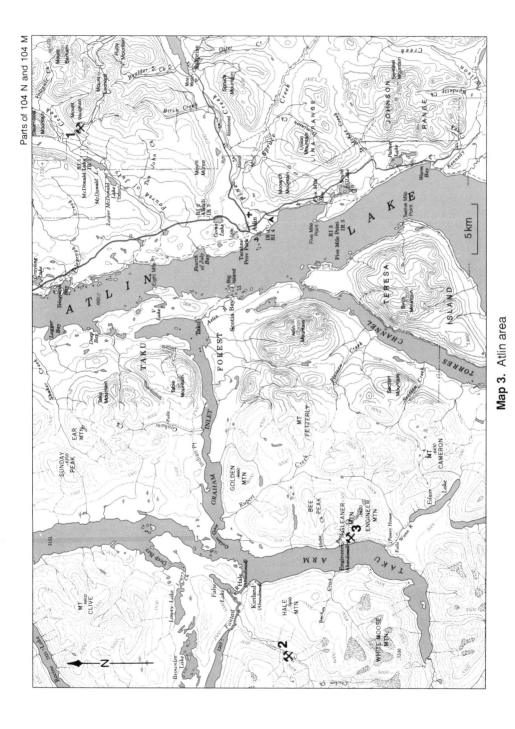

Map 3. Atlin area

1. Atlin-Ruffner Mines   2. Bighorn occurrence   3. Engineer Mines

km	0	Junction of the Alaska Highway and Highway 7; proceed south along Highway 7.
km	1.6	Junction; take the road on the left to Atlin Lake (road on right leads to Carcross). The entire 95 km road to Atlin Lake is within the Yukon Plateau. The road follows the east shore of Little Atlin Lake, then the valley of Lubock River, and finally the east shore of Atlin Lake. Mountains along the road reach elevations of about 1372 m near Little Atlin Lake, and close to 2135 m at Atlin Lake. Between the Alaska Highway and the northern end of Atlin Lake, the mountains are composed of Paleozoic sedimentary rocks while granitic rocks of Mesozoic age comprise the mountains along the northern half of Atlin Lake.
km	5-8	Road-cuts on left expose buff-coloured, compact limestone. Little Atlin Lake is on right.
km	42	Atlin Lake on right.
km	86.7	Junction, road on left to Fourth of July Creek and to Atlin-Ruffner Mine.
km	88.6	Bridge over Fourth of July Creek.
km	97.3	Atlin, at junction. The road on left leads to the shore of Atlin Lake. The rugged Boundary Ranges of the Coast Mountains form a back drop at the south end of the Lake. Also visible is the giant Llewellyn Glacier that sprawls for a distance of over 30 km from the south end of Atlin Lake to the Alaska border. To continue the road log, turn left at the junction.
km	97.7	Junction. The road straight ahead leads to Surprise Lake; turn right.
km	100.1	Bridge over Pine Creek.
km	113.3	Bridge over McKee Creek. Grey chalcedony and red and greyish jasper pebbles and boulders occur in the bed of the creek.
km	113.4	Road on left leads 1.6 km to the McKee Creek placer gold workings (see page 36).
km	120.3	Warm Bay. Hot springs are located about 6 km by trail south of Warm Bay.

Atlin-Ruffner Mine

GALENA, SPHALERITE, ARSENOPYRITE, CHALCOPYRITE, PYRITE, QUARTZ, CALCITE, ANKERITE

In shear zone in lamprophyre dykes

Galena, sphalerite and arsenopyrite occur with minor chalcopyrite and pyrite in a matrix of quartz, calcite and ankerite.

The deposit has been known since 1901 and was worked between 1921 and 1933; exploration work has since been done by various concerns including Atlin-Ruffner Mines Limited and Interprovincial Silver Mines Limited. The workings consisted of several shafts, adits and open-cuts. Gold, silver, lead and zinc were produced.

The mine is located at the 1190 m level on the northwestern slope of Leonard Mountain; it overlooks Fourth of July Creek. Access is by a rough 16 km road leading east from the Atlin Road at km 86.7 (see page 35).

Refs.:   2 p. 71-72; 3 p. 266-270; 38 p. 15A-24A; 131 p. 202.

Maps: (T):   104 N/12 Atlin
                    104 N Atlin
            (G):   1082A Atlin, Cassiar district, British Columbia (1 inch to 4 miles)

Atlin Placer Deposits

GOLD, IRIDOSMiNE, WOLFRAMITE

In placers

Gold has been produced from the stream gravels in the Atlin Lake area since 1898. The gravels of the following streams have yielded gold: Pine, Spruce, McKee, Birch, Ruby, Otter, and Wright creeks, and O'Donnel River. All localities are on the east side of Atlin Lake. Mining was done by pits, shafts and by hydraulic methods. Most of the activity was concentrated on Pine, Spruce and Birch creeks. The largest nuggets were obtained from Spruce and Birch creeks; nuggets weighing 2581 and 1120 g each were recovered from Spruce Creek. Iridosmine was reported from the black sand of Ruby Creek, and wolframite was recovered from Boulder Creek. In the period 1898 to 1945 Pine Creek was the highest producer with a yield of slightly over 4 000 000 kg for a value of 2.25 million dollars. Boulder Creek ranked second with about one half the yield, followed closely by Ruby and McKee creeks. The peak years of production were between 1900 and 1910. The discovery of gold in the Atlin area is credited to two prospectors from Juneau, Fritz Miller and Kenneth McLaren. Both the discovery and initial work were on Pine Creek, but other streams were soon being worked as a result of a prospecting rush that occurred a few months after the original discovery. By 1899 the population of Atlin included about 4,000 miners along with some 1,000 non-miners; various commercial operations owed their existence to the mining boom. The production of gold in the area has declined since 1946 and at present only a few operators work the deposits.

The gold-bearing creeks are indicated on Map 3. The most accessible of the old workings are those of Pine Creek along the road to Surprise Lake.

Road log from Atlin

km	0	Junction at Atlin; proceed east toward Surprise Lake.
km	0.3	Junction; continue straight ahead.
km	5.6	Junction; road on right leads to the Spruce Creek placers. Follow road on left.
km	8.8	Discovery. This is a former gold-mining centre which in the early days was known as Pine City. A few buildings dating back to 1898-99 remain on the site amid gravel tailings of former mining operations.

Refs.:   2 p. 74-77; 5 p. 121-179; 97 p. 80-81.

Maps: (T):   104 N/5 Teresa Island
                    104 N/11 Surprise Lake
                    104 N/12 Atlin
            (G):   1082A Atlin, Cassiar district, British Columbia (1 inch to 4 miles)

Atlin Lake Occurrence

JASPER, SERPENTINE

Along lake shore

Pebbles of red and brownish red jasper, and of dark green serpentine were noted along the shore of Atlin Lake in the vicinity of Atlin village. The serpentine is veined with chrysotile and contains tiny grains of magnetite.

Maps: (T):   104 N Atlin
        (G):   1082A Atlin, Cassiar district, British Columbia (1 inch to 4 miles)

Engineer Mine

GOLD, CALAVERITE, ANTIMONY, PYRITE, CHALCOPYRITE, LIMONITE, QUARTZ CRYSTALS, CALCITE, ALLEMONTITE, ROSCOELITE

In veins cutting shale and greywacke

Native gold in the form of grains, scales and leaves (measuring up to 2 cm in diameter) was formerly mined from this deposit. It was associated with calaverite, native antimony, pyrite, chalcopyrite and limonite in quartz-calcite veins. Slender crystals of quartz were found in vugs and calcite crystals in cavities in the veins. Large reniform masses of allemontite and flaky masses of green roscoelite have been reported from the underground workings.

The mine was originally worked from 1899 to 1906 by the Engineer Mining Company. Although rich pockets of gold were encountered, the mine was never an important producer. It was worked spasmodically until 1952 by various individuals and companies including: Captain James Alexander, Neil Forbes, T.J. Kirkwood and Walter Sweet; Engineer Gold Mines Limited. The property was mined by several tunnels and shafts and a mill was installed at the mine-site. Gold and silver were extracted from the ore.

An occurrence of native gold (flakes measuring up to 30 mm across) on Bighorn Creek was explored by adits in about 1910. Gold is associated with galena, chalcopyrite and pyrite in quartz veins cutting amphibolite.

The Engineer Mine is on the east shore of Taku Arm of Tagish Lake, 48 km from Atlin. The workings begin at the shore and extend 800 m eastward. Some of the old buildings remain on the site. Access is by boat from Atlin.

Refs.:   28 p. 74-99; 40 p. 13-14; 54 p. A60-A61; 69 p. C112-C114; 111 p. 95-101; 127 p. A39.

Maps: (T):   104 M/8 Edgar Lake
             104 M Skagway
        (G):   94 A Taku Arm, Atlin district, British Columbia (1 inch to 4 miles)

This is the last occurrence in the Atlin area; the road log along the Alaska Highway is resumed.

Part of 105 D

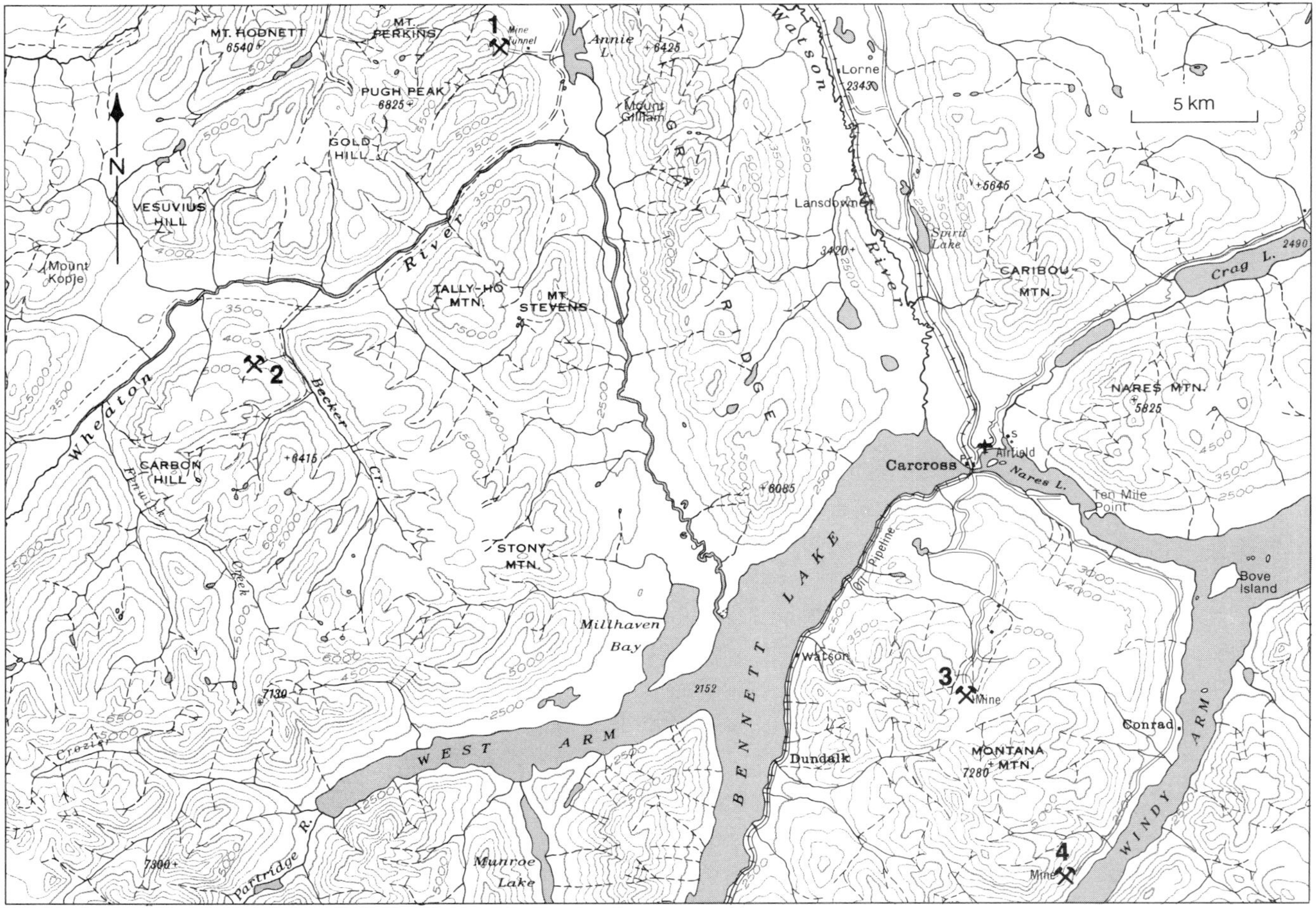

Map 4. Carcross area

1. Union Mines 2. Yukon antimony Mine 3. Arctic Caribou Mines 4. Venus Mine

km	1393	Jake's Corner; junction, road to Atlin (Highway 7).
km	1456	Junction, road to Carcross (Highway 2).

Side trip to Carcross

km	0	From **km 1456** Alaska Highway, proceed south along the Carcross Road.
km	18	Junction, Annie Lake Road to the Union Mines and to Yukon Antimony Mine (see page 40); road log continues straight ahead.
km	50	Junction; road on left leads 53 km to **km 1393** on the Alaska Highway. Continue straight ahead.
km	51.2	Junction; road on right leads to the Arctic Caribou Mine (see page 40). Road log continues along road on left.
km	68.1	Conrad. A few log buildings at the road-side mark the site of a former town that existed during mining activity in the Montana Mountain area. Stores, churches, several hotels and restaurants, and a mining recorder's office served the district. When active mining ceased in about 1912, Conrad became a ghost-town.
km	70.8	Venus Mine mill (on left) on the shore of Windy Arm.
km	72.4	Venus Mine. (See page 41).

Union Mines

GALENA, ARSENOPYRITE, SPHALERITE, PYRITE, CHALCOPYRITE, QUARTZ CRYSTALS

In quartz-calcite veins cutting greywacke

Arsenopyrite and galena are the most common minerals at this former silver-lead mine. The galena occurs in massive form and as aggregates of tiny cubes. Dark brown sphalerite and small amounts of pyrite and chalcopyrite are associated with the galena and arsenopyrite. Vugs in massive quartz are lined with transparent crystals of quartz.

The deposit was staked in 1908 by W.F. Schnabel and Mr. Northrop, and was worked briefly from a 41 m crosscut at the 1067 m level on the east side of Idaho Hill which overlooks Annie Lake. The mine was connected by an aerial tramway to the camp on Schnabel Creek at an elevation of 884 m.

Access is by a steep 1.6 km trail leading west from the Annie Lake road at a point 21.7 km from its junction with the Carcross road at km 18 (see above road log).

Refs.:　27 p. 129-139; 120 p. 135-136.

Maps:	(T):	105 D/6 Alligator Lake
		105 D/7 Robinson
	(G):	1093A Whitehorse, Yukon Territory (1 inch to 4 miles)

Yukon Antimony Mine

STIBNITE, GALENA, SPHALERITE

In shear zone in granitic and volcanic rocks

Stibnite, in massive form and as crystals measuring several cm long, occurs at this property. It is associated with quartz and is also found in a grey to black clayey material. Minor amounts of galena and sphalerite are associated with the ore.

The deposit is located on the east slope of Carbon Hill at an elevation of 1555 m near the head of Conglomerate Creek, a tributary of Becker Creek. The earliest exploratory work on the Carbon Hill deposits was performed in 1893 by two prospectors from Juneau, Frank Corwin and Thomas Rickman, who are also credited with the discovery of the Union Mines. These prospectors died shortly after their discoveries and the exact locations of the deposits were unrecorded. In 1906, the old workings were relocated and staked by H.E. Porter, and a prospecting rush ensued. The deposit was later staked by Theodore Becker and Howard Cochran. Intermittent development work was done exposing the deposit by trenches, stripping and tunnelling. The most recent work was conducted by Yukon Antimony Corporation Limited in 1965-66.

Road log from km 18 (see page 39) of Carcross Road (Highway 5):

km	0	Turn right onto the road to Annie Lake.
km	21.7	Turn-off to Union Mines; continue straight ahead.
km	27.0	Wheaton Creek crossing; from this point the road may be impassable for motor vehicles. The road follows the Wheaton River.
km	37.8	Becker Creek crossing; turn left and proceed along Becker Creek.
km	42.6	The road leaves Becker Creek and turns to the right (west).
km	46.7	Mine.

Refs.:   27 p. 3-4; 31 p. 43-49; 55 p. 52-55; 120 p. 132; 130 p. 380.

Maps: (T):   105 D/3 Wheaton River
               105 D/6 Alligator Lake
        (G):   1093A Whitehorse, Yukon Territory (1 inch to 4 miles)

Arctic Caribou (Big Thing) Mine

ARSENOPYRITE, PYRITE, GALENA, CHALCOPYRITE, STIBNITE, SPHALERITE, SCORODITE, QUARTZ CRYSTALS

In veins cutting granodiorite

Arsenopyrite, as finely to coarsely crystalline masses, occurs with minor pyrite and galena in quartz veins which in places contain vugs lined with small quartz crystals. Chalcopyrite, stibnite and sphalerite have also been reported. Scorodite is common.

The deposit was worked for gold and silver at various intervals since 1905 when Col. J.H. Conrad commenced work on this and other properties in the Windy Arm area. The original openings consisted of a 137 m inclined shaft and a 708 m adit. The most recent work was done in 1965 by Arctic Gold and Silver Mines Limited (formerly Arctic Mining and Exploration Limited). Some of the old workings were reopened, a new adit was driven and some trenching was done. A mill near the mine commenced production in 1968. Operations ceased in 1971.

The mine is located above timber line at an elevation of about 1708 m on the west side of Sugarloaf Hill, a peak on the north side of Montana Mountain. A rough road that leaves the Carcross Road at km 51.2 (see page 39) leads 6 km to the mill and continues for another 6 km to the mine. Visitors may collect specimens from the dumps, but the underground workings are dangerous and should not be entered.

Refs.:   25 p. 24-25; 55 p. 55-62; 20 p. 127; 131 p. 37.

Maps: (T):   105 D/2 Carcross
         (G):   1093A Whitehorse, Yukon Territory (1 inch to 4 miles)

Venus Mine

ARSENOPYRITE, PYRITE, GALENA, SPHALERITE, CHALCOPYRITE, CHALCOCITE, JAMESONITE, MALACHITE, YUKONITE, CERUSSITE

In quartz-carbonate veins cutting volcanic rocks

Arsenopyrite, pyrite and galena are the most common minerals in the deposit; sphalerite, chalcopyrite and chalcocite occur in minor amounts. Jamesonite, malachite, yukonite, cerussite and antimony ochre were found during early mining operations. The arsenopyrite carries values in gold, the galena carries silver.

This deposit was originally exploited by Col. J.H. Conrad in 1905. Ore was obtained from adits driven into the eastern slope of Montana Mountain above Windy Arm (Tagish Lake) and was transported to a mill on the shoreline by an aerial tramway. The ore was then carried by boat to the railway at Carcross. Between 1905 and 1915, 5442 t of ore are reported to have been mined and shipped to smelters. Underground work was resumed in 1966 by Venus Mines Limited. A mill was installed and commenced operations in 1970. The mine was closed in 1971. It is located on Highway 2 at km 72.4 (see page 39).

Refs.:   25 p. 25; 50 p. 62-64; 120 p. 129-130; 131 p. 386.

Maps: (T):   105 D/2 Carcross
         (G):   1093A Whitehorse, Yukon Territory (1 inch to 4 miles)

The road log along the Alaska Highway continues.

km	1455.8	Junction Carcross Road (Highway No. 5).
km	1467.1	Turn-off (right) to Miles Canyon. The Yukon River flows through Miles Canyon, a gorge 915 m long and 27 m wide; in passing through the canyon, the river drops 5 m. The rocks exposed along the almost vertical walls of the canyon are basalt. From the Robert Lowe footbridge that bridges the canyon, the well-developed columnar jointing of the basalt can be observed. Pebbles of nephrite jade have been reported from the gravels of the Yukon River in the vicinity of Miles Canyon (Ref.: 42 p. 38B).
km	1468.7	Turn-off (left) to Whitehorse copper mines.

Whitehorse Copper Mines

CHALCOPYRITE, BORNITE, TETRAHEDRITE, CHALCOCITE, CUPRITE, MELACO-
NITE, COVELLITE, NATIVE COPPER, VALERIITE, CHRYSOCOLLA, MALACHITE,
AZURITE, BROCHANTITE, POSNJAKITE, PYRITE, MAGNETITE, HEMATITE, MO-
LYBDENITE, PYRRHOTITE, ARSENOPYRITE, STIBNITE, GALENA, SPHALERITE,
EPIDOTE, GARNET, DIOPSIDE, PLAGIOCLASE, SERPENTINE, TREMOLITE-ACTI-
NOLITE, CALCITE, SCAPOLITE, WOLLASTONITE, STILBITE, LAUMONTITE, CH-
ABAZITE, VESUVIANITE, TALC, ARAGONITE, CHLORITE, QUARTZ CRYSTALS,
JAROSITE, GOETHITE, TITANITE, PEROVSKITE, ORTHOCLASE, ZOISITE

In a skarn zone at the contact of limestone and granitic rocks

Chalcopyrite and bornite are the chief ore minerals of the Whitehorse copper deposits which consist of a number of properties that extend along a northwest-trending belt for 30 km, from the Cowley Lakes to Porter Creek. Other copper minerals associated with the deposits are tetrahedrite, chalcocite, cuprite, melaconite, covellite, native copper and valeriite. Colourful specimens of secondary copper minerals can be found on the dumps; included are: chrysocolla, as bright blue and bright green porcelain-like crusts and botryoidal encrustations; malachite, as dull to bright green finely granular and acicular aggregates; azurite, as bright blue powdery coatings; brochantite, as bright green crusts; posnjakite, as greenish blue powder. The brochan-tite was found at the War Eagle Mine, the posnjakite at the Copper King Mine. Metallic minerals are: pyrite, magnetite, hematite (specularite), molybdenite, pyrrhotite, arsenopyrite, stibnite, galena and sphalerite. Of these, magnetite and hematite are the most common. A number of nonmetallic minerals occur in the skarn zone. The most abundant are light yellow to yellowish green prismatic crystals and crystalline aggregates of epidote, yellowish to reddish brown massive garnet, green diopside, plagioclase, yellowish green to olive-green serpentine, grey and light to dark green tremolite-actinolite and white and salmon-pink calcite. Scapolite, as white columnar aggregates (fluoresces pink under "short" ultraviolet rays), and wollastonite, as colourless to light yellow and white prismatic aggregates, are less abundant. The following have also been identified from the deposit: stilbite, as colourless and white, radiating blade-like and botryoidal aggregates; laumontite, as white, striated flat crystal aggregates on feldspar; chabazite, as tiny transparent rhombs in cavities in a garnet-epidote matrix; vesuvianite, in light brown transparent massive form; talc, as white flaky masses; aragonite, as a white waxy crust on garnet and pyroxene; dark green chlorite; "micro" crystals of colourless quartz in cavities; colourless to light brown mica; yellow powdery jarosite; rusty brown powdery goethite; titanite, as dark brown grains associated with garnet; perovskite (rare), as shiny black grains in serpentine and calcite; and pink orthoclase. Attractive pink massive zoisite was found in the dumps of the Little Chief mine; it is intimately associated with white plagioclase and green pyroxene, producing a mottled effect. It takes a good polish and can be used for jewellery. Blotches of brown garnet are scattered throughout this rock. Massive greenish yellow serpen-tine speckled with magnetite grains also occurs at the Little Chief Mine; it is suitable for ornamental purposes. At the Pueblo Mine dumps, specimens of specular hematite and of secondary copper minerals (chrysocolla, malachite) are abundant. Wollastonite, garnet and serpentine (yellow-green, olive-green, amber) are common in the dumps of the Copper King Mine.

Outcrops of copper-bearing rocks in the Whitehorse copper belt where first noted by miners en route to the Klondike during the gold rush of 1897. The first claim was staked in 1898 by Jack McIntyre on the Copper King deposit. Other claims staked in 1898 were the Ora by John Hanly, the Anaconda by W.A. Puckett, and the Big and Little Chief by Wm. McTaggart and Andrew Oleson. In 1899, the Pueblo, Best Chance, Arctic Chief, Grafter, Valerie, War Eagle and others were claimed, and development of the Copper King, Anaconda and Pueblo commenced. The first shipment of ore was made in 1900 by Messrs McIntyre and Granger from the Copper King

Plate X

Miles Canyon, Yukon River; basalt is exposed along the vertical canyon walls. (GSC 159528)

Mine. In the next four years, production was also recorded from the Valerie and Arctic Chief mines, and development work was performed on several other properties. A 20 km railway spur was built in 1909 from McRae to the Pueblo Mine to connect the mines to the White Pass and Yukon Railway. Production was recorded from the mines from 1929 to 1930. In 1963, New Imperial Mines Limited (renamed later as Whitehorse Copper Mines Limited) commenced work on several of the old properties; work consisted of open pits at the Little Chief, Arctic Chief, Black Cub and War Eagle properties, and underground development of the little Chief and Middle Chief orebodies. A mill near the Little Chief Mine began operations in 1967, and a road was built connecting it to the War Eagle pit. Operations closed at the end of 1982 due to ore exhaustion.

The mill is located 3.7 km by road from **km 1468.7** of the Alaska Highway (see page 41).

Road log to Copper King Mine and Pueblo Mine from **km 1479** of the Alaska Highway:

km	0	Junction of the Alaska Highway and the road to Fish Lake; proceed onto road to Fish Lake.
km	1.3	Copper King Mine on left just before the bridge over McIntyre Creek.
km	4.2	Intersection; continue straight ahead.
km	4.5	Junction; turn right.
km	4.7	Pueblo Mine.

Part of 105 D

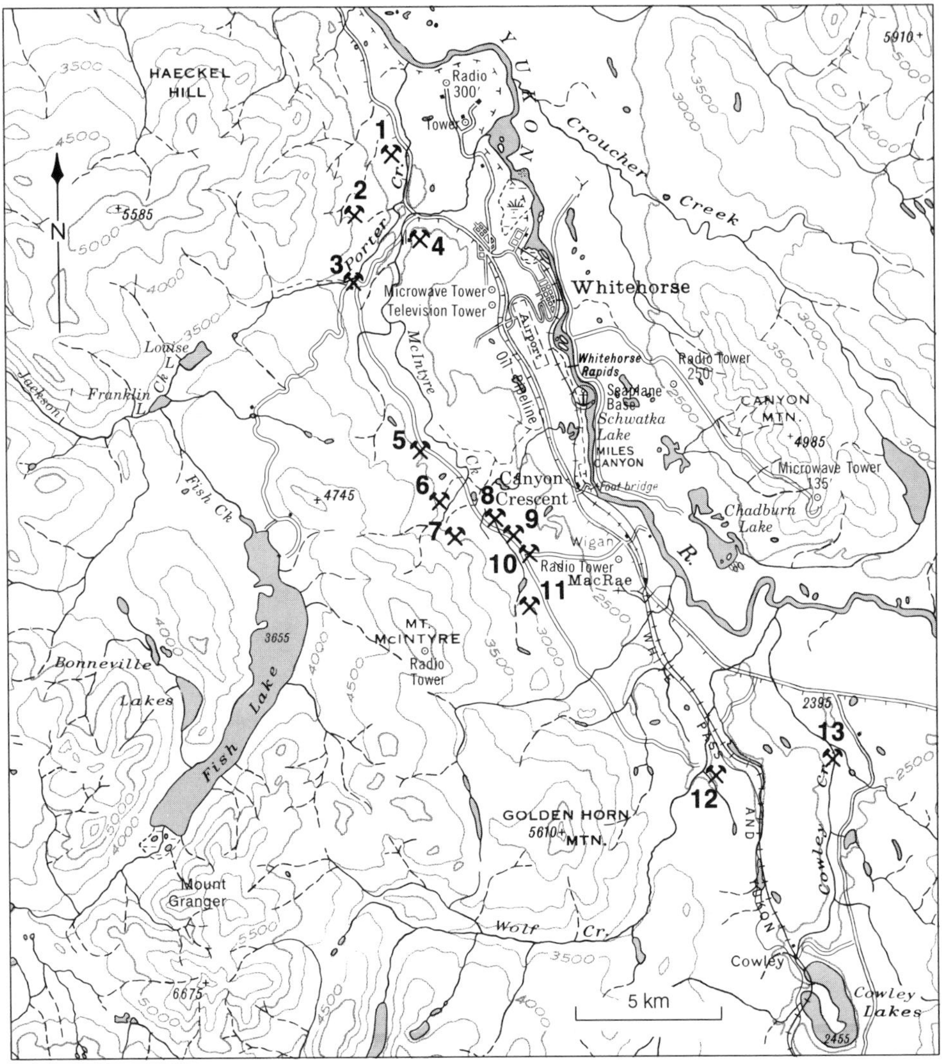

Map 5. Whitehorse copper belt properties.

1. Anaconda
2. War Eagle
3. Pueblo
4. Copper King
5. Best Chance
6. Grafter
7. Arctic Chief
8. Big Chief
9. Middle Chief
10. Little Chief
11. Valerie
12. Keewenaw
13. Cowley Park

Refs.:   39 p. 48-49; 50 p. 49-54; 55 p. 50-51; 57 p. 33-39; 88 p. 1-3, 20-58; 120 p. 137-142; 131 p. 267-268.

Maps: (T):   105 D/10 MacRae
                105 D/11 Whitehorse
                105 D/14 Upper Laberge
         (G):   1093A Whitehorse, Yukon Territory (1 inch to 4 miles)
                49-1962 Whitehorse Copper Belt (1 inch to 1 mile)

| km | 1476 | Turn-off to Whitehorse. The city of Whitehorse is situated in the broad valley of the Yukon River. Here, the valley is about 6 km wide and is bordered on the east by a long limestone ridge known as Canyon Mountain which reaches an elevation of 1520 m above sea level. On the west side, are granitic peaks with elevations of about 1677 m, including Golden Horn Mountain, Mount McIntyre and Haeckel Hill. (The treeline is at 1311 m above sea level). Between these ridges and the Yukon River, deposits of silt and boulder clay form walls that are remnants of the valley occupied by the Yukon River in preglacial times. After the ice retreated, the river incised the old valley floor to a depth of 61 m and resumed its course along the old channel except for a section above Whitehorse, from Miles Canyon to the Whitehorse Rapids, where it cut a new channel through basalt (Ref.: 88 p. 3-6). |

The section of the Yukon River from Marsh Lake to Lake Laberge was formerly known as the Lewes River; in 1949 it was officially named the Yukon River by the Canadian Board on Geographical Names. The name Yukon was first applied in 1846 by Mr. J. Bell of the Hudson's Bay Company to the portion below the mouth of the Porcupine River at Fort Yukon as it was the name used by the local Indians. The portion above Fort Yukon was referred to as the Pelly or the Lewes; in maps resulting from an expedition on the Yukon River in 1883, explorer Frederick Schwatka referred to the river from its mouth to its source as the Yukon. The Yukon, being navigable from the Bering Sea to Whitehorse Rapids played a vital role in early exploration and was used by stern-wheel steamers to transport supplies to Dawson during the Klondike gold rush and until 1948 when the Alaska Highway was completed. The distance from Whitehorse to Dawson is 724 km and to the Bering Sea, 3253 km (Ref.: 42 p. 14B-21B; 88 p. 3).

Whitehorse Rapids Occurrence

ARAGONITE, CALCITE, OLIVINE

In basalt

Vesicles in basalt contain white radiating tufts of acicular aragonite crystals and white botryoidal calcite. Dog-tooth crystals of calcite occur with the botryoidal calcite, and brownish yellow olivine occurs as small masses in the amygdules.

The basalt is exposed along the Yukon River at the rapids at the Whitehorse power dam in Whitehorse.

Plate XI

Amygdaloidal basalt exposures on Yukon River at Whitehorse Rapids. (GSC 159529)

Maps: (T):   105 D/11 Whitehorse
       (G):   1093A Whitehorse, Yukon Territory (1 inch to 4 miles)

km	1479	Junction (left), road to Fish Lake. Access to the Pueblo and Copper King mines is from this junction.
km	1480	Junction (left), road to War Eagle Mine. The mine is 2.2 km from this point.

Road-cut at km 1480

MALACHITE, CHRYSOCOLLA, AZURITE, BORNITE, MOLYBDENITE, GARNET, SERPENTINE

Plate XII

Copper King Mine, Whitehorse, c. 1900. (National Archives of Canada/PA 122786).

In limestone

Vividly coloured secondary copper minerals occur midway up a steep road-cut which marks the northern extension of the Whitehorse copper belt (see page 42). This occurrence is part of the Anaconda property. The copper minerals include: malachite, as bright green radiating fibres forming tiny hemispheres; chrysocolla, as light blue finely fibrous and blue-green finely granular masses; azurite, as bright royal blue finely fibrous and granular aggregates; and massive bornite. Molybdenite, light brown massive garnet and greenish yellow to dark green massive serpentine are associated with the copper mineralization. The road-cut is about 80 m beyond the junction at **km 1480**.

Maps: (T):   105 D/14 Upper Laberge
           (G):   1093A Whitehorse, Yukon Territory (1 inch to 4 miles)

km	1488	Junction Klondike Road (Highway 2). At about this junction, the Alaska Highway leaves the Yukon River valley and, as it proceeds westward along the valley of the Takhini River, the northern extension of the Boundary Ranges (elevations to 2135 m) of the Coast Mountains is visible to the south, and the south end of the Miners Range (elevations to 2045 m) can be seen north of the Highway. The route is within the Yukon Plateau, an upland area that is cut by valleys and that encloses some mountain ridges; it follows the old Whitehorse-Kluane wagon road built in 1904. For the road log along the Klondike Road see page 74.

km	1506	This point marks the crossing of the old Dawson road over Takhini River. The old Dawson road followed the west side of the Miners Range and was joined by the present Whitehorse-Stewart Crossing Road at **km 95**.
km	1522.6	Bridge over Takhini River.
km	1541	Junction, road to Kusawa Lake. Takhini River and Kusawa Lake form the northern border of the Boundary Ranges that extend southeastward along the east side of the British Columbia-Alaska border to Stewart. Granitic rocks form the core of these mountains.

On the north side of the Highway, deposits of sand and gravel are exposed along the lower slopes of the mountain ridges; these deposits are remnants of an old shoreline of a glacial lake that developed from glacial meltwaters towards the close of Pleistocene time when glacial ice covered the entire region except for peaks above 1830 m. As the Highway continues its course westward to Haines Junction, deposits of stratified silts can be seen along road-cuts and river banks. These deposits settled at the bottom of a glacial lake (upon which the Highway has been constructed) and were deeply incised by several streams including Mendenhall, Aishihik and Dezadeash rivers. A conspicuous white layer of volcanic ash can be observed at numerous places along the sides of the Highway and near the surfaces of road-cuts and of stream banks (Ref.: 76 p. 14-17).

km	1557	Bridge over Mendenhall River.
km	1567	Champagne, at the intersection of the historic Dalton Trail, formerly used by miners en route to the Klondike during the gold rush. This trail leads south along Dezadeash Lake and thence to Haines, Alaska; north from Champagne it follows the valley of Nordenskiold River and connects to the Whitehorse-Stewart Crossing Road at **km 23**. Champagne was established as a trading post in 1902 and is now an Indian community. It is situated on the west side of a north-trending ridge 6 km long, 500 to 1500 km wide and 30 to 60 m high. The ridge is composed of sand, gravel, and boulders, and is believed to be a terminal moraine formed by the retreat of a glacier. It is mantled by sand dunes resulting from Recent geological activity. Indian artifacts have been found in the dunes south of the village. The Alaska Highway traverses the moraine across its width. (Ref.: 76 p. 3, 8, 20, 24.)
km	1602	Junction, Aishihik Road. This road leads north along the valley of Aishihik River and to the northern end of Aishihik Lake. Otter Falls, a scenic attraction on the Aishihik River 27 km from this junction, is a picturesque scene that resembles the one formerly featured on the Canadian five dollar currency. At the falls, the water tumbles over granitic rocks at the outlet of the Aishihik River on Canyon Lake. The rounded hills forming a backdrop to the falls rise to elevations of about 1525 m and are composed of metamorphic and granitic rocks.

Plate XIII

Otter Falls, Aishihik River. (GSC 159485)

Aishihik Lake Area Occurrences

AGATE; CHALCOPYRITE, MALACHITE

In basalt; in skarn

Pale blue agate occurs in geodes in basalt at localities immediately north of Vowel Mountain (61°17′N, 136°58′W), and on the east flank of Mount Cooper (61°14′N, 136°09′W). The geodes are reported to weather readily from the basalt. Vowel Mountain is located on the west side of Nordenskiold River about 48 km east of Aishihik Lake, and Mount Cooper is on the south side of the river, about 32 km east of the south end of Aishihik Lake.

Colourful chalcopyrite and malachite specimens are found in skarn near Hopkins Lake (61°17′N, 136°58′W).

Ref.: Pers. Comm., D.J. Tempelman-Kluit (G.S.C.)

Maps: (T): 115 H/1 Mount Cooper
115 H/7 Hopkins Lake
115 H/8 Vowel Mountain
(G): 192 A Aishihik Lake area, Yukon (1 inch to 4 miles)

km	1620	Bridge over Marshall Creek. Small grains of pink garnet occur in biotite schist occurring as pebbles along the bed of the creek. The rock is derived from the metamorphic rocks forming the Ruby Range on the north side of the Highway.
km	1635	Haines Junction, at the junction of Haines Road (Highway 3).

The Haines Road

The Haines Road links the Alaska Highway to the Pacific Ocean at Haines, Alaska. It passes through parts of Yukon Territory, British Columbia and Alaska.

Road log along the Haines Road:

km	0	Junction Haines Road and the Alaska Highway at **km 1635**. The Haines road is within the Shakwak Valley to km 63, and is bound on the west side by the Kluane Ranges to km 82.
km	11	Junction, bush road on left to Kathleen River asbestos occurrence (see page 52).
km	25.4	Bridge over Kathleen River.
km	27.3	Junction, road on right to Johobo Mine (see page 52).
km	27.7	Junction, road to Kathleen Lakes. A valley glacier emanating from Lowell Glacier (in the St. Elias Mountains) entered the Shakwak Valley in Pleistocene time via Kathleen Lake. The ice-carved basin of this lake was later dammed by the deposition of sand and gravel at the mouth of Victoria Creek resulting in the formation of two lakes – the Kathleen Lakes. The larger of the two is near the Haines Road, and the smaller is west of it (Ref.: 76 p. 14). The Kluane Ranges on either side of the lakes reach elevations of about 2290 m above sea level.
km	38	The road parallels the west side of Dezadeash Lake for the next 16 km.
km	54.7	Junction, road on right to Shorty Creek and Beloud Creek placer deposits. (See page 52).
km	58	The ridges along both sides of the road are eskers composed of gravel, sand and boulders left by glaciers.
km	63	From about this point to Haines, the highway more or less follows the old Dalton Trail, a pack trail cut by Jack Dalton in the 1890s. It was an overland route to the Klondike.
km	65.1	Junction, road on left to Klukshu village. For the next 16 km the Haines Road parallels Klukshu River which separates the Kluane Ranges from the Boundary Ranges of the Coast Mountains. A batholithic mass of granitic rocks of Cretaceous age underlies the Coast Mountains (Ref.: 76 p. 25). The Boundary Ranges extend south to Stewart, British Columbia.
km	85.3	Junction, road on right to Silver Creek and Squaw Creek placers (see page 52) and to Dalton Post, a trading post established in 1892 on the Tatshenshini River by Jack Dalton, explorer and pioneer.

km	92	Eskers (narrow ridges of sand and gravel) lie along the road; they are 15 to 30 m high and up to 3 km long, and form parallel clusters on the west side of the road.
km	95	For the next 22 km, the road follows the broad, drift-filled valley of Tatshenshini River which separates the Alsek Ranges of the St. Elias Mountains on the west side of the road from the Boundary Ranges on the east side. This river as well as succeeding river valleys that the Haines Road parallels to Alaska, has entrenched its course in a northwest-trending plateau, the Duke Depression, which extends from Alaska to and along the southwestern side of the Kluane Ranges.
km	105	Yukon-British Columbia border.
km	114.2	Junction, road on right to Squaw Creek placers. From this point to Rainy Hollow, the Dalton Trail follows an old footpath used by the Chilkat Indians as a trade route from Klukwan, Alaska to the Yukon.
km	115	For the next 15 km most of the area traversed by the highway is untimbered; the elevation ranges from about 884 to 915 m above sea level. A similar stretch is encountered between km 146 and km 167.
km	132	The highway crosses a gravel fan with abandoned stream channels built up by Datlasaka Creek and the headwaters of Nadahini Creek. Kelsall Lake is on the east side of the highway, and 2379 m Mount Kelsall at its northeastern end is the highest peak along the British Columbia portion of the highway. The Datlasaka Range (Alsek Ranges) on the west side of the road contains numerous large glaciers.
km	138	The remaining section of the Haines Road is entirely within the Alsek Ranges, the southeastern front of the St. Elias Mountains. Their peaks, mantled with ice and snow, reach elevations close to 2745 m.
km	151	Chilkat Pass, at an elevation of 1065 m above sea level.
km	164	Three Guardsmen Pass and Three Guardsmen Mountain (on left) with its three granite peaks reaching elevations of over 1830 m.
km	167	From this point to about km 175, the highway passes through Rainy Hollow, a broad forested depression occupied by Klehini River and its tributary, Seltat Creek.
km	172.2	Junction, road (on right at hairpin turn) to Mineral Mountain-Copper Butte mines (see page 53). From about this junction to km 193, the road parallels the valley of Klehini River. Gold was found in the gravels of the river, but not a paying quantities (Ref.: 119 p. 39).
km	191	British Columbia-Alaska boundary at Pleasant Camp.
km	256	Haines, Alaska.

Maps: (T): 115 A Dezadeash
            114 P Tatshenshini River

Kathleen River Asbeston Occurrence

ASBESTOS, SERPENTINE

In peridotite

Slip-fibre asbestos occurs with massive serpentine in peridotite; the fibre is commonly 1 cm long but occurs up to 5 cm in length.

The deposit is located at an elevation of 839 m between two knolls situated 4 km northwest of Kathleen River at the mouth of Quill Creek. Asbestos float was discovered there in 1953 by V. Noble of Whitehorse. The deposit was exposed by trenches and bulldozer cuts.

Access is via a bush road, 10.5 km long, leading east from the Haines Road at km 11 (see page 50).

Ref.:　　57 p. 29-31.

Maps:　(T):　115 A/11 Kathleen Lakes
　　　　(G):　1019 A Dezadeash, Yukon Territory (1 inch to 4 miles)

Johobo Mine

BORNITE, CHALCOPYRITE, PYRITE, MALACHITE, CHALCOCITE

In faults and shear zones in andesite

Bornite and chalcopyrite occur as lenses, veinlets, and disseminated grains in andesite. Minor amounts of pyrite, malachite and chalcocite are associated with the copper ore minerals.

Bornite was discovered at an elevation of 1083 m on the south side of Bornite Creek (5.6 km southwest of Kathleen Lakes) in 1953 by Dr. E.D. Kindle of the Geological Survey of Canada during a geological investigation of the area. It was staked by H. Honing and associates in 1958; small-scale mining was conducted in 1958-59. A similar deposit was discovered by Honing in 1959 at a locality 3915 m north of Bornite Creek. In the same year, Johobo Mines Limited operated the deposit and shipped 680 t of ore averaging about 15 per cent copper. A further shipment to Japan of 7011 t of ore averaging 26.5 per cent copper and 62 g of silver per tonne was made in 1961. The ore was mined from open-cuts. In 1961 the property was optioned to Dominion Explorers Limited which explored the deposit with two adits and diamond-drilling.

A 29 km truck road connects the mine to km 27.3 (see page 50) on the Haines Road; it follows the south side of the Kathleen Lakes, crossing Goat and Victoria creeks.

Refs.:　76 p. 57-58; 105 p. 28-30; 106 p. 27-29.

Maps:　(T):　115 A/5 Cottonwood Lakes
　　　　　　　115 A Dezadeash
　　　　(G):　1019A Dezadeash Yukon Territory (1 inch to 4 miles)

Dezadeash Area Placers

GOLD, COPPER

In placers

Placer gold has been recovered intermittently from the streams southwest of Dezadeash Lake since 1898. It was discovered by miners travelling along the Dalton Trail to the Klondike in the 1890s. Gold was recovered from Tatshenshini River and its tributaries, Silver and Squaw

(Dollis) creeks; from Beloud, Victoria, Goat and Shorty creeks; from Bates River and its tributaries, Iron and Wolverine creeks; and from Mush and Shaft creeks. The most productive creeks have been Shorty, Beloud and Squaw creeks. Coarse gold was found on Squaw Creek in 1927 by Paddy Duncan of Klukshu. In a prospecting rush that followed, a number of claims were staked and worked by Indians from Klukshu and Champagne. In the British Columbia portion of the creek, numerous nuggets weighing 124 to 280 g were found; one nugget weighing a little over 1430 g was found in 1937 by E. Peterson and B. Turbitt. At Beloud Creek, copper nuggets ranging in weight from a few grams to 12.6 kg were recovered by B. Beloud of Whitehorse during placer operations in 1938-39.

Access to the Shorty Creek and Beloud Creek placers is by a road leading west from km 54.7 (see page 50) on the Haines Road; to the Silver Creek, Squaw Creek and Tatshenshini River placers by the road leading to Dalton Post from km 85.3 (page 50) on the Haines Road. An alternate road to Squaw Creek leaves the Haines Road at km 114.2.

Since panning is prohibited on staked claims, the status of the placers should be determined by consulting the Mining Recorder, Indian and Northern Affairs Canada at Whitehorse, or the Gold Commissioner, Department of Energy, Mines and Petroleum Resources at Victoria.

Ref.:   <u>76</u> p. 48-54.

Maps: (T): 114 P Tatshenshini River
             115 A/6 Mush Lake
             115 A/3 Dalton Post
             115 A Dezadeash
     (G): 1019A Dezadeash, Yukon Territory (1 inch to 4 miles) Squaw Creek-Rainy Hollow Area, northwestern British Columbia (B.C. Dept. Mines, Petrol. Res., 1 inch to 2 miles)

Mineral Mountain-Copper Butte Mines

BORNITE, CHALCOCITE, CHALCOPYRITE, SPHALERITE, GALENA, MAGNETITE, WITTICHENITE, PYRRHOTITE, PYRITE, COVELLITE, MALACHITE, AZURITE, GARNET, MONTICELLITE, ZOISITE, WOLLASTONITE, DIOPSIDE, CLINOZOISITE, VESUVIANITE, ANORTHITE, GAHNITE, TITANITE, CALCITE

In a skarn zone at the contact of marble with argillite, quartzite, gneiss or schist

Copper-silver and lead-zinc mineralization occurs in deposits on Mineral Mountain and on Copper Butte located northwest and north respectively of the hairpin turn at km 172.2 (see page 51) on the Haines Road. The ore minerals are bornite, chalcocite, chalcopyrite, sphalerite (dark brown to black) and galena; they occur as veinlets, lenses and disseminations in skarn. Magnetite, wittichenite, pyrrhotite, covellite and pyrite are associated with the ore, and malachite and azurite form stains and crusts on the copper minerals. The minerals comprising the skarn include yellowish green and brown garnet (andradite), white monticellite, medium to dark green zoisite, white to grey wollastonite, white diopside, light brown clinozoisite, pink and green vesuvianite, anorthite, blue gahnite, titanite and calcite. Most of the skarn rock is medium-grained. The small, high-grade deposits were explored on the steep southwest side of Mineral Mountain and on the west side of Copper Butte; the former is a long, iron-stained ridge with an elevation of 1562 m above sea level, the latter a low rounded dome.

Copper float was found at Rainy Hollow near the Dalton Trail in 1898 by miners enroute to the Klondike. Numerous claims were staked in that and in the following year on Mineral Mountain and Copper Butte. Exploration of the deposits continued from about 1908 to 1922, and shipments of lead-silver ore were made from the Maid of Erin Mine between 1911 and 1922,

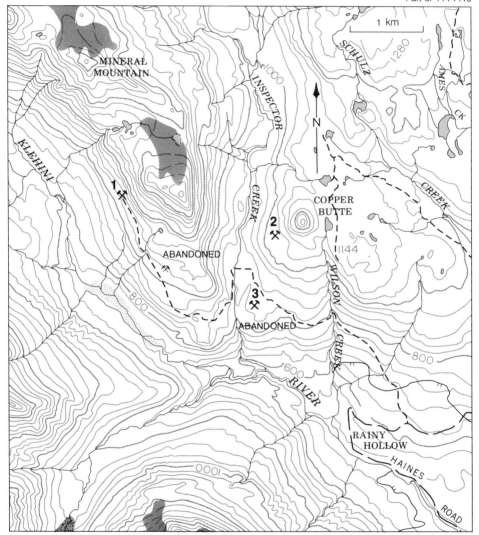

Map 6. Rainy Hollow area

1. Maid of Erin Mines   2. State of Montana Mine   3. Victoria Mine

and from the State of Montana Mine in 1908 and 1909. Most of the work was done on the Maid of Erin Mine which yielded 349.46 kg (77.658 pounds) of copper, 181921 g (5,849 ounces) of silver and 187 g (6 ounces) of gold from 142 t of sorted ore. The mine, located at an elevation of 1100 m on the steep southwestern slope of Mineral Mountain, consisted of an incline, two short adits,a vertical shaft and open cuts. A trial shipment of a few t of ore was made from the State of Montana Mine located at an elevation of 1067 m at the western base of Copper Butte; the workings consisted of a trench, open cuts and an adit. Both the Maid of Erin and State of Montana mines are above timberline. The Victoria Mine, about 800 m south of the State of Montana Mine, was explored by an adit and surface cuts; shipments were not recorded from this nor from several other properties in the area.

Access to the mines is by an overgrown old tractor road that leaves the Haines Road at the hairpin bend at km 172.2 (see page 51). About 3 km from the junction, the road forks; one fork crosses Inspector Creek and continues 2.5 km to the Maid of Erin Mine, the other leads northeast for a distance of 800 m above timberline to the State of Montana Mine. The Victoria Mine is on the northeast side of the trail just before reaching the fork.

Refs.:   <u>89</u> p. 30-32; <u>119</u> p. 11-13, 10-57.

Maps: (T):   114 P/10 Nadahni Creek
                 114 P Tatshenshini River
        (G):   Squaw Creek-Rainy Hollow area, northwestern British Columbia (B.C. Dept.
                 Mines, Petroleum Resources,1 inch to 2 miles)

The Polaris-Taku Mine, the Tulsequah Chief Mine and the Big Bull Mine are located in the Taku River area, northwestern British Columbia and are accessible by air or by a water route from Juneau. The descriptions of them follow.

Polaris-Taku Mine

ARSENOPYRITE, PYRITE, STIBNITE, PYRRHOTITE, MAGNETITE, FUCHSITE

In sheared volcanic rocks

Gold-bearing arsenopyrite and pyrite are finely disseminated in quartz-carbonate veins; the arsenopyrite commonly occurs as needle-like crystals. Stibnite occurs as coarse bladed crystals. Small amounts of pyrrhotite and magnetite are associated with the arsenopyrite and pyrite. Fuchsite, a green chrome mica, is a conspicuous constituent of the veins.

The Polaris-Taku Mine is a former gold producer. The deposit was discovered and staked in 1929 by Art Hedman, Ray Walker, Ray Race and associates of Juneau. Initial exploration of the property was conducted by the N.A. Timmins Corporation in 1930-32 and by the Alaska Juneau Gold Mining Company in 1932-34. In 1936, the Polaris-Taku Mining Company Limited acquired the property and brought it into production in 1937. Operations were suspended in 1942, reopened in 1946, and closed in 1950. The mill was installed in 1937. The mine was developed by four adits at elevations of 177 m, 111 m, 75 m and 41 m above sea level, and by a shaft sunk from the adit at the 75 m level. It produced 7 203 579 g of gold, 365 771 g of silver and 79 853.5 kg of copper.

The mine is on the southern slope of Whitewater Mountain in the Coast Mountains of British Columbia. It is on the west side of Tulsequah River about 10 km upstream from its mouth on Taku River which in turn is about 95 km via the Taku River and Taku Inlet from Juneau. A 10 km road along the west side of Tulsequah River connected the mine to Taku River; during mining operations, barges transported the concentrates from the end of the road to deep-sea freighters at the head of Taku Inlet. The settlement of Tulsequah was located at the mouth of the Tulsequeh River. This river is characterized by a broad, steep gravel base and a continually changing course; it is fed by Tulsequah Glacier and every few years it is flooded by a sudden draining of Tulsequah Lake through a channel beneath Tulsequah Glacier.

The mine is 65 km by air from Juneau; it is the property of New Taku Mines Limited.

Refs.:   6 p. A62-A68; 74 p. 1-2, 4, 63-65; 80 p. B19-B28; 104 p. 65-69; 107a p. 53-55.

Maps: (T):   104 K/12 Tulsequah River
                      104 K Tusequah
              (G):   931A Taku River, British Columbia (1 inch to 2 miles)
                      1262A Tulsequah and Juneau, Cassiar district, British Columbia
                      (1 inch to 4 miles)

Tulsequah Chief, Big Bull Mines

SPHALERITE, CHALCOPYRITE, PYRITE, GALENA, BORNITE, TENNANTITE, HEMATITE, JASPER

In sheared volcanic rocks

The Tulsequah Chief Mine and the Big Bull Mine were formerly worked for zinc, copper and lead. The most abundant ore minerals were sphalerite (light brown to yellow), chalcopyrite and pyrite. Galena was intimately associated with sphalerite. Bornite and tennantite were also present. Hematite and jasper occurred at the Big Bull Mine.

The Tulsequah Chief deposit was staked prior to 1923 by W. Kirkham of Juneau; the brownish yellow stain on the bluffs attracted prospectors to the outcrops which were at an elevation of 488 m (above sea level) on the steep slope that forms the northeast side of the Tulsequah Valley. The mine is 12 km above the mouth of the river. The Big Bull deposit was discovered in 1929 by V. Manville and is at the foot of Mount Manville on the east side of Tulsequah River and 8 km southeast of Tulsequah Chief Mine. The properties were explored intermittently by various interests and were brought into production by Tulsequah Mines Limited in 1951. The mine workings consist of shafts and adits. The ore was processed at the mill at the Polaris-Taku Mine on the opposite side of the river. The concentrates were shipped by barge to ocean freighters at Taku Inlet. Operations ended in 1957. The mines produced a total of 2 931 582 g of gold, 105 774 211 g of silver, 12 325 162 kg of copper, 12 197 414 kg of lead, 5 648 586 kg of zinc and 205 658 kg of cadmium.

The Tulsequah Chief Mine is located about 5 km northeast of the Taku-Polaris Mine, the Big Bull Mine 6 km southeast of it. Roads connected the mines to the Tulsequah River.

Refs.:   6 p. A68-A70; 67 p. 7-16; 74 p. 6-7, 58-63; 107a p. 53-55.

Maps: (T):   104 K/12 Tulsequah River
                      104 K Tulsequah
              (G):   931A Taku River, British Columbia (1 inch to 2 miles)
                      1262A Tulsequah and Juneau, Cassiar district, British Columbia
                      (1 inch to 4 miles)
The road log along the Alaska Highway is resumed.

km	1635	Haines Junction, at the junction of Haines Road. The Alaska Highway enters Shakwak Valley which it follows to White River. The valley is a geological fault zone, 3 to 15 km wide and 320 km long; it extends in a northwesterly direction from the westernmost point of Kusawa Lake to and beyond White River, and it separates the geologically younger rock formations of the St. Elias Mountains to the south from the older rocks of the Yukon Plateau on its north side. The Shakwak Valley is mantled with Pleistocene and Recent deposits of till, gravel, sand, silt and volcanic ash; it encloses Kluane, Kathleen and Dezadeash lakes and is incised by numerous streams (Refs.: 15 p. 5, 8-9; 76 p. 11-12).

The St. Elias Mountains

Visible in the distance from the Highway (to the southwest), are the broad, rugged, snowy summits of the Ice Field Ranges of the St. Elias Mountains, Canada's highest mountains, crowned by 6054 m Mount Logan. These mountains are described by Dr. H.S. Bostock of the Geological Survey of Canada (Ref.: 14 p. 92): "Above a sea of lesser peaks and wide ice-fields the great peaks stand solitary or in compact, isolated groups. Besides their colossal size, this individual aloofness adds much to the impressiveness of their vast, wild, and icy beauty, and contrasts them sharply with the jumbled rivalry of summits around many of the main peaks of the coast, Rocky, and Mackenzie Mountains, and other mountains of the Canadian Cordillera. Many of these individual peaks and groups are block-like in form, rising on nearly every side with precipitous cliffs, not to pinnacle-like tops, but to broad, still steep, though relatively gentler, summit areas. This gives them an appearance of stupendous massiveness from all directions. Another outstanding feature is the mantle of snow and ice that even in summer cloaks a great part of them. It spreads unbroken over their gentler, summit areas, smoothing the contours of their upper slopes and concealing bedrock. As the slopes steepen downward, it overhangs the edges of precipices in great cliffs of ice from which it cascades in mighty avalanches thousands of feet to the broad fields of snow and ice below, where it feeds the glaciers that lead away from between the peaks. Almost the only exposures of rock in all the vast expanse of white and blue around the great peaks are in their precipices. Below these dazzling monarchs a sea of lesser peaks, mighty themselves in other company, form a jagged and rocky platform. such is a general picture of the dominant features of these great mountains beside which the better known ranges of Canada are dwarfed to relative insignificance."

The mountain system derives its name from Mount St. Elias which was discovered and named on July 20, 1741 (St. Elias being the patron saint of that day) by Vitus Bering and Alexei Cherikof while exploring the Pacific Coast for Russia. At the time, and for many years thereafter, it was believed to be the highest mountain of the system. In 1890, a three-man expedition led by I.C. Russell and sponsored by the National Geographic Society and the United States Geological Survey, investigated the St. Elias Mountains, and discovered and named Mount Logan, the highest peak in the range. The first description of the mountain was made by Dr. Russell: "The clouds parting toward the northeast revealed several giant peaks not before seen, some of which seem to rival in height St. Elias itself. One stranger, rising in three white domes far above the clouds, was especially magnificent. As this was probably the first time its summit was ever seen, we took the liberty of giving it a name. It will appear on our maps as Mount Logan, in honor of Sir William E. Logan, founder and long director of the Geological Survey of Canada." (Ref.: 100 p. 58, 141.)

In 1967, a mountain range in the St. Elias Mountains was designated by the Canadian Permanent Committee on Geographical Names as the Centennial Range to mark the centenary of the Canadian Confederation. The range straddles the Alaska-Yukon boundary and extends in an easterly direction for about 35 km from it. Its peaks (about 3050 to 3660 m above sea level) have been named for each of the ten provinces, for the two territories, and one peak was named Centennial Peak; their location in the range from west to east corresponds to the geographical position of the provinces and territories they represent. The valley along the north side of the range is occupied by Chitina Glacier, the valley along the south side by Walsh Glacier. Mount Lucania is located immediately northeast of the range.

Maps: (T):   115B & 115C Mount St. Elias
                M.C.R. 7 Centennial Range

Plate XIV

St. Elias Mountains viewed from 3 750 m looking southeast up Slims River which is bridged by the Alaska Highway at km 1705. (National Air Photo Library T6-119L)

km	1635	**The Kluane Ranges**

Adjacent to the Highway, on the south side, between Haines Junction and White River, are the Kluane Ranges which constitute the outer front of the St. Elias Mountains. From the Highway, the ranges have the appearance of a steep, wall-like, serrated ridge of fairly uniform elevation (up to 2440 m) with slopes furrowed by talus-ridden valleys and containing small alpine glaciers; they are dissected by mountain streams, some carrying gold in their gravels. The Kluane Ranges are composed predominantly of volcanic and sedimentary formations with some granitic rocks. The Ruby Range which borders the north side of the Highway from the Aishihik River (**km 1602**) to the Kluane River (**km 1791**) is underlain by granitic rocks, schists and gneisses. In contrast to the rugged Kluane Ranges, the Ruby Range presents a more subdued topography with peaks reaching elevations of up to 2290 m above sea level; some of its streams have been worked for placer gold. The limit of forest growth in both ranges is at an elevation of 1220 m.

km	1640	A Dominion Experimental Farm was formerly located on left.
km	1644.5	Trail to Sugden Creek on left, just west of the bridge over Bear Creek.

Dezadeash River Olivine Occurrence

OLIVINE, DIOPSIDE

In peridotite

Crystals of olivine measuring 7 to 10 cm in length occur with light green tabular crystals of diopside in peridotite. The olivine is blackish green due to the inclusion of microscopic particles of magnetite.

The peridotite occurs along the mountain slope on the west side of Dezadeash River. The Sugden Creek trail, which leads south from the Alaska Highway, passes the occurrence at a point 12.9 km from **km 1644.5**. Access is possible in late summer by vehicles equipped with 4-wheel drive. The trail continues an additional 11 km to the Sugden Creek placer deposits that were worked for gold and platinum.

Ref.:   76 p. 37-38, 48, 54.

Maps: (T):   115 A/10 Mount Bratnober
                115 A Dezadeash
         (G):   1019A Dezadeash, Yukon Territory (1 inch to 4 miles)

km	1657-1660	Lying astride the Highway are a series of ice-block ridges left by ice sheets that moved in a northeasterly direction during Pleistocene time. The ridges are only a few m high, up to 300 m long, and are composed of gravel, sand and silt (Ref.: 76 p. 21.)
km	1689	Boutillier Summit. This is the highest point (elevation 1000 m) on the Alaska Highway west of Whitehorse.
km	1695	Bridge over Silver Creek, at the south end of Kluane Lake.

Plate XV

Williscroft Creek, **km 1716**, with the Kluane Ranges behind the Alaska Highway. (GSC 159481)

Kluane Lake Placers

GOLD

Kluane Lake, measuring about 65 km in length and 3 to 10 km in width, is the largest lake in the Yukon and is the deepest part of Shakwak Valley. Its elevation is 785 m above sea level and it is drained into the Bering Sea via Kluane, Donjek, White and Yukon rivers. Near the mouth of Silver Creek, a settlement known as Kluane or Silver City was at one time the centre of activity serving the mining district of Kluane; it sprang up as a result of the discovery of placer gold in the area.

On July 4, 1903, Dawson Charlie of Cariboo Crossing (now Carcross) staked the discovery claim on Fourth of July Creek in the Ruby Range, 24 km to the northeast. A prospecting rush ensued and by 1905 most of the gold placers now known had been staked. Except for Gladstone, Cultus and Fourth of July creeks, the gold placers were in the streams to the south of the

Shakwak Valley, including Sheep, Bullion, Burwash and Arch creeks and Koidern River (Edith Creek). Although mining activity was of short duration, the interest was revived in the 1912-14 period when gold was discovered in the Chisana district of Alaska. Intermittent production of gold has been realized from the Kluane district since that time. The locations of the placer workings are indicated on Map 1177A, Kluane Lake (Geological Survey of Canada); those accessible from the Alaska Highway are mentioned in the road log on pages 63, 65.

Refs.: 15 p. 40; 92 p. 1-3, 105-108).

Maps: (T): 115 G and 115 F Kluane Lake
          (G): 1177 A Kluane Lake, Yukon Territory (1 inch to 4 miles)

| km | 1705 | Bridge over Slims River. Slims River is a swiftly flowing mountain stream fed by the Kaskawulsh Glacier located in a valley of the Icefield Range to the southwest. Fine glacial silts that mantle the river flats are whipped up into dust clouds by prevailing winds, and the valley becomes a funnel through which the silt is transported and deposited in the mouth of the river and at the southern end of Kluane Lake. This accumulation is a continuing phenomenon and has resulted in a shifting of the shoreline at this end of the lake: as seen from the bridge, dry mud flats occupy the former lake shore (Refs.: 15 p. 6-8; 92 p. 2-3).

Although the Alaska Highway parallels the shore of Kluane Lake to **km 1759**, the lake is visible from it for only the next 32 km. The Ruby Range forms a backdrop to the north side of the lake. The longest unbroken ridge of the Kluane Ranges borders the left (southwest) side of the Highway and Kluane Lake, from Slims River to **km 1767** where it is interrupted by the broad valleys of the Duke River and Burwash Creek; this is the highest section of the Kluane Ranges and contains several alpine glaciers. The road-cuts along the Highway at **km 1707** and the outcrops on the peninsula at **km 1709** expose volcanic rocks of Triassic age. |
km	1712.6	Turn-off (on right) to Horseshoe Bay Camp-site. Pebbles of grey chert, maroon and brownish yellow jasper, and a brownish red volcanic rock streaked with green epidote are found along the shoreline at the camp-site.
km	1716.0	Bridge over Williscroft Creek. Pebbles of brown to red jasper and epidote rock (epidote and quartz in grey and purplish volcanics) occur in the bed of the creek and along the shore of the lake.
km	1718-1725	**Kluane Lake shoreline** Pebbles of red jasper are common along the shore and in the bed of Congdon Creek (**km 1724.4**). Small black specks of hematite occur in some jasper pebbles. Some grey chert and epidote-quartz pebbles were also noted. The jasper pebbles are most numerous at the Goose Bay Camp-site at **km 1725**.
km	1734.8	Bridge over Nines Creek. Pebbles of red, orange-red, maroon-red and brown jasper occur in the bed of the creek along with pebbles composed of quartz and epidote, calcite and epidote, and purple and grey andesite and basalt containing blotches and veinlets of epidote. Epidote commonly occurs in amygdules in grey and maroon volcanics that are also found as pebbles along the creek.

Plate XVI

Kluane Lake shoreline, **km 1719**, with the Ruby Range in the background. Jasper pebbles are abundant along the shore. (GSC 159479)

km	**1735.8**	Bridge over Mines Creek.
km	**1738.2**	Bridge over Bock's Creek. Pebbles, similar to those occurring at Nines Creek, are found in the beds of Mines and Bock's creeks.
km	**1758**	Kluane Historical Society Museum on right. Local rock and mineral specimens and artifacts are displayed in the Museum.
km	**1767.5**	Bridge over Duke River. Pebbles of epidote (in quartz matrix) and of amygdaloidal basalt occur in the broad flats near the bridge.
km	**1772**	On the left side of the Highway, the Donjek Range can be seen through a wide gap in the Kluane Ranges. The gap is occupied by the valleys of Duke River and Burwash Creek separated by an upland area. Conspicuous in the foreground of the Donjek Range, is Amphitheatre Mountain with its flat cap of Tertiary volcanic rock overlying Tertiary sedimentary strata. Coal (lignite) seams occur in light brown and grey shale that outcrops along the slopes below the lava cap; fossil leaves occur

in the shale. The Donjek Range contains small glaciers along its slopes which rise to peaks 2440 m to 3050 m high; the range parallels the Kluane Ranges and separates them from the Icefield Ranges, the backbone of the St. Elias Mountains. The Duke River drains the Donjek Range and carries unconsolidated sediments to its mouth on the Kluane River. At times the accumulation is large and clogs the Kluane River thus choking the outlet of Kluane Lake and causing a rise in the level of the lake; fluctuations of up to 3 m in the mean annual level have been reported (Refs.: 15 p. 6; 92 p. 81, 84, 113).

km	1776.2	Bridge over Burwash Creek. Pebbles composed of epidote with quartz, of purple volcanic rock containing irregular patches of green epidote, and of amygdaloidal basalt containing epidote, calcite, quartz and chalcedony in the cavities are found in the bed of the creek. The epidote and volcanic pebbles are colourful and take a good polish.
km	1776.2	Trail on left leading up Burwash Creek.

Burwash Creek Placers

GOLD, PLATINUM, SILVER, COPPER

In placers

Coarse gold was found in 1904, in the lower canyon and for 12 km above it; a 155 g nugget and several nuggets weighing about 30 g were recovered. Platinum, native silver and native copper have been reported from the concentrates. The gold and platinum occurred as flat plates and nuggets. Burwash Creek was worked at intervals since the discovery of gold there in 1904 by Messrs. Altamose, Ater, Smith and Bones. It has been the most productive placer creek in the Kluane district and it exceeded the combined total of gold from all other streams in the district. Until 1914, total production from the creek was estimated at between $30,000 and $40,000. After 1914, mining activity declined. Since 1945 mining has been conducted by Burwash Mining Company Limited between the lower end of the canyon and the mouth of Tatamagouche Creek, as well as along the latter creek. A sluicing plant is used to recover the gold. For a brief period (1948-51), Kluane Dredging Company operated a floating separation plant on the lower part of Burwash Creek.

A 10-km road leads to the deposit from the Alaska Highway. Panning the placers of this stream or of any other stream is permitted only in locations not held by claims; details of ownership can be obtained from the Mining Recorder, Indian and Northern Affairs Canada, Whitehorse.

Refs.: 29 p. 22-24; 50 p. 112-113; 55 p. 120-121; 85 p. 1A, 15A-16A; 92 p. 106-107; 97 p. 108-111.

Maps: (T): 115 G/6 Duke River
       (G): 1177A Kluane Lake, Yukon Territory (1 inch to 4 miles)

km	1787.6	Turn-off on left to Wellgreen Mine.

Plate XVII

Edith Creek, **km 1845**, with Kluane Ranges in background. Pebbles of jasper, chalcedony, and volcanic rock occur in bed of stream. (GSC 159474)

Wellgreen Mine

PYRRHOTITE, PENTLANDITE, CHALCOPYRITE, SPHALERITE, VIOLARITE

In serpentinized peridotite

The sulphide minerals occur as solid masses closely associated with each other in the host rock. The ore contains, in addition to copper and nickel, values in platinum and palladium. The deposit was discovered and staked by W.B. Green and C.A. Aird in 1952, and later acquired by the Hudson-Yukon Mining Company. Underground work consisting of an adit and shafts was conducted by the company and a mill was constructed near the Alaska Highway (**km 1787.6**), about 16 km by road from the mine. The mine is located on a slope of the Kluane

Ranges overlooking Nickel Creek, a tributary of Quill Creek. It produced nickel, copper, cobalt and platinum metals from May to July, 1972.

Refs.:   32 p. 953-959; 92 p. 110-111; 131 p. 189, 190.

Maps: (T):   115 G/5 Steele Creek
        (G):   117A Kluane Lake, Yukon Territory (1 inch to 4 miles)

km	**1789**	Bridge over Quill Creek. Pebbles and boulders of jasper in various shades of red and green occur along the creek. Jasper and grey chalcedony occur as masses about 5 cm across in amygdaloidal basalt which occurs as small boulders. Also occurring are pebbles of fine grained purple volcanic rock containing veinlets and irregular masses of epidote, and of epidote in a matrix of quartz; these pebbles as well as the jasper pebbles are attractive when polished and can be used for ornamental purposes. Epidote also occurs in granitic rock pebbles.
km	**1791**	Kluane River on right. For the next few km, the Highway follows the west bank of Kluane River. Pebbles similar to those occurring at Quill Creek are found in the broad river flats.
		On the north side of the Highway, moraines formed of glacial drift are a feature of the topography between the Kluane and Donjek rivers; the mountains from this point to White River reach elevations of up to 1830 m.
km	**1822.2**	Bridge over Donjek River. Geodes filled with chalcedony and quartz occur among the gravels and boulders in the river flats.
		The Donjek River is fed by Donjek Glacier and by Steele Glacier, known locally as the Galloping Glacier because of its 488 m surge in one month in 1966-67. The river deposits large accumulations of gravel, sand and silt on the ever-shifting channels that carve the valley-floor which in Pleistocene time was occupied by a large glacier. The valley with its broad flood plains cuts a conspicuous intermontane gap in the Kluane Ranges and marks the western boundary of the Donjek Range. To the south, beyond the opening, are the snow-covered Icefield Ranges with their numerous glacier-filled valleys. As in the Slims River valley, off-glacier winds whip up the fine silts creating great dust-clouds in the valley of the Donjek River.
		The Highway continues in a northwesterly direction in its final course along the Kluane Ranges; a series of sluggish streams and quiet lakes occupy a low-lying area on the left (southwest) side of the Highway. The steep wall-like front of the Kluane Ranges is composed of volcanic and sedimentary rocks of Paleozoic age, while the mountains on the right are underlain by older granitic and metamorphic rocks including schists, gneisses and quartzites. (Refs.: 92 p. 2-3; 136 p. 1a.)
km	**1844.9**	Bridge over Edith Creek (Koidern River). Pebbles, similar to those found at Quill Creek, occur in the bed of this creek in the vicinity of the bridge. Placer gold has been recovered at various times from this stream. (Ref.: 15 p. 40.)

Plate XVIII

White River at Canalask Mine, Miners Ridge on right and the Nutzotin Mountains in distant background. (GSC 159475)

km	**1878**	Koidern.
km	**1879.1**	Junction, road on left to Canalask Mine.

Canalask Mine

PYRRHOTITE, PENTLANDITE, CHALCOPYRITE, SPHALERITE, PYRITE, MARCASITE, ZOISITE, GYPSUM, MALACHITE, BROCHANTITE, CHRYSOCOLLA, HEXAHYDRITE, ROZENITE, SERPENTINE, MICA

In altered volcanic rocks

The sulphide minerals - pyrrhotite, pentlandite, chalcopyrite, sphalerite, pyrite, and marcasite - occur as fine disseminations and as small massive lenses; they are associated with a carbonate-zoisite matrix. Secondary minerals are common on specimens occurring in the rock dumps, the most abundant being gypsum and malachite. Gypsum occurs as transparent, colourless striated tabular crystal aggregates, elongated plates, rounded encrustations, and as fine granular masses; it is closely associated with malachite and is commonly stained light green or blue. Malachite forms light to medium dark green, powdery to finely crystalline coatings on the specimens. Other secondary minerals identified from the deposit include: brochantite, as bluish green crusts; chrysocolla, as light blue vitreous encrustations on calcite; hexahydrite, as white sugary crusts and spherical aggregates; rozenite, as a white powder. Olive-green serpentine and dark brown to black mica were also found in the rock dumps.

The deposit was discovered in 1952 by Prospectors Airways Company Limited. In 1954, it was acquired by Canalask Nickel Mines Limited which conducted exploratory work on the property until 1958. An adit was driven into the east bank of the White River at the 820 m level. Subsequent surface exploration was performed by various companies but there was no production. The deposit is located on the east side of the White River overlooking Miners Ridge and the Nutzotin Mountains (Kluane Ranges).

Access is by a single lane 4.5 km road leading south from the Alaska Highway at **km 1879.1**.

Refs.: 50 p. 65-68; 92 p. 111.

Maps: (T): 115 F/15 Canyon City
(G): 1177A Kluane Lake, Yukon Territory (1 inch to 4 miles)
1012A Northwest Shakwak Valley, Yukon Territory (1 inch to 4 miles)

Canyon City Copper Deposit

NATIVE COPPER, CHALCOCITE, CUPRITE, CHALCOPYRITE, BORNITE, COVEL-LITE, NATIVE SILVER

In amygdaloidal basalt

Large slabs of native copper have been found at this locality; one is reported to measure 2.5 m by 1 m and 12 cm thick, and to weigh 1165 kg. In the winter of 1957-58, it was transported to Whitehorse where it is displayed outside the Yukon Historical Society's MacBride Museum. The copper slabs are believed to have weathered out of fractures in Triassic basalt. Native copper also occurred as bunches and small masses. The host rock is traversed by calcite veins carrying chalcocite, native copper, cuprite and chalcopyrite. Bornite, covellite and native silver also occur in the rock.

Original reports of copper in the upper White River district were made by the Indians who utilized the metal for utensils and weapons, and who related to explorers the occurrence of masses of copper the size of a log cabin. Native copper was subsequently found by prospectors, although not in these sizes. The first reported occurrence of native copper was made by C.W. Hayes of the United States Geological Survey, who with Lieutenant Frederick Schwatka and prospector Mark Russell visited the region in 1891 on their way from Fort Selkirk, at the confluence of Pelly and Yukon rivers, to the Alaskan coast. They found small nuggets on Kletsan Creek, 15 to 25 km southwest of Canyon City. Using caribou horns, the Indians extracted from the rock copper nuggets averaging several grams in weight; the odd nugget weighed up to 4.5 kg. The bedrock copper deposit at Canyon City was discovered in May 1905 by Solomon Albert who staked it along with Joseph R. Slaggard and M.C. Harris. It was known as Discovery Copper grant and was located on the southeast bank of the Upper Canyon of White River nearly opposite the mouth of Boulder Creek and 2.5 km upstream from the abandoned settlement of Canyon City.

Plate XIX

Native copper slab with Joseph Slaggard, at its source near Canyon City, 1913. (GSC 25598)

Early work consisted of three adits, and some open-cuts and trenches on the steep valley wall 30 to 60 m above the river. Between 1967 and 1975, Silver City Mines Limited explored the deposit and discovered a new copper showing near the old adits. There was no production during this time. A 32 km tote-road was built; this branches off from the Canalask Mine road at a point 3 km south of the Alaska Highway. Native copper was also found in the gravels of Generc River, and in streams on the Alaska side of the boundary.

Refs.:   30 p. 4-5; 133-141; 50 p. 68-70; 86 p. 25; 92 p. 108-110; 131 p. 343.

Maps: (T):   115 F/15 Canyon City
        (G):   1177A Kluane Lake Yukon Territory (1 inch to 4 miles)
               1012A Northwest Shakwak Valley, Yukon Territory (1 inch to 4 miles)

| km | 1880.3 | Junction, road on right to White River flats. Small boulders of amygdaloidal basalt are common in the dry river flats. The amygdules are filled with stilbite, prehnite, chalcedony, quartz, calcite, serpentine and plagioclase feldspar. Other boulders are composed of a mixture of quartz and epidote, and of quartz and chlorite. Charcoal-grey and red marble containing crinoid fossils was also found. |

Plate XX

The same slab at the MacBride Museum, Whitehorse. (GSC 159491)

km	1881.2	Bridge over White River, at the Lower Canyon. The river was so named in 1850 by Robert Campbell of the Hudson's Bay Company because of its milky colour. Its waters originate in the Klutlan Glacier to the south and in the Russell Glacier in Alaska; fine silt and white volcanic ash suspended in the water give it the white turbidity. The steep river banks cut through the Kluane Ranges on the south side of the bridge, and on the north side, the river enters a broad flood plain characterized by shifting bars and quick sands. (Ref.: 30 p. 4, 59.)

Upper White River Gold Deposits

NATIVE GOLD

In placers

Gold was formerly obtained from the placers of Pan, Bowen and Hidden creeks which drain the southwestern side of the Nutzotin Mountains, about 15km west of the White River bridge. Although some coarse gold has been found in these creeks, they were not considered to be economic.

The gold-bearing placers of Pan Creek were discovered in the winter of 1912-13 by William E. James, Peter Nelson and Frederick Best of Dawson City. Because of water problems, mining was not feasible and James and Nelson moved on to Alaska after being told by a White River Indian, named Joe, about placer gold occurrences there; on May 3, 1913, they discovered the gold placers in the Chisana district, about 50 km west of the Alaska-Yukon border. In the staking rush that followed, prospectors stampeded from the north and from Burwash Landing via the Kluane Lake-Canyon City trail which followed a chain of stream valleys along the southwestern edge of the Kluane Ranges. From Canyon City, the trail continued to the Pan Creek area placers and then along Beaver Creek to the Chisana district. This trail was within the Duke Depression – a plateau-like area separating the Kluane Ranges and the Coast Mountains from the main mass of the St. Elias Mountains, including the Donjek Range.

Refs.: 14 p. 95; 15 p. 10-11; 29 p. 11, 29-30; 30 p. 125-133; 92 p. 107.

Maps: (T): 115 F/15 Canyon City
115 K/2 Dry Creek
(G): 1177A Kluane Lake, Yukon Territory (1 inch to 4 miles)
1012A Northwest Shakwak Valley, Yukon Territory (1 inch to 4 miles)

Volcanic Ash

White volcanic ash occurs throughout most of southern Yukon Territory. It can be observed as a mantle covering road-sides and lower slopes of mountains, as a thin layer beneath top-soil and rooted in vegetation, and as a thin band in road-cuts and scarped bands of streams and rivers. Its white colour contrasts strikingly with the enclosing soil or underlying rocks. It forms a single horizontal layer varying in thickness from a few cm in most areas to about 60 cm. On the east side of Grafe Creek (**km 1844.4**), the layer is about 58 cm thick and on the west bank of Donjek River, about 30 cm. It forms a conspicuous snow-white covering along the ditches and between trees and shrubs along the Alaska Highway between Pickhandle Lake (**km 1866**) and Whitehorse, and along the Whitehorse-Stewart Crossing Road between **km 113** and **km 145** (page 75).

The ash is composed of pumice that resembles white sand; fragments of pumice up to 10 cm long have been reported. The deposit is believed to have originated from a volcanic explosion in the vicinity of the Natazhat Glacier at the head of Kletsan Creek, about 48 km southwest of the White River bridge. At the source, dunes of ash several hundred m high were noted by geologists. At the time of the eruption, winds distributed the ash over two elongated lobe-shaped areas: one extending north along the International Border to the Ogilvie Mountains, the other east to the Mackenzie Mountains. The thickness of the deposit decreases progressively with increase in distance from the source. Because of its fairly uniform distribution over a wide area, geologists believe that the ash was deposited tranquilly as in a gentle snowfall, and that the fall was of short duration lasting not more than a few days at most. The event is believed to have taken place less than 2,000 years ago.

The occurrence of volcanic ash in the Yukon was first reported by Frederick Schwatka during his exploration of the Yukon River in 1883. Along the steep banks of the river between Five Finger Rapids and Fort Selkirk, he observed "a conspicuous white stripe some two or three inches in width" which he identified as volcanic ash. It has since been recorded by geologists investigating the Yukon Territory.

Refs.: 15 p. 36-39; 30 p. 107-111; 42 p. 43B-46B; 92 p. 90-92; 102 p. 196.

Maps: (T): 115 K/2 Dry Creek
(G): Figure 1, Map of upper Yukon River basin in Yukon Territory, and adjacent parts of Northwest Territories and northern British Columbia, showing distribution and thickness of Recent volcanic ash deposit. (In G.S.C. Memoir 267).

km	1889	Horsecamp Hill, on right, is composed of sedimentary and granitic rocks.

km	1895	Bridge over Sanpete Creek. Pebbles of epidote mixed with quartz, and pebbles of a deep red volcanic rock cut by veinlets of epidote occur in the bed of this creek, and at Dry Creek and Beaver Creek.

The Alaska Highway completes its long course within the Shakwak Valley and enters the Yukon Plateau which it traverses to the Yukon-Alaska border. The Shakwak Valley extends northwestward along the Nutzotin Mountains (Kluane Ranges) into Alaska, and the Yukon Plateau occupies a wide area as far north as Dawson City.

km	1900	Dry Creek No. 1 bridge.

km	1905	Dry Creek. Siwash Ridge on right. Between Dry and Snag creeks, the Highway is within the Wellesley Basin – a lowland with scattered, irregularly contoured knobs, ridges and small mountains rising 150 to 460 m above its floor which decreases in elevation from about 730 m (above sea level) in the southern part to 580 m in the north. The hills and ridges are composed mostly of resistant volcanic and granitic rocks, and schists, gneisses and quartzites; their slopes and the basin floor are thickly mantled with glacial deposits of sand, gravel, till and silt. The lowland is traversed by the White and Donjek rivers, and by Sanpete, Dry, Beaver and Snag creeks. Numerous small lakes and ponds occupy kettle holes between moraines, ridges, and mounds of glacial debris. Muskeg is a feature of some poorly drained areas. (Refs.: 14 p. 72; 15 p. 10; 30 p. 54-55, 58-60.)

km	1911	Snag Junction. A 27 km road leads to Snag on the White River at the mouth of Beaver Creek. A meteorological station was maintained at Snag from 1943 until 1966. Elkland Mountain (1456 m) is prominent to the west of the junction.

During the gold rush to the upper White River and Chisana districts, two routes travelled by prospectors and explorers from the north converged at Snag and continued overland to the southwest. One route followed the White River from its mouth on the Yukon River to Beaver Creek; the other was a pack trail from the Yukon River via Coffee Creek and Wellesley Lake to Snag. The shallow, swiftly flowing White River was navigated from its mouth to Beaver Creek by poling-boats and to the Donjek River by river-boats. Year-round roadhouses supplying accommodation and meals were established at regular intervals of 32 to 40 km along the White River and along the trail to the Alaskan gold placers; one was located at Snag which, due to the gold rush, grew rapidly from a two-cabin settlement to one with 250 cabins. A Royal Northwest Mounted Police detachment was established at Snag to patrol the route. (Ref.: 30 p. 11-13, 23-25.)

km	1923	Macauley Ridge is on right. It is formed of volcanic rocks.

km	1932	Bridge over Beaver Creek.

km	1934	Beaver Creek. This is the last settlement on the Canadian section of the Alaska Highway.

km	**1937**	Hill on left is formed of Tertiary rhyolite and latite lavas. (Ref.: 15 p. 35.)
km	**1944**	Bridge over Snag Creek. The creek is so named due to the great piles of driftwood it gathers along its banks during spring floods. Some of the logs become partly lodged in the creek bed producing snags; because of the turbidity of the water, they can not be seen and make navigation treacherous. Snags are also a common feature along Beaver Creek. (Ref.: 30 p. 59-60.)
		Outcrops of Paleozoic sedimentary rocks (shale, limestone, cherty slate, and sandstone) occur on both sides of the Alaska Highway from the Snag Creek bridge to about km 1951, the rocks are folded and intersected by faults. (Ref.: 30 p. 19.)
km	**1947**	The Alaska Highway emerges from the Wellesley Basin, and the topography to the north is characterized by undulating hills that reach elevations of about 915 m. For the next 8 km, the Highway is bordered by a swampy area occupied by Mirror Creek on the left, and by gentle hills on the right. Thick deposits of glacial drift occur along the road.
km	**1950**	Psilomelane was found in a vein cutting white-bedded rhyolite tuff on the north side of the Alaska Highway approximately 220 m east of **km 1950**. When discovered in 1949, the vein measured 50 cm wide and was exposed over a length of 7.6 m. The deposit was staked by W.T. Batrick and W. Hammond. (Ref.: 15 p. 44-45.)
km	**1955**	The broad area to the north of this point is unglaciated and lacks glacial deposits and other evidence of glaciation. This is because the Pleistocene ice-sheets that originated in the Icefield Ranges and moved into and north from the Shakwak Valley reached their northern limit at about this point.
km	**1965**	Alaska-Yukon border. The Alaska Highway continues to Fairbanks, Alaska where it terminates at Mile 1523.

There's gold, and it's haunting and haunting;
It's luring me on as of old;
Yet it isn't the gold that I'm wanting
So much as just finding the gold.
It's the great, big, broad land 'way up yonder,
It's the forests where silence has lease;
It's the beauty that thrills me with wonder,
It's the stillness that fills me with peace.

From "The Spell of the Yukon",
Robert W. Service

Plate XXI

Rocking for gold, Gold Hill, Bonanza Creek, 1899. (National Archives of Canada/PA 16223)

Plate XXII

Volcanic ash, **km 113** Whitehorse-Dawson Road, appears as white patches on the ground. (GSC 159494)

THE KLONDIKE ROAD

The Klondike Road links the Alaska Highway to Dawson. It consists of two sections: the Whitehorse-Stewart Crossing section, and the Stewart Crossing-Dawson section for a total distance of 540 km. The Klondike Road is within the Yukon Plateau. It leaves the Alaska Highway at **km 1488**, 18 km east of the original Dawson trail. The old Dawson trail proceeds north along the west side of the Miners Range to Carmacks; it is joined by the Klondike Road at **km 95**.

The Klondike Road: Whitehorse-Stewart Crossing Section

km	0	Junction, Alaska Highway at **km 1488**. The road log proceeds along the Klondike Road.
km	4.0	Bridge over Takhini River. The Takhini River flows from Kusawa Lake to the Yukon River; its steep banks expose glacial sand and silt. A thin layer of volcanic ash, about 5 cm wide, forms a white horizontal line which is visible near the top of the river banks.
km	5.9	Turn-off (left) to Takhini Hot Springs. The hot springs are located 10 km from the highway.
km	29	For the next 55 km the highway parallels the eastern flank of Miners Range, so named by G.M. Dawson of the Geological Survey of Canada for the miners ("...good fellows all of them" Ref.: 42 p. 157B) that he encountered during his geological reconnaissance of the Yukon in 1887. Pilot Mountain (at **km 29**), at an elevation of 2055 m, is the highest peak in the Miners Range. These mountains are composed of Mesozoic volcanic rocks. On the east side of the highway, the Yukon River widens to form Lake Laberge which is 50 km long and up to 7 km wide. White limestone of Triassic age is conspicuously exposed along the slopes of hills and ridges on the east side of the lake.
		Lake Laberge is a part of the 740 km waterway from Whitehorse to Dawson; sternwheel steamboats formerly maintained a regular service between these centres during the summer months. The lake was named for Michael Laberge of Montreal, an explorer for the Western Union Telegraph Company, who ascended the Yukon River in 1867. (Refs.: 42 p. 142B, 156B; 126 p. 21).

Big Salmon River Placers

GOLD

In placers

Gold was discovered in the bars of Big Salmon River by G. Langtry, P. McGlinchey and two other prospectors in 1881. Gold was subsequently found and worked in placers of Lewes (Yukon) and Teslin rivers, and Livingstone, Summit, Lake, Cottoneva, Little Violet and other creeks. The Livingstone Creek placers were the most productive with a high proportion of nuggets weighing over 30g, and one weighing 590g; native copper, magnetite, garnet and cinnabar were associated with the gold. Production from the district declined after 1920. A 64 km trail leads northeast from the east side of Lake Laberge (opposite Jackfish Bay), to the gold placers of the Livingstone Creek area in the Big Salmon Range.

Refs.:   20 p. 22-27; 42 p. 180B-181B.

Maps: (T):   105 E Laberge
                    372A Laberge sheet, Yukon Territory (1 inch to 4 miles)

km	**32.7**	Junction, single lane road to the Lake Laberge camp-site.
km	**56**	Fox Lake is on left with Miners Range in the background. The lake and the ridges adjacent to the highway are underlain by Jurassic sedimentary rocks consisting of conglomerate, sandstone, argillite, greywacke. (Ref.: 20 p. 13-14).
km	**89**	Junction, road to Braeburn Lake. The highway follows the valley of Klusha Creek for the next 30 km.
km	**95**	The old Whitehorse-Dawson Road joins the Klondike Highway at this point.
km	**96**	Conglomerate Mountain (1025 m) on the right is representative of the broad rounded mountains that rise from the fairly flat upland surfaces of Yukon Plateau. The mountain is composed predominantly of conglomerate of Jurassic age. (Ref.: 26 p. 33-34).
km	**113**	A layer of white volcanic ash can be observed as a white line or band near the top of gravel banks at the side of the highway for the next 30 km. It is also seen as a white carpet in adjacent forests.
km	**115**	Emerald (Twin) Lake.
km	**123**	The Dalton Trail from Champagne joined the old Dawson Road about here. From this point to Carmacks, the highway parallels the broad, steep-walled valley in which the Nordenskiold River cuts a meandering course isolating numerous oxbow lakes. This river was named by explorer Frederick Schwatka of the United States for Arctic explorer Baron von Nordenskiöld of Sweden. Lieutenant Schwatka, in the course of his 1883 expedition of the Yukon River from its source to its mouth, named numerous geographical features in honour of other explorers and geographers. (Ref.: 102 p. 190).
km	**124**	Montague roadhouse was formerly operated here to provide accommodation for miners and explorers using the Dalton Trail and the Whitehorse-Dawson Road. Other roadhouses, located at 30-40 km intervals, included one at the north end of in Braeburn Lake, at Emerald (Twin) Lake, at Carmacks, and at Minto.

km	135	Montague Mountain on right. Sedimentary rocks form the lower slopes near the highway, and andesite forms the upper slopes as well as Andesite Mountain to the north. A series of similar hills border the east side of the highway to Carmacks.
km	140	Porter Mountain, on the right side of the highway, is formed predominantly of syenite porphyry.
km	150	Bushy Mountain on right.
km	156	Mount Berdoe is on right. Bushy Mountain and Mount Berdoe are underlain by basalt and tuffs of Tertiary age.
km	164	Bridge over the Yukon River at Carmacks. The town was named in honour of George Carmack, a discoverer of gold in the Klondike.
		From Carmacks to Minto the highway follows the east bank of the Yukon River departing from the course of the old Dawson Road which was along the west bank.

Dawson Range Mines

GOLD, ARSENOPYRITE, PYRITE, TOURMALINE, GALENA, SPHALERITE, FREI-ESLEBENITE, ACANTHITE, NATIVE SILVER, ANDORITE, TETRAHEDRITE, STIB-NITE, SCORODITE; CHALCEDONY

In quartz veins cutting granitic and metamorphic rocks; in volcanic rocks

Gold and gold-silver deposits occur in the Mount Nansen-Freegold Mountain area at the eastern end of the Dawson Range, west of Carmacks. Lode gold was discovered on Freegold Mountain in 1930 by prospector P.F. Guder of Carmacks, and T.C. Richards of Whitehorse worked the Laforma Mine on the southern slope of Freegold Mountain in 1939-40. The gold occurs with arsenopyrite, pyrite and tourmaline in quartz veins. The workings at the mine consisted of three adits at elevations of 1190, 1106 and 1081 m; a mill was installed in 1938 and 2613g of crude gold (with a 20 per cent silver content) was recovered and made into a brick, believed to be the first gold brick made from a lode-gold deposit in the southern Yukon. Between 1939 and 1940, 44695g of gold were recovered.

The gold-silver properties are located on a ridge between Nansen and Victoria creeks. The quartz veins carry arsenopyrite with pyrite, galena, sphalerite, native silver, stibnite and the silver-bearing minerals freieslebenite, acanthite, andorite and tetrahedrite. Green scorodite, as a stain on the veins, was also reported. The gold-silver mineralization was discovered in 1962 by prospector, G.F. Dickson of Whitehorse. Mount Nansen Mines Limited and Brown-Mc-Dade Mines Limited opened the deposits by means of a number of adits. A mill was installed and operated by Mount Nansen Mines Limited from 1968 to 1969; gold, silver and lead were produced.

From Carmacks, a 68 km rough road leads to Freegold Mountain, and a 64 km road to the Nansen Creek-Victoria Creek area leaves the Freegold Mountain road about 65 km west of the Nordenskiold River bridge in Carmacks.

Along the old Mount Nansen road, leading south from about km 50 of the Freegold Mountain road, chalcedony geodes occur in volcanic rocks. An occurrence was staked by P.F. Guder at a point 6.4 km from the Freegold Mountain road.

76

Refs.:   10 p. 22-26; 50 p. 35-38; 55 p. 29-31, 34-38; 56 p. 8; 105 p. 33-36.

Maps: (T):   115 I/3 Mount Nansen
              115 I/6 Stoddart Creek
          (G):   340A Carmacks, Yukon Territory (1 inch to 4 miles)

km	166.7	Junction Campbell Highway (Highway 4).

Anvil Mine

GALENA, SPHALERITE, PYRITE, PYRRHOTITE, CHALCOPYRITE, MARCASITE,
MAGNETITE, TETRAHEDRITE, BOURNONITE, ARSENOPYRITE, ANGLESITE,
GOETHITE, GYPSUM

In phyllitic rocks

The ore consists of a massive assemblage of pyrite, pyrrhotite, galena and sphalerite with minor
chalcopyrite, marcasite and magnetite. Other minerals reported from the deposit include
tetrahedrite, bournonite, arsenopyrite, marcasite, anglesite, goethite and gypsum.

The deposit was discovered in 1965 by Dynasty Explorations Limited using geophysical and
geochemical surveys and geological mapping. In 1965 Anvil Mining Corporation Limited was
formed to continue the exploration and to bring the deposit into production. The ore was
estimated to contain 9.1 per cent combined lead-zinc, and 37.3g of silver per ton with reserves
of 57 million t. Mining was from an open pit. The mill began production in 1969, and the
lead-zinc concentrates were shipped to West Germany and Japan. The concentrates were
transported by truck to Whitehorse thence by rail to Skagway where they were transferred to
ships. From 1975 to 1982, Cyprus Anvil Mining Corporation operated the deposit. Curragh
Resources Inc. was the operator from 1986 to 1991 when the mine was closed.

The mine is located in the Anvil Range at an elevation of about 1220 m near Faro Creek, a
tributary of Rose Creek. As a result of mining activity, the new town of Faro came into
existence.

Road log from the Whitehorse-Stewart Crossing Road at **km 166.7**:

km	0	Proceed east onto the Campbell Highway. This road successively follows the valleys of the Yukon, Little Salmon, Magundy and Pelly rivers to Ross River settlement.
km	27	The highway follows the Salmon River Valley.
km	84	Little Salmon Lake on right. The lake is 34 km long and about 2.5 km wide. The ridges that rise abruptly from both sides of the lake are composed of schist, quartzite, limestone, greenstone and argillite of Paleozoic age. The ridges reach elevations of about 1960 m. Little Salmon Range, a unit of the Pelly Mountains, parallels the north shore of the lake, and its south shore marks the northern boundary of the Big Salmon Range.
km	119	The highway continues eastward between Magundy River and the southern end of the Glenlyon Range of the Pelly Mountains. Glenlyon Peak (Mount Hodder) at 2191 m and Truitt Peak at 2074 m (opposite km 122) are the highest peaks of the range which is underlain by a granitic batholith of Mesozoic age.

| km | 170 | Faro Junction, and turn-off to Faro and to the Anvil Mine. The road leads 29 km to the mine. At about this point the highway enters the Tintina Valley which it follows to Ross River which separates the Anvil Range on its northeast side from the St. Cyr Range on its southwest side. |

Refs.:   1 p. 400-405; 33 p. 39, 40, 42-43, 71-72; 50 p. 43-44; 110 p. 43-52; 112 p. 39; 131 p. 36; 138 p. 127.

Maps: (T):   105 K/6 Mount Mye
               (G):   13-1961 Tay River, Yukon Territory (1 inch to 4 miles)

The road log along the Whitehorse-Dawson road continues below.

| km | 167 | Tantalus Butte on right. |

Tantalus Butte Mine

COAL

High volatile bituminous coal has been produced intermittently from this mine since about 1923. The coal seam ranges in thickness from 2.5 to 6 m and occurs in a rock formation consisting of conglomerate with some sandstone and shale. The rocks are of Mesozoic age and form the butte into which an adit was driven to extract the coal. The portal overlooks the Yukon River and is visible from the highway.

The mine was originally operated to supply coal for domestic heating in Dawson; it was later operated by the Anvil Mining Corporation Limited for use in its operations at the Anvil Mine in Faro.

Refs.:9 p. 59-62; 50 p. 114.

Maps:(T):115 I/1 Carmacks

(G):340 A Carmacks sheet, Yukon Territory (1 inch to 4 miles)

km	172	For the next 8 km, the highway circles the eastern half of Five Finger Mountain which is underlain by volcanic rocks of Tertiary age. Its elevation is 897 m above sea level. At the northern base of the mountain on the east bank of the Yukon River, the Five Finger coal mine was formerly operated. (Ref.: 9 p. 62-63).
km	187	**Five Finger Rapids**
		The rocks beneath the rapids are conglomerate and sandstone of Jurassic age. The rapids are caused by these resistant strata which have a braking effect on the swiftly flowing (estimated at about 6.5 km per hour) Yukon River, above and below the rapids the river maintains an unobstructed course through a heavily drift-filled valley. Friable shale is associated with these rocks in exposures along the steep river banks and in the cliffs forming the shoreline of the islands. Fossils including shells and plants, and flat cherty concretions measuring up to 25 cm long, occur in the shale. Ammonites and pelecypods have been found in the shale lying beneath the sandstone and conglomerate on the east side of the river, just above

Plate XXIII

Five Finger Rapids, Yukon River; Dawson Range in the backgorund. (GSC 159527)

the rapids. These rapids were considered to rank second only to the Whitehorse Rapids in the dangers they presented to navigation along the Yukon River. In the distant background (looking west from the highway viewpoint) is the smooth-topped Dawson Range with elevations to about 1982 m. (Refs.: 9 p. 21-27; 42 p. 144B-147B).

km	204	The highway meets the original Dawson-Whitehorse Road and follows its course to Minto. The old Dawson Road crossed the Yukon River at Yukon Crossing, the site of the roadhouse.

Volcanic ash is visible along the highway from about this point to Minto. The ridge bordering the highway is underlain by volcanic and granitic rocks. The resistant volcanic rocks form the highest peaks of the Dawson Range to the southwest. (Ref.: 9 p. 29-30).

km	238	Minto. The old Dawson Road continued along the Yukon River to Pelly River and then to Dawson. The ill-fated Hudson's Bay Company post of Fort Selkirk was located at the junction of the Yukon and Pelly rivers, 37 km downstream from Minto. The post was established in 1848 by Robert Campbell on a point of land between the Pelly and Yukon rivers but, due to spring floods at this location, it was moved to the opposite (south) side of the river in 1852. The construction was nearly completed when the post was pillaged and burnt by hostile Coast Indians in spite of the vigilance of friendly local Indians. Parts of the old buildings and chimneys, built of basalt blocks, mark the site on the south side of the Yukon River about 2.5 km downstream from the Pelly River. Although at the

time this was the Company's most important post west of the Rockies, it was not re-established. (Refs.: 9 p. 1; 42 p. 135B-136B, 139B; 95 p. 46).

The Yukon River upstream from Fort Selkirk was until 1949 known as the Lewes River. It was named in 1842 by Robert Campbell in honour of John Lee Lewes, an official of the Hudson's Bay Company.

The highway leaves the Yukon River Valley and proceeds north along a drift-filled depression occupied by Von Wilczek Creek and Von Wilczek Lakes named by Schwatka in honour of Graf von Wilczek of Vienna. (Ref.: 102 p. 200).

| km | 270 | Pelly Crossing. The Pelly River was named by Robert Campbell for Sir John Henry Pelly of the Hudson's Bay Company. On the south side of the river and east of the highway is 1493 m. Ptarmigan Mountain underlain by mica schist and granite gneiss with some limestone on the northeastern side. (Refs.: 9 p. 16; 42 p. 137B). On the west side of the highway between Pelly and Stewart rivers, the Willow Hills form a ridge with elevations between 1190 m and 1372 m above sea level. In the distance, east of **km 328**, Grey Hunter Peak, at 2216 m, is the highest summit of the McArthur Group mountains which are formed of granitic rocks of Mesozoic age. These rocks have intruded older strata consisting mainly of slate. (Ref.: 12). |

| km | 330 | Junction, road to Ethel Lake. The highway crosses the Tintina Valley. |

| km | 343 | Bridge over Stewart River at Stewart Crossing. A rock-cut at the north end of the bridge exposes metamorphic rocks believed to be of Precambrian or early Paleozoic age (Ref.: 18). These rocks form the ridges to the northwest and northeast of the bridge. From Stewart Crossing to Dawson the highway route is within the Tintina Valley. |

The Stewart River is one of the principal tributaries of the Yukon River; it was named for James G. Stewart of the Hudson's Bay Company who explored it in 1849. It was navigable for river-boats for a distance of 320 km from its mouth to Fraser Falls, about 65 km upstream from Mayo.

Galena Hill-Keno Hill Mines

GALENA, SPHALERITE, FREIBERGITE, QUARTZ CRYSTALS, ARSENOPYRITE, PYRITE, SIDERITE, MARCASITE, CHALCOPYRITE, PYRRHOTITE, PYRARGYRITE, ACANTHITE, BOULANGERITE, JAMESONITE, BOURNONITE, MENEGHINITE, STEPHANITE, POLYBASITE, NATIVE SILVER, NATIVE ZINC, NATIVE GOLD, COVELLITE, CHALCOCITE, LIMONITE, WAD, ANGLESITE, CERUSSITE, MALACHITE, AZURITE, AURICHALCITE, BROCHANTITE, GYPSUM, PLUMBOJAROSITE, ROZENITE, GUNNINGITE, SENARMONTITE, BEUDANTITE, BINDHEIMITE, DUNDASITE, SCORODITE, SZOMOLNOKITE, SZMIKITE, ILESITE, HAWLEYITE, ARAGONITE, BARITE, TOURMALINE, KAOLINITE, MICA, MINIUM, STIBNITE

In fault veins cutting quartzite, phyllite, schist and greenstone

Galena, sphalerite and freibergite are the principal ore minerals of the silver-lead-zinc deposits in the Elsa-Galena Hill-Keno Hill area. Galena and amber to dark brown sphalerite occur as fine grained and coarsely crystalline aggregates, as groups of crystals, and as individual crystals. Dark grey to almost black metallic freibergite is generally found as grains and small irregular masses in the galena and sphalerite. Quartz, arsenopyrite, pyrite and brownish white to dark

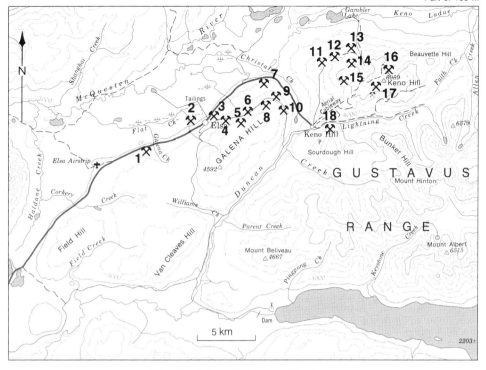

Map 7. Galena Hill-Keno Hill mines.

1. Silver King	10. Tin Can
2. Husky	11. Ladue
3. Elsa	12. Sadie-Friendship
4. Dixie	13. Lucky Queen
5. Hector-Calumet	14. Lake
6. Arctic	15. Shamrock
7. Formo	16. Nabob
8. Galkeno	17. No. 9
9. Bluebird	18. Mount Keno

brown and black siderite are commonly associated with these minerals, and in places occur as well-developed crystals occupying vugs. A number of metallic minerals occur less commonly in the ore zones. These include: marcasite, chalcopyrite, stibnite (rare), pyrrhotite, pyrargyrite (in cleavages in galena), acanthite (small fibrous masses and films associated with pyrargyrite and native silver), and the sulphosalts, boulangerite, jamesonite, bournonite, meneghinite, stephanite and polybasite. The sulphosalts are generally indistinguishable in the hand specimen. Native silver has been found in leaf, scale, arborescent and filament form in ice, and associated with quartz crystals in some of the underground operations that reach the zone of permafrost. Native zinc (rare), as tiny grey metallic plates was found with siderite, limonite and wad at the Elsa Mine. Grains, scales and tiny nuggets of native gold have been obtained by panning the residual soils of the area. Covellite and chalcocite have been reported as rare alterations of chalcopyrite. Limonite is common as yellow to brown earthy to botryoidal masses. Wad, an intimate intergrowth of hydrous manganese oxides (pyrolusite, psilomelane,

81

Plate XXIV

Husky Mine, Elsa. Mount Haldane in left background and foothills of Ogilve Mountain in right background. (GSC 159525)

manganite), occurs as black dendritic films and as coatings and botryoidal masses on vein minerals and on the host rocks. Secondary minerals forming coatings or encrustations include: light to dark grey banded anglesite on galena; white to grey cerussite, as earthy and tabular crystal aggregates associated with anglesite; malachite, azurite, aurichalcite (rare) and brochantite associated with freibergite and chalcopyrite; gypsum, as colourless to white crystal aggregates; yellow to rust-coloured earthy plumbojarosite; dull white rozenite, on pyrite; finely powdered white gunningite, on sphalerite; greyish to white earthy senarmontite, on jamesonite; greenish to yellowish brown beudantite, associated with galena, freibergite and other lead minerals; greenish yellow to brownish yellow bindheimite, associated with freibergite, jamesonite, galena and boulangerite; white to yellowish dundasite, as felt-like crusts and radiating crystals; yellowish to greyish and brownish green scorodite and yellowish green to yellowish brown pharmacosiderite, associated with arseonopyrite; and the sulphates szomolnokite, szmikite and ilesite. Hawleyite occurs as a bright yellow powdery coating on sphalerite, galena and siderite, it was first (1955) described from the Hector-Calumet Mine. Transparent crystals of gypsum associated with aragonite crystals (rare) line cavities in siderite, and crystals of barite have been found in cavities in dolomite. Other minerals reported from the deposit include tourmaline, kaolinite, mica and minium.

The rich silver-lead deposits of the Galena Hill-Keno Hill area were for a number of years Canada's most important source of these metals. The original discovery of argentiferous galena was made in 1906 on Galena Creek by H.W. McWhorter; this deposit became the Silver King Mine which was worked from 1913 until 1918. The discovery of a similar deposit near the summit of Keno Hill by Louis Beauvette in July, 1918, led to a prospecting rush which resulted in the staking of a number of claims in the area. The first production from the Keno Hill deposits was realized in 1920-21 by Keno Hill, Limited. During a 20-year period beginning in 1921, the Treadwell Yukon Company under geologist Livingston Wernecke, brought into production the Ladue, Sadie-Friendship and Lucky Queen mines on Keno Hill, and the Hector-Calumet, Arctic and Mastiff, Elsa, and Silver King mines on Galena Hill. In 1946, the present operator, United Keno Hill Mines, Limited, acquired the properties and since then has been almost the sole producer in the area, the others being MacKeno Mines, Limited on Galena Hill (1953-58) and Bellekeno Mines, Limited on Sourdough Hill (1952-54). Later, geologists of United Keno Hill Mines, Limited discovered the Husky and several other ore-bodies. The deposits are worked by open pit and underground methods. Over the years, large quantities of silver, lead, zinc and cadmium have been produced, and the district has been one of the leading producers of silver in Canada.

Visitors wishing to collect specimens from the mine dumps must apply to the personnel office of the Company at Elsa.

Road log from bridge over Stewart River at Stewart Crossing:

km	0	Proceed onto the road to Mayo (Highway 11). The highway parallels the north side of the Stewart River for 50 km.
km	53	Junction; turn left. The road on right leads to Mayo.
km	58	Junction, road on left, to the hydro-electric dam.
km	70.6	Junction, Minto Lake Road on left.
km	70.7	Junction, Mayo Lake Road on right. The lake is about 30 km from this junction. The lake, the river that drains it, and the town were named for Frank Mayo by Alexander McDonald, a miner and explorer who prospected in the Mayo area in 1887. Mr. Frank Mayo was a partner in the trading firm of Harper, McQuesten and Company.
km	78.3	Junction, road on left to Mount Haldane; continue straight ahead to Elsa.
		On the northwest side of Mount Haldane, at an elevation of 1067 m, galena-bearing veins similar to those at the Galena Hill-Keno Hill deposits were developed in 1918-20; the location is shown on topographical map 105 M/13.
km	94.6	Silver King Mine on right, overlooking the valley of the South McQuesten River and the foothills of the Ogilvie Mountains.
km	97.8	Elsa, at a junction. The road on right leads to the mine offices; to reach Keno Hill, turn left.
km	103.6	Junction, McQuesten-Hansen Lakes Road; continue straight ahead.
km	106.8	Formo Mine on right. On left to the north of Mount Haldane is a distant view of the Ogilvie Mountains. The mountains were named in honour of William Ogilvie, a Canadian government surveyor who surveyed much of the Yukon in the 1880s.
km	110.2	Galkeno Mill road. Straight ahead is a view of the Gustavus Range (elevation to 2044 m) which borders the north side of Mayo Lake.
km	112.3	Keno City, at a junction. The road on right leads to the Bellekeno Mine, the road on left to the Keno Hill mines.

Refs.: <u>22</u> p. 1-2, 7, 79, 113-164; <u>36</u> p. 3-5; <u>50</u> p. 20-24; <u>131</u> p. 380-381.

Maps: (T):   105 M/13 Mount Haldane
              105 M/14 Keno Hill
        (G):   1147A Keno Hill-Galena Hill area, Yukon Territory (1 inch to 4 miles)

Mayo Area Placer Deposits

GOLD, SCHEELITE, WOLFRAMITE, CASSITERITE, TOURMALINE, SCORODITE, NATIVE BISMUTH, HEMATITE, CINNABAR, GARNET

In placers

Numerous gold-bearing creeks were discovered between 1898 and 1903 when hundreds of prospectors stampeded into the Mayo area in search of the rich gold placers rumoured to exist in the vicinity of the Stewart River. The Haggart Creek placers had already been discovered in 1895, and those of the Stewart River prior to that date. Prospecting activity was accelerated after the discovery of the Duncan Creek placers in 1898 by the Gustaveson family (father and two sons), pioneers of the district; the gold was found in the canyon of the creek in the Gustavus Mountains and in its tributary, Lightning Creek. Gold was also recovered from the placers of Dublin Gulch, Secret Creek and Lynx Creek, all tributaries of Haggart Creek; from Minto Creek, Minto Lake (the northeastern end), McLagen Creek, a tributary of Minto Lake, and Highet Creek, a tributary of Minto Creek; from Johnson Creek, a tributary of McQuesten River; from Thunder Gulch, a tributary of Lightning Creek; and from Ledge and Davidson creeks, near Mayo Lake. Coarse nuggets have been reported including some the size of lima beans, and one weighing about 124g was found at Duncan Creek. Gold has been won from some of the streams in the district each year since 1898; the coarse gold is purchased by jewellers for use in the manufacture of attractive gold nugget jewellery.

Scheelite occurs as a white sand in the gold concentrates. It first became an important byproduct of gold mining during World War I when tungsten was in short supply, and its production has continued. For a number of years Dublin Gulch was the principal source of tungsten in the Yukon; other scheelite-bearing placers include Haggart, Lynx, Secret, Johnson, Scheelite, Sabbath (Swede) and Highet creeks. Wolframite is associated with the scheelite in some of the placers.

In addition to gold and tungsten ores, the creeks of the district have yielded the following minerals: yellowish to greenish brown tourmaline-cassiterite nodules (with sugary texture) measuring up to several cm in diameter, at Dublin Gulch and at Haggart and Arizona creeks; scorodite, as green bunches and irregular masses, at Dublin Gulch; native bismuth, as small grains and cleavage pieces, at Dublin Gulch and at Haggart Creek; cassiterite at Ledge Creek; siliceous hematite (Black Diamond) pebbles, at Dublin Gulch; pebbles of siliceous hematite containing jasper, at Duncan and Lightning creeks; cinnabar, at Canyon Creek; and garnet, at Dublin Gulch. The cassiterite-tourmaline nodules are derived from a vein deposit that has been trenched near the top of a hill overlooking Haggart Creek and Dublin Gulch.

Before panning in any of these placers, visitors should check with the Mining Recorder at Mayo to determine whether claims on them are held. Access to the creeks in the Minto Lake area is via the Minto Lake Road, to the Highet Creek-Johnson Creek area via a road branching off from the Minto Lake Road, to the Dublin Gulch-Haggart Creek area via a road branching off from the South McQuesten Road, to the Sourdough Hill area (Thunder Gulch, Duncan Creek, etc.) via a road leading south from Keno City.

Refs.: 11; 17 p. 19-30; 22 p. 84-85, 139-141, 163-164; 31 p. 13-26; 50 p. 106-112; 57 p. 74-82; 71 p. 18-20, 25-41; 101 p. 13-14.

Maps: (T): 105 M Mayo
             106 D Nash Creek
             105 P McQuesten
       (G): 1147A Keno Hill-Galena Hill area, Yukon Territory (1 inch to 4 miles)

The Klondike Road: Stewart Crossing-Dawson Section

km	**0**	Junction, at the bridge over Stewart River; proceed onto the road to Dawson. From this junction to the Clear Creek bridge, the highway parallels the Stewart River which has entrenched its course in the heavily drift-covered floor of the Tintina Valley, a broad trench across the Yukon Plateau. On the southwest side of the Stewart River, the uniform, rolling upland is broken by the White Mountains which project over 300 m above the surface, and on the opposite side of the river, long ridges border the highway; a network of deep valleys cut the plateau on both sides of the highway. The rocks comprising the ridges bordering the northeast side of the highway as far as **km 7.5** are predominantly interbedded quartz-mica schist and quartzite; similar metamorphic rocks forming the White Mountains have been intruded by basic rocks that cap the peaks. (Ref.: 13 p. 4, 9).
km	**47**	Bridge over the McQuesten River. This river bears the name of Leroy Napoleon McQuesten, a trader originally with the Hudson's Bay Company, and later with the Alaska Commercial Company. (Ref.: 102 p. 281, 284).
		The McQuesten River joins the Stewart River about 1.5 km west of the bridge; formerly, a detachment of the Royal North-West Mounted Police was located at the mouth. Opposite the mouth, Chest Mountain rises from the river level (457 m) to an elevation of 1188 m; it is underlain by granitic rocks.

Stewart River Placer Deposits

GOLD

In placers

The Stewart River was one of the first rivers in the Yukon to attract gold miners. Gold was recovered in paying quantities from its bars for many years beginning in 1883; the production reached a peak between 1885 and 1887. The bars were auriferous from the mouth of Mayo River to almost the mouth of the Stewart. Steamboat Bar, about 6 km below the mouth of McQuesten River, was the richest placer on the Stewart and was reported to yield $140 per day per man using a rocker. In 1886, a few of the miners sluiced the gravels using water pumped up by engines from the "New Racket" steamboat; each miner earned $1,000 in less than a month, after paying an equal sum to the owners of the boat. In 1910 and 1911, two dredges worked the bars but this operation proved to be financially unsuccessful.

The gold was fine and was localized in small areas near the head of each bar; the gold-bearing gravels were shallow, less than 60 cm thick.

Refs.:   31 p. 10, 13-14; 72 p. 5C-6C; 94 p. 40-43.

Maps: (T):   115 P McQuesten
        (G):   1143A McQuesten, Yukon Territory (1 inch to 4 miles)

km	54	Partridge Creek. A hot spring is located on the east side of Partridge Creek approximately 25 km upstream from the highway. The temperature of the water issued by the spring is 24°C.
km	57.4	Turn-off (left) to airstrip on the shore of Stewart River opposite Steamboat Bar.
km	60.5	Bridge over Clear Creek. Placer gold has been recovered from the placers in the upper sections of Clear Creek since 1895. Clear Creek Placers Company Limited operated a dredge on their claims in the 1940s. (Refs.: 13 p. 10-11; 17 p. 19; 72 p. 5C).
km	76.1	Junction, Clear Creek Road leading approximately 40 km to the Clear Creek placers. Before proceeding to this area, visitors should check with the Mining Recorder at Dawson to determine whether claims are held; panning in such claims is prohibited.
km	89	Gravel Lake on right. Beyond the lake, in the distance to the northwest is a view of the snow-clad, serrated ridges of the Ogilvie Mountains whose foothills rise abruptly from the northeastern side of the Tintina Valley. The peaks of these mountains are fairly uniform in elevation reaching up to about 2135 m above sea level. Between Gravel Lake and the Klondike River (km 129), Tintina Valley is occupied by Flat River; in this section, the valley reaches its maximum width of about 22 km. The southwest side of the valley is bordered by the Klondike Plateau, a unit of the Yukon Plateau.
km	120	The highway begins a 10 km descent to the mouth of Flat Creek on the Klondike River; it drops from an elevation of 760 m at km 119 to 460 m at Flat Creek.
km	129.5	Bridge over Flat Creek. From the Flat Creek bridge, the highway parallels the south bank of the Klondike River to its mouth on the Yukon River at Dawson.

On the left (south) side of the highway, rounded, dome-shaped hills rise to elevations of about 760 m to 915 m. They are underlain by metamorphic rocks (schists, gneisses and quartzites) of Precambrian or early Paleozoic age. |

Plate XXV

The Royal Northwest Mounted Police taken after their return from their search for Inspector Fitzgerald and party, Dawson, 1911. From left to right: Constable F. Twiner, Corporal W.J.D. Dempster, Constable J.F. Fyfe (R.C.M.P. Photo Library 4314).

The Dempster Highway

This 720 km highway links Arctic Red River at about km 1450 of the Mackenzie Highway and Inuvik to **km 142** on the Dawson-Stewart Crossing Road. The highway crosses the Ogilvie Mountains, the Taiga Ranges of the Mackenzie Mountains, and the Richardson Mountains. Initially, the road parallels the North Klondike River and crosses the Tintina Valley before entering the Ogilvie Mountains at about km 25. It reaches an elevation of about 1330 m at the North Fork Pass at km 80.

Plate XXVI

Prospectors and miners on a mountain slope near Chilkoot Summit enroute to the Klondike, c 1897. (National Archives of Canada/C 28646)

Plate XXVII

Mining operations at Grand Forks, a settlement that flourished during the Gold Rush and was located at the junction of Bonanza and Elodorado creeks; sluice boxes and timber shafts in foreground. (National Archives of Canada photo C-14544).

The peaks near the road are about 2135 m above sea level, and a 2364 m peak about 16 km southwest of the pass is the highest peak of the Ogilvie Mountains. Sedimentary strata intruded by granitic rocks comprise these mountains. From the pass, the highway descends to the valley of Blackstone River, bridges it at km 117, then proceeds past Chapman Lake and along Blackstone River. The section along Blackstone River (about 50 km) follows the route of an old trail formerly used by Indians in trading with Dawson, and for trapping and hunting in the vicinity of the Blackstone, Hart and Wind rivers. During construction of the highway, a number of Indian graves were discovered there (Pers. comm.: S.P. Baker). The trail was also used by the Royal North-West Mounted Police on their regular patrol from Dawson to Fort McPherson; the patrols reported caribou, mountain sheep, moose, ptarmigan and rabbits in the area.

Before reaching the Ogilvie River at km 198, the highway crosses the Taiga Ranges (elevations 1525 to 1738 m above sea level) via Windy Pass at km 160, and enters Porcupine Plateau. From km 177, permafrost conditions were encountered by the construction crew. Porcupine Plateau, a vast region of smoothly rounded hills and ridges with a maximum relief of 275 m, separates the mountains to the south and to the west from the Richardson Mountains. Within the plateau, the highway follows the valleys of the Ogilvie and Peel rivers, then heads in a northerly direction, bridges Eagle River, and crosses the Arctic Circle before proceeding through the Richardson Mountains and into the Peel Plateau to Fort McPherson. Between the plateau, the rugged Richardson Mountains rise abruptly to elevations of about 1220 m above sea level; the mountain system is 257 km long and 25 to 80 km wide, and is composed of folded sedimentary rocks. The final section of the highway is through the low-lying, lake-dotted Peel Plain (30 to 60 m above sea level) to Arctic Red River settlement at the mouth of the Arctic Red River on the Mackenzie River, then to Inuvik.

The highway was named in honour of Inspector W.J.D. Dempster who, as an officer of the Royal North-West Mounted Police, served at various posts in the Yukon from 1898 until 1934. From 1907 until 1911, he was a member of the Dawson-McPherson dog-sled patrol which left Dawson once each winter transporting mail to and from Fort McPherson, Herschel Island, Kittygaruit and Arctic Red River; the outgoing trip took 4 to 5 weeks, the return 3 to 4 weeks. The 765 km route followed the Yukon and Twelvemile rivers to Seely Pass, then proceeded along Blackstone River to the Hart, Wind and Peel rivers to Fort McPherson. It was also used as a trade route by the Indians, some preferred to trade at Dawson, others at Fort McPherson. Inspector Dempster is remembered in the Yukon for his arduous search in 1911 for the ill-fated "Lost Patrol", a McPherson-Dawson patrol that was lead by Inspector F.J. Fitzgerald but failed to reach Dawson; the tragic patrol had lost its way and perished, and was found by Dempster's patrol only about 50 km from Fort McPherson.

The first post established by the North-West Mounted Police (since 1920, the Royal Canadian Mounted Police) was at Fortymile in 1895; the force has since maintained law and order at various posts in the Yukon. Their intimate knowledge of the country, gained in the course of their patrols, was freely passed on to grateful miners, prospectors and explorers venturing into the unknown land. Their reports contain observations on prospecting and mining activity, on the native population, on game and timber, on traders, explorers and missionaires, and on trails and routes of accessibility – valuable information for the various concerns engaged in opening the North.

Refs.: 19 p. 20, 21, 23, 24, 25; 43 p. 248-253; 44 p. 245-251; 45 p. 232-239; 46 p. 256-262; 47 p. 293-301; 48 p. 200-209; 51 p. 44-47; 52 p. 2-3, 4; 81 p. 66-69; 117 p. 326-332; 134.

Maps: (T): 116 B and 116 C   Dawson
             116 G and 116 F   Ogilvie River
             116 H   Hart River
             116 I   Eagle River
             116 P   Bell River
             106 M   Fort McPherson
             106 N   Arctic Red River
             107 B   Aklavik
       (G): 900 A   Principal mineral areas of Canada (1:7,603,200)

The road log along the Klondike Road is resumed

km	165.7	Bridge over Hunker Creek. Between Hunker Creek and Bonanza Creek, extensive tailings from former placer operations line the highway. The Klondike Hills parallel the south side of the highway from Hunker Creek to the Yukon River.
km	166.5	Junction, Hunker Creek Road leading to the Dominion Creek area placers.
km	171.1	Junction, Bear Creek Road.
km	179.5	Junction, Bonanza Creek Road. This road leads to the Bonanza Creek-Eldorado Creek placers.
km	180.2	Bridge over the Klondike River.
km	182	Dawson, at the junction of the Klondike river with the Yukon River. Formerly the capital of Yukon Territory, it sprang into existence during the Klondike gold rush, rapidly attaining a population of 30,000; some of its buildings are now National Historic Sites. Dawson, or Dawson City, was surveyed by William Ogilvie and named by him in honour of Dr. George Mercer Dawson, the third director of the Geological Survey of Canada, and leader of the Yukon Expedition of 1887-88 which combined geological (under Dawson and R.G. McConnell) and surveying (under William Ogilvie) investigations that laid the groundwork for our knowledge of the geography and geology of much of Yukon Territory. The report of Dr. Dawson's explorations provided vital information to the miners and prospectors who stampeded to the Klondike in search of gold.

Plate XXVIII

A miner of the late 1890's at his shaft on a hill opposite Claim 58 below Bonanza Creek. (National Archives of Canada photo PA-16945)

Klondike Gold fields

GOLD, CASSITERITE, SILICEOUS HEMATITE

In placers

The phenomenally rich placer goldfields of the Klondike district ranked among the greatest in mining history. The Klondike creeks accounted for most of the Yukon Territory's placer gold production which, from 1866 to the end of 1970, was estimated (by the Dominion Bureau of Statistics) at 345243 kg valued at nearly 262 million dollars; over one-third of this value was realized in the period from 1898 to 1903. Production from the Klondike declined steadily after 1900, and dropped sharply when dredging operations ceased in 1966. In recent years, the annual production has been 187 to 250 kg obtained by hydraulicking and by sluice operations; the coarse nuggets are used by jewellers in the Yukon for fashioning into attractive gold nugget jewellery, and related articles.

The gold-bearing creeks are located southeast of Dawson in an area bound by the Yukon River on the west, the Klondike River on the north, Flat and Dominion creeks on the east, and Indian River on the south. They radiate from King Solomon Dome, on the Hunker Creek Road about 30 km south of the Klondike Road; some, including Bonanza, Eldorado, Bear and Hunker creeks flow into the Klondike River, and others including Quartz, Dominion, and Sulphur creeks flow into the Indian River. The most productive creeks have been Bonanza, Eldorado, Hunker and Dominion creeks. Eldorado creek was regarded as one of the richest placer creeks ever discovered and its first thirty-seven claims (each 152 m long and numbered from the mouth) yielded in the first 5 years an estimated value of 20 to 25 million dollars; the gold was coarse with numerous nuggets valued at 400 to 1,000 dollars each (assay value of $15.50 to $15.75 per ounce). At Hunker Creek, along a 1.6 km stretch, the yield was about $3,000 per running metre of the valley; nuggets were numerous in places. The original discoveries of large quantities of gold were made on Bonanza Creek, and a yield of nearly half a million dollars

Plate XXIX

Dredge and tailings, Bonanza Creek, 1971. (GSC 159500)

was reported from some of the richer claims on Dominion Creek. Other streams that have yielded gold in paying quantities include Bear, Allgold, Sulphur, Gold-Run, Last Chance, Gold Bottom, Quartz, Eureka and Adams creeks, and many of their gulches and pups. Most of the gold was in the form of flakes, grains and nuggets; it was alloyed with silver and its grade varied from $12.50 to $17.50 per ounce. The highest values were reported from Allgold Creek.

Cassiterite pebbles measuring up to 3 cm in diameter have been found in the gravels of Hunker, Dominion, Bonanza and Sulphur creeks; the pebbles are light to medium brown with black bands. They are known as wood-tin or "Yukon diamonds". Siliceous hematite ("Black diamond") occurs as pebbles at Hunker and Bonanza creeks. Both the cassiterite and the hematite take a high polish and are used locally for jewellery. Tusks of fossil mammoths and of bisons have been found in the gravels of Bonanza and Eldorado creeks.

The gold is believed to be derived from quartz veins and stringers associated with the mica and quartz schists comprising the country rocks that underlie the stream gravels. During a long unbroken period of erosion since Tertiary times, the quartz veins and the enclosing rock disintegrated and the gold accumulated in concentrations in the beds of streams and along their valley slopes. Since the Klondike area was not glaciated, the gold accumulations remained undisturbed until their discovery by miners. The auriferous gravels occur in the valley bottoms and on the benches along the lower valley slopes; the bench gravels are composed mostly of white quartz and are referred to as the "White Channel" gravels. Most of the gold was found in the gravels within 60 cm of bedrock and in crevices in the bedrock. The gravel is mantled with a layer of muck or peat usually from 1 to 2.4 m thick, but in places 15 m thick.

93

Plate XXX

Tourists' gold-panning operations, Bonanza Creek. (GSC 159503)

The original mining methods were by sinking a shaft to bedrock and by open-cuts. Because permafrost extends to 60 m or more in the Dawson area, the gravels had to be thawed before the gold-bearing gravels could be extracted. Thawing was achieved in the bottom of the shaft by various methods including wood fires, hot stones, steam thawers and water pumps; the thawed gravels were hoisted up and sluiced. The layer of muck insulated the underground workings preventing collapse of the walls; large chambers could thus be excavated, and one on Dominion Creek was reported to measure 42 by 70 m with no pillars for support. In the open-cut method, the muck was removed by directing naturally flowing water over a desired area in the spring, causing it and the gravels beneath to thaw. Hydraulicking was also used but lack of a water supply hindered operations. In about 1900, a dredge from the Lewes (Yukon) River was put into operation on Bonanza Creek. In 1923 the Yukon Consolidated Gold Corporation Limited was formed from 8 companies operating in the Klondike placers, and until 1966 it mined various creeks using electrically-driven dredges and bulldozer-sluicing plants. One of the dredges remains on Bonanza Creek and has been designated an Historic Site. Since 1966, placer mining has been conducted by individual operators, mostly by sluicing.

Plate XXXI

Yukon gold nugget bracelet. (GSC 202514-Z)

The discovery of spectacularly rich gold placers in the Klondike sparked a world-wide interest in the area, and drew the greatest stampede of miners and prospectors in the history of mining in Canada. Miners abandoned their placer operations in other parts of the Yukon and Alaska, and were joined by hundreds of others who made the long hazardous journey from more distant points to share in the wealth of the Klondike. Although the rush began in 1896, miners worked the bars of Indian Creek as early as 1894 and recovered gold from Quartz Creek in 1895. In the summer of 1896, Robert Henderson, who began prospecting in the area in 1894, found his richest yield in a stream he named Gold Bottom Creek, and invited a miner - George W. Carmack - to prospect the creek; the latter did so, but not being encouraged by the results, returned to Klondike (a settlement, now abandoned, at the mouth of the Klondike River) pausing on the way to prospect some of the creeks. He and his two Indian associates, Tagish Charlie and Skookum Jim, made a rich strike on Muffler Creek (later named Bonanza Creek by the miners); on August 17, 1896 he staked the Discovery Claim, a double claim, for himself and one for his companions, and related the news to miners at Forty Mile. As a result of these discoveries, claims were rapidly staked along the whole of Bonanza Creek, its tributaries and gulches, and in other creeks in the area. By 1899, most of the gold placers in the district were discovered, and the town of Dawson City became the commercial, social and mining centre of the area. The Discovery Claim on Bonanza Creek has been designated a Historic Site by the Department of Indian and Northern Affairs.

Most of the miners made their way to the Klondike along the Trail of '98: from Skagway on foot across the Boundary Ranges of the Coast Mountains via the Chilkoot Pass to Lake Bennett where they embarked on the Yukon River to take them to Dawson; lacking a local supply of boats, the earliest miners constructed their own craft from pine and spruce trees at Lake Bennett. The sudden demand for transportation services resulted in a ship-building boom at the settlement of Bennett, in the installation of river-boat services from Bennett Lake to Dawson, and in the construction of the White Pass and Yukon Railway from Skagway to Whitehorse. With the completion of the railway in 1900, Bennett became a ghost-town and the stern-wheel steamer route to Dawson originated at Whitehorse. A network of roads connected the placer operations to Dawson City.

Before panning any of the placers, visitors should check with the Mining Recorder in Dawson to determine whether claims are held. A check should also be made on the condition of the roads. Access to the creeks is as follows: Allgold Creek, from Flat Creek at **km 129.5** on the Dawson - Stewart Crossing Road; Hunker, Dominion, Gold Run, Sulphur, Eureka, Quartz, Gold Bottom and Last Chance creeks, from the Hunker Creek Road; Bonanza, Eldorado and Adams creeks, from the Bonanza Creek Road. The dredge on the Bonanza Creek Road is located 16 km from the highway. Tourist facilities for panning gold are set up at points on the Bonanza Creek Road; since the locations may vary from year to year, visitors should consult the local tourist office.

Refs.:   5 p. 147; 21 p. 352-354; 50 p. 91-103; 84 p. 5B-69B; 87 p. 12-14; 90 p. 55A-62A; 95 p. 79, 87-88, 119; 101 p. 13-14; 125 p. 21-22, 36.

Maps: (T):   115 O/10 Granville
115 O/14 Grand Forks
115 O/15 Flat Creek
116 B/3 Dawson
(G):   711A Ogilivy, Yukon Territory (1 inch to 4 miles)
1011 Auriferous gravels on Bonanza and Hunker creeks, Klondike Mining district Yukon (1 inch to 1/2 mile)
688 Klondike gold fields (1 inch to 2 miles)

The Sixtymile Road

The Sixtymile road links the Klondike Highway to Alaska. Its route is along the crest of a long, flat-topped ridge underlain by schists and quartzites; the ridge separates the Yukon River and Fortymile Creek to the north from Swede Creek and Sixtymile River to the south. Much of the road is above timberline which is at about 1067 m above sea level. It traverses the northern part of Klondike Plateau (a unit of Yukon Plateau), an unglaciated region of widespread discontinuous permafrost. In travelling along the road, a top-of-the-world view unfolds a seemingly endless series of long, flat-topped ridges of fairly uniform elevation, that have been dissected into a maze of deep gently curved V-shaped valleys whose floors are 457 to 915 m below the crests. This topography is the result of long continuous erosion since Tertiary times and the absence of glacial action.

Road log along the Sixtymile Road from Dawson:

km	0	Ferry landing on the west side of the Yukon River, opposite Dawson. The Moosehide Hills form a ridge north of Dawson, and about 10 km downstream, is the site of Fort Reliance, a former trading post on the Yukon River operated by Harper, McQuesten and Company.
km	11	The highway, in reaching the crest of the ridge, has climbed from an elevation of about 335 m above sea level at the ferry landing to 1067 m. Swede Creek is on left, and the Yukon River with the Ogilvie Mountains in the distance on the right.
km	48	The castle-like formation along the north side of the road is composed of quartzite; the less resistant surrounding rocks have been weathered leaving these block-like forms.
km	53	Junction, road to Clinton Creek and Fortymile River (so-named because it is 40 miles from Fort Reliance). The description of the Clinton Creek Mine is given on page 98.

The discovery in the autumn of 1886 of coarse gold on Fortymile River caused a migration of miners from all other camps to the area. Gold was found along a 160 km stretch from the mouth of the river, and some miners were reported to recover nearly $100 worth of gold per day. Platinum was also found. Most of the productive bars were located in the Alaska section of the river.

In the spring of 1887, a trading post was established at the mouth of Fortymile River on the Yukon River by Harper and McQuesten. A town sprang up and included blacksmith shops, and dance, billiard and opera houses, a cigar factory, bakeries, breweries, distilleries, and a detachment of the Royal North-West Mounted Police. It became a ghost town when the Klondike attracted the miners away from the area.

The road log continues along the Sixtymile Road.

km	55	Swede Dome on left.
km	79	Junction, road to the Sixtymile gold fields.
km	92	The road at this point is at an elevation of about 1310 m, the highest in its course.
km	95	Junction, road to Sixtymile goldfields. A description of the Sixtymile goldfields is given on page 99.
km	97	Yukon-Alaska border.

Refs.: 16 p. 69-71; 19 p. 22-23; 24; 37 p. 37-48, 52; 42 p. 181B-182B; 55 p. 105-107; 58 p. 15; 83 p. 139D-140D; 95 p. 72; 125 p. 37, 41.

Maps: (T): 116 B & 116 C Dawson
(G): 1284A Dawson, Yukon Territory (1 inch to 4 miles)

Plate XXXII

Clinton Creek Mine, 1971. (GSC 159495)

Clinton Creek Mine

ASBESTOS, SERPENTINE, MAGNETITE PICROLITE, MAGNESITE, TREMOLITE, HY-DROMAGNESITE, BRUCITE, ARAGONITE, PYROAURITE, OPAL, FUCHSITE, CHAL-COPYRITE, GARNIERITE

In serpentinite intruding schist, quartzite, gneiss and crystalline limestone

Golden-green cross-fibre asbestos occurs in light to medium green massive serpentine; the fibres measure up to 3 cm long but average much less. Grains, crystals and pods of magnetite occur in the serpentine. Yellowish green picrolite is also present. Other minerals associated with the serpentine are: magnesite, as compact white translucent to chalk-like masses and veins; tremolite, as white to grey radiating fibrous aggregates; hydromagnesite, as white microscopic discs; brucite, as white to greyish white fibrous masses with fibres several cm long; aragonite, as coarse white, vitreous radiating fibrous aggregates; and pyroaurite, as colourless silky, flaky patches on serpentine. Common opal has been found near the surface of the pit; it varies in colour from pea-green to olive-green and from brownish red to brown, and each background colour is mottled with tones of the other colours. Fuchsite, garnierite and chalcopyrite were found in the deposit.

The deposit was discovered in 1957 by G. Walters of Dawson and the staking was financed by the Caleys, also of Dawson. In 1960, Cassiar Asbestos Corporation Limited acquired the property and put it into production from 1967 to 1978. The mine is about 225 km south of the Arctic Circle; it is located at an elevation of 488 m on Porcupine Hill which overlooks Clinton Creek. The mill was situated on Trace Hill, on the opposite side of Clinton Creek, and ore was transported via a 1.6 km aerial tramline. The fibre was transported by truck to Whitehorse, by rail to Skagway, and finally by container-ships to the Company's warehouses in Vancouver. In winter months when ferry service is discontinued on the Yukon River at Dawson, the fibre was unloaded and transported over the Yukon River by an aerial tramline, then reloaded onto trucks. The mine consists of three pits: the main pit which is 272 m deep, the Creek pit which is located 450 m east of the main pit, and the Snowshoe pit, located 360 m east of the Creek pit.

Road log to the mine from Sixtymile Road at km 53 (see page 97):

km	0	Proceed onto Clinton Creek Road.
km	31	Bridge over Fortymile River. The old town of Fortymile was located approximately 5 km downstream from this bridge.
		The new town of Clinton Creek has been established on the northwest side of the bridge.
km	44	Mine

Refs.:   35 p. 216-220; 50 p. 31-32; 57 p. 19-21.

Maps: (T):   116 C/7 Forty Mile
116 B & 116 C Dawson
(G):   1284A Dawson, Yukon Territory (1 inch to 4 miles)

Sixtymile River Goldfields

GOLD, CINNABAR, GALENA

In placers

Gold was discovered in the Sixtymile district in 1892 by C. Miller on Miller Creek, about 5 km from its mouth. Subsequent discoveries were made at Glacier, Big Gold, Little Gold, Bedrock and Matson creeks, and at Sixtymile River. Both fine and coarse gold were recovered and nuggets valued at up to $8 each were found at the Miller Creek and Sixtymile River placers. Gold at that time was valued at $20.64 per ounce.

Gold was mined from gravels in the Valley bottoms and on benches or terraces along the streams. The workings consisted of opencuts, shafts and dredging. Mining was done at the following locations: Sixtymile River, between the mouth of Miller Creek and the mouth of Big Gold Creek; Miller Creek, for a distance of about 5 km beginning at its mouth; Glacier Creek, about 5 km from its mouth, Matson Creek, near the mouth of Weide Gulch, (about 8 km above the forks of the creek); Big Gold Creek, from the mouth of Glacier Creek to Sixtymile River. Original operations were conducted on Miller Creek by Nolasque Tremblay, Joe Lemay, Joe Roi and Louis Boucher. Production reached a peak in 1895. Two dredges operated in the area, one on Miller Creek (1915-16) and on Sixtymile River (between 1929 and 1941), and the other on Big Gold Creek (between 1947 and 1959). Fragments of cinnabar (measuring up to 1 cm) and galena were recovered from the placers in Sixtymile River near the mouth of Miller Creek. The goldfields are about 16 km from the Sixtymile Road.

Refs.:　16 p. 69-71; 37 p. 37-48, 52; 42 p. 181B-182B; 55 p. 105-107; 58 p. 15; 95 p. 72; 125 p. 37, 41.

Maps:　(T):　115 N/9 Matson Creek
　　　　　　115 N/15 Crag Mountain
　　　　　　116 C/2 Sixtymile
　　　　(G):　1812 Sixtymile and Ladue rivers, Yukon Territory (1 inch to 4 miles).

ADRESSES FOR MAPS AND REPORTS PUBLISHED BY VARIOUS GOVERNMENT AGENCIES

Geological reports published by Government of Canada

*Publications Office,
Geological Survey of Canada,
Department of Energy, Mines and Resources,
601 Booth Street,
Ottawa, Ontario,
K1A 0E8 (613-995-4342)

Publishing Centre
Supply and Services Canada
Hull, Quebec
K1A 0S9 (613-997-2560)

or

Authorized agents (See Book dealers, yellow pages of telephone book)

Geologial maps published by Government of Canada

*Publications Office,
Geological Survey of Canada,
Department of Energy, Mines and Resources,
601 Booth Street,
Ottawa, Ontario,
K1A 0E8 (613-995-4342)

Geological maps and reports published by Government of British Columbia

Crown Publications,
546 Yates Street,
Victoria, British Columbia
V8W 1K8 (604-386-4636)

Topographic maps

*Canada Map Office,
Department of Energy, Mines and Resources,
615 Booth Street
Ottawa, Ontario
K1A 0E9 (613-952-7000)

*Prepayment is required for all orders; cheques should be made payable to the Receiver General of Canada.

Road maps and travel information

Tourism British Columbia,
1117 Wharf Street,
Victoria, British Columbia,
V8W 2Z2 (604-387-1428 or 1-800-663-6000)

Tourism Yukon,
Government of Yukon,
P.O. Box 2703
Whitehorse, Yukon,
Y1A 2C6 (403-667-5340)

MINERAL, ROCK DISPLAYS

Indian and Northern Affairs Canada,
200 Range Road,
Whitehorse, Yukon.

Kluane Historical Society Museum,
Burwash Landing,
Mile 1093, Alaska Highway,
Yukon.

MacBride Museum,
Whitehorse, Yukon.

Yukon Chamber of Mines,
412 Main Street,
Whitehorse, Yukon.

The Dawson City Museum,
Dawson, Yukon.

Keno Mining Museum
Keno, Yukon.

SELECTED REFERENCES

1 Aho, A.E.
1969:   Base metal province of Yukon; Bulletin, Canadian Institute of Mining and Metallurgy, v. 62, no. 684, p. 397-409.

2 Aitken, J.D.
1959:   Atlin map-area, British Columbia; Geological Survey of Canada, Memoir 307.

3 Alcock, F.J.
1930:   Zinc and lead deposits of Canada; Geological Survey of Canada, Economic Geology Series 8.

4 Bates, Robert L. and Jacson Julia A.
1987:   Glossary of Geology, 3rd Ed; American Geological Institute.

5 Bilsland, W.W.
1952:   Atlin 1889-1910: the story of a gold boom; British Columbia Historical Quarterly, v. 16, no. 3-4, p. 121-179.

6 Black, J.M. and Hemsworth, F.J.
1948:   Taku River; British Columbia Minister of Mines, Annual Report, 1947, p. A61-A64.

7 Blusson, S.L.
1968:   Geology and tungsten deposits near the headwaters of Flat River, Yukon Territory and southwestern district of Mackenzie, Canada; Geological Survey of Canada, Paper 67-22.

8
1965:   Catalogue of type invertebrate fossils of the Geological Survey of Canada, v. II; Geological Survey of Canada.

9 Bostock, H.S.
1965:   Carmacks district, Yukon; Geological Surv.ey of Canada, Memoir 189.

10
1941:   Mining industry of Yukon, 1939 and 1940; Geological Survey of Canada, Memoir 234.

11
1943:   Upper McQuesten River, Yukon; Geological Survey of Canada, Preliminary map 43-9 (1 inch to 2 miles).

12
1947:   Mayo, Yukon Territory; Geological Survey of Canada, Map 890A (1 inch to 4 miles).

13
1948:   McQuesten, Yukon Territory (Prel. Map); Geological Survey of Canada, Paper 48-25.

14
1948:   Physiography of the Canadian Cordillera, with special reference to the area north of the fifty-fifth parallel; Geological Survey of Canada, Memoir 247.

15
1952:   Geology of the northwest Shakwak Valley, Yukon Territory; Geological Survey of Canada, Memoir 267.

16
1957:   Yukon Territory, selected field reports of the Geological Survey of Canada, 1898 to 1933; Geological Survey of Canada, Memoir 284.

17
1959:   Yukon Territory, in Tungsten deposits of Canada; Geological Survey of Canada, Economic Geology Series 17, p. 14-37.

18
1964:   Geology of McQuesten, Yukon Territory; Geological Survey of Canada, Map 1143A (1 inch to 4 miles).

19
1970:   Physiographic subdivisions of Canada, in Geology and Economic Minerals of Canada; Geological Survey of Canada, Economic Geology Series 1, 5th Ed., p. 11-32 and Map 1254A.

20 Bostock, H.S. and Lees, E.J.
1938:   Laberge map-area, Yukon; Geological Survey of Canada, Memoir 217.

21 **Bostock, H.S., Mulligan, R. and Douglas, R.J.W.**
    1957:   The Cordilleran region, in Geology and Economic Minerals of Canada; Geological Survey of Canada, Economic Geology Series 1, 4th Ed., p. 283-392.

22 **Boyle, R.W.**
    1965:   Geology, geochemistry and origin of the lead-zinc-silver deposits of Keno Hill-Galena Hill area, Yukon Territory; Geological Survey of Canada, Bulletin 111.

23 **Brown, C.J.**
    1961:   The geology of the Flat River tungsten deposits, Canada Tungsten Mining Corporation Limited; Bulletin, Canadian Institute of Mining and Metallurgy, v. 54, no. 591, p. 510-513.

24 **Brown, R.J.E.**
    1967:   Permafrost in Canada; Geological Survey of Canada, Map 1246A (1 inch to 120 miles).

25 **Cairnes, D.D.**
    1907:   Explorations in a portion of the Yukon, south of Whitehorse; Geological Survey of Canada, Summary Report for 1906, p. 22-34.

26 1910:   Lewes and Nordenskiold rivers coal district, Yukon Territory; Geological Survey of Canada, Memoir 5.

27 1912:   Wheaton district, Yukon Territory; Geological Survey of Canada, Memoir 31.

28 1913:   Portions of Atlin district, British Columbia; Geological Survey of Canada, Memoir 37.

29 1915:   Explorations in southwestern Yukon; Geological Survey of Canada, Summary Report for 1914, p. 10-33. (Reprinted in Bostock, 1957, p. 354-380.)

30 1915:   Upper White River district, Yukon; Geological Survey of Canada, Memoir 50.

31 1916:   Mayo area-Scroggie, Barker, Thistle, and Kirkman creeks - Wheaton district, Yukon Territory; Geological Survey of Canada, Summary Report for 1915, p. 10-49.

32 **Campbell, Finley A.**
    1960:   Nickel deposits in the Quill Creek and White River areas, Yukon; Bulletin, Canadian Institute of Mining and Metallurgy, v. 53, p. 953-959.

33 **Campbell, R.B.**
    1967:   Geology of Glenlyon map-area, Yukon Territory; Geological Survey of Canada, Memoir 352.

34 **Challinor, John**
    1961:   A dictionary of geology; University of Wales Press, Cardiff.

35 **Christian, J.D.**
    1966:   The Clinton Creek asbestos project and its effect on Yukon; Western Miner, v. 39, no. 4, p. 216-220.

36 **Cockfield, W.E.**
    1920:   Mayo area, Yukon; Geological Survey of Canada, Summary Report for 1919, pt. B, p. 3-7.

37 1921:   Sixtymile and Ladue Rivers area, Yukon; Geological Survey of Canada, Memoir 123.

38 1926:   Silver-lead deposits in Atlin district, British Columbia; Geological Survey of Canada, Summary Report for 1925, pt. A, p. 15-24.

39 **Cockfield, W.E. and Bell, A.H.**
    1926:   Whitehorse district, Yukon; Geological Survey of Canada, Memoir 150.

40 **Cooke, H.C.**
    1946:   Canadian lode gold areas (summary account); Geological Survey of Canada, Economic Geology Series 15.

41 **Dana, Edward Salisbury**
    1904:   The system of mineralogy of James Dwight Dana, 6th Ed., John Wiley and Sons.

42   **Dawson, George M.**
1888:   Report on an exploration in the Yukon district, Northwest Territories and adjacent northern portion of British Columbia; Geological Survey of Canada, Annual Report, New Series, v. III, pt. 1, p. 1B-277B.

43   **Dempster, W.J.D.**
1909:   Constable W. Dempster, Patrol, Dawson to Fort McPherson; Royal North West Mounted Police, Annual Report, 1908, Appendix F, p. 248-253.

44   1910:   Constable W. Dempster, Patrol, Dawson to Fort McPherson; Royal North West Mounted Police, Annual Report, 1909, Appendix C, p. 245-251.

45   1911:   Report of Constable W.J. Dempster on patrol from Dawson to Fort Macpherson (winter); Royal North West Mounted Police, Annual Report, 1910, Appendix D, p. 232-239.

46   1913:   Sergeant W.J.D. Dempster's patrol from Dawson to Fort Macpherson and return; Royal North West Mounted Police, Annual Report, 1912, Appendix D, p. 256-262.

47   1914:   Sergeant W.J.D. Dempster's patrol, from Dawson to Fort Macpherson and return; Royal North West Mounted Police, Annual Report, 1913, Appendix C, p. 293-301.

48   1953:   The lost patrol; RCMP Quarterly, v. 18, no. 3, p. 200-209. (As told to George Black).

49   **Douglas, R.J.W., Gabrielse, H., Wheeler, J.O., Stott, D.F. and Belyea, H.R.**
1970:   Geology of western Canada in Geology and Economic Minerals of Canada; Geological Survey of Canada, Economic Geology Series 1, 5th Ed., Chap 8, p. 367-488, and Chart III.

50   **Findlay, D.C.**
1969:   The mineral industry of Yukon Territory and southwestern district of Mackenzie, 1967; Geological Survey of Canada, Paper 68-68.

50a   **Fleischer, Michael and Mandarim, Joseph A.**
1991:   Glossary of Mineral Species 1991; The Mineralogical Record Inc., 6th ed.

51   **Forrest, A.E.**
1908:   Constable A.E. Forrest, patrol, Dawson to Fort Macpherson; Royal North West Mounted Police, Annual Report, 1907, Appendix D, p. 44-47.

52   **Gabrielse, H.**
1957:   Geological reconnaissance in the northern Richardson Mountains, Yukon and Northwest Territories; Geological Survey of Canada, Paper 56-6.

53   1963:   McDame map-area, Cassiar district, British Columbia; Geological Survey of Canada, Memoir 319.

54   **Graham, Charles**
1947:   Notes on metal mines; British Columbia Minister of Mines, Annual Report, 1946, p. A60-A61.

55   **Green, L.H.**
1966:   The mineral industry of Yukon Territory and southwestern District of Mackenzie, 1965; Geological Survey of Canada, Paper 66-31.

56   1968:   Lode mining potential of Yukon Territory; Geological Survey of Canada, Paper 67-36.

57   **Green, L.H. and Godwin, C.I.**
1964:   The mineral industry of Yukon Territory and southwestern District of Mackenzie, Northwest Territories, 1963; Geological Survey of Canada, Paper 64-36.

58   **Green, L.H. and Roddick, J.A.**
1962:   Dawson, Larsen Creek, and Nash Creek map-areas, Yukon Territory; Geological Survey of Canada, Paper 62-7.

59 Hage, C.O.

1944: Geology adjacent to the Alaska Highway between Fort St. John and Fort Nelson, British Columbia; Geological Survey of Canada, Paper 44-30.

60 Hanson, G. and McNaughton, D.A.

1936: Eagle-McDame area, Cassiar district, British Columbia; Geological Survey of Canada, Memoir 194.

60a Harris, Donald C., Roberts, Andrew C., Thorpe, Ralph I., Jonasson, I.R., Criddle, Alan J.

1984: Lapieite $CuNiSbS_3$, a new mineral species from the Yukon Territory, in Canadian Mineralogist, v. 22, p. 561-564.

61 Holland, Stuart St.

1950: Placer gold production in British Columbia; British Columbia Department of Mines, Bulletin 28.

62 1960: Notes on metal mines, Alaska Highway; British Columbia Minister of Mines, Annual Report for 1959, p. 19-21.

63 1962: Jade in British Columbia; British C.olumbia Minister of Mines and Petroleum Resources., Annual Report for 1961, p. 119-126.

64 Howell, J.V.

1960: Glossary of geology and related sciences, 2nd Ed., American Geological Institute, Washington.

65 Hughes, J.E.

1967: Geology of the Pine Valley, Mount Wabi to Solitude Mountain, northeastern British Columbia; British Columbia Department of Mines and Petroleum Resources, Bulletin 52.

66 Irish, E.J.W.

1958: Charlie Lake, west of sixth meridian, British Columbia; Geological Survey of Canada, Map 17-1958 and descriptive notes (1 inch to 4 miles).

67 Irvine, W.T.

1957: Tulsequah Chief and Big Bull mines; in Structural geology of Canadian ore deposits, Congress volume; Canadian Institute of Mining and Metallurgy, 6th Commonwealth Mining and Metallurgical Congress.

68 Jambor, J.L. and Boyle, R.W.

Gunningite, a new zinc sulphate from Keno Hill-Galena Hill area, Yukon; Canadian Mineralogist, v. 7, pt. 2, p. 209-218.

69 James, H.T.

1928: Northwestern mineral survey district (no. 1); British Columbia Minister of Mines, Annual Report for 1927, p. C57-C115.

70 Johnston, W.A.

1926: Gold placers of Dease Lake area, Cassiar district, British Columbia; Geological Survey of Canada, Summary Report for 1925, pt. A, p. 33-74.

71 Keele, Joseph

1905: The Duncan Creek mining district, Stewart River area, Yukon; Geological Survey of Canada, Summary Report for 1904, pt. A, p. 18-41.

72 1906: The Upper Stewart River region; Geological Survey of Canada, Annual Report for 1904, v. XVI, p. 1C-23C.

73 Kerr, F.A.

1926: Dease Lake area, Cassiar district, British Columbia; Geological Survey of Canada, Summary Report for 1925, pt. A, p. 75-99.

74 1948: Taku River map-area, British Columbia; Geological Survey of Canada, Memoir 248.

75   **Kindle, E.D.**
      1945:   Geological reconnaissance along the Canol Road, from Teslin River to MacMillan Pass,
              Yukon; Geological Survey of Canada, Paper 45-21.

76   1953:   Dezadeash map-area, Yukon Territory; Geological Survey of Canada, Memoir 268.

77   **Lang, A.H.**
      1970:   Prospecting in Canada; Geological Survey of Canada, Economic Geology Series 7, 4th
              Ed.

78   **Laudon, Lowell R. and Chronic, B.J. Jr.,**
      1947:   Mississippian rocks of Meramec age along Alcan Highway, northern British Columbia;
              Bulletin, American Association of Petroleum Geologists, v. 31, no. 9, p. 1608-1618.

78a   **Leaming, S.F.**
      1978:   Jade in Canada; Geological Survey of Canada, Paper 78-19.

79   **Lord, C.S.**
      1944:   Geological reconnaissance along the Alaska Highway between Watson Lake and Teslin
              River, Yukon and British Columbia; Geological Survey of Canada, Paper 44-25.

80   **Mandy, Joseph T.**
      1937:   Northwestern mineral survey district (no. 1); British Columbia Minister of Mines,
              Annual Report for 1936, p. B1-B63.

81   **Mapley, H.G.**
      1906:   Report of Constable H.G. Mapley, patrol, Dawson to Fort Macpherson; Royal North
              West Mounted Police, Annual Report 1905, Appendix E, p. 66-69.

82   **McCammon, J.W.**
      1952:   Asbestos; British Columbia Minister of Mines, Annual Report for 1951, p. A208-
              A214.

83   **McConnell, R.G.**
      1891:   Report on an exploration in the Yukon and Mackenzie basins, Northwest Territories;
              Geological Survey of Canada, Annual Report New Series v. IV, 1888-89, p. 1D-163D.

84   1905:   Report on the Klondike gold fields; Geological Survey of Canada, Annual Report for
              1901, New Series, v. XIV, p. 5B-71B (Reprinted in Bostock, 1957, p. 64-113).

85   1905:   The Kluane mining district, southwest Yukon; Geological Survey of Canada, Annual
              Report for 1904, v. XVI, p. 1A-18A. (Reprinted in Bostock, 1957, p. 114-126)

86   1906:   Headwaters of the White River; Geological Survey of Canada, Summary Report for
              1905, p. 19-26. (Reprinted in Bostock, 1957, p. 144-151)

87   1907:   Report on gold values in the Klondike high level gravels; Geological Survey of Canada,
              Publication 979. (Reprinted in Bostock, 1957, p. 217-238)

88   1909:   The Whitehorse copper belt, Yukon Territory; Geological Survey of Canada, Publica-
              tion 1050.

89   1914:   Rainy Hollow mineral area, British Columbia; Geological Survey of Canada, Summary
              Report for 1913, p. 29-33.

90   **McConnell, R.G. and Tyrrell, J.B.**
      1899:   Preliminary note on the gold deposits and gold mining in the Klondike region;
              Geological Survey of Canada, Annual Report for 1898, New Series v. XI, p. 55A-62A
              (Reprinted in Bostock, 1957, p. 17-23).

91   **McLearn, F.H. and Kindle, E.D.**
      1950:   Geology of northeastern British Columbia; Geological Survey of Canada, Memoir 259.

92   **Muller, J.E.**
      1967:   Kluane Lake map-area, Yukon Territory; Geological Survey of Canada, Memoir 340.

93   **Muller, J.E. and Christie, R.L.**
1966:   Geology, Kluane Lake, Yukon Territory; Geological Survey of Canada, Map 1177A (1 inch to 4 miles).

94   **Ogilvie, William**
1890:   Exploratory survey of part of the Lewes, Tat-on-duc, Porcupine, Bell, Trout, Peel, and Mackenzie rivers; Canada, Department of the Interior, Annual Report for 1887-88, pt. 8.

95   1898:   The Klondike official guide, Canada's great gold field, the Yukon district; The Hunter, Rose Co., Limited, Toronto; W.H. Smith and Sons, Limited London.

96   **O'Grady, B.T.**
1951:   Asbestos; British Columbia Minister of Mines, Annual Report for 1950, p. A207-A217.

97   **O'Neill J.J. and Gunning, H.C.**
1934:   Platinum and allied metal deposits of Canada; Geological Survey of Canada, Economic Geology Series 13.

98   **Palache, C., Berman, H. and Frondel, C.**
1944:   Dana's system of mineralogy, 7th Ed., volumes I and II; John Wiley and Sons.

99   **Plumb, W.N.**
1968:   The geology of the Cassiar asbestos deposit; pamphlet, Cassiar Asbestos Corporation, Limited.

100   **Russell, Israel C.**
1892:   An expedition to Mount St. Elias, Alaska; National Geographic Magazine v. III, 1891, p. 53-203.

101   **Sabina, Ann P.**
1964:   Rock and Mineral collecting in Canada, v. I, Yukon, Northwest Territories, British Columbia, Alberta, Saskatchewan and Manitoba; Geological Survey of Canada, Miscellaneous Series 8.

102   **Schwatka, Frederick**
1898:   Along Alaska's great river; George M. Hill Company, Chicago, New York.

103   **Selwyn, Alfred R.C.**
1877:   Report on exploration in British Columbia; Geological Survey of Canada, Report of Progress 1875-76, p. 28-87.

104   **Sharpstone, D.C.**
1948:   Polaris-Taku Mine (Whitewater Claims); in Geological Survey of Canada, Memoir 248.

105   **Skinner, R.**
1961:   Mineral industry of Yukon Territory and southwestern District of Mackenzie, 1960; Geological Survey of Canada, Paper 61-23.

106   1962:   Mineral industry of Yukon Territory and southwestern District of Mackenzie, 1961; Geological Survey of Canada, Paper 62-27.

107   **Smitheringale, Wm. V.**
1957:   The mine of Cassiar Asbestos Corporation Limited, Cassiar, B.C. in The geology of Canadian industrial mineral deposits; Canadian Institute of Mining and Metallurgy, Congress vol., 6th Commonwealth Mining and Metallurgical Congress, p. 49-53.

107a   **Souther, J.G.**
1971:   Geology and mineral deposits of Tulsequah map-area, British Columbia; Geological Survey of Canada, Memoir 362.

108   **Stelck, C.R. and Wall, J.H.**
1954:   Kaskapau foraminifera from Peace River area of western Canada; Research Council of Alberta., Report 68.

109 Sutherland, P.K.
1958: Carboniferous stratigraphy and rugose coral faunas of north-eastern British Columbia; Geological Survey of Canada, Memoir 295.

110 Templeman-Kluit, D.J.
1968: Geological setting of the Faro, Vangorda and Swim base metal deposits, Yukon Territory (105K); in Report of Activities, pt. A, 1967; Geological Survey of Canada, Paper 68-1A, p. 43-52.

111 Thomson, Ellis
1937: A review of the occurrence of tellurides in Canada; University of Toronto Studies, Geological Series no. 40, 1936-1937; p. 95-101.

112 Thurmond, Robert E.
1971: Problems of mine production in Canada's far north; Western Miner, v. 44, no. 5, p. 39-46.

113 Tidsbury, A.D.
1970: Toad River; Geology, exploration, and mining in British Columbia, 1969; British Columbia Department of Mines and Petroleum Resources, p. 51-52.

114 Traill, R.J.
1983: A catalogue of Canadian minerals; Geological Survey of Canada, Paper 80-18.

115 Traill, R.J. and Boyle, R.W.
1955: Hawleyite, isometric cadmium sulphide, a new mineral; American Mineralogist, v. 40, p. 555-559.

116 Tyrrell, J.B.
1901: Yukon district; Geological Survey of Canada, Annual Report, New Series, v. XI, 1898, p. 36A-46A.

117 Ward, E.
1917: Corporal E. Ward - Dawson to McPherson and return; Royal North West Mounted Police, Annual Report, 1916, Appendix E, p. 326-332.

118 Warren, P.S. and Stelck, C.R.
1955: New Cenomanian ammonites from Alberta; Research Council of Alberta, Report 70, Appendix.

119 Watson, K. de P.
1948: The Squaw Creek-Rainy Hollow area, northern British Columbia; British Columbia Department of Mines, Bulletin 25.

120 Wheeler, J.O.
1961: Whitehorse map-area, Yukon Territory; Geological Survey of Canada, Memoir 312.

121 White, L.G.
1963: The Canada Tungsten property, Flat River area, Northwest Territories; Bulletin, Canadian Institute of Mining and Metallurgy, v. 56, no. 613, p. 390-393.

122 Whiteaves, J.F.
1877: Notes on some fossils collected during the expedition; Geological Survey of Canada, Report of Progress 1875-76, p. 96-106.

123 Williams, M.Y.
1944: Geological reconnaissance along the Alaska Highway from Fort Nelson, British Columbia to Watson Lake, Yukon; Geological Survey of Canada, Paper 44-28.

124 Williams, M.Y. and Bocock, J.B.
1932: Stratigraphy and palaeontology of the Peace River valley of British Columbia; Transactions, Royal Society of Canada, 3rd ser., v. 20, sec. IV, p. 197-224.

125 Wilson, V.
1895: Guide to the Yukon gold fields; Calvert Company, Seattle.

110

ANONYMOUS

126   1899:   First annual report, 1898; Geographic Board of Canada.

127   1953:   Annual Report, 1952; British Columbia Minister of Mines.

128   1953:   Gazeteer of Canada; British Columbia: Canadian Board on Geographical Names.

129   1971:   Gazeteer of Canada, Yukon (Provisional); Canadian Board on Geographical Names.

130   1970:   Canadian Mines Handbook 1969-70; Northern Miner Press.

131   1971:   Canadian Mines Handbook 1971-72; Northern Miner Press.

132   1971:   Geology, exploration and mining in British Columbia in 1970; British Columbia Department of Mines and Petroleum Resources.

133   1971:   The Northern Miner; v. 57, no. 33.

134   1971:   WAC C-9 World aeronautical chart; Canada, Surveys and Mapping Branch.

135   1971:   WAC D-12 World aeronautical chart; Canada, Surveys and Mapping Branch.

136   1972:   The Whitehorse Star; v. 72, no. 16.

137   1988:   Canadian Mines Handbook 1988-89; Northern Miner Press.

138   1991:   Canadian Mines Handbook 1991-92; Northern Miner Press.

GLOSSARY

Acanthite. Ag_2S. H=2-2½. Iron-black metallic, prismatic aggregates. Sectile. Low temperature form of silver sulphide, argentite being the high temperature form. Ore of silver associated with other silver minerals.

Actinolite. $Ca_2(Mg, Fe)_5Si_8O_{22}(OH)_2$. H=5-6. Bright green to greyish green, fibrous or radiating prismatic aggregates. Variety of amphibole.

Allemontite. SbAs. H=3-4. Tin-white to reddish grey metallic, fibrous, lamellar, reniform, mammillary or finely granular masses. Tarnishes to grey or brownish black. Perfect cleavage in one direction. Fuses to a metallic globule. Occurs in veins with other arsenic and antimony minerals, and in pegmatites containing lithium minerals. Renamed stibarsen.

Alunogen. $Al_2(SO_4)_3.17H_2O$. H=1½-2. White fibrous to powdery. Vitreous to silky lustre. Acid, sharp taste. Secondary mineral associated with pyrite or marcasite.

Amphibole. A mineral group consisting of complex silicates including tremolite, actinolite and hornblende. Common rock-forming mineral.

Andesite. A dark coloured volcanic rock composed mainly of plagioclase feldspar with amphibole or pyroxene.

Andorite. $PbAgSb_3S_6$. H=3-3½. Dark grey metallic, striated prismatic or tabular crystals; massive. Conchoidal fracture. Black streak. Soluble in HCl. Associated with sulphides and other sulphosalts.

Anglesite. $PbSO_4$. H=2½-3. Colourless to white, greyish, yellowish or bluish tabular or prismatic crystals, or granular. Adamantine or resinous lustre. Characterized by high specific gravity (6.36 to 6.38) and adamantine lustre. Effervesces in nitric acid. Secondary mineral formed generally from galena. Ore of lead.

Ankerite. $Ca(Mg, Fe)(CO_3)_2$. Variety of dolomite from which it cannot be distinguished in the hand specimen.

Anorthite. $CaAl_2Si_2O_8$. A plagioclase feldspar.

Antigorite. $Mg_3Si_2O_5(OH)_4$. H=2½. Green translucent variety of serpentine having lamellar structure.

Antimony. Sb. H=3-3½. Light grey metallic, massive, granular, lamellar, or radiating. Occurs with other antimony minerals. Used as a component of lead alloys for manufacture of storage batteries, cable coverings, solders, bearing metal; also for flame-proofing textiles, paints and ceramics.

Apatite. $Ca_5(PO_4)_3(F,Cl,OH)$. H=5. Green, blue, colourless, brown, red hexagonal crystals, or granular, sugary massive. Vitreous lustre. May be fluorescent. Distinguished from beryl and quartz by its inferior hardness; massive variety is distinguished from calcite, dolomite by its superior hardness and lack of effervescence in HCl, and from massive diopside and olivine by its inferior hardness. Used in the manufacture of fertilizers and detergents.

Aragonite. $CaCO_3$. H-3½-4. Colourless to white or grey and, less commonly, yellow, blue, green, violet, rose-red, prismatic or acicular crystals; also columnar, globular, stalactitic aggregates. Vitreous lustre. Transparent to translucent. Distinguished from calcite by its cleavage and higher specific gravity (2.93). Effervesces in dilute HCl.

Argentite. Ag_2S. H=2-2$\frac{1}{2}$. Dark grey cubic, octahedral crystals; arborescent, massive, metallic. Very sectile. Occurs in sulphide deposits with other silver minerals. Inverts to acanthite at temperatures below 180°C.

Argillite. A clayey sedimentary rock without a slaty cleavage or shaly fracture.

Arsenopyrite. FeAsS. H=5$\frac{1}{2}$-6. Light to dark grey metallic, striated prisms with characteristic wedge-shaped cross-section; also massive. Tarnishes to bronze colour. Ore of arsenic; may contain gold or silver.

Asbestos. Fibrous variety of certain silicate minerals such as serpentine (chrysotile) and amphibole (anthophyllite, tremolite, actinolite, crocidolite) characterized by flexible, heat- and electrical-resistant fibres. Chrysotile is the only variety produced in Canada; it occurs as veins with fibres parallel (slip fibre) or perpendicular (cross-fibre) to the vein walls. Used in the manufacture of asbestos cement sheeting, shingles, roofing and floor tiles, millboard, thermal insulating paper, pipecovering, clutch and brake components, reinforcing in plastics, etc.

Aurichalcite. $(Zn, Cu)_5(CO_3)_2(OH)_6$. H=1-2. Light green to blue silky to pearly acicular or lath-like crystals forming tufted, feathery, plumose, laminated or granular encrustations. Transparent. Soluble in acids and in ammonia. Secondary mineral occurring in oxidized zones of copper and zinc deposits, associated with other secondary copper and zinc minerals.

Axinite. $Ca_2 (Fe, Mn) Al_2BSi_4O_{15}(OH)$. H=7. Violet, pink, yellow to brown wedge-shaped crystals or massive, lamellar. Vitreous lustre. Fuses readily with intumescence. Occurs commonly in contact-altered calcareous rocks. Transparent varieties used as gemstones.

Azurite. $Cu_3(CO_3)_2(OH)_2$. H=3$\frac{1}{2}$-4. Azure-blue to inky blue tabular or prismatic crystals; also massive, earthy, stalactitic with radial or columnar structure. Vitreous, transparent. Secondary copper mineral. Effervesces in acids. Ore of copper.

Barite. $BaSO_4$. H=3-3$\frac{1}{2}$. White, pink, yellowish, blue tabular or platy crystals; granular massive. Vitreous lustre. Characterized by a high specific gravity (4.5) and perfect cleavage. Used in the glass, paint, rubber, and chemical industries, and in oil-drilling technology.

Basalt. Dark coloured, fine grained volcanic rock or lava composed predominantly of an amphibole or pyroxene with plagioclase. Amygdaloidal basalt is one that contains cavities which may be occupied by one or more minerals.

Batholith. A very large body of coarse-textured igneous rocks such as granite or diorite.

Beudantite. $PbFe_3 (AsO_4)(SO_4)(OH_6)$. H=3$\frac{1}{2}-4\frac{1}{2}$. Dark green, brown, black rhombohedral crystals; also yellow earthy or botryoidal masses. Vitreous, resinous to dull lustre. Secondary mineral occurring in iron and lead deposits. Difficult to distinguish in hand specimen from other yellowish secondary minerals.

Bindheimite. $Pb_2Sb_2O_6(O,OH)$. H=4-4$\frac{1}{2}$. Yellow to brown, white to grey or greenish powdery to earthy encrustations; also nodular. Secondary mineral found in antimony-lead deposits. Difficult to identify except by X-ray methods.

Bismuth. Bi. H=2-2$\frac{1}{2}$. Light grey metallic reticulated crystal aggregates; also foliated or granular. Iridescent tarnish. Used as a component of low melting-point alloys and in medicinal and cosmetic preparations.

113

"Black diamond". A siliceous hematite which, when polished, takes a high, mirror-like lustre. Used as a gemstone.

Bog iron ore. Loose, porous iron ore formed by precipitation of water in bogs or swampy areas. Ore consists of limonite, goethite, and/or hematite.

Bornite. Cu_5FeS_4. H=3. Reddish brown metallic. Usually massive and tarnished to iridescent blue, purple, etc. Known as peacock ore, variegated copper ore purple copper ore or vitreous copper. Ore of copper.

Boulangerite. $Pb_5Sb_4S_{11}$. H=2½-3. Dark bluish grey metallic, striated, elongated prismatic to acicular crystals; also fibrous, plumose aggregates. Fibrous cleavage is distinguishing characteristic. Occurs in veins with lead minerals. Ore of antimony.

Bournonite. $PbCuSbS_3$. H=2½-3. Grey to blackish grey metallic. Short prismatic or tabular crystals with striated faces; massive. Occurs in veins with sulphides and sulphosalts. Not readily identified in hand specimen.

Brochantite. $Cu_4(SO_4)(OH)_6$. H=3½-4. Vitreous emerald-green acicular crystal aggregates; massive, granular. Secondary mineral formed by oxidation of copper minerals. Distinguished from malachite by lack of effervescence in HCl.

Brucite. $Mg(OH)_2$. H=2½. White, grey, light blue or green tabular, platy, foliated or fibrous aggregates, also massive. Pearly or waxy lustre. Soluble in HCl. Distinguished from gypsum and talc by its superior hardness and lack of greasy feel. Resembles asbestos but lacks silky lustre. Is more brittle than muscovite. Used for refractories and as a minor source of magnesium metal.

Cabochon. A polished gemstone having a convex surface; transluscent or opaque minerals such as opal, agate, jasper, and jade are generally cut in this style.

Calaverite. $AuTe_2$. H=2½-3. Brass-yellow to silver-white metallic, bladed, lath-like or striated short prisn.atic crystals. Fuses readily; on charcoal gives bluish green flame and gold globules. Ore of gold. Occurs in veins with pyrite, native gold.

Cassiterite. SnO_2. H=6-7. Yellow to brown prismatic crystals; twinning common. Also radially fibrous, botryoidal, or concretionary masses; granular. Adamantine, splendent lustre. White to brownish or greyish streak. Distinguished from other light coloured nonmetallic minerals by its high specific gravity (6.99); from wolframite by its superior hardness. Ore of tin. Concentrically banded variety used as a gemstone.

Cerussite. $PbCO_3$. H=3-3½. Transparent white, grey or brownish tabular crystals with adamantine lustre; also massive. High specific gravity (6.5) and lustre are distinguishing features. Secondary mineral formed by oxidation of lead minerals. Fluoresces in shades of yellow in ultraviolet light. Ore of lead.

Chabazite. $CaAl_2Si_4O_{12}$. $6H_2O$. H=4. Colourless, white, yellowish or pinkish square crystals. Vitreous lustre. Occurs in cavities in basalt. Distinguished from other zeolites by its almost cubic crystal form; distinguished from calcite by its superior hardness and its lack of effervescence in HCl.

Chalcedony. SiO_2. H=7. Translucent micro-crystalline variety of quartz. Colourless, grey, bluish, yellowish, reddish, brown. Formed from aqueous solutions. Attractively coloured chalcedony is used for ornamental objects and jewellery. Varieties include agate, carnelian, jasper, etc.

114

Chalcocite. Cu_2S. H=$3\frac{1}{2}$-4. Dark grey to black metallic; massive. Tarnishes to iridescent blue, purple, etc. Also referred to as vitreous copper, sulphurette of copper or copper glance. Soluble in HNO_3. Black colour and slight sectility distinguish it from other copper sulphides. Ore of copper.

Chalcopyrite. $CuFeS_2$. H=$3\frac{1}{2}$-4. Brass-yellow massive, or tetrahedral crystals. Iridescent tarnish. Brass colour distinguishes it from pyrrhotite. Distinguished from pyrite by its inferior hardness, from gold by its superior hardness and lower density. Also called copper pyrite and yellow copper. Ore of copper.

Chert. Massive opaque variety of chalcedony; generally drab coloured in various tints of grey or brown.

Chlorite. $(Mg, Fe, Al)_6(Al,Si)_4O_{10}(OH,O)_8$. H=2-$2\frac{1}{2}$. Transparent green flaky aggregates. Distinguished from mica by its colour and non-elastic flakes.

Chrysocolla. $(Cu, Al)_2H_2Si_2O_5(OH)_4 \bullet nH_2O$. H=2-4. Blue to blue-green earthy, botryoidal, or fine-grained massive. Conchoidal fracture. Secondary mineral found in oxidized zones of copper-bearing veins. Often intimately mixed with quartz or chalcedony, producing attractive patterns; because of it being mixed with quartz, the resultant superior hardness renders it suitable for use in jewellery and ornamental objects. Minor ore of copper.

Chrysotile. Fibrous variety of serpentine (asbestos).

Cinnabar. HgS. H=2-$2\frac{1}{2}$. Red to brownish red rhombohedral, tabular or short prismatic crystals; also granular or earthy. Adamantine to metallic or dull lustre. Bright red streak. Sectile. Perfect cleavage. Volatile before blow-pipe. Alters to native mercury and mercury minerals. Occurs in veins, or fractures in sandstone or quartizite. Ore of mercury.

Cirque. Semicircular basin along mountain slopes formed by glaciers.

Clinozoisite. $Ca_2Al_3(SiO_4)_3(OH)$. H=7. Pale green to greenish grey prismatic crystals; also granular or fibrous masses. Vitreous lustre. Perfect cleavage. Member of epidote group. Occurs in metamorphic rocks.

Columbite-Tantalite. $(Fe, Mn)Nb_2O_6$-$(Fe, Mn)Ta_2O_6$. H=5-7. Brownish black to black prismatic or tabular crystals forming parallel groups; also massive. Submetallic lustre. Occurs in pegmatites. Ore of niobium which is used in high-temperature steel alloys, and of tantalum which is used in electronics.

Concretion. Rounded mass formed in sedimentary rocks by accretion of some constituent (iron oxides, silica, etc.) around a nucleus (mineral impurity, fossil fragment, etc.).

Conglomerate. A sedimentary rock formed of rounded pebbles or gravel.

Copper. Cu. H=$2\frac{1}{2}$-3. Massive, filiform or arborescent; cubic or dodecahedral crystals. Hackly fracture. Ductile and malleable. Occurs in lava.

Covellite. CuS. H=$1\frac{1}{2}$-2. Inky blue iridescent in shades of brass yellow, purple, coppery red. Massive; crystals (hexagonal plates) rare. Metallic lustre. Distinguished from chalcocite and bornite by its perfect cleavage and colour.

Cubanite. $CuFe_2S_3$. H=$3\frac{1}{2}$. Brass- to bronze-yellow tabular crystals or massive. Distinguished from chalcopyrite by its strong magnetism. Associated with other copper-iron sulphides. Rare mineral.

Cuprite. Cu_2O. H=3½-4. Red to almost black crystals (octahedral, dodecahedral or cubic), massive, earthy. Adamantine, submetallic or earthy lustre. Brownish red streak. Distinguished from hematite by its inferior hardness, from cinnabar and proustite by its superior hardness. On charcoal it is reduced to a metallic globule of copper. Soluble in concentrated HCl. Associated with native copper and other copper minerals. Ore of copper.

Diabase. Dark coloured igneous rock composed mostly of lath-shaped crystals of plagioclase and of pyroxene. Used as building, ornamental and monument stone.

Diopside. $CaMgSi_2O_6$. H=6. Colourless, white to green monoclinic variety of pyroxene.

Diorite. A dark coloured igneous rock composed mainly of plagioclase and amphibole or pyroxene.

Dolomite. $CaMg(CO_3)_2$. H=3½-4. Colourless, white, pink, yellow or grey rhombohedral or saddle-shaped crystals; also massive. Vitreous to pearly lustre. Slightly soluble in cold HCl. Ore of magnesium which is used in the manufacture of lightweight alloys.

Dundasite. $PbAl_2(CO_3)_2(OH)_4 \bullet H_2O$. H=2. White, silky to vitreous radiating crystals, spherical aggregates, matted encrustations. Effervesces in acids. Secondary mineral associated with lead minerals.

Dyke. A long narrow body of igneous rocks that cuts other rocks.

Epidote. $Ca_2(Al,Fe)_3(SiO_4)_3(OH)$. H=6-7. Yellowish green to deep green prismatic crystals, also fibrous or granular masses. Vitreous lustre. Yellow-green colour is distinguishing feature. Occurs in metamorphic and granitic rocks, and in basalt.

Esker. A long stream-deposited ridge or mound formed by the accumulation of sand, gravel, and boulders left by retreating glaciers.

Fault. Structural feature produced by the movement of one rock mass relative to another; shear zone, brecciated zone, fault zone refer to the region affected by the movement.

Feldspar. A mineral group consisting of alumino-silicates of potassium and barium (monoclinic or triclinic), and of sodium and calcium (triclinic). Orthoclase and microcline belong to the first group, plagioclase to the second. Used in the manufacture of ceramics, porcelain-enamel, porcelain, scouring powders, and artificial teeth.

Fluorescence. Property of certain substances to glow when exposed to light from an ultraviolet lamp. It is caused by impurities in the substance or by defects in its crystal structure. Two wavelengths are commonly used to produce fluorescence: long wave (320 to 400 n), short wave (254 n).

Fluorite. CaF_2. H=4. Transparent, colourless, blue, green, purple or yellow, cubic or, less commonly, octahedral crystals; also granular massive. Vitreous lustre. Good cleavage. Often fluorescent; this property derives its name from the mineral. Used in optics, steelmaking, ceramics.

Freibergite. $(Ag,Cu,Fe)_{12}(Sb,As)_4S_{13}$. A silver-rich variety of the tetrahedrite-tennantite mineral series.

Freieslebenite. $AgPbSbS_3$. H=2-2½. Grey metallic striated prismatic crystals. Grey streak. Associated with silver and lead ores.

Fuchsite. An emerald-green chromium-rich muscovite.

116

Gabbro. A dark, coarse-grained igneous rock composed mainly of calcic plagioclase and pyroxene. Used as a building and monument stone.

Gahnite. $ZnAl_2O_4$. H=7$\frac{1}{2}$-8. Dark blue-green, yellow or brown octahedra, rounded grains, massive. Vitreous lustre. Occurs in granite pegmatite and in marble.

Galena. PbS. H=2$\frac{1}{2}$. Dark grey metallic cubic crystals or crystal aggregates; also massive. Perfect cleavage. Distinguished by its high (7.58) specific gravity and perfect cleavage. Ore of lead.

Garnet. (Ca, Fe, Mg, Mn)$_3$ (Al, Cr, Fe, Mn)$_2$. H=6$\frac{1}{2}$-7$\frac{1}{2}$. Transparent red dodecahedral crystals, or massive granular; also yellow, brown, green. Distinguished by its crystal form. Used as an abrasive. Transparent garnet is used as a gemstone. Mineral group consisting of several species including almandine, pyrope, grossular.

Garnierite. A general term for green hydrous nickel silicates.

Geode. A hollow nodule whose shell is composed of chalcedony from which crystals, commonly of quartz, project into the interior.

Gneiss. A coarse grained foliated metamorphic rock composed mainly of feldspar, quartz and mica. Used as a building and monument stone.

Goethite. FeO(OH). H=5-5$\frac{1}{2}$. Dark brown, reddish or yellowish brown, earthy, botryoidal, fibrous, bladed or loosely granular masses; also prismatic, acicular, tabular crystals or scaly. Has characteristic yellowish brown streak. Weathering product of iron-rich minerals. Ore of iron.

Gold. Au. H=2$\frac{1}{2}$-3. Yellow metallic, irregular masses, plates, scales, nuggets. Rarely as crystals. Distinguished from other yellow metallic minerals by its hardness, malleability, high specific gravity (19.3). Precious metal.

Gossan. A decomposed or weathered rusty covering on masses of pyrite or in upper zone of veins; consists of hydrated iron oxides.

Granite. Grey to reddish coloured relatively coarse-grained igneous rock composed mainly of feldspar and quartz. Used as a building and monument stone.

Granodiorite. An igneous rock intermediate in composition between granite and diorite.

Graphite. C. H=1-2. Dark grey to black metallic, flaky or foliated masses. Flakes are flexible. Greasy to touch. Black streak and colour distinguish it from molybdenite. Usually occurs in metamorphic rocks. Used as a lubricant, in "lead" pencils, and refractories.

Greenstone. A metamorphosed volcanic rock composed mainly of chlorite.

Greywacke. Sedimentary rock containing large amounts of amphibole or pyroxene and feldspar.

Gunningite. $ZnSO_4 \cdot H_2O$. H=2$\frac{1}{2}$. White powder occuring as an efflorescence on sphalerite from which it has oxidized. First described from the Keno Hill deposits, it was named in 1962 for Dr. H.C. Gunning, a former geologist with the Geological Survey of Canada, and later, Head of the Geology Department, University of British Columbia.

Gypsum. $CaSO_4 \cdot 2H_2O$. H=2. White, grey, light brown, granular massive; also fibrous (satin spar), or colourless, transparent (selenite). Distinguished from anhydrite by its inferior hardness. Occurs in sedimentary rocks. Used in the construciton industry for plaster, wallboard, cement, tiles, paint, and as a soil conditioner and fertilizer. Satin spar and alabaster (fine grained translucent variety) are used for carving into ornamental objects.

Hawleyite. CdS. Bright yellow powdery coating; earthy. Associated with sphalerite and siderite. First described from the lead-silver-zinc deposit at the Hector-Calumet Mine in Elsa, Yukon. Named for Professor J.E. Hawley of Queen's University, Kingston.

Hematite. Fe_2O_3. H=$5^{1/2}$-$6^{1/2}$. Reddish brown to black massive, botryoidal, or earthy, with greasy to dull lustre; also foliated or micaceous with high metallic lustre (specularite). Characteristic red streak. Ore of iron.

Hexahydrite. $MgSO_4 \cdot 6H_2O$. Colourless or white, finely fibrous, columnar; also globular encrustations. Pearly to vitreous lustre. Bitter, saline taste. Occurs sparingly as an alteration product of epsomite. Originally found at a Bonaparte River locality in British Columbia. Associated with other sulphates from which it is not readily distinguished.

Hoodoos. Pillars or tower-like forms resulting from erosion of horizontal strata.

Hornblende. $Ca_2(Mg, Fe)_4Al(Si_7Al)O_{22}(OH,F)_2$. H=6. Member of amphibole group. Dark green, brown, black prismatic crystals or massive. Vitreous lustre. Common rock-forming mineral.

Hydromagnesite. $Mg_5(CO_3)_4(OH)_2 \cdot 4H_2O$. H=$3^{1/2}$. Colourless or white, transparent, flaky, acicular or bladed crystal aggregates forming tufts, rosettes or encrustations; also massive. Vitreous, silky or pearly lustre. Associated with serpentine, brucite, magnesite. Effervesces in acids. Distinguished from calcite by its habit.

Igneous. Rocks that have crystallized from magma or from the melting of other rocks; usually composed of feldspar and quartz, with hornblende, pyroxene or biotite.

Ilesite. $(Mn, Zn, Fe)SO_4 \cdot 4H_2O$. Green to white loose prismatic crystal aggregates. A secondary mineral formed by oxidation in sulphide veins.

Iridosmine. (Os, Ir). H=6-7. Light grey metallic, tabular or, rarely, short primatic crystals; flakes, flattened grains. Perfect cleavage. Associated with gold and platinum placer deposits.

Jade. See Nephrite.

Jamesonite. $Pb_4FeSb_6S_{14}$. H=$2^{1/2}$. Dark grey metallic, acicular, fibrous, columnar or plumose aggregates commonly striated. Iridescent tarnish. Decomposes in HNO_3. Occurs in veins with other lead sulphosalts and sulphides.

Jarosite. $KFe_3(SO_4)_2(OH)_6$. H=$2^{1/2}$-$3^{1/2}$. Yellow to brown pulverulent coating associated with iron-bearing rocks and with coal. Distinguished from iron oxides by giving off SO_2 when heated.

Jasper. An opaque deep red to brown, yellow, green or mauve variety of quartz. Used as an ornamental stone and as a gemstone.

Kaolinite. $Al_2Si_2O_5(OH)_4$. H=2. Chalk-white, greyish, yellowish or brownish earthy masses. Dull lustre. Clay mineral formed chiefly by decomposition of feldspars. Becomes plastic when wet. Used as a filler in paper, and in the manufacture of ceramics.

Lamprophyre. Fine-grained dark-coloured dyke rock composed of plagioclase feldspar, amphibole and/or pyroxene.

Lapieite. $CuNiSbS_3$. Grey metallic microscopic grains associated with pyrite, polydymite, gersdorffite and millerite in a matrix consisting of quartz with altered spinel, magnesite and bright green mica. The mineral was named in 1984 for the Lapie River, which was named for an Indian guide to explorer Robert Campbell.

Laumontite. $CaAl_2Si_4O_{12} \bullet 4H_2O$. H=4. White to pink or reddish white, vitreous to pearly, prismatic crystal aggregates; also friable, chalky due to dehydration. Characteristic alteration distinguishes it from other zeolites.

Lazulite. $MgAl_2(PO_4)_2(OH)_2$. H=5$\frac{1}{2}$-6. Blue pyramidal or tabular crystals; massive. Vitreous lustre. soluble in hot acids. Transparent variety used as a gemstone.

Limestone. Soft, white, grey or buff sedimentary rock formed by the deposition of calcium carbonate. Dolomitic limestone contains variable proportions of dolomite and is distinguished from calcium limestone by its weaker (or lack of) effervescence in HCl. Used as a building stone and as road metal. Shell limestone (coquina) is a porous rock composed mainly of shell fragments. Crystalline limestone (marble) is a limestone that has been metamorphosed and is used as a building, monument and ornamental stone.

Limonite. Field term referring to natural hydrous iron oxides composed mainly of goethite. Yellow-brown to dark brown earthy, porous, ochreous masses; also stalactitic or botryoidal. Secondary product of iron minerals.

Magnesite. $MgCO_3$. H=4. Colourless, white, greyish, yellowish to brown, lamellar, fibrous, granular or earthy masses; crystals rare. Vitreous, transparent to translucent. Distinguished from calcite by lack of effervescence in cold HCl. Used in the manufacture of refractory bricks, cements, flooring, and for making magnesium metal.

Malachite. $Cu_2CO_3(OH)_2$. H=3$\frac{1}{2}$-4. Bright green granular, botryoidal, earthy masses; usually forms coating with other secondary copper minerals on copper-bearing rocks. Distinguished from other green copper minerls by effervescence in HC1. Ore of copper.

Marble. See limestone.

Marcasite. FeS_2. H=6-6$\frac{1}{2}$. Pale bronze to grey metallic radiating, stalactitic, globular or fibrous forms; twinning produces cockscomb and spear shapes. Yellowish to dark brown tarnish. Massive variety is difficult to distinguish from pyrite in the hand specimen.

Melaconite. CuO. Dull powdery coatings or masses; lustrous, resembling coal; reniform or colloform masses. Soluble in HCl or HNO_3. Known as copper pitch ore. Name has been changed to tenorite.

Meneghinite. $Pb_{13}Sb_7S_{24}$. H=2$\frac{1}{2}$. Blackish grey metallic. Slender, striated prismatic crystals, fibrous, massive. Oxidized by HNO_3. Associated with sulphides and sulphosalts.

Microcline. $KAlSi_3O_8$. H=6. White, pink to red, or green (amazonite) crystals or cleavable masses. Member of feldspar group. Distinguished from other feldspars by X-ray or optical methods.

Minium. Pb_3O_4. H=2$\frac{1}{2}$. Bright red to brownish red, earthy, pulverulent masses with greasy to dull lustre. Orange-yellow streak. Affected by HCl and HNO_3. Secondary mineral formed by the alteration of galena or cerussite.

Molybdenite. MoS_2. H=1-1$\frac{1}{2}$. Dark bluish grey metallic tabular, foliated, scaly aggretates or hexagonal crystals; also massive. Sectile with greasy feel. Distinguished from graphite

119

by its bluish lead-grey colour and by its streak (greenish on porcelain, bluish grey on paper). Ore of molybdenum.

Monticellite. $CaMgSiO_4$. H=5. Colourless, grey, small prismatic crystals or grains. Vitreous lustre. Occurs in calcite and crystalline limestone. Related to olivine group. Not readily identifiable in hand specimen.

Moraine. An accumulation of sand, gravel, boulders carried and deposited by glaciers.

Nephrite. $Ca_2(Fe, Mg)_5Si_8O_{22}(OH)_2$. H=6. Dense, compact fibrous variety of tremolite-actinolite group. Green to black, grey, white. Occurs in metamorphic rocks, in periodotite or serpentinite. Very tough. Nephrite is one type of jade used as a gemstone and ornamental stone.

Olivine. $(Mg, Fe)_2SiO_4$. H=6$\frac{1}{2}$. Olive-green, vitreous, granular masses or rounded grains; also yellowish to brownish black. Distinguished from quartz by its cleavage; from other silicates by its olive-green colour. Soluble in hot dilute HCl. Used in manufacture of refractory bricks. Transparent variety (peridot) is used as a gemstone.

Opal. $SiO_2 \cdot nH_2O$. H=5$\frac{1}{2}$-6$\frac{1}{2}$. Colourless, green, grey to black with waxy lustre, and iridescence in gem varieties. Common, or non-gem variety, lacks the iridescence, is translucent to opaque, colourless to white, red, brown, grey, green, yellow, etc. Massive, botryoidal, mammillary or pisolitic forms. Distinguished from chalcedony by its inferior hardness, lower specific gravity. Formed at low temperatures by silica-bearing waters seeping into fissures and cavities in sedimentary and volcanic rocks.

Orthoclase. $KAlSi_3O_8$. H=6. Red, pink or white feldspar. Short prismatic crystals. Vitreous lustre. Perfect cleavage. Distinguished from plagioclase feldspar by absence of twinning striations.

Pegmatite. A very coarse grained dyke rock.

Pentlandite. $(Fe, Ni)_9S_8$. H=3$\frac{1}{2}$-4. Light bronze-yellow massive, granular aggregates. Octahedral parting and nonmagnetic property distinguish it from pyrrhotite with which it is commonly associated. Ore of nickel.

Peridotite. An igneous rock consisting almost entirely of olivine and pyroxene with little or no plagioclase feldspar.

Permafrost. Permanently frozen ground. The zone may be a few inches to several hundred m thick and may be thousands of years in this state.

Perovskite. $CaTiO_3$. H=5$\frac{1}{2}$. Reddish brown to black cubic or octahedral crystals; also granular massive. Adamantine to metallic lustre. Uneven fracture. White to grey streak. Distinguished from titanite by its crystal form, from pyrochlore by its lustre and streak.

Phyllite. A lustrous metamorphic rock with a texture between that of a schist and a slate.

Picrolite. A non-flexible fibrous variety of antigorite (serpentine).

Placer. Sand or gravel deposit containing gold and/or other mineral particles; generally refers to deposits in paying quantities.

Plagioclase. $(Ca, Na)Al(Al, Si)Si_2O_8$. H=6. White or grey tabular crystals or cleavable masses having twinning striations on cleavage surfaces. Vitreous to pearly lustre. Distinguished from other feldspars by its twinning striations.

Platinum. Pt. H=4-4$\frac{1}{2}$. Grey metallic, grains, scales, nuggets, cubic crystals (rare). Hackly fracture. Malleable and ductile. Occurs in basic and ultrabasic igneous rocks, and in placers.

Plumbojarosite. $PbFe_6(SO_4)_4(OH)_{12}$. Yellowish brown to dark brown, dull to silky, powdery, earthy, or compact encrustations; microscopic hexagonal plates. Soft and feels like talc. Dissolves slowly in acids. Oxidation product of lead ores. Not readily identified in hand specimen.

Polybasite. $(Ag, Cu)_{16}Sb_2S_{11}$. H=2-3. Black metallic tabular crystals or massive. Thin splinters are deep red in colour. Decomposed by HNO_3. Occurs with silver-bearing minerals in veins.

Porphyry. A dyke rock consisting of distinct crystals (phenocrysts) in a fine-grained matrix.

Posnjakite. $Cu_4(SO_4)(OH)_6 \cdot H_2O$. Minute, blue flaky and radiating sheaf-like aggregates. Associated with other secondary copper minerals; not readily distinguished from them in the hand specimen.

Prehnite. $Ca_2Al_2Si_3O_{10}(OH)_2$. H=6$\frac{1}{2}$. Light green globular, stalactitic, masses with fibrous or columnar structure. Vitreous lustre. Colour and habit are distinguishing features.

Psilomelane. $(Ba,H_2)Mn_5O_{10}$. H=5-6. Black massive botryoidal, stalactitic, or earthy. Dull to submetallic lustre. Black streak, and amorphous appearance. Ore of manganese. Name has been changed to romanechite.

Pyrargyrite. Ag_3SbS_3. H=2$\frac{1}{2}$. Deep red prismatic crystals, massive. Adamantine lustre. Deep red streak. Occurs in veins carrying other silver minerals. Known as ruby silver. Ore of silver. Colour is identifying characteristic.

Pyrite. FeS_2. H=6-6$\frac{1}{2}$. Pale brass-yellow metallic crystals (cube, pyritohedrons, octahedrons), or massive granular. Iridescent when tarnished. Distinguished from other sulphides by its colour, crystal form, and superior hardness. Source of slulphur.

Pyroaurite. $Mg_6Fe_2(CO_3)(OH)_{16} \cdot 4H_2O$. H=2$\frac{1}{2}$. Colourless, yellowish, blue, green, or white flaky, nodular or fibrous. Pearly or waxy lustre. Crushes to talc-like powder. Effervesces in HCl. Becomes golden yellow and magnetic when heated.

Pyroxene. A mineral group consisting of Mg, Fe, Ca and Na silicates related structurally. Diopside, enstatite, aegirine, jadeite, etc. are members of the group. Common rock-forming mineral.

Pyroxenite. An igneous rock composed mainly of pyroxene with little or no feldspar.

Pyrrhotite. $Fe_{1-x}S$. H=4. Brownish bronze massive granular. Black streak. Magnetic; this property distinguishes it from other bronze sulphides.

Quartz. SiO_2. H=7. Colourless, yellow, violet, pink, brown, black, six-sided prisms with transverse striations or massive. Transparent to translucent with vitreous lustre. Rock forming mineral. Occurs in veins in ore deposits. Used in glass and electronic industries. Transparent varieties used as gemstones.

Quartzite. A quartz-rich rock formed by the metamorphism of a sandstone. Used as a building and monument stone, and, if colour is attractive, as an ornamental stone; high purity quartzite is used in the glass industry.

Rhodonite. $MnSiO_3$. H=6. Pink to rose-red massive, commonly veined with black manganese minerals. Conchoidal fracture, very tough. Resembles rhodochrosite from which it is distinguished by a superior hardness and lack of effervescence in HCl. Associated with manganese ores. Used as a gemstone and an ornamental stone.

Rhyolite. A fine-grained volcanic rock with composition similar to granite.

Roscoelite. A vanadium-bearing muscovite. Reddish brown to greenish brown.

Rozenite. $FeSO_4 \cdot 4H_2O$. White or greenish white, finely granular, botryoidal or globular encrustations. Metallic astringent taste. Difficult to distinguish in hand specimen from other iron sulphates with which it is associated.

Sandstone. Sedimentary rock composed of sand-sized particles (mostly quartz).

Scapolite. $Na_4Al_3Si_9O_{24}Cl$-$Ca_4Al_6Si_6O_{24}(CO_3,SO_4)$. H=6. White, grey, or less commonly, pink, yellow, blue, green prismatic and pyramidal crystals; also massive granular with splintery, woody appearance. Vitreous, pearly to resinous lustre. Distinguished from feldspar by its square prismatic form, prismatic cleavage, and splintery appearance on cleavage surfaces. May fluoresce under ultraviolet rays. Transparent varieties may exhibit chatoyancy (cat's - eye effect) when cut into cabochon stones.

Scheelite. $CaWO_4$. H=4$\frac{1}{2}$-5. White, yellow, brownish; transparent to translucent massive. Also dipyramidal crystals. High specific gravity (about 6). Generally fluoresces bright bluish white under "short" ultraviolet rays; this property is utilized in prospecting for scheelite, an ore of tungsten.

Schist. Metamorphic rock composed mainly of flaky minerals such as mica and chlorite.

Scorodite. $FeAsO_4 \cdot 2H_2O$. H=3$\frac{1}{2}$-4. Green, greyish green to brown crusts composed of tabular or prismatic crystals; also massive, earthy, porous or sinter-like. Vitreous to subresinous or subadamantine lustre. Soluble in acids. Secondary mineral formed by oxidation of arsenopyrite.

Senarmontite. Sb_2O_3. H=2-2$\frac{1}{2}$. Colourless to greyish white, transparent; octahedral crystals or granular, massive. Forms crusts. Resinous to subadamantine lustre. Soluble in HCl. Secondary mineral formed by the oxidation of antimony minerals. Minor ore of antimony.

Serpentine. $Mg_3Si_2O_5(OH)_4$. H=2-5. White, yellow, green, blue, red, brown, black massive; may be mottled, banded or veined. Waxy lustre. Translucent to opaque. Asbestos (chrysotile) is the fibrous variety. Formed by the alteration of olivine, pyroxene, amphibole, or other magnesium silicates. Found in metamorphic and igneous rocks. Used as an ornamental building stone (verde antique) and for cutting and/or carving into ornamental objects.

Serpentinite. A metamorphic rock consisting almost entirely of serpentine.

Shale. Fine-grained sedimentary rock composed of clay minerals.

Shear zone. See fault.

Siderite. $FeCO_3$. H=3$\frac{1}{2}$-4. Brown rhombohedral crystals, cleavable masses, earthy, botryoidal. Distinguished from calcite and dolomite by its colour and higher specific gravity, from sphalerite by its cleavage. Ore of iron.

Siltstone. A very fine grained sedimentary rock composed predominantly of quartz grains.

Silver. Ag. H=2½-3. Grey metallic arborescent, wiry, leafy, platy or scaly forms; crystals (cubic, octahedral, dodecahedral) are rare. Tarnishes to dark grey or black. Hackly fracture. Ductile, malleable. Colour, form and sectility are identifying characteristics.

Skarn. An altered rock zone in limestone and dolomite in which calcium silicates (garnet, pyroxene, epidote, etc.) have formed.

Slate. A fine-grained metamorphic rock characterized by a susceptibility to split into thin sheets.

Specularite. Black variety of hematite having a high lustre.

Sphalerite. ZnS. H-3½-4. Yellow, brown or black, granular to cleavable massive; also botryoidal. Resinous to submetallic. Honey-brown streak. Soluble in HCl, and gives off H_2S. Ore of zinc.

Stephanite. Ag_3SbS_4. H=2-2½. Black metallic, striated prismatic or tabular crystals, or massive. Decomposed by HNO_3. Occurs in veins in silver deposits.

Stibnite. Sb_2S_3. H=2. Dark grey metallic (bluish iridescent tarnish), striated prismatic crystals; also acicular crystal aggregates, radiating columnar or bladed masses; granular massive. Soluble in HCl. Most important ore of antimony.

Stilbite. $NaCa_2Al_5Si_{13}O_{36} \bullet 14H_2O$. H=4. Colourless, pink, white, platy crystal aggregates commonly forming sheaf-like aggregates. Vitreous, pearly lustre. Transparent. Sheaf-like form distinguishes it from other zeolites with which it is associated.

Syenite. An igneous rock composed mainly of feldspar with little or no quartz. Used as a building and monument stone.

Szmikite. $MnSO_4 \bullet H_2O$. H=1½. White to pink, reddish, stalactitic, botryoidal masses. Earthy. Secondary mineral found with manganese minerals.

Szomolnokite. $FeSO_4 \bullet H_2O$. H=2½. White to pinkish white fine hair-like aggregates or finely granular encrustations; also botryoidal, globular crusts. Vitreous lustre. Metallic taste. Associated with pyrite and other iron sulphates from which it is not readily distinguishable in the hand specimen.

Talc. $Mg_3Si_4O_{10}(OH)_2$. H=1. Grey, white, green finely granular or foliated. Translucent; feels greasy. Massive varieties are known as steatite and soapstone, and because of their suitability for carving, are used for ornamental purposes. Formed by alteration of magnesium silicates (olivine, pyroxene, amphibole, etc.) in igneous and metamorphic rocks. Used in cosmetics, ceramics, paint, rubber, insecticide, roofing and paper industries.

Tetrahedrite – Tennantite. $Cu_{12}Sb_4S_{13}$ - $Cu_{12}As_4S_{13}$. H=3½-4. Dark-grey to iron-black, metallic, tetrahedral crystals; also massive granular to compact. Brown, black, or deep red streak. Ore of copper; may contain silver, antimony values.

Titanite. $CaTiSiO_5$. H=6. Brown, wedge-shaped crystals; also massive granular. May form cruciform twins. Adamantine lustre. White streak. Distinguished from other dark silicates by its crystal form, lustre and colour. Also known as sphene.

Topaz. $Al_2SiO_4(OH, F)_2$. H=8. Colourless, white, pale blue, yellow, brown, grey, green, prismatic crystals with perfect basal cleavage; also massive granular. Vitreous, transparent. Distinguished by its crystal habit, cleavage, hardness. Used as a gemstone.

123

Tourmaline. Na(Mg, Fe)$_3$Al$_6$(BO$_3$)$_3$Si$_6$O$_{18}$(OH)$_4$. H=7$\frac{1}{2}$. Black, green, blue, pink, brown, yellow prismatic crystals; also columnar, massive granular. Prism faces are striated vertically. Vitreous lustre. Conchoidal fracture. Distinguished by triangular cross-section, striations, fracture. Used in the manufacture of pressure gauges; transparent variety used as a gemstone.

Tremolite. Ca$_2$Mg$_5$Si$_8$O$_{22}$(OH)$_2$. H=5-6. White, grey, striated prismatic crystals, bladed crystal aggregates, fibrous. Perfect cleavage. Vitreous lustre. Generally occurs in metamorphic rocks. Fibrous variety is used for asbestos; transparent crystals are sometimes used as a gem curiousity.

Tuff. A rock formed from volcanic ash.

Valleriite. 4(Fe, Cu)S•3(Mg,Al)(OH)$_2$. Massive, platy, bronze-black. Perfect cleavage. Occurs in copper deposits.

Vesuvianite. Ca$_{10}$MgAl$_4$(SiO$_4$)$_5$(Si$_2$O$_7$)$_2$(OH)$_4$. H=7. Yellow, brown, green, violet, transparent prismatic or pyramidal crystals with vitreous lustre; also massive, granular, compact od pulverulent. Distinguished from other silicates by its tetragonal crystal form; massive variety distinguished by its ready fusibility and intumescence in blowpipe flame. Also known as idocrase. Transparent varieties may be used as a gemstone.

Wad. A field term used for substances consisting mainly of manganese oxides.

Wittichenite. Cu$_3$BiS$_3$. H=2-3. Grey metallic tabular crystals or columnar, acicular aggregates; massive. Fuses easily. Soluble in HCl and gives off H$_2$S; decomposed by HNO$_3$. Alters readily to yellowish brown, red, blue colours, and eventually forms covellite.

Wolframite. (Fe, Mn)WO$_4$. H=4-4$\frac{1}{2}$. Dark brown to black, short prismatic striated crystals, lamellar or granular. Submetallic to adamantine lustre. Perfect cleavage in one direction. Distinguishing features are colour, cleavage, and high specific gravity (7.1-7.5). Ore of tungsten.

Wollastonite. CaSiO$_3$. H=5. White to greyish white, compact, cleavable, or fibrous masses with splintery or woody structure. Vitreous to silky lustre. May fluoresce under ultraviolet rays. Distinguished from tremolite (H=6) and sillimanite (H=7) by its inferior hardness and by its solubility in HCl. Used in ceramics and paints.

"Yukon diamond". A term used in the North for concentrically banded black, dark brown, tan-coloured cassiterite pebbles found in placers of the Yukon. Also known as wood tin. Used as a gemstone.

Yukonite. Ca$_3$Fe$_3$ (AsO$_4$)$_4$OH• 12H$_2$O. H=2-3. Black to dark brown irregular concretions. Decrepitates at low heat and when immersed in water. Easily fusible. Found originally at Tagish Lake, Yukon.

Zinc. Zn. H=2. White to light grey metallic crystals, scales. Brittle.

Zoisite. Ca$_2$Al$_3$(SiO$_4$)$_3$(OH). H=6$\frac{1}{2}$. Grey, brownish grey, yellowish brown, mauvish pink, green aggregates of long prismatic crystals (striated); also compact fibrous to columnar masses. Vitreous to pearly lustre. Transparent to translucent. Massive variety distinguished from amphibole by its perfect cleavage. Transparent varieties used as gemstones; pink variety known as thulite, deep blue variety as tanzanite.

CHEMICAL SYMBOLS FOR CERTAIN ELEMENTS

Ag - silver

Al - aluminum

As - arsenic

Au - gold

B - boron

Ba - barium

Be - beryllium

Bi - bismuth

C - carbon

Ca - calcium

Cb - columbium (niobium)

Ce - cerium

Cl - chlorine

Co - cobalt

Cr - chromium

Cu - copper

Er - erbium

F - fluorine

Fe - iron

H - hydrogen

K - potassium

La - lanthanum

Li - lithium

Mg - magnesium

Mn - manganese

Mo - molybdenum

Na - sodium

Nb - niobium

Ni - nickel

O - oxygen

P - phosphorus

Pb - lead

Pt - platinum

R - rare-earth elements

S - sulphur

Sb - antimony

Se - selenium

Si - silicon

Sn - tin

Sr - strontium

Ta - tantalum

Te - tellurium

Th - thorium

Ti - titanium

U - uranium

W - tungsten

Y - yttrium

Yb - ytterbium

Zn - zinc

Zr - zirconium

INDEX OF MINERALS ROCKS AND FOSSILS

DATE DUE

	261-2500		Printed in USA

The Well-Tun'd Word

The Well-Tun'd Word

Musical Interpretations
of
English Poetry
1597-1651

Elise Bickford Jorgens

University of Minnesota Press, Minneapolis

Publication of this book was assisted by a grant
from the publications program of the National Endowment
for the Humanities, an independent federal agency,
and a grant from
Western Michigan University

Published by the University of Minnesota Press,
2037 University Avenue Southeast,
Minneapolis, Minnesota 55414
Printed in the United States of America

Library of Congress Cataloging in Publication Data

Jorgens, Elise Bickford.
    The well-tun'd word.

    Bibliography: p. 6
    Includes index.
    1. Music and literature. 2. Songs, English—
History and criticism. 3. Music—History and
criticism—17th century. 4. English poetry—Early
modern, 1500-1700—History and criticism.
I. Title.
ML3849.J67   784.3'001'5   81-13090
ISBN 0-8166-1029-0   AACR2

The University of Minnesota
is an equal-opportunity educator
and employer.

For Catherine and Elisabeth

Foreword

Our very notions of music and poetry depend upon a profound difference between the two arts, even to the fascinating question whether poetic texts rightly share with musical sound the empire of the ear at all, or whether writing is not by nature a trope for absent sound, and in a way in which actual musical notation is not. And yet since classical times, each art has appealed to its kinship with the other—in defining itself, in defending itself against attack, and in expounding itself to students and admirers. That kinship has been figured in many ways: a prelapsarian couple in the Paradise of Antiquity that declined, in some cultural Fall, into the striving, loving pair we know today; or, as in Aristophanes' fable and in Plato's *Symposium*, an original whole of melody and word intermingled that cracked apart into two beings who live out the history of human culture in quest of each other. John Milton calls "Voice and Verse" "Sphere-born harmonious Sisters," but it is their offspring, or emanations—word and melody —which he invokes as he urges them, in "At a Solemn Music," to "Wed your divine sounds, and mixt power employ" in order to animate inert matter, like the breath of the Creator. The wedding of music and poetry took place for Milton in this poem, in church, which is to say that the harmonizing of *lexis* and *melos* into an echo of a greater *logos* was a religious, not an aesthetic matter. For secular verse and music, the momentary reunion is consummated in the bed of love-song; for meditative lyric in German, in the field of *Einsamkeit*. In opera, the two remain an old theatrical couple, words allowing

music to take star billing, but always remembering that it was because of (in this case) her that the whole enterprise was launched in six-teenth-century Italy to begin with. But whether the connection is that of marriage, companionship, friendly combat, or whatever, it is in secular song that the relation is made manifest, and tested.

From a literary point of view, the relation is susceptible to a va-riety of ad hoc interpretations as well. Paul Valéry could call attention to the ways in which the manipulations of speech sound and its patterns in romantic and later poetry internalized, or troped, an accompanying music, by wryly remarking that "adding music to a good poem is like using a stained-glass window to light a painted picture." John Donne complains that, after he has himself been fool enough to write of his amatory grief in verse, some composer will come along to compound the foolishness, and "sett and sing my paine," thereby augmenting the world's grief: here, "adding music" to a poem is a kind of emotional broadcasting. But the musical setting of a text can be a very different matter indeed. For Schopenhauer, in a passage which Nietzsche quotes at length in *Birth of Tragedy*, the "deep relation which music has to the true nature of all things also explains the fact that suitable music played to any scene, action, event, or surrounding seems to dis-close to us its most sacred meaning, and appears as the most accurate and distinct commentary upon it." Opera is clearly the question here, but later on Schopenhauer includes poems as "events," and the implied relation of music to words in art-song is that of in-terpreter to text, the interpretation by no means being confined to an elicitation of feelings (Donne's "sing my paine"—not "sing *about* it"), but to a revelation of meaning.

Yet if a musical setting is to be thought of as a kind of hermeneutic activity performed on a poem, another kind of interpretive activity—a hermeneutic of musical setting—must apply itself to song and reveal the way in which, within it, the music is discoursing on the meaning of the words. This is, of course, the work of the critic who must under-stand not only the character of the text but of that of the music. And this in turn means knowing a good deal about the history of each, and, particularly, about the history of the conventions that bear upon the poem or music in question. Furthermore—and this is the most im-portant—the analyst of song must understand the history of various conventions of setting themselves, of the many ways in which and by

which the music is—as Valéry wittily and distortingly puts it—"added to" the poem. A text can do anything, from remaining silent on the margins of the musical page (in which case it will have "inspired" or otherwise helped to generate the textless music) to reducing the music to the serviceable role of punctuating declamation. But in every case, there is considerable room within the convention's ground-rules for exploration, invention, originality. And this, again, the interpreter of song must explore.

But perhaps we should say "interpreter of settings," for it is the set words, the text as glossed by the homily of the music, which is at issue. We are most accustomed to the analysis of the rhetoric of setting, as it were: how Schumann's treatment of Heine's *"Ich hab im Traum geweinet"* in *Dichterliebe* propounds a lunging, roaring passion which it claims to find hidden or suppressed in the bitter almost muttered ironies of Heine's last stanza, for example. And we are more familiar, in musicological analyses of song, with being shown how structural units of the verse engage those of the conventions of musical form from which the texture of the setting is derived—whether these engagements are those of conjunction or tension. We know well of notions of "expression," and how a word or phrase may have the latent feeling plucked out of it by melody, harmony, or rhythmic entity; and we know how, in larger, through-composed works, inner voices, recurring motives, thematic material transformed but recognizably so, may become tropes of memory and other operations of consciousness.

But the minute details of what happens to the very stuff of English verse, in particular, when set to some kind of music in some kind of way, has been far less well explored. The linguistic peculiarities of our language make for a complex interrelation of word-stress, syntax and diction: leading English word and phrase stress into viable roles in our accentual-syllabic verse system is a little like setting speech to a kind of declamatory music to begin with. English poetry develops its own linguistic and graphic rhythms, and musical settings can ignore, or attend to, these, but only up to a point. The way in which a musical setting of an English phrase can resolve a syntactic ambiguity present in the written form of it is a kind of atom of musical interpretation of speech; once the language has been given additional structure by verse, the possibilities grow more ramified.

The period from about 1590 to about 1660 is a classic age for the history of song in English, and the setting of texts to music during

that period was attended to with practical care and with theoretical underpinnings that did not reappear until the modernist decades. The details of that famous renaissance and baroque marriage of poem and music have been much studied. Musicologists like Wilfred Mellers, whose own sensibility embodied a harmonious meeting of literary critic and musical analyst, and purely literary theorists like Angus Fletcher and Jerome Mazzaro, possessed of considerable musical sophistication, have written interestingly about English song itself and about the condition of poetry during the years of its great accord with music, which seemed to terminate with the death of Purcell and the rise of Pope. But the minute details of the terrain of the set word—semantically, grammatically, and rhetorically considered—have been overflown (rather than overlooked) by the surveyors.

Elise Jorgens is just such a grammarian and rhetorician of musical setting. She brings to this splendid study of English solo song from Dowland to Lawes a linguistic and poetic, as well as a musical, understanding. She is not content with tired clichés about the English language being less "musical" or "singable" than Italian or even German, but applies to her discussion of what makes for interpretive setting a sophisticated grasp of English phonology, and of the schemata of English verse with their conventional significance. The result is that we are forced to revise the question "Why is English 'unmusical'"' into "Just *how* is it 'musical' in its own way?" No such detailed examination of the intricate workings of seventeenth-century English song has been attempted before. Until Dr. Jorgens's work, the real significance, for example, of Milton's praise of Henry Lawes as one who "First taught our English music how to span / Words with just note and accent" could not fully be grasped: Milton's own enjambment can "span" the words of the lines' beginnings and endings, and he praises Lawes as a composer who can indeed somehow manage to set enjambment itself, to give in the setting a sense both of line termination and of syntactical and musical flow at once. This book provides a useful taxonomy of the genera and species of seventeenth-century English song even as it attentively and lovingly explores the behavior of particular different creatures.

This book is of great value not only for students of English music and literature of the seventeenth century, but, much more widely, for anyone interested in the relation of text to music, in that it provides a splendid model for all such investigations and raises questions

of a general nature. Lovers of English poetry will be pleasantly surprised to come across settings of old friends, and be made to ponder on the way in which the setting's reading of text differs from their own. Or they will come across such amusing anomalies as the setting by Henry Lawes of the eighth sonnet of Spenser's *Amoretti* — hardly an expected poem for a Caroline composer — and imagine his friend Milton, perhaps, urging it on him.

It is through her lively and meticulous analyses of what is going on in musical settings at any particular moment that the very concept of setting itself is illuminated. What Milton meant, in "At a Solemn Music," by "That undisturbèd Song of pure concent" was both "that song about pure harmony" and "that purely harmonious song" — in other words, music and poetry harmoniously joined and celebrating the harmony of that relationship. For the active and inquiring spirit, there is no greater celebration than devoted, intense, informed analysis, and Dr. Jorgens's book, an illuminating job of work on its material, is as well an act of love.

John Hollander
New Haven, Connecticut

Acknowledgments

This book emerged first, I suppose, from my having grown up in a household where both words and music were constantly present, from having had parents who loved the printed word, and who both taught English at one time or another, and a father who was a singer as well. Next, it grew from my own vacillations, from an undergraduate major in English literature, from graduate studies in music, and from my own love of singing. In the process of deciding that my equilibrium lay in combining these often warring devotions, and of finding a way in which I could do so, I have incurred many debts.

First I must thank Barry S. Brook and the Doctoral Program in Music at The City University of New York for the open-mindedness that allowed a project like this to begin under the aegis of work toward a Ph.D. in Music. Second I would like to thank Stoddard Lincoln of the CUNY Department of Music, whose interests lay in similar directions and who offered assistance and encouragement. Others who have read the manuscript in various stages and have contributed generously with helpful comments and queries include Walter R. Davis, Andrew J. Sabol, Stanley Boorman, Gary Schmidgall, H. Wiley Hitchcock, Murray Lefkowitz, Hugo Weisgall, and Ruth H. Rowen.

My thanks go also to the many libraries, in this country and in England, which have made their resources available to me, and especially to the Folger Shakespeare Library in Washington, D.C., for a Fellowship to support my work there in the spring and summer of 1976.

Portions of Chapters 1 and 2 appeared in an article entitled "On Matters of Manner and Music in Jacobean and Caroline Song" in *English Literary Renaissance*, 10:2 (Spring, 1980). I am grateful for their permission to reprint that material.

Staff members of the University of Minnesota Press who have helped get the book into print deserve commendation along with my deep thanks; they have spent many hours on the special problems that arise in the production of a cross-disciplinary book like this.

The deepest gratitude is often the most difficult to express. It is gratitude of that kind that I offer here to John Hollander. First in his teaching, and later in his unfailing support and encouragement at every stage in the progress of the work, he has been the provoker, the taskmaster, and the muse who made it possible for me to write this book.

Despite the helpful criticism of friends and colleagues, I know that there will be errors or questionable judgments in these pages. For these I assume full responsibility; indeed, I do so with some content since I have often found most stimulating the work of scholars with whom I do not always agree. Thus I willingly leave it now to my readers to find and correct my shortcomings, and I end with the hope that at the very least I will have raised some new questions.

Elise Bickford Jorgens
Kalamazoo, Michigan

Contents

Musical Examples

Chapter 3

Chapter 4

Chapter 5

Chapter 6

Footnotes

The Well-Tun'd Word

Introduction

Thomas Campion declared that his aim was "to couple [his] Words and Notes lovingly together."[1] This famous statement has been taken as a manifesto of the impeccable union of poetry and music during the late Renaissance in England, and much has been written about the celebrated coupling by scholars of both music and literature.[2] Most of these investigations have approached the subject from the point of view of genres of song, and the differences between madrigal and lute song (which were considered synonymous at the start of the twentieth century) are now quite well understood with regard to both music and poetry. However, little formulation has been made of the means through which words and notes *may* be joined or of the ways in which a composer may provide a specific interpretation of a poem. This study focuses on a medium, the solo song, rather than on a genre. It concerns conventions of setting a poetic text to music—the specific musical techniques with which a composer indicates particular interpretations of poetry—and how changes in musical style in Jacobean and Caroline England are related to these conventions.

These lines from Campion's "Now winter nights" present the traditional Orphean association of words and music:

> Let well-tun'd words amaze
> With harmony divine.

In a metaphorical sense we may also read the lines as suggesting a more practical alliance, and "well-tun'd" may be interpreted as "well-

set"—a reading especially appropriate for verse by Campion. In this metaphorical sense, Campion's lines express an attitude underlying the relationship between music and poetry in virtually every solo art song in the first half of the seventeenth century. Two points are made: It is the words that will amaze; but if they are "well-tun'd"— which we shall now interpret as being set to music in an appropriate manner—their power to amaze will be increased, and the harmony made by words and music together will be nothing short of divine. This is the philosophy of musical humanism and is, at least in theory, the guiding principle of most vocal music of the late sixteenth and seventeenth centuries. But Campion does not indicate *how* the words are to be "well-tun'd," and on this question composers of the period differed widely. Their varying methods of setting a text, as well as the resultant musical styles, depend on their attitudes toward the text and reflect the specific facets of the text they felt it was the province of music to "tune." Interpretive devices often span the boundaries of genres and may be considered instead in sets determined by the elements of poetic composition a composer wishes to represent. Although presumably the same set of possible correlations is available, not all composers emphasize the same methods of linking the two arts, and differences in musical style consequently may have a definite relationship to composers' interpretive goals and to their selection of techniques for accomplishing them. The evolution of song styles during the first half of the seventeenth century will therefore be viewed here as a function of particular attitudes composers may adopt toward the desirable relationship between music and poetry.

The musical developments I wish to trace are closely related to changing styles in Elizabethan, Jacobean, and Caroline lyric poetry and to composers' efforts to respond appropriately to them. These musical changes are best seen in the solo songs of the period. Although the English madrigal provides a wealth of evidence of careful interpretation of poetry well before the turn of the century, there are important reasons for limiting this study to the solo song and for starting with the first publication of lute songs in 1597. The first reason is a musical one. By 1625, the polyphonic art of the madrigal had virtually disappeared in England. The solo lute song, however, which had fully established the solo medium alongside the polyphonic by 1600, suffered a less precipitous decline, gradually yielding place

in the 1620s to the solo continuo song. The shift from the lute song to the continuo song was a radical one, but the continuity in the solo medium enables us to observe the musical change in relation to changing tastes in poetry and to composers' attempts to meet those changing tastes.

Another deciding factor lies in the texts characteristically chosen by composers of polyphonic and solo vocal music. It is generally agreed that the poetry of the English madrigal is not the best the period had to offer.[3] Although the madrigalists set a few poems by major Elizabethan poets, most of the madrigal texts were either translation of Italian poetry or frothy lyrics by minor English poets of the period. The lutenists, however, set some of the best lyric poetry of Elizabethan and Jacobean England. The serious influence of *English* poetry on English music thus began with the lute song.

Finally, the musical differences between the lute song and the continuo song, as clear and well-defined as they are at both ends of the spectrum, did not appear overnight. The elements of poetic and musical taste that would shape the new style of the continuo song began to appear in some of the early lute songs, and their growing significance for the joining of music and poetry can be traced through this corpus of English song.[4]

The choice of 1651 as a cutoff date is perhaps a little more arbitrary. Just as English solo song did not begin with the lutenists, neither did it end at the Commonwealth, as the songs of Henry Purcell will attest. The composers of continuo songs, however, held characteristic attitudes toward musical interpretation of poetry and made characteristic choices of conventions of setting that indicate those attitudes. These were not significantly carried on in the songs of Purcell and later English song writers. The reasons for this change lie at least in part in some of the features of the continuo song and its poetry that I shall discuss below: the tendency of solo song to a marked cleavage between simple, tuneful airs and heavy-handed declamatory songs, and the prevailing taste in serious poetry at mid-century that no longer favored a linguistic context easily represented with music. Furthermore, the songs of Purcell and his contemporaries leaned increasingly toward the stage and thus represent a tradition somewhat different from that of the solo art song.

Caroline composers were prolific: Manuscript sources, datable roughly between 1610 and 1650, provide us with well over fifteen

hundred continuo songs. None of these were printed, however, until John Playford's first collection appeared in 1651.[5] The contents of Playford's volume, and of those that followed it, are drawn largely from the earlier manuscripts.[6] Thus, although it is clear that Caroline continuo songs remained popular well into the second half of the century, it is equally clear—and can be demonstrated by correlation with manuscript sources—that the majority of these songs were written before 1651.

This book is divided into two sections: Part I concerns the poetry and its possibilities for musical representation; Part II discusses the songs in categories defined by attitudes toward textual interpretation. Realizing that an interdisciplinary investigation of this sort will have readers with varying kinds of expertise, I have begun these two large sections with overviews of the poetry and the music respectively, to establish the context for the detailed discussions that follow. Such surveys may seem more or less cursory depending on the reader's field; nonetheless, it seemed advisable to include them, both for the convenience of a divided audience and in the hope that the book will be useful to students at various levels.

Part I, focusing on the poetry, is an introduction to the materials of the study. It will identify and explain those aspects of poetry that can be interpreted musically (both the mechanics of poetic composition and the words themselves—their literal meaning and their rhetorical and thematic implications) and will describe in detail various technical means with which music can provide such interpretation. It will outline a set of interpretive techniques that could, for the most part, be applied to the songs of virtually any period. Further, it will provide a working vocabulary that will be used in Part II in discussing specific approaches to textual interpretation.[7]

Part II concerns the ways in which these conventions of setting a text actually are used in English solo song of the first half of the seventeenth century. Each chapter focuses on a particular attitude toward which aspects of a text *should* be interpreted with music. Chapter 3 concerns the ideals and the practical results of musical humanism in France, where the emphasis is on representing external verse structure, and the development in English song of the attitude toward the text espoused by the French humanists. This attitude, and its musical effluence, eventually lost its original relationship to the text, but the survival of the musical style—and in many cases its

external relationship to the text as well — is evident in the light-hearted tuneful and dance-related songs discussed in Chapter 4. In Chapter 5, the stances toward music and text inherent in the Italian humanistic movement, with emphasis on thematic structure and dramatic presentation, will be related to the development of the monodic and declamatory styles in England.

These three chapters reflect three basic positions toward musico-poetic correlation adopted in early seventeenth-century England — three stances that may be recognized through particular sets of musical conventions. Obviously, though, not all songs of the period will fit neatly into one or another of these categories. Chapter 6, therefore, concerns those songs with elements of more than one attitude — the strophic, declamatory lute songs and continuo airs — which are a peculiarly English amalgam. These songs, which more than any of the others combine the resources of several sets of conventions to represet the rhetoric of emotions, are of especial interest; they seem to have flowered during the first half of the seventeenth century and then died, yielding place to more rarefied types developing from the styles considered in Chapters 4 and 5.

At the beginning of the period to be covered, music and poetry were considered "sister arts"; the poetry of the period — indeed, well into the second half of the century — is full of references to the union of music and poetry. But well before mid-century they were no longer so closely united. Poets were profuse in their praise of Henry Lawes' ability to set their verse, but history has not found the match an equal one, as it has in Dowland's songs. The disintegration of the celebrated union between the two arts seems to coincide with the shift from the lute song to the continuo song. What constituted that perfect union and what brought about its dissolution — with reference to changes in prevailing musical styles, changes in the kinds of poetry set, and especially the ways these factors affected or were affected by the attitudes composers held toward their texts — is the subject of Part II. A brief concluding chapter reviews the historical development that emerges from such considerations.

Campion, Dowland, the brothers Lawes, and Lanier — all sought to "amaze" with their joining of words and music. That they could have such dramatically different results is evidence that the "well-tun'd word" was by no means clearly defined. With a perspective that they could not have had, I shall try in the chapters that follow to offer some definitions.

Part I Poetry and Music

Prologue

Between 1597 and 1651, the predominant styles of both lyric poetry and music in England changed significantly, and there is evidence in the solo songs that modes of musical interpretation of poetry changed too, in response to alterations in poetic taste. But major changes in style or shifts in interpretive emphasis appear as general changes only from a historical perspective. I wish to look at them not as major breaks but as parts of a continuing reevaluation of various attitudes composers held toward musico-poetic relationships, as they brought those attitudes to new musical tastes and new kinds of poetry. The conventions of musical setting that could represent the metrical structure or the rhetoric of emotions in lyric poetry in 1600 might no longer be appropriate to the poetry of the next generation. The adaptation of techniques of musical interpretation to meet new poetic tastes then becomes an important factor in any change in musical style.

Composers of vocal music usually choose the poetry of their own contemporaries or near contemporaries to set to music.[1] It seems also to be true that music often lags about a generation behind the other arts in adopting conventions that can be related to a "period" style. In periods when vocal music is in the vanguard, a case could be made that this lag is, at least in part, directly related to the time required for composers to assimilate new literary tastes before they can begin to respond creatively to them. With Jacobean composers this argument is strong, for they tended to select either the work of poets in the generation just before their own or that of their conservative

rather than progressive contemporaries—i.e., poetry for which there was some degree of established precedent for musical interpretation.

Some of the poetry set by the lutenist composers goes well back into Elizabeth's reign, and most of the rest is stylistically related to it. Thus the developments in poetic style that originated with Elizabethan lyric poets had a decisive influence on the relationship between words and music in the next fifty years. The Petrarchan movement that hit English lyric poetry during the second half of the sixteenth century was largely responsible for the poetic style of the Elizabethan lyric. This style is decorative in contrast to the plain or what C. S. Lewis called the "drab" style of the earlier court poets. The essence of the Petrarchan lyric is its refined and decorative use of language in the description of the physical beauty and moral purity of the beloved. Whereas the lover, the persona, is subject to alternating fits of hope and despondency, the love affair itself is always idealized and the passions so standardized as to be universal. The tendency to write about impersonal, generalized subjects and the requisite glorification of the lady encouraged reliance on the conventions of rhetoric—figures of speech and elaborate conceits—and on a stock of descriptive images. These features made the style a "literary mannerism." In the best instances, such a set of expectations gave rise to poetry of great lyric beauty whose linguistic artistry is its own justification, regardless of any failing in thematic originality. But rhetorical devices and decorative language, the source of the special charm of the best of this poetry, became so characteristic as to risk becoming primary substance in the hands of lesser poets. Some poems became exercises in the curious (in the Elizabethan sense) and in the poet's ability to create things of beauty with words; the words are important in their own right, not simply as grammatical elements.

This ornate, conventional style was particularly important in the song poetry in Elizabethan England;[2] indeed, its models, the *Canzoniere* of Petrarch, were love songs. The subjects of Petrarchan lyrics are general and impersonal partly because the linguistic style itself removes them from direct experience. Music is an abstract language, and setting a poem to music also tends to remove it from direct personal utterance. Thus, to set a lyric poem of this kind to music is only to underline its poetic context. It is unnecessary for the composer to try to interpret the poem as a personal statement; and since linguistic conventions are so much a part of the poetic style, it

is not only appropriate but desirable for a musical setting to dwell on its means of expression—the individual word or phrase, or the line of verse—as both madrigal and lute song do.

A poem can be interpreted musically in a number of ways. In seventeenth-century England, a musical setting might portray drama or tension in the poem through harmony or, in polyphonic genres, by means of elements such as textural contrast; the tone of the poem might be reflected in the rhythmic or harmonic language of the setting; and most of the aspects of the organization of sound patterns in time—the characteristic that music and poetry have most clearly in common—could be coordinated. A musical setting might correlate, or even reshape, a poetic structure with a musical form; the organization of words into lines could be reflected in musical phrasing; and in English, certain features of the elements of prosody in a poem might be interpreted through the handling of musical rhythm.

Prosody and the other mechanical aspects of the craft of poetic composition were matters of concern to Elizabethan poets, enjoying a new emphasis with the late Renaissance interest in humanistic thinking about poetry. Part of the humanistic idea was a return to the poetic style of the ancient Greeks, and the "New Poetry" that appeared in Italy, France, and England was representative of this movement. To some, it meant experimentation with Classical quantitative poetic meters, but even more, it meant an increased awareness of poetic meter as a part of the craft of versification. Among the Elizabethans, Sidney's poetry is most remarkable in this respect; not only did he compose some quantitative verses, but his accentual poetry introduced new metric norms (he used trochaic as well as iambic accentual patterns, for instance, and reintroduced feminine rhymes to English verse) and featured a great variety of line and stanza forms. The mechanics of versification have a direct effect on the sounds of poetry, and this sensitivity to the "music of poetry" is a characteristic of Elizabethan lyric verse—in particular that verse thought of as poetry for music—that is carried into the seventeenth century, notably in the work of Campion. Thus not only the characteristic linguistic and thematic features, but the mechanical elements of Elizabethan song verse, and of some lyric poetry that followed it, were conducive to musical realization; i.e., Elizabethan song verse demanded of musical rhythm that it reinforce the intricacies of poetic rhythm and meter that were integral parts of the poetic style.

If the Petrarchan lyric and the New Poetry represented major changes from the plain style of the Tudor poets, metaphysical poetry was at least as dramatic a revolution; although very little metaphysical verse was set to music, its effects on the relationship between music and poetry were perhaps even more far-reaching through their influence on the literary tastes of succeeding generations. Elizabethan lyric poets were generally courtiers, noblemen who spent their idle hours composing verse and who typically disdained publication. Their art was a courtly one, and like all the other courtly arts was designed in part to win favor for the artist. The principal writers of metaphysical poetry, on the other hand, beginning with John Donne, were not courtiers but churchmen. Their verse did not have to conform to the tastes of court or monarch; they were not dependent on popularity for their positions; and they were free to express personal sentiments in a personal style. For our purposes, the most important aspect of this new role was an attitude of apparent unconcern with musical setting. Although metaphysical poets also gave lip service to the union of music and poetry (Donne, for instance, entitled a number of his verses "Song"), many features of the metaphysical style made poetry very difficult to set to music.

One of these features was the personal character of metaphysical verse. Where the Elizabethan song lyricist wrote of idealized or universal situations, the metaphysical poet was far more likely to write about personal experience. The persona often seems to assume the voice of the poet himself, and a completely different tone results from the poet's attitude toward his subject. Since musical setting lends abstraction or distance from direct statement, it was difficult for a composer to adopt an appropriate stance toward poetry of this kind. At best, he was compelled to seek a way for singer and persona to be identified.

Another characteristic of metaphysical poetry troublesome for musical interpretation was its particular use of the conventions of rhetoric—its emphasis on irony and its frequently argumentative character. Whereas Elizabethan lyric verse used the conceits and the figures of speech of rhetoric in a decorative manner, often for descriptive purposes, metaphysical poetry partook of the persuasive aspect of Classical rhetoric, adopting decisive stances with regard to its subjects, sometimes becoming didactic. This emphasis, too, reflected the poet's changing attitude toward his own verse and made it

more difficult for a composer to adopt an interpretive goal. Irony and argument are rhetorical appeals to the emotions, but unlike decorative language that appeals to those emotions triggered by the senses, these devices appeal to cognitive processes that, in turn, will produce an emotional response.

Many of the mechanical aspects of metaphysical poetry seem designed to enhance the sense of direct personal statement and to facilitate the presentation of argument or ironic stance. Donne's poetic rhythms, for instance, have been called rough and unmusical, close to those of natural speech rhythms, in striking contrast to the smooth, metrical flow of most Elizabethan lyric verse.[3] His poetic meters are extremely varied, the surface texture of his verse depends more on complex diction and syntax than on regularity of versification, and his lines often feature strong enjambments. Speech rhythms could be represented clearly with varied musical rhythms, but the metaphysical avoidance of regular poetic meters was symptomatic of other changes that would force reassessment of music's relationship to poetry, especially in its larger dimensions. The rough rhythms, for example, made the sense of personal statement in the poem stronger, but they made strophic composition nearly impossible. Elizabethan lyricists who expected their poetry to be sung seem to have constructed the stanzas of their verse so that the same musical setting could serve for all. Such organization is feasible and appropriate where versification is a creative goal in itself; but where rhythm and meter are subordinate to syntax and narrative structure, strict allegiance to stanzaic patterns is unlikely at best.

Strophic setting is similarly discouraged by the thematic structure of much metaphysical poetry. The stanzas of the Elizabethan song poem often were parallel statements, with little or no narrative continuity from one stanza to the next and without appreciable change in tone, so that the same musical interpretation would be appropriate for all stanzas and musical structure would reinforce poetic structure. Metaphysical poetry, on the other hand, is more likely to have a dialectical or narrative thematic structure, so that even where stanzas correspond to logical divisions in the development of the theme, to sing succeeding stanzas to the same music as the first is in a sense a contradiction of the poetic structure. This is particularly apparent where irony is present on a structural level—where, for instance, the tone of a second or third stanza is so changed as to demand that the

reader reevaluate his reading of the first. In such cases, strophic musical structure is an external imposition and does not grow out of consideration of the text.

Understandably, little of this poetry found its way into the lute song books contemporary with its appearance. But the technical features of metaphysical poetry soon entered the poetic vocabulary. Although many of the lyric verses of Jacobean and Caroline poets—poems that *were* set to music with great frequency—do not adopt the intensely personal tone of Donne's verse, they do take on the rough diction and strongly enjambed lines of metaphysical verse, and their structural models, though externally similar to the Elizabethan stanzaic patterns, more often contain a thematic structure that is narrative or ironic. Cavalier poetry is derived primarily from the influence of Ben Jonson, whose style is characterized by a greater sense of taste and decorum than metaphysical verse, but without the decorative language of the Petrarchan lyric. Literary historians point out that whereas Donne's lines override the verse structure, Jonson's have a careful disposition of image and phrase within the line, making them more "songlike." This linear balance is usually maintained by Cavalier poets like Suckling and especially Herrick (whose poems were texts for countless simple, tuneful airs in the second quarter of the century), but less consistently by poets such as Lovelace and Carew, who often allowed syntax to overflow the linear structure of their verse and whose poetry therefore presented problems to the composer similar to those of metaphysical verse.

The social nature of much Cavalier poetry made it, like Elizabethan lyrics, more appropriate in subject than metaphysical poetry for musical interpretation, but it was typically more argumentative than flattering, and ironic statement is much more common than in earlier lyrics. The clichés of rapturous adoration that are primary substance in Petrarchan verse become terms of persuasion in the Cavalier lyric. Thomas Carew's "Hee that loves a Rosie cheeke," for instance, uses images of physical beauty that were standard descriptive conceits in the Petrarchan rhetoric of flattery, but Carew makes them part of an argument to the would-be lover to look beyond physical beauty. A musical setting that emphasizes such devices must be able to represent their ironic as well as their merely descriptive function.

If a poet put personal emotion and argument above finely detailed

craft, or if versification itself involved roughness designed to further thematic content, then the composer too had to seek ways to handle larger complexities than those involving only syllables and words. Nonetheless, not only metaphysical poetry but especially its more songlike Jacobean and Caroline successors did become the primary sources of texts; composers did look for techniques to represent words and syllables *and* the more complicated larger dimensions of poetry. But the challenge was enormous.

Chapter 1
Music for Meter and Rhythm

Definitions of Rhythm and Meter in Music and Poetry

Music and poetry are both structured temporal arts, depending on some kind of recurrence for the perception of their organization. They differ from the spatial arts in that their formal structures must be grasped in process, and the listener is not free to return his attention to specific events, except in memory.[1] Recurrence is therefore particularly crucial to the perception of temporal structure because there must be features that can, at some level, be recalled as determinants of form. But temporal organization involves nonrecurrent features as well. The term "rhythm" is often used in a broad sense to refer to the organization of time, encompassing both recurrent and nonrecurrent factors. "Rhythm," thus loosely defined, describes all of the nonpitched, nonvocalized elements of a temporal form, and includes the concepts of accent and meter as well as duration. But although both arts use some combination of duration and stress for a significant part of their surface effects, this broad sense is the only one in which "rhythm" can be used with respect to both music and poetry. In trying to isolate rhythmic conventions, we will have to be specific as to which are functions of a more precise definition of rhythm, and which are functions of the related elements of duration and meter; for in a narrower sense, although "rhythm" and "meter" are essential to a discussion of either poetry or music, they are not synonymous in the two arts.

"Rhythm" and "meter" are so common in talk of music that they would hardly seem to require defining. Yet the words often are used

loosely, and even musicians do not always agree on their meaning.[2] The following definitions, therefore, are intended primarily to indicate the way in which I will use "rhythm" and "meter" in the pages that follow.

In Western music, the organization of time occurs on several levels, beginning with a series of pulses, equally accented and of equal duration; the relation of these pulses to physical time, the speed at which they pass, is the "tempo." "Meter" is the arrangement of pulses into regularly recurring groups, indicated by the presence of an implied stress or metric accent on the first pulse of each group. Today we tend to think of musical meter as indicated by the time signature and bar lines in a score, and by the mid-seventeenth century, these external features of metric organization were in general use. But meter, thus carefully laid out, is present only in the dance-related music in the early part of the seventeenth century. Yet it is wrong to assume that no sense of meter exists in the less strongly metric songs, for at some level there is almost always (except in the truly unmetered styles associated with recitative) an implied meter or unit of measurement. We are hardly ever in doubt as to what constitutes the beat, and all other note values are experienced as functions of that beat; the organization of note values is thus regulated by the "measuring" of time into recurrent units. Such grouping is sometimes implied in the music of the sixteenth and seventeenth centuries by harmonic rhythm, with chord changes corresponding to the organization of beats, and in the song literature it is usually apparent also in the rate of declamation of syllables.

"Rhythm" refers to the durational organization of the notes in a piece of music into multiples or divisions of the pulse. Although note values may be organized without regard to a metric regulation (again as in free recitative), our perception of temporal organization in music most often involves meter and rhythm simultaneously, and it is sometimes difficult to separate the effects into these components. Nonmetric stresses implied through harmonic or melodic writing or the rhythmic accents indicated by lengthened notes (agogic accents) encumber strict differentiation. Nevertheless, we will want to identify a particular musical or declamatory effect as achieved through metric organization (regularly recurrent accent), rhythmic organization (the manipulation of the relative durations of notes and syllables), or the application of extraneous accents.

Poetic meter is the organizing principle on which verses are constructed. Like musical meter, a poetic meter must present some kind of recurrence for the listener or reader to perceive organization, but the basis of poetic meter will vary from one language to another, or sometimes even from one poem to another in the same language, depending on what particular element is recurrent and whether it recurs at regular or irregular intervals. In English, the primary basis of poetic meter is accent (accentual meter), although the exact pattern of stresses is the poet's choice. Most English poetry of the seventeenth century is also syllabic (i.e., with the same number of syllables per line, sometimes throughout the poem, sometimes in couplets or quatrains). We shall have to look at various kinds of poetic meter in more detail later on, for they have quite different effects on the relationship to musical settings. For the moment we must stress that, regardless of its basis, poetic meter is a constructional norm, and absolute conformity to such a norm is usually neither possible nor altogether desirable.

"Rhythm" in poetry is the actual pattern of durations and stresses made by the words of the poem. Unlike poetic meter, poetic rhythm is not an absolute. Its pattern cannot be defined, for in any language rhythm is subject to the demands of syntax and speech inflection. In English, for instance, where accent is the determinant of both meter and rhythm, a simple prepositional phrase may present different rhythmic patterns depending on the context. The sentence "The man is in the house" will have quite different rhythms in response to the questions "Where is the man?" (The mán is in the hoúse), or "Why isn't the man in the house?" (The mán ís in the hoúse), or again "Is he indoors or out of doors?" (The mán is ín the hoúse). The rhythm of English accentual, syllabic poetry, then, is variable in its handling of changing accentual patterns required by syntax.

A common conflict between poetic rhythm and meter in English arises in connection with phrase rhythms, like those discussed in the preceding paragraph. Although in general the natural rhythm of the language is iambic, there are many short phrases—typically prepositional phrases ("in the air"), infinitive phrases ("to be loved"), or possessives ("of my heart")—that we normally accent thus: ⏑ ⏑ ∕ . Because the unstressed words in such phrases are monosyllables, however, their intrinsic accentuation is not fixed, and as we have

seen, the rhythmic articulation may vary. In the context of a strong iambic meter, the first syllable may take on an accent:

A silent bird was hov'ring in the air;

whereas in another (anapestic) line, a speech-like rhythm might prevail:

An eagle was gliding high up in the air.

Meter and rhythm in accentual poetry represent two planes of temporal organization that apply not only to the arrangement of syllables into metric or rhythmic accentual patterns, but also to the larger dimensions—to the arrangement of words into lines (versification) and grammatical units (phrases and sentences), and to the arrangement of lines and phrases into stanzaic patterns, sonnets, and the like, or into thematic or narrative structures. We might call these planes the *formal* (meter, versification, stanzaic pattern) and the *semantic* (rhythm, grammar or syntax, and thematic or narrative structure).[3] On any dimension they may be coincident, or they may involve conflicts like those between speech rhythms and poetic meter.[4] A setting of a poem must use the materials of musical organization of time in some kind of relationship to the elements of temporal organization in poetry. But music does not have a readily identifiable semantic plane of organization as distinct from its formal plane. Because it is "formalized" in musical notation, a musical setting of a poem *acts* like the formal frame of the poem, regardless of which level of the poem's own organization it represents. It is thus of some importance to musical setting whether the formal and semantic levels of the poem are in agreement, for if they are not, the composer will have to choose between them. Musical interpretation of phrases like "in the air" in the lines above may then depend on the composer's understanding of the difference between rhythm and meter in poetry, on the one hand, or on the other, on some degree of calculated disregard of the metrical handling of speech rhythms.

Whether such decisions are made consciously or as part of a composer's intuitive sense of how he will set a poem, we can identify three fundamental attitudes that determine how the temporal organization of music and poetry may be related: (1) the adoption of a technique that will represent the formal arrangement of syllables and

words on one or more dimension; (2) the choice of a technique that coordinates musical elements with the semantic plane of poetic organization; and (3) the selection of a style that imposes purely musical criteria (such as dance rhythms) over those of poetry. In any of these possible choices, part of the effectiveness of a setting will depend on the composer's understanding of the nature of the language he is setting and of the ways in which the characteristics of the language are conventionally used in the formal and semantic organization of its poetry.[5]

The neoclassical movement, which spread over Europe in the sixteenth century, brought with it not only experimentation with poetic meters, but a desire to unite music and poetry in what was believed to be the manner of the ancient Greeks.[6] The main goal of *musical* humanism was a search for the means to re-create the moral and emotional effects ascribed to ancient music. This idea included— at least in the writings of theorists such as Zarlino, Pontus de Tyard, Vincenzo Galilei, and Girolamo Mei—discussion of the possibility of reviving ancient musical practices regarding intonation and the use of the modes. But in practice, only in the belief that it was ultimately through the words that music could produce such effects,[7] and in the consequent emphasis on a close alliance of music and text, did humanism have any real impact on musical history.

The close union of the two arts sought by late Renaissance musical theorists and composers thus derived inspiration from what they thought was originally an inseparable union of music and poetry in the Greek lyric. No general agreement, however, existed as to what form the union should take, and two quite different sets of attitudes and techniques grew in France and in Italy as responses to the same theory. The French humanists sought to join the formal plane of poetic organization (in this case, meter) with musical notation as they believed was done in the Greek lyric, whereas the Italians worked toward a synthesis of the musical language with the semantic organization and the meaning of the poem, or even of the individual word, striving to re-create the effects of ancient practice. Both positions had, in turn, an influence on solo song in England where, although the desire to emulate Greek practice was not so abundantly spelled out as it was on the continent, we can nevertheless see evidence of striving for the same ideals. The French theories are particularly interesting for their overt connections with music; but to deal

with them, as we shall in detail in Chapter 3, we must briefly consider the metric principles of Classical Greek and Latin lyric poetry, their transfer to sixteenth- and seventeenth-century French poetry, and the effects they had on Elizabethan and early seventeenth-century English poets and composers.

Quantitative Poetic Meters

Classical Greek poetry was organized in quantitative meter, a system of durational patterns governed by the length of syllables as determined by the length and placement of the vowels. A long syllable was assigned a duration twice that of a short syllable, and verses were constructed so as to yield a recurrent pattern corresponding to a musical rhythm involving only two note values. For example, the durations of three feet of poetry that scan as $-\smile\smile\ |-\smile\smile\ |--$ on the basis of syllable length may be rendered by the following musical notation: ♩ ♩ ♩ | ♩ ♩ ♩ | ♩ ♩. It is generally believed that such a system corresponded to the actual pronunciation of long and short syllables in Classical Greek, and that accentuation or inflection of Greek words was based on pitch differentiation rather than dynamic stress.

Renaissance neoclassicists, however, derived their interpretation of quantitative verse primarily from the Romans. Classical Latin poetry represents an attempt to impose the Greek quantitative system on a language that was pronounced with dynamic accent determined by syllable placement rather than syllable length. As in Greek poetry, the metric organization of Latin poetry is based on a pattern derived from the determination of long and short syllables, according to specific rules of vowel length and position with regard to the number of following consonants; but since the application of these rules often violates the principles of accentuation, especially the rule that a Latin word must not be accented on the last syllable, it seems unlikely that Latin poetry was recited quantitatively.[8] The best-known line of Latin poetry will illustrate the problem:

> Arma virumque cano, Troiae qui primus ab oris

A vowel followed by one consonant is considered short, and one followed by two consonants is long; thus, length by position in a quantitative scansion turns the normally "vírŭmquĕ" into "virŭm-quē," and the normally "cáno" into "cănō." Latin use of quantita-

tive meter is therefore best understood as a constructional principle having nothing to do with pronunciation or declamation of the poem. As G. L. Hendrickson says of both the Latin usage and that of the Elizabethan practitioners of Classical meter, "The poet himself was of course conscious of his painstaking and orderly sequence of dactyls and spondees, and in the privacy of his closet may well have 'scanned and proved' their correctness; but surely it was not part of his purpose that his readers would share that consciousness."[9] Lines like the above were read with normal accentuation, and the quantitative system, which was audible in the sense of a musical rhythm in Greek poetry, became essentially a mechanical means of constructing verse and rarely audible in Latin poetry.

Although Renaissance poets' knowledge of Classical meters was derived mainly from Latin, the primarily constructional function of the system apparently was not always recognized by those poets who experimented with quantitative verse. In France, the poets of the *Pléiade* were important neoclassicists; Ronsard, in particular, had humanistic ideas about music and poetry. But it was Jean-Antoine de Baïf, founder of the *Académie de poésie et de musique,* who worked with the rules of Classical prosody, applying them arbitrarily to the syllables of French poetry to produce his *vers mesurés.* For Baïf, quantitative meter was obviously more than a constructional norm; he fully intended that it be an audible part of his verse, and an association with music was fundamental to the conception of Classical poetry as practiced by the *Académie.* Long syllables, as in the Greek system, were considered to be twice the duration of short; the notation of music was used to show precisely how the duration of syllables was to be measured and how the syllables were to be spoken or sung.[10]

Example 1.1.

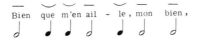

Bien que m'en ail – le, mon bien,

Jacques Mauduit, "Bien que m'en aille." From *Chansonettes mesurées de Ian-Antoine de Baïf* (1586); *Les Maîtres musiciens de la renaissance française,* Vol X, p. 78. Ed. M. Henry Expert. Repr., n.d. Reproduced by permission of Broude Bros., Ltd., New York.

This kind of union of music and poetry, based on an auditory con-

ception of poetic meter, represents a completely arbitrary imposition of a system onto French verse, as much a constructional procedure as it was for the Romans, but obviously taken a step further in the insistence that it be heard as well. Yet the relationship to the language is fundamentally different, for French is not an accentual language as Latin is. Thus, where to pronounce the quantitative scansion of Latin verse is frequently to distort the natural accentual patterns of the language, such pronunciation has no comparable effect on the French language. Since there is no word stress, the imposition of a rhythmic pattern—whether spoken or sung—cannot seriously distort the normal pronunciation of the words.[11] This principle will come up repeatedly, especially in Chapter 3, for it is deeply involved in the possibility of transfer of any kind of musical style from French texts to those in an accentual language, such as English. For the French to measure their verse according to the arbitrary rules of quantitative meter was no more nor less an exercise than for the Romans to do so; but the French, because of the character of their language, were more at liberty than the Romans to realize the resultant meters in musical notation and thereby maintain the musico-poetic structure of the Greek lyric.

In England the introduction of quantitative meters aroused considerable controversy, partly attributable to uncertainty as to whether the meters were to be considered constructional models or models of sound patterns.[12] Sir Philip Sidney was one of the most ardent disciples of quantitative experiments and wrote some poems based on Latin models; Spenser, Harvey, and Stanyhurst also tried using Classical meters. The poems, however, were disagreeable to many critics because they did not scan like English poetry, and the quantitative scansion, if treated as an audible rhythmic pattern, violated the normal English accentuation, just as it did in Latin. One major difficulty was that no set rules existed for determining syllable length in English. Harvey and Drant both composed sets of rules, but of course their rules—like those of their Latin counterparts—had nothing to do with the accentual pronunciation of English. Spenser and Harvey himself seem to have been the most uncertain of the effects of the Classical meters. Their famous correspondence centers on the illogical and ungainly effects of accenting those syllables that are long by position according to the quantitative rules. Hendrickson points out that, as in the Latin models, correspondence of length and accent is nowhere implied by the rules;[13] but it is apparent in the controversy

that English poets were unable to divorce syllable length from accent.

The Elizabethans do not seem generally to have equated quantitative meters with actual musical rhythms as the French did; but they were undoubtedly acquainted with the French experiments, and the knowledge that Classical meters were used in another language as models for sound patterns in poetry may have been an additional source of confusion. Whereas the nonaccentual nature of the French language made it possible for a musical rhythm derived from poetic meter to be applied to the French words, the highly accentual character of English did not lend itself to this kind of interpretation. The frequent failure of length and accent to coincide made it difficult to conceive of the meters as sound patterns, and consequently less practicable to use the quantitative meter as the basis for a musical setting.

At the very end of the movement, however, Thomas Campion, whose *Observations in the Art of English Poesie* appeared in 1602, tried to work out a system for determining quantity that would also coincide with word stress. At the start of his chapter on determining syllable length he says, "But above all the accent of our words is diligently to be observ'd, for chiefly by the accent in any language the true value of the sillables is to be measured."[14] In his experimental verses, Campion did succeed in aligning accent and syllable length, and his one musical setting which equates quantitative meter with musical rhythm ("Come let us sound," No. 21 in *Rosseter's Book of Airs*, 1601) might have offered a direction for quantitative experiments in English in line with the French efforts. In fact, however, although some of Campion's later songs show some effects of these experiments, he did not follow his own rules with any consistency, and in the early decades of the seventeenth century, the movement withered.

The experiments with quantitative meters were thus a minimal factor in Elizabethan poetry. But the underlying association of poetic meter and musical rhythm, inherent in the original Greek meters and in the French movement, did have some effect on musical settings of poetry in England, especially in the work of Campion. The use of quantitative meters in French practice was ultimately of less importance to English poets and composers than the emphasis on poetic meter itself. In England, as well as in France and Italy, the nature of the respective languages, and the poetic meters that had

grown out of the characteristics of those languages, were important in the development of musical styles.

Syllabic Poetic Meter

Most French and Italian poetry of the Renaissance is written in syllabic meter, with syllable count as the organizing principle. The French alexandrine and the Italian *endecasillabo* are syllabic meters. The regularly recurring element is the number of syllables in the line, and accent is not a factor; the line is usually broken by a caesura after a prescribed number of syllables, but there is otherwise no articulation until the end of the line. Since the French language has no accent, the line will flow without interruption, first to the caesura, then to the end. This metric structure is often carefully rendered in musical rhythm in certain kinds of *airs de cour* of the late sixteenth and early seventeenth centuries. In this setting of a poem by Bussy d'Amboise, probably composed in the 1570s or 1580s, the traditional *coupe* after the sixth syllable and the ends of lines of verse are indicated by a slowing down of musical rhythm:[15]

Example 1.2.

[Guillaume Tessier?] "Amans qui vous plaignés." From *Airs de cour pour voix et luth (1603-1643)*, p. 48. Ed. André Verchaly, 1961. Reproduced by permission of the Société Française de Musicologie.

The combination of a nonaccentual language and a syllabic verse structure allows the composer setting a French text to manipulate the musical durations and stresses according to any chosen criteria—whether the application of Classical meters, the strictly musical logic of a dance rhythm, or the dictates of fancy—without impairing either the normal pronunciation of the text or its metric structure.

The Italian language does have penultimate stress, but because it is predictable, this accent is less prominent in Italian than in Germanic languages and is not the basis of its poetic meter. Since a syllabic

meter in Italian poetry prescribes nothing but the number of syllables per line, often a median pause, and the placement of an accent on the penultimate syllable of the line, the pattern of the remaining accents may be different in every line. A musical setting of an Italian poem can represent the accentual pattern of its *speech* rhythms in musical rhythm and, at the same time, outline its formal syllabic meter in musical phrasing.

These characteristics of poetic rhythm and meter in Italian have direct bearing on one of the most significant reactions to musical humanism in Italy: the Florentine *Camerata* that flourished in the 1570s and 1580s. For the musical theorists of this group (especially Vincenzo Galilei), the neoclassical desire to link music and poetry emphasized expressive and dramatic projection of the moral or emotional content of the text rather than its surface texture. Intelligibility of the text was crucial to Galilei, since the words, ultimately, carried the content, and intelligibility was deemed best served in monodic settings that imitated the rhythms of speech. But also included in the humanists' dicta was the requirement that poetic meter be carefully preserved; D. P. Walker points out that Galilei "clearly implies that the 'effetti' will not be forthcoming if the metre of the verse is not perceptible when it is sung."[16]

As we have seen, and will see further in the course of this investigation, if the language were English, the composer trying to adhere to these doctrines might face conflicts. But since the syllabic meter of Italian poetry can accommodate speech rhythms without suffering distortions to the perception of metrical organization, a setting made on this basis can work with both its semantic organization (speech rhythms) and its formal organization (syllabic meter). Some composers were greatly influenced by this strain of humanistic ideas about music and poetry and, in particular, by the thinking of the members of the *Camerata*. Giulio Caccini, for instance, was one of the most vociferous of the exponents of the new style if not always its most radical musical interpreter. Caccini's setting of the following line of poetry by Rinuccini is representative of the way the formal and semantic levels of Italian verse could be set, with musical rhythm and ornament used to interpret the textual rhythm, but with a durational pause (though not a break in the musical line) at the caesura and at the end of the line as seen in example 1.3.

Many of Caccini's settings, especially those from the 1590s and

Example 1.3.

Giulio Caccini, "Fillide mia." From *Le Nouve musiche*, pp. 129-30. Ed. H. Wiley Hitchcock, 1970. Reproduced by permission of A-R Editions, Inc., Madison, Wisconsin.

early 1600s, do reflect the metrical form of the poetry, often with the added emphasis of an embellishment on the line-defining penultimate syllable. But like other Italians, Caccini believed that the passions presented in the text must take precedence over all else. In the service of emotional expressiveness, he was not always careful to preserve the caesura, and the syllabic structure of individual lines is sometimes sacrificed if the grammatical phrase encompasses a couplet. Rarely, however, does Caccini go further in distorting the formal organization of poetry; nor, again, does he need to, for the flexibility of the characteristic syllabic meter in Italian poetry allows for representation of semantic structure in speech rhythms and of formal structure in phrasing.

Accentual Poetic Meter

English lyric poetry of the late sixteenth and early seventeenth centuries usually has a syllabic linear structure too. But the relationship of versification (the organization of lines of verse) to poetic meter is complicated by the strength of accent in English. Compared with the nonaccentual character of French and the predictable and unemphatic stresses of Italian, accentuation in the English language is very strong, falling most commonly into the alternation of stressed and unstressed syllables that form an iambic rhythm. Because of this characteristic of the language, the normal poetic meter of English poetry is accentual; the recurrent feature in the temporal organization is the number and placement of accents in the line, whether the regularity applies to pairs of lines, alternate lines, or any arrangement the poet may choose. In its strictest interpretation, accentual meter does not regulate the number of syllables in the line, but most of the

Elizabethan and Jacobean poetry with which we will deal (i.e., the poetry that was set to music) is accentual syllabic verse.

Since the Tudor period, the most common poetic meter in English has been iambic:

> The silver swan, who living had no note,
> When death approached, unlocked her silent throat,[17]

But other possibilities exist: Sidney is credited with introducing the trochaic meter to English prosody:

> Onely joy, now here you are,
> Fit to heare and ease my care:
> Let my whispering voyce obtaine,
> Sweete reward for sharpest paine:
> Take me to thee, and thee to me.
> 'No, no, no, no, my Deare, let be.'[18]

And, although it is much less common, we shall have occasion to see some English verse that uses the three-syllable grouping of a dactylic meter. But whatever the particular pattern of stresses, their regular presence and their function in the perception of poetic structure are crucial for the relationship to music.

The use of accent as the organizational basis of poetic structure, in addition to its function in the articulation of speech rhythms, will, of course, pose a considerably different set of problems for the composer setting English poetry to music than for one setting the syllabic meters of French or Italian. Poetic rhythm, for instance, is not likely to coincide regularly with the constructional norm of an accentual meter (in fact, if it does, the surface effects of the poem are not very interesting). The composer therefore will have to choose whether to work with the rhythm or the meter of the text. Should poetic meter be chosen, the use of musical accent (including the implied stresses of musical meter) and musical rhythm (particularly the agogic accent implied by longer note values) will be greatly limited by the regular recurrence of word stress. And since accentual meter is closely related to the normal accentual rhythms of the language, a setting that renders poetic rhythm in musical notation will have similar restrictions, even though much greater variety is available and it will be possible to consider the thematic context of the text.

In setting an English accentual syllabic poem to music, a composer is giving us an interpretation of the poem that is unique in the relative permanence of its handling of poetic rhythm and meter. The rhythm and meter of the poem, though clearly perceptible to a reader, are imprecise in that their essential elements—duration and stress—have not been fixed. Because we have no notation to represent these elements of language, the poet cannot be certain that any reader will give the same inflections, the same stresses and durations to his words that he does. Poetic rhythm, even more than meter, involves syntax and inflection and is open to interpretation. An oral reading of a poem is an interpretation that, like a musical setting, works with the rhythm and meter of the poem to give the reader's own emphases to the original poem. But a reader's interpretation cannot be crystallized in such a way that it could be duplicated, any more than the poet's original rhythmic intentions can. (An oral reading can, of course, be reproduced electronically, but it cannot be duplicated in another reading.) A performance of a song is like an oral reading insofar as those elements left open to the performer's interpretation cannot be duplicated. But much more of the interpretation of the poem has been determined by the time it gets to a singer. A composer combines the meter of the poem, the rhythm of the poem, the meter of the music, and the rhythm of the music to produce the musical declamation of the text, the primary level at which a musical setting may be said to interpret a text,[19] formalizing the relative durations of syllables in musical rhythm and linking the effects of the various kinds of musical accent (though less precisely fixed in musical notation than duration) to particular syllables.

Given the initial premise that most English poetry is organized on the basis of a recurrent two-syllable stress pattern, either iambic or trochaic, we can see that the possible strict and regular interpretations of its poetic meter with musical meter are limited. A poem may be set very simply in a duple meter with metric accent coinciding with word stress:

The   peace-full   wes-terne   winde

or, if duration is added as a reinforcement of word stress, in a triple musical meter, or in a duple meter with dotted rhythms:

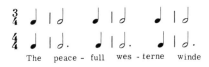

The peace - full   wes - terne   winde

The line used here is Campion's, and, in fact, his own interpretation of it is very close metrically to the first version:[20]

Example 1.4.

The peace-full wes-terne winde   The win-ter stormes hath tam'd.

Thomas Campion, "The peacefull western winde." Excerpt from *The Works of Thomas Campion*, p. 101. Ed. and with introduction by Walter R. Davis. Copyright © 1967 by Doubleday and Co., Inc. and Faber and Faber, Ltd. Reprinted by permission of the publishers.

Campion often worked this closely with poetic meter, with results that usually are simple and direct without descending to the trite. But except for his songs and a few others from the lutenists' corpus, most of the airs that give a faithful rendition of poetic meter are of a lighter, dance-related genre and are more often than not in a triple meter like the second version.

The triple meter in music, though it was felt to be "perfect" in the Middle Ages, is probably not as natural a temporal organization as a duple meter; we walk and run normally to a duple meter, but it takes a conscious effort to coordinate our steps in a triple meter, and the three-beat pattern is often associated with such coordination in the form of dancing. The triple time also is more consciously experienced even when the physical act of dancing is not present.[21] In contrast to a duple meter, which presents a simple alternation of stress and nonstress, a triple meter requires more of the listener's participation to make a distinction, at some level of perception, between the single stressed beat and two unstressed beats. A triple meter is thus more strongly felt than a duple meter and makes meter

itself a prominent feature of musical organization. This feature will have a definite bearing on the effect of setting the meter of English poetry to a ternary beat, for the prominence of the musical meter draws attention to the declamation of the textual meter coincident with it. Furthermore, the effect is strengthened by the rhythmic articulation necessary to coordinate the three-beat musical pattern with a two-syllable unit of verse; the continued use of the following pattern adds rhythmic repetition to that of both musical and poetic meter: ♩ |♪ ♩ |♪ ♩ |♪ The combination also invites tedium and triviality in textual interpretation.

One of the difficulties with a setting that coordinates poetic meter with a triple musical meter is that since the composer is now using both metric accent and duration to reinforce the metric regularity of the poem, no readily available interpretive element is left to set the rhythm of the poem. The agogic accent will be less effective if the listener is already accustomed to a steady alternation of long and short note values, and the tendency to continue setting primarily the meter of the text is very strong. It is usually only when other elements of the works are important that such pieces can escape being merely pleasant trifles. One possible factor—a frequent one, it might be added, in the early years of the seventeenth century—is the presence of the dance. Dowland's "Frog Galliard" is quite characteristic in its rather mechanical representation of poetic meter in music, but the well-known bass line of the piece and its associated dance rhythm suggest physical participation with the music (example 1.5). If the listener is aware of the aligning of rhythm, meter, and poetic structure, it is as a reinforcement of the function of the rhythm for dancing, not as a detraction from the metrical niceties of the text.

Although some light-hearted and dancelike songs use a two-beat musical pattern to represent poetic meter, the duple meter is generally less likely to suggest triviality in setting English accentual meter than a triple one, because it does not require rhythmic differentiation of syllables in addition to metric; and use of the duple meter, of course, leaves rhythm available for interpretive purposes, as we shall consider shortly. But even if rhythm is not so used, even if the declamation is a strict correspondence of poetic meter with musical meter, a setting in duple meter does not impose its own metric organization as strongly as a triple does, and the auditor can be aware of the semantic organization of the text. This, I think, is an important reason that serious texts in English are almost invariably set to a duple meter.[22]

Example 1.5.

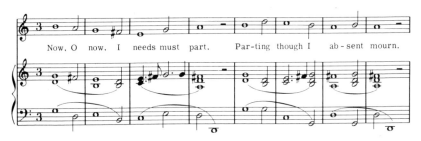

John Dowland, "The Frog Galliard." From *The First Book of Ayres* (1597); *The English Lute-Songs*, Series I, Vol. 1/2, p. 12. Ed. Edmund H. Fellowes. Rev. Thurston Dart, 1965. Reproduced by permission of Stainer and Bell, Ltd. and Galaxy Music Corp.

and we may justifiably consider a choice of musical meter an aspect of the composer's interpretation of the poetry. Notice, for instance, the difference in interpretation that the choice of meter makes in these two versions of a setting by William Lawes of Robert Herrick's "Gather ye rosebuds":

Example 1.6a.

William Lawes, "Gather ye rosebuds." From *William Lawes Autograph Manuscript*; Additional MS 31432, ff. 33v-34. Reprinted with permission of The British Library, Department of Manuscripts.

The melody is virtually the same in both versions, and in both cases poetic meter is represented in the musical notation, with hardly any specific musical interpretation of the words. The triple time version,

Example 1.6b.

Ga - ther your rose - buds whilst you _____ may. Old

time is still a - fly - ing: For that same flow'r that

smiles to - day, To - mor - row will be dy - ing.

William Lawes, "Gather your rosebuds." From Drexel MS 4041, f. 43. Reproduced with permission of the Music Division, The New York Public Library, Astor, Lenox, and Tilden Foundtions.

however, makes a stronger *musical* statement: It is very lyrical and smoothly flowing—seductive is perhaps the word—but the appeal is definitely musical. The duple time setting, on the other hand, provides a clear and firm articulation of the words, letting the poet's text speak for itself.

It may be noticed that the last line in the triple-time version of Lawes's song, and the punch line of Herrick's argument, is set to a broader triple-time pattern (hemiola), with declamation in the duple subdivision. The introduction of a hemiola pattern like this one, shifting the accent momentarily from a triple to a duple organization, is one of the simplest and most frequent gestures at avoiding the monotony of metrical settings in triple time. Hemiola is often used as a purely musical convention and is frequently related to the harmonic framework and characteristic rhythms of the dance that underlie many of these songs. But sometimes it is demanded by the rhythms of the text, which refuse to be forced into a triple meter. To sing a line like Campion's in the next example, for instance, in the

Example 1.7.

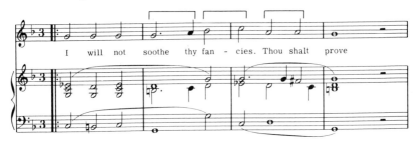

Thomas Campian, "Thou art not faire." From *The Songs from Rosseter's Book of Airs* (1601); *The English Lute-Songs,* Series I, Vol. 4/13, p. 22. Ed. Edmund H. Fellowes. Rev. Thurston Dart, 1969. Reproduced by permission of Stainer and Bell, Ltd. and Galaxy Music Corp.

triple meter as it is written would outrageously distort the accentuation. That Campion realized the necessity for a hemiola adjustment here is shown by the harmonic rhythm of the bass line, which suggests this grouping in the placement of the whole notes and the rhythm of the tonal cadence in g minor:[23]

The most frequent occasion for hemiola, however, seems to be to provide variety in setting iambic verse to a triple meter. William Corkine, in this lute song (example 1.8), uses a continual alternation of the simple triple meter and the broader triple of a hemiola to avoid the repetitive rhythm that the textual meter would require in the simple ternary pattern:

The alternative would be the mechanical kind of setting suggested below:

Example 1.8.

William Corkine, "Truth-trying Time." From *Second Book of Ayres* (1612); *The English School of Lutenist Song Writers,* Second Series, p. 6. Ed. Edmund H. Fellowes, 1927. Reproduced by permission of Stainer and Bell, Ltd. and Galaxy Music Corp.

Corkine's adoption of the hemiola, though in itself conventional, at least avoids this kind of monotony.

Except for Herrick-Lawes "Gather ye rosebuds," the examples of English songs used thus far have been Elizabethan or early Jacobean poems, and the characteristic emphasis on metrics in the poetry makes expected and appropriate this toying with the possibilities for representing the accentual meter. But most of the poetry is also stanzaic and most of the songs strophic. Thus another of the composer's considerations, at least theoretically, is the relationship of poetic meter to stanzaic verse structures. The metric formula of a poem in English acts in effect like a musical setting; it provides a standard pattern based on the first stanza, of which all other stanzas are essentially *contrafacta.* Yet even within the regular meters of Elizabethan lyrics (and even more in the poetry of succeeding generations) poetic rhythm often varies within the imposed pattern of poetic meter, and it is unlikely that the rhythms of successive stanzas will be identical to those of the first.

Again, the difference between setting a French strophic text and an English one is instructive. The two French lines quoted on page 27, for instance, because they have the same number of syllables and the caesura in the same position, could be interchanged musically without distortion; setting a French strophic verse to music is thus essentially a mechanical matter and strophic songs in French generally are quite satisfactory from the point of view of declamation. But consider these lines by the Earl of Pembroke:

> Disdain me still, that I may ever love,
> For who his Love enjoys, can love no more;
> The war once past, with peace men cowards prove,
> And ships returned do rot upon the shore:
> > Then though thou frown, I'll say thou art most fair,
> > And still I'll love, though still I must despair.
>
> As heat's to life, so is desire to love,
> For these once quenched, both life and love are done:
> Let not my sighs, nor tears, thy virtue move;
> Like basest metals, do not melt too soon.
> > Laugh at my woes, although I ever mourn,
> > Love surfeits with rewards, his nurse is scorn.[24]

The accentual iambic meter provides a frame into which most of the words can fit, but the actual rhythms in the two stanzas are quite different. The first line of the second stanza, for instance, requires a reversal to make the syntactical structure clear:

> As heat's to life, so is desire to love,
> Meter: ◡ / ◡ / ◡ / ◡ / ◡ /
> Rhythm: ◡ / ◡ / / ◡ ◡ / ◡ /

and its rhythm is therefore not the same as that of the comparable line in the first stanza.

The equation of poetic meter with music, with either accent or duration equivalent to word stress, will have an advantage over less regularized handling of texts in making strophic settings feasible. In this sense, metrical settings may be considered careful renditions of the poem, for in such songs it is at least conceivable that the composer is taking into account that there is more to a poem than the first stanza. The point is again particularly relevant to Campion. The two-strophe poetic structure was a favorite with Campion, the second stanza typically introducing a reversal or a clinching argument

to complete the first; and his simple, metric settings make possible the equally well-declaimed recitation of both stanzas. His "I must complain," for instance, adds an ironic aspect in the second stanza, in contrast to the typical lover's complaint of the first:

> I must complain, yet doe enjoy my Love;
> She is too faire, too rich in lovely parts:
> Thence is my grief, for Nature, while she strove
> With all her graces and divinest Arts
>> To form her too too beautifull of hue,
>> She had no leasure left to make her true.
>
> Should I, agriev'd, then wish shee were lesse fayre?
> That were repugnant to mine owne desires:
> Shee is admir'd, new lovers still repayre;
> That kindles daily loves forgetfull fires.
>> Rest, jealous thoughts, and thus resolve at last:
>> She hath more beauty then becomes the chast.[25]

The simple setting allows this thematic interest to come through since both stanzas are well set with respect to poetic meter:

Example 1.9.

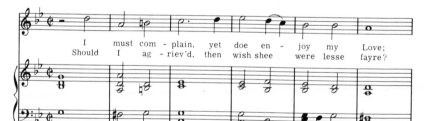

Thomas Campion, "I must complain." Excerpt from *The Works of Thomas Campion*, p. 185. Ed. and with introduction by Walter R. Davis. Copyright © 1967 by Doubleday and Co., Inc. and Faber and Faber, Ltd. Reprinted by permission of the publishers.

But of course Campion's strophic setting is possible only because the musical statement is necessarily very generalized and makes little, if any, rhythmic interpretation of its own. A representation of poetic meter, especially of an English accentual meter, in musical rhythms would theoretically be acceptable for any poem of the same metric

structure, and the effect of the setting would be to smooth over the differences in poetic rhythm that give the verses their individuality. Sometimes the choice of a noninterpretive setting seems particularly appropriate when, for example, surface details other than rhythm (such as assonance or internal rhyme) are present and would be enhanced by an even, metric declamation,[26] or when the subject matter is definitely contemplative rather than emotional, dramatic, or expostulatory, as in some of Campion's religious songs. In most cases, however, because of the characteristic alternation of stressed and unstressed syllables, the mechanical setting of English poetic meters accompanies verses that are of regular meter and often not very interesting as poetry. The combination of regular verse and simple setting is most typical of popular styles where interpretation of the text is not a primary consideration.

Musical Representation of Poetic Rhythm

Where textual interpretation is important, composers will find ways of avoiding the repeated coincidence of poetic meter with musical meter, and seek to work with the semantic plane of organization — the rhythms of the text. To accomplish this, the nonmetric resources of musical rhythm may be added to the effects of meter, or musical meter itself may be altered to provide the necessary variety. Accentual poetic rhythms usually are represented with some kind of alternation of relatively longer and shorter note values. Some of the songs from the sixteenth and seventeenth centuries do not have a regular duple or triple musical meter, so textual rhythm may be freely represented with musical rhythm. The line shown in example 1.10 from Dowland's "Love stood amazed," for example, is not regularly divided with bar-lines and is clearly neither duple nor triple, but a combination, as indicated by the harmonic rhythm as well as the declamatory rhythms. The rhythms of the line are determined, not by a preconceived, regular scheme of poetic or musical meter, but by Dowland's interpretation of the rhythms of the text.[27]

Of course, such free rhythmic correlation is possible only in the absence of regular musical meter. Nonetheless, variations in musical rhythm can accommodate textual rhythms even within a regular metric scheme. If, in a song with a regular musical meter, the setting does not align musical meter with poetic meter, the stress patterns of musical meter and poetic rhythm may conflict. This is particularly

Example 1.10.

John Dowland, "Love stood amazed." From *The Third Booke of Songs* (1603); *The English Lute-Songs*, Series I, Vol. 10/11, p. 20. Ed. Edmund H. Fellowes. Rev. Thurston Dart and David Scott, 1970. Reproduced by permission of Stainer and Bell, Ltd. and Galaxy Music Corp.

apparent in the dance-related songs in the seventeenth century, where the musical meter must be strictly maintained, regardless of textual accentuation. Occasionally, such conflicts are present in songs in which poetic rhythm seems to have been taken into consideration. In such cases, correct word stress must be imposed without the reinforcement of musical accent. In performing Dowland's "Lacrimae," for example, a good singer would not distort "pity" and "deprived" as Dowland's musical indications seem to suggest, but would bring out the cross-rhythm implied by the duple meter of the pavane in the accompaniment and the triple of the declamatory rhythm.

But this apparent carelessness is relatively infrequent in songs of the seventeenth century. Normally, a composer will give some indication of avoidance of the metric accent, so that the force of regular musical stress patterns will not intrude on the declamation of the text. In this line from "Blame not my cheeks," for example, Campion makes use of a common hemiola pattern to prevent an undue accent on the first syllable of "distressed," lengthening the preceding "by"

Example 1.11.

John Dowland, "Flow my tears." From *The Second Book of Songs* (1600); *The English Lute-Songs*, Series I, Vol. 5/6, pp. 4-5. Ed. Edmund H. Fellowes. Rev. Thurston Dart, 1969. Reproduced by permission of Stainer and Bell, Ltd. and Galaxy Music Corp.

so that the strong chord change also will not coincide with "dis-":
Difficulties with the placement of syllables within a musical meter

Example 1.12.

Thomas Campian, "Blame not my cheeks." From *The Songs from Rosseter's Book of Airs* (1601); *The English Lute-Songs*, Series I, Vol. 4/13, p. 26. Ed. Edmund H. Fellowes. Rev. Thurston Dart, 1969. Reproduced by permission of Stainer and Bell, Ltd. and Galaxy Music Corp.

also may be handled with rests, avoiding the coincidence of an un-accented syllable with a metric accent. In example 1.13a, a phrase

Example 1.13a.

Henry Lawes, "Love thee! Good sooth, not I." From *Select Ayres and Dialogues, The Third Book*, p. 17. London: John Playford, 1669. Facsimile ed. Ridgewood, N.J.: Gregg Press, Inc., 1966.

from a song by Henry Lawes, the placement of syllables within the metric structure clearly shows the composer's interpretation of the opening words. He reads them "Love *thee!*" (rather than someone else) and not "*Love* thee!" (rather than hate thee) as he might have with a rhythmic interpretation like the following:

Example 1.13b.

Since poetic meter is derived ultimately from the natural rhythms of the language, to set the rhythm of the words in accentual verse to music most often does not violate the stress patterns of its meter; thus a rhythmic setting at most will make the surface texture rough as compared with the evenness and regularity of a metric setting. But as we noted above, phrase rhythms in English do often conflict with poetic meter, and with certain kinds of phrases the composer must choose between a rhythmic or a metric interpretation. A couplet like this one from Campion's "Masque of Squires" presents some inter-esting problems:

> Come ashore, come merry mates,
> With your nimble heels and pates,

The trochaic meter, if rigorously followed, would not place an accent on the second "come." This is clearly wrong, and Campion himself, acknowledging the need for counting the silences in scanning accentual poetry,[28] provides for a freer rhythmic interpretation of the line:

Come ashore,   come merry mates,

| Meter: | / ⌣ / ⌣ / ⌣ / |
| Rhythm: | / ⌣ / ⌣ / / ⌣ / |

Giovanni Coperario's musical setting handles the rhythm of the first line well. But notice what Coperario does with the phrase "with your nimble heels and pates." This second line is treated as though the regular trochaic meter were the sole determinant of musical rhythm, although he could easily have avoided accenting "with" and provided as accurate a phrase rhythm here as he did for "come merry mates," as in example 1.14b.

Such small details can make a significant difference in determining a

Example 1.14a.

John Coprario, "Come ashore." From *The Masque of Squires* (1614); *The English Lute-Songs*, Series I, Vol. 17, p. 40. Ed. Gerald Hendrie and Thurston Dart, 1959. Reproduced by permission of Stainer and Bell, Ltd. and Galaxy Music Corp.

Example 1.14b.

composer's attitude toward the text. Where conflicts between phrase rhythms and poetic meter occur, the choice will be made according to the composer's interpretive goal.

Long note values in the context of shorter ones (the agogic accent) tend to give prominence to syllables set to them. A composer can make an interpretation of a phrase of text apparent with musical rhythm by setting particular syllables to long notes and drawing attention to those words or syllables in the context of the phrase. In example 1.13a, for instance, the rest before "Love thee!" not only avoids the metric accent, but reinforces the composer's interpretation of the meaning by, in effect, shortening the duration of "Love" and making "thee" longer by comparison. An even better example is this line from the famous "Lacrimae."

Example 1.15a.

Nev - er may my woes be re - liev - ed.

John Dowland, "Flow my tears." From *The Second Book of Songs* (1600); *The English Lute-Songs*, Series I, Vol. 5/6, p. 4. Ed. Edmund H. Fellowes. Rev. Thurston Dart, 1969. Reproduced by permission of Stainer and Bell, Ltd. and Galaxy Music Corp.

Dowland puts emphasis on "Never" and "woes" with long notes. It is a logical and beautiful interpretation, and because the song is so well known, it seems difficult to imagine any other.[29] But the composer might have written something like this:

Example 1.15b.

Nev-er may   my   woes be___   re - liev   -   ed,

In this hypothetical setting, the emphasis is shifted from "woes" to the possessive "my" and from the despairing "Never" to the desired condition, "be relieved."

We have thus far been concerned only with nonpitched elements, but either harmony or melody may be involved in promoting syllables. Harmonic rhythm sometimes is made to coincide with declamatory rhythms, as in Dowland's "Love stood amazed" (see p. 41). When harmonic rhythm is used in this way, as it often is in settings emphasizing poetic meter as well, the chord changes are simply a reinforcement of the rhythms of syllabic declamation and do not add any particular stresses of their own. But harmony also can be used as an interpretive device, both affectively (as we shall see in Chapter 6) and as a determinant of interpretive stress patterns. In the next example, although the declamatory rhythms suggest a speechlike accentuation, the harmonic rhythm adds interpretive accent with a chord change on "tarry," while the unchanging harmony of the first measure reduces the stress on "call":

Example 1.16.

John Dowland, "Come when I call." From *The Third Booke of Songs* (1603); *The English Lute-Songs*, Series I, Vol. 10/11, p. 42. Ed. Edmund H. Fellowes. Rev. Thurston Dart and David Scott, 1970. Reproduced by permission of Stainer and Bell, Ltd. and Galaxy Music Corp.

In the monodic settings that began to appear in England around 1610, the rate of harmonic rhythm tends to be much slower than declamatory rhythm, and in such songs the placement of *any* chords will have the effect of emphasis. In example 1.17, a setting by Henry Lawes of Suckling's poem, the first syllable to coincide with a chord is "*her*etic," giving added accentuation to this startling epithet. We might compare this setting with the anonymous one of the same text, shown in example 1.18, where the stresses are much more em-

phatically on "No, no" because of the placement of the accompanying chords.

Henry Lawes' setting of "No, no, fair heretic" shows other possibilities in the use of harmony. The stress on "heretic" is accompanied by a chord change with root movement by fifth (d minor to A major). Although tonal harmony had not been systematically established in the early seventeenth century, it is nonetheless often apparent that such "functional" chord progressions were felt to be stronger than those with root movement by second or third; the re-

Example 1.17.

No, no, fair__ he - re-tic,   It can-not be   But an

ill   love in me   And worse   for thee;

Henry Lawes, "No, no, fair heretic." From *Henry Lawes Autograph Manuscript*; Additional MS 53723, ff. 52v-53. Reprinted with permission of The British Library, Department of Manuscripts.

maining chord changes in the example, though they support the textual rhythm, do not provide the same kind of emphatic stress as that on "heretic." At the end of the example is an interesting

Example 1.18.

No,   no, fair   he - re-tic

[Anonymous], "No, no, fair heretic." From Drexel MS 4041, f. 8v. Reproduced with permission of the Music Division, The New York Public Library, Astor, Lenox, and Tilden Foundations.

harmonic device common in this period, combining coloristic and declamatory functions. "And worse for thee" obviously requires a strong accentual pattern because of its thematic implications, and the harmonic root movement of the phrase is again from d minor to A major. But Lawes also introduces an unprepared suspension, making the bass line pass through the lower third (B♭) while maintaining the fifth of the d minor triad in the melody; the listener thus hears the harsh dissonance of a major seventh—nicely coincident with "worse"—en route to the strong chord progression governing the phrase.

Melody, too, may be an important factor in the handling of the rhythms of the text. A rise in pitch often acts as a dynamic accent, and any melodic leap over a large musical interval is likely to function as an accent in drawing attention to the syllables set to the leap. Both Dowland's version and the hypothesized version of "Never may my woes be relieved" (p. 45) use rises in pitch and upward leaps to reinforce the rhythmic placement of stress; and in Campion's "Blame not my cheeks" (p. 42), the correct accentuation of "distressed" is emphasized by a descending melodic line to "dis-" and a leap up to the accented second syllable. Melodic direction alone, however, is not sufficient to indicate word stress; the effect of melody on declamation is always a reinforcement of musical rhythm.

The realization of the rhythms and meters of accentual poetry in the notation of musical rhythm is, in a fundamental sense, what it means to set an English poem to music. A composer must assign notes to the syllables of the text, and whether or not he has consciously chosen a declamatory style that will represent the temporal organization of the syllables in a particular way, the relation of the musical rhythms and meter to those of the words will be heard in performance. The conventions of setting a text to music can have specific effects on declamation, but there is in addition a broader sense in which a declamatory style is an important interpretive element. As we look at songs from the first fifty years of the seventeenth century, it will be apparent that a wide range of rhythmic declamation is possible, from the simple settings of Campion and others, in which virtually all syllables are set to the same note value, to the extremely varied rhythms of Dowland in his later songs and Henry Lawes in his most dramatic songs, in which note values set to syllables may range from double whole note to sixteenth note in the same song.

The effects of these extremes in style are obviously quite different, and the style of declamation will be one of the composer's most effective means of establishing a rhetorical stance toward the poem. Our concern here, however, is the relationship to the rhythms of the language. Because of the deeply rooted iambic conventions of English accentual, syllabic verse, the relative durations of its syllables are more varied than the equal note values of a Campion setting, but usually do not run to the extremes of rhythm in the dramatic or declamatory songs. A composer wishing to reflect normal speech patterns of English probably will be most successful working with a relatively even distribution of longer and shorter note values and with not more than a threefold or fourfold ratio between the longest and shortest notes. Any deviation from such speech norms will be perceived as an interpretive distortion. Systematically equalized metric settings tend to sound removed from the content of the text; the listener cannot become emotionally involved in the text, because its declamation is so artificially smooth that the words themselves have lost some of the force of syntactical inflection that gives them meaning. Surface texture and elements of versification, however, are well served in settings of this type, and we shall find that promotion of these features sometimes seems to be the focus of such songs. When we move to the other end of the spectrum, the effect is the opposite: A declamation that greatly exaggerates the varying durations of normal speech rhythms will tend to suggest a highly oratorical or dramatic reading of the text, one that seeks to emphasize the narrative and/or the emotional character of the text at the expense of its surface texture, and to make the content of the text appear "larger than life."

The smoothest, most naturally convincing declamation will merge the stress patterns of poetry and music and will use the rhythmic and metric resources of music, as well as the reinforcement of applied accents and the effects of melody and harmony, to promote the composer's interpretation of the text. But the particular balance of all of these elements will depend not only on the conventions of the period and the composer's individual style and conception of the poem, but also on the characteristics of the poetry chosen and the composer's view of the function of the poem in the song. The syllabic, solo settings typical of Jacobean and Caroline song use all of the devices discussed above to render an intelligible and effective setting. It is the proportion in the use of these and other conventions,

however, that can make one song a more precise rendition of a text than another, or one composer's style quite different from another's. And that proportion is determined to a large extent by the composer's attitude toward the text—conscious or unconscious—in any given song.

Chapter 2
Music for Lines and Stanzas

The musical handling of poetic rhythm and accentual meter in song is inevitable. Without declamation—the actual setting of the syllables of the text—there would be no song. However, the treatment of the larger dimensions of poetic composition shows the depth of a composer's understanding of a poem's organization. Without interpretation of lines and stanzas, phrases, sentences and paragraphs, the words *could* be sung, but the result would be largely recitation, not art song. With the larger dimensions, the musician can begin to expand interpretive goals in more purely musical directions, for sensitive representation of the larger structural features of poetry *can* become much less a mechanical exercise and more an artistic one of re-creation.

Versification

Versification, the arrangement of words into lines or, technically, verses, is a convention of the poet's craft, comparable to accentual meter in that it imposes a limiting, formal frame. In the poetry of the lute songs and the continuo songs, versification tends to be regular and predictable. Syllabic meter specifies the number of syllables in a line and in the poetry of sixteenth- and seventeenth-century English songs is an important part of versification. So, too, is the use of end-rhymes, which audibly signal the limits of lines. These formal conventions of versification lend themselves readily to musical representation of the simplest, most mechanical sort.[1] One need only

think of a Campion tune, or one like this by John Bartlet, in which syllabic[2] declamation counts out the length of the lines and the end-rhymes are reinforced by longer note values:

Example 2.1.

Who doth be - hold my mis - tress' face And
Who hears her speak and marks her grace . . . .

se - eth not, good hap hath he
. . . .

John Bartlet, "Who doth behold my Mistress' face." From *A Book of Ayres* (1606); *The English School of Lutenist Song Writers*, Second Series, p. 7. Ed. Edmund H. Fellowes, 1925. Reproduced by permission of Stainer and Bell, Ltd. and Galaxy Music Corp.

In addition to the strictly formal conventions of versification, the arrangement of words is determined by syntactical and grammatical concerns—the semantic organization. The relationship of linear structure to grammatical structure is of especial interest in the lyrics written with music in mind because of the formalizing effect of a musical setting. In the poetry of the English lute song, that relationship usually is almost as predictable as versification itself. Lines are most often end-stopped; grammatical structure is so arranged as to correspond to versification, and semantic and formal planes of organization coincide.

In many poems of the period, the grammatical coherence of each line is so great that the lines might almost be interchanged without severe damage to the poem. "Disdain me still" is such a poem (see p.

38). Not only are grammatical units and lines identical in length, but the line lengths and rhyme scheme are regular and the grammatical units self-contained. Rearrangement would hardly affect any aspect of the poem's organization. Such lines are, of course, ideally suited for musical representation in the conventional manner of the period. In Dowland's setting of this poem, the mechanical counting-out of the syllabic linear structure is avoided, with lively musical rhythms interpreting the rhythms of the text; but the end of each line of the poem is indicated clearly, both voice and accompaniment (or all four voices in the alternative version) coming to rest on a sustained note:

Example 2.2.

John Dowland, "Disdain me still." From *A Pilgrimes Solace* (1612); *The English Lute-Songs*, Series I, Vol. 12/14, p. 2. Ed. Edmund H. Fellowes. Rev. Thurston Dart, 1969. Reproduced by permission of Stainer and Bell, Ltd. and Galaxy Music Corp.

Because the formal and semantic arrangements are congruent, the composer is free to interpret the semantic organization—the rhythms and grammatical structure—while giving a faithful representation of the formal. Notice, for instance, the separation of the grammatical phrases "Disdain me still, / that I may ever love" in the vocal line, with the lute providing musical continuity that corresponds to the unifying effect of linear structure.

Melodic shape, rather than rhythm, is sometimes used to articulate grammatical phrases within the linear structure. In the next example, the grammatical phrasing is delineated with melodic direction:

Example 2.3.

O   no, I tell thee no;   though from thee   I must go,

Yet my heart says not so:

Nicholas Lanier, "Unwilling Parting." From *Select Ayres and Dialogues, The Second Book*, p. 57. London: John Playford, 1669. Facsimile ed. Ridgewood, N.J.: Gregg Press, Inc., 1966.

The sense of the text is clear, because the phrasing has been carefully articulated with melody; and because the lines are end-stopped, the formal linear structure is also reinforced by the parallel melodic phrasing.

Syntax

Of course, not all poetry has end-stopped lines. Syntax sometimes overrides the linear structure and the lines are said to be enjambed; formal and semantic planes of organization are then in conflict, and musical setting will encounter some difficulties. The composer's choices at the outer limits seem to be fairly clear-cut. Dowland, in the song in example 2.4 simply ignores the enjambment and adheres to the formal structure of versification, marking the division between lines with a rest. At the other extreme, as seen in example 2.5, Henry Lawes, in his setting of Thomas Carew's "When thou, poor excommunicate," ignores versification, determining his musical rhythms and phrases entirely by the grammatical structure of the lines and setting the text as though it were prose.

Strong enjambments of this kind are much more common in the songs of Caroline composers than in those of Jacobean composers, but even in Caroline songs, both poets and composers seem to make

Example 2.4.

John Dowland, "Wilt thou, unkind, thus reave me." From *The First Book of Ayres* (1597); *The English Lute-Songs*, Series I, Vol. 1/2, p. 30. Ed. Edmund H. Fellowes. Rev. Thurston Dart, 1965. Reproduced by permission of Stainer and Bell, Ltd. and Galaxy Music Corp.

some attempt to compromise. Although there are some exceptions in which syntax overrides even the couplet structure (such as the preceding example), in the lyrics used as song texts, enjambments occur most often *within* couplets, as in the following:

> God of winds, when thou art growne
> Breathles and hast spent thy store,
> When thy Raging blasts are gone
> I can furnish thee with more.
> I can lend thee sighs that are
> Fitter for thy Churlish Warre.[3]

The grammatical self-containment of individual lines in "Disdain me still" is here applied to units of two lines, closed couplets. This arrangement usually presents little difficulty to musical setting, for the composer can simply set the lines two at a time, maintaining the formal structure of the couplets. The strength of versification—the regularity of the couplets and the force of the rhyme scheme—make such enjambments a means of tightening the formal structure, and a musical setting that corresponds to this organization acts as further formal control. William Lawes seems to make a gesture toward representing the poet's balance of versification and syntax in his musical setting. The grammatical structure of the couplets is suggested by the absence of rests after "growne" and "gone," but the linear structure is also made audible with the sustained notes on the rhyming words. Lawes's gesture may, in fact, be only a visual one, for any but the

Example 2.5.

Henry Lawes, "When thou, poor excommunicate." From *Henry Lawes Autograph Manuscript*; Additional MS 53723, f. 110. Reprinted with permission of the British Library, Department of Manuscripts.

most skilled of singers would surely be literally too "breathles" to make the connection. But it is at least a reminder to the singer that the syntax is not broken at the end of every line of the poem.

Example 2.6.

William Lawes, "God of Winds." From *William Lawes Autograph Manuscript*; Additional MS 31432, f. 31. Reprinted with permission of The British Library, Department of Manuscripts.

But such musical balancing of formal and semantic structures works only if the composer has fully understood the relationship between them and if the poet has provided the appropriate auditory

signals of formal design. In another of William Lawes' songs (see example 2.7), we can see an example of improper balance between formal and semantic representation that can result if either, or in this case both, of those conditions is not met. The pattern of enjamb-ment is the same as in the last example, but the couplets are not joined by an interlocking rhyme scheme but are rhymed aabb. From the standpoint of the poem there is no problem: if anything,

Example 2.7.

William Lawes, "He that will not love." From *The Treasury of Musick, Containing Ayres and Dialogues, Book I*, p. 8. London: John Playford, 1669. Facsimile ed. Ridgewood, N.J.: Gregg Press, Inc., 1966.

the enjambed couplets are held together more strongly by rhyme. But the musical effect is wrong, and Lawes's setting falls square-ly into its trap. The composer has set lines 1-2 and 3-4 as two par-allel phrases of four measure each. Gramatically this is quite cor-rect, and the rhymes of "be" and "me" and "fears" and "ears" are heard as internal rhymes—if at all. But the formal effect, created by the musical setting of the first couplet, is to make it sound like some sort of distorted ballad meter (a trochaic pentameter line, "He that will not love, must be my Scholar," followed by a short tro-chaic line). This pattern establishes an expectation of a rhyme scheme that joins the couplets to each other rather than separating them. In the *musical* context it is quite startling to hear "ears" at the end of the second phrase where the strength of the formal arrange-ment suggested by the musical structure leads us to expect a rhyme for "me." Lawes might have alleviated the difficulty by bringing out

the rhyming words as he did in the previous example, but then the
grammatical coherence—especially of the first couplet—would have
been weakened. There seems to be no easy solution that would maintain the poet's balancing of versification and syntax.

Nevertheless, this is a relatively simple kind of imbalance between
formal and semantic organization, and one that exists only in the
context of musical setting. Imbalance intended by the poet for
thematic reasons may present problems that are much more interesting. "Parting, *Celia* Weepes" by Thomas Carew was set to music
by Henry Lawes, but it presents so many difficulties to musical
representation that it might well be used as a case study. For the
present, we wish to look at its enjambments, which include various
degrees of conflict between its formal and semantic organization.

> Weepe not (my deare) for I shall goe
> Loaden enough with mine owne woe;
> Adde not thy heavinesse to mine:
> Since Fate our pleasures must dis-joyne,
> Why should our sorrowes meet? if I
> Must goe, and lose thy company,
> I wish not theirs; it shall relieve
> My griefe, to thinke thou dost not grieve.
> Yet grieve, and weepe, that I may beare
> Every sigh, and every teare
> Away with me, so shall thy brest
> And eyes discharg'd, enjoy their rest.
> And it will glad my heart to see,
> Thou wer't thus loath to part with mee.[4]

Only one line (line 3) is grammatically self-contained in the way that
every line of "Disdain me still" was; the others are all to some degree
linked to each other, from the adverbial function of line 2 joining it
to line 1, and the incompleteness of the conditional clause in line 4
necessitating line 5, to the strong grammatical link between lines 5
and 6: "if I/Must goe." Furthermore, the linking is not confined to
the couplet structure but crosses it at lines 4-5 and 10-11. With this
parrying of the two kinds of organization of his words, the poet has
built into his verse a tension appropriate to his subject.

The poem is a strange one because, although it has the shorter
tetrameter lines common in "songs" and is in rhymed couplets
throughout, it has a sonnetlike thematic structure, with a clear division into octave and sestet. Yet Henry Lawes, perhaps lured away

from the semantic structure by the songlike formal features, chose to set it as a strophic song. In Lawes' manuscript, the text appears as three four-line stanzas with an additional couplet (a not uncommon arrangement in some of Carew's other "songs" such as "Hee that loves a Rosie cheeke") although the composer provides no music for the final couplet. In the printed source,[5] lines 11 and 12 have been omitted to make three equal stanzas, and the poem appears as follows:

Example 2.8.

Henry Lawes, "Weep not, my dear." From *Select Ayres and Dialogues, The Second Book*, p. 40. London: John Playford, 1669. Facsimile ed. Ridgewood, N.J.: Gregg Press, Inc., 1966.

The strophic setting, of course, obliterates the sonnetlike thematic structure, but that is a problem to be considered later. Here we must observe what the decision to write a strophic song does to the poet's precariously balanced lines. Lawes has tried to reconcile the demands of versification and syntax, setting the couplets as continuous phrases with just enough pause midway to make the rhymes audible. But because he has set the poem as four-line stanzas, he cannot connect lines 4-5: "Since Fate our pleasures must disjoyne,/Why should our

sorrows meet?" Instead, so as not to leave "Since Fate our Pleasures must disjoyne" dangling uncompleted at the end of a stanza, he has joined the only self-contained line of the poem (line 3) to line 4: "Add not thy heaviness to mine,/Since Fate our pleasures must disjoyn."

Formal Structure

With the last example, we have moved into a yet more interesting aspect of versification, its relation to the way a whole poem is put together. Syllabic linear structure and rhyme scheme are recurrent elements, like accentual meter, that give formal shape to a poem; and this shape, like the other formal conventions of poetic composition, is relatively easily translated into musical form. The sonnetlike structure of "Weep not, my dear" is not articulated in its formal conventions (there is, for example, no change of rhyme scheme at the sestet); and except for omitting two lines, Henry Lawes' setting—for all its difficulties with grammatical structure—did no violence to the succession of rhymed couplets of the external, formal structure of the poem. The syllabic linear structure and the rhyming couplets are clearly and audibly represented in musical structure.

Such mechanical representation of form is extremely common in early seventeenth-century songs. In fact, many songs go further, making some change in the musical language—which will be perceived as a component of musical form—coincide with changes in the elements of articulation of formal design in poetry. Thomas Campion, for instance, is always careful to reflect the pattern of rhyme scheme and the lengths of lines with appropriate musical repetitions. His setting of "I must complain" correlates the rhyme scheme with melodic phrases like this:

Music	Rhyme
A	⌈a ⌊b
A	⌈a ⌊b
‖: B :‖	‖: c c :‖

Literally dozens of lute songs have a similar aligning of rhyme scheme and melodic repetition. A slightly more subtle kind of articulation, but having a similar correlation with formal poetic structure, appears in Dowland's setting of the same poem. There the first four lines (abab) are set to a polyphonic texture and the last two (cc) to a homophonic texture.

In the second quarter of the seventeenth century, it became a common practice to represent changes in rhyming pattern or in the lengths of lines with a change in musical meter,[6] most often (but not always) from duple to triple. Thus, in a song by the Caroline composer Roger Hill, the correlation is like this:

	Admit, thou Darling of mine Eyes,
2	I serve some Idol lately fram'd;
2	That underneath a false disguise,
	Our true Loves might the less be fam'd:
3	Canst thou that know'st my Heart suppose
2	I fall from Thee to worship Those.[7]

Thematic Structure

In songs where the external, formal structure of the poem seems to have no significant correlation with the thematic arrangement, those formal features may themselves be the determinants of the dimensions of musical structure. But the formal organization of a poem often does have thematic significance. Many of the lyrics have a sonnetlike structure in which the final couplet is in some sense a consequence of what has gone before—a reply or riposte, the conclusion of a condition set up in the preceding lines, or sometimes a summing-up. Such coincidence of form and content makes musical representation of structural divisions more interesting too, for the musical differentiation can set off the thematic divisions even more effectively than can the formal elements of poetry.

In Thomas Carew's "Hee that loves a Rosie cheeke" the thematic structure of each stanza is embedded in the formal organization of the lines:

> Hee that loves a Rosie cheeke,
> Or a corall lip admires,
> Or from star-like eyes doth seeke
> Fuell to maintaine his fires;

> As old *Time* makes these decay,
> So his flames must waste away.
>
> But a smooth, and stedfast mind,
>   Gentle thoughts, and calme desires,
> Hearts, with equall love combind,
>   Kindle never dying fires.
> Where these are not, I despise
> Lovely cheekes, or lips, or eyes.[8]

The quatrain, abab, establishes the conditions, and the couplet, cc, presents the result. Two musical settings of this piece exist, one by Henry Lawes and one by Walter Porter,[9] and both make use of changes of musical meter in this way. The musical change calls attention to the poetic one, and thus makes clearer the thematic organization.

The formalizing effect of musical setting, which can reinforce formal and thematic structures that are coincident, can of course be utilized even when the formal structure of a poem is not so clearly designed to further the perception of thematic structure. In the following poem, the formal structure is simply a succession of rhymed couplets of lines of equal length:

> If the quick spirit of your Eye
> Now languish, and anon must dye;
> If every sweet and every grace
> Must flye from that forsaken face:
>   Then Celia let us reap our joys,
>   E're time such goodly fruit destroys.
>
> Or if that Golden Fleece must grow,
> For ever free from aged Snow;
> If those bright Suns must know no shade,
> Nor your fresh Beauty ever fade;
>   Then Celia feare not to bestow,
>   What still being gather'd, still must grow.
>
>   Thus either Time his sickle brings
>   In vain, or else in vain his wings.[10]

But the thematic structure is obviously the same quatrain-couplet antithesis as in "Hee that loves a Rosie cheeke." The musical setting, which changes meter as the other one did at the thematic division, formalizes the thematic structure and makes it easier for the casual

listener to grasp. Campion's "I must complain," like some of his other songs, seems to be a special case, for the thematic implications of the final couplet are relevant only to the second stanza. The musical differentiation of that couplet is then perceived as related to formal structure the first time around, and to both formal and thematic the second.

It is appropriate here to recall that we are talking about poetry as *song;* we are concerned with its aural perception, not its visual perception. In this context, the reinforcing, formalizing effects of musical setting can be of considerable importance. A reader can go back to the quatrain and quickly reformulate the structural implications if he has missed them the first time around. A listener cannot so easily do that, and therefore any auditory clues as to the significance of poetic structure will perform a function similar to indentation or italics on the printed page.

Such reinforcement, of course, assumes at least some kind of harmony between formal and semantic structures and considers that the composer's interpretation of the thematic organization is framed in formal terms analogous to those of poetry. Composers can, however, add musical interpretation of thematic structure that is outside the formal conventions of poetry. For example, Henry Lawes has represented a particular kind of thematic shape in "Break heart in twain" with the shape of his melodic line. The poem reads like this:

> Break heart in twain! Fair Ronile may see
> How much her cruelty hath injur'd thee;
> Thy tears and sighs so powerless have been
> That laughter they from her, not pity win.
> Wert thou once dead 'tis like she would lament,
> And seem to sigh, to show some discontent;
> Not that she lov'd, but to preserve her fame,
> And shun the title of a murd'rer's name.[11]

The first six lines describe the pain of the injured lover; and the last couplet, in the common formal-thematic pattern, twists the point of view to show us his sardonic bitterness as well. Lawes, however, has given the poem a climactic shape independent of the formal structure of the poem, building his melodic line gradually higher and higher to the fateful last verse, as seen in example 2.9.

Similarly, John Dowland, in his setting of "Sweet stay awhile," has interpreted thematic shape independent of formal structure. The

Example 2.9.

Not that she lov'd. but to pre-serve her fame.

And shun the tit-le of a mur - d'rer's name.

Henry Lawes, "Break heart in twain!" From *Henry Lawes Autograph Manuscript;*
Additional MS 53723, f. 31. Reprinted with permission of The British Library,
Department of Manuscripts.

familiar quatrain-couplet structure governs the poem's formal and
thematic organization, but except for a cadence after the quatrain,

Example 2.10.

O stay. or else my joys. my joys, my joys, must

die, And pe - rish in their in - fan - cy.

John Dowland, "Sweet stay awhile." From *A Pilgrimes Solace* (1612); *The English
Lute-Songs*, Series I, Vol. 12/14, p. 5. Ed. Edmund H. Fellowes. Rev. Thurston Dart,
1969. Reproduced by permission of Stainer and Bell, Ltd. and Galaxy Music Corp.

Dowland's setting does not make much of this. Instead, Dowland interprets the fifth line as the climactic one and builds musical intensity by increasing textural complexity up to this line, stretching the line itself to twice the duration of the others with musical elaboration, and falling back to the original level for the *dénouement* of the last line.

The Strophic Problem

All that has been said in the last two sections is relevant to the organization of single stanzas of poetry, or to poems that are not divided into stanzas but presented as continuous structures. In either case, the relationships of musical setting to poetic structure—formal or semantic—is usually direct correlation. That is, the musical setting is some kind of representation of the first stanza in a strophic song, or of the entire poem in a longer, nonstrophic song.[12] Because the large majority of early seventeenth-century songs are strophic, however, the relationship between the formal and semantic organization of stanzaic poetry is a very important concern, perhaps even more important in its larger implications than in its effect on poetic rhythm and meter. Most of the song lyrics are truly strophic texts: not only is the formal structure passed on from one stanza to the next, but more significantly, the thematic structure is fully coincident with the formal division into stanzas.

This structure is most clearly seen in a simple song like "Now what is love," in which each stanza is a completely self-contained statement on the central topic, in this case the enormous topic of "love":

> Now what is love I pray thee tell,
> It is that fountaine and that well
> Where pleasures and repentance dwell,
> It is perhaps that sancesing bell
> That towles all in to heav 'n or hell,
> And this is love as I heare tell.

> Now what is love I praie thee saie,
> It is a worke on holy daie,
> It is December match't with Maie,
> When lustie blood in fresh arraie,
> Heare ten monethes after of their plaie,
> And this is love as I heare saie.

> Etc.[13]

A poem like this one, set to music by Robert Jones, could go on forever; in fact some versions have up to nineteen stanzas in varying arrangements.[14] This open-endedness is a direct concomitant of the genuinely strophic character of both formal and semantic organization. The overall thematic structure of such poems may be described as cumulative,[15] or the piling-up of statements, none of which is dependent on any others. More sophisticated examples of the same procedure are common in the lute songs and include poems like "Disdain me still"[16] and another of Robert Jones' texts, "The Fountains smoke," where the effect is strengthened by the refrainlike last line:

> The fountaines smoake, And yet no flames they shewe,
> Starres shine all night Though undesern'd by day,
> And trees doe spring, yet are not seene to growe,
> And shadowes moove, Although they seeme to stay,
> In Winters woe, Is buried Summers blisse,
> And Love loves most, when love most secret is.
>
> The stillest streames descries the greatest deepe,
> The clearest skie is subject to a shower,
> Conceit's most sweete, when as it seemes to sleepe,
> And fairest dayes doe in the morning lower,
> The silent Groves sweete Nimphs they cannot misse,
> For love loves most, where love most secret is.
>
> The rarest jewels, hidden vertue yeeld,
> The sweete of traffique, is a secret gaine,
> The yeere once old doth shew a barren field,
> And Plants seeme dead, and yet they spring againe,
> Cupid is blind, the reason why, is this,
> Love loveth most, where love most secret is.[17]

Strophic musical setting is ideally suited to such texts. The formalizing effect of the setting, combined with the musical repetition of a strophic song, reinforces the repetitive formal structure and emphasizes that these are parallel statements on a single topic. The effect of both music and poetry is additive rather than developmental.

In some poems, the stanzaic formal pattern is matched with a thematic structure that we might call associative. The individual stanzas in such structures are usually relatively self-contained, but

their order is more clearly directed by an associative linking from one to the next.[18]

> What poore Astronomers are they,
> Take womens eies for stars
> And set their thoughts in battell ray
> To fight such idle warres,
> When in the end they shal approve,
> Tis but a jest drawne out of love.
>
> And love it selfe is but a jeast,
> Devisde by idle heads,
> To catch yong fancies in the neast,
> And lay it in fooles beds.
> That being hatcht in beauties eyes,
> They may be flidge ere they be wise.
>
> But yet it is a sport to see
> How wit will run on wheeles,
> While wit cannot perswaded be
> With that which reason feeles:
> That womens eyes and starres are odde,
> And love is but a fained god.
>
> But such as will run mad with will,
> I cannot cleare their sight:
> But leave them to their studie still,
> To looke where is no light.
> Till time too late we make them trie,
> They study false Astronomie.[19]

The central conceit of each stanza is suggested in the preceding one giving the poem a thematic structure that is congruent with the formal strophic one but that uses it in a manner different from "The fountaines smoake." Failure to hear the associative link from stanza to stanza will in this instance greatly weaken the poem, and rearrangement or omission of any of the stanzas would destroy the progression.

Strophic musical setting of a poem like this must be seen in a different light, even though the semantic and formal organizations are both stanzaic. The formalizing of rhythm and meter, rhyme scheme and so on will not be inappropriate to the structural organization, for although it may create some awkwardness in declamation

or in syntactical organization, it does emphasize that these statements are presented in the same frame, both formally and thematically. And furthermore, the associative structure that links the stanzas will be as audible as it would in an aural reading. Nevertheless, the *implication* of a strophic setting—which is admittedly subtle and is most often ignored in an age when strophic setting is the norm— is that the stanzas set to the same music are separate but equal units, each one as complete as the accompanying musical structure. The listener is taken back to the beginning of the musical statement with each new stanza. But in a poem whose thematic organization is associative, each stanza does not begin anew, but takes its cue from what came before. A strophic setting of such a poem is thus not quite in keeping with the structure of the poem itself.

This problem becomes most critical and paradoxically is most overtly ignored, when the thematic structure is narrative. Again the problem is most clearly seen in the simplest examples. Campion's balladlike song, "It fell on a sommers day," exhibits many of the characteristics of a folk ballad:

> It fell on a sommers day,
> While sweete Bessie sleeping laie
> In her bowre, on her bed,
> Light with curtaines shadowed;
> Jamy came, shee him spies,
> Opning halfe her heavie eies.
>
> Jamy stole in through the dore,
> She lay slumbring as before;
> Softly to her he drew neere,
> She heard him, yet would not heare;
> Bessie vow'd not to speake,
> He resolv'd that dumpe to breake.
>
> First a soft kisse he doth take,
> She lay still, and would not wake;
> Then his hands learn'd to woo,
> She dreamp't not what he would doo,
> But still slept, while he smild
> To see love by sleepe beguild.
>
> Jamy then began to play,
> Bessie as one buried lay,
> Gladly still through this sleight

> Deceiv'd in her owne deceit;
> And, since this traunce begoon,
> She sleepes ev'rie afternoone.[20]

Campion is obviously having fun with the implications of the popular ballad, for his own witty style does enter, especially in the epigrammatic final couplet. Nonetheless, a conflict arises between formal and semantic organization that is no less apparent for being consciously done. The thematic structure is narrative. As is characteristic of the ballad, it tells a single event in a story, in the person of an objective narrator; its language is active, using many verbs and only a minimum of the decorative, descriptive language (filled with adjectives and adverbs) of the courtly lyric. The formal structure is also balladlike, though not quite the "ballad meter" of true folk songs. The tetrameter couplets are grouped in six-line stanzas, and Campion's musical setting corresponds to this arrangement. But there is no thematic justification for this stanzaic pattern. It could as well be four- or eight-line stanzas, or not stanzaic at all. The musical setting, ignoring the narrative character of the thematic structure, intensifies the deceptive but artful simplicity of Campion's song by associating it still further with the popular ballad. The setting makes of the formal pattern a norm of recitation which can represent the tone of the poem, but not its "story."

Another, more serious, Campion poem, however, will show us a less coy imbalance between formal and semantic organization:

> When thou must home to shades of under ground,
> And there ariv'd, a newe admired guest,
> The beauteous spirits do ingirt thee round,
> White Iope, blith Hellen, and the rest,
> To heare the stories of thy finisht love,
> From that smoothe toong whose musicke hell can move;
>
> Then wilt thou speake of banqueting delights,
> Of masks and revels which sweete youth did make,
> Of Turnies and great challenges of knights,
> And all these triumphes for thy beauties sake:
> When thou hast told these honours done to thee,
> Then tell, O tell, how thou didst murther me.[21]

The formal organization is easily described: two identical, six-line stanzas of iambic pentameter, with the familiar quatrain-couplet division articulated in the rhyme scheme. The strophic musical

setting represents this formal pattern in Campion's conventional manner (as described on p. 59).

But Campion's thematic structure does not conform to the pattern suggested by the rhyme scheme, nor to the stanzaic division. It has, rather, a shape that transcends the formal structure and is derived from two "When . . . then . . . " sentences: "When thou must home" (lines 1-6), "Then wilt thou speake" (lines 7-10); "When thou hast told" (line 11), "Then tell" (line 12). The first builds to the climactic point of "all these triumphs for thy beauties sake," and the second brings in the Campion riposte, "Then tell how thou didst murther me." Except that the first "When" clause ends with the first stanza, the narrative, climactic progression is outside the formal structure. Furthermore, the ironic effect of the second sentence is dependent in part upon retrospection—upon the reader's or listener's ability to recognize the parallel construction of the two sentences and to compare this short sentence with the longer one that preceded it.

Campion's strophic musical setting seems to have little to do with these features of poetic structure, although his poising of the thematic against the formal in the poem is surely as careful as Carew's in "Weepe not, my deare." Indeed, it is difficult to imagine a musical setting that *could* adequately represent both kinds of organization in a poem like this. A through-composed setting could indicate the thematic shape, but would still leave hidden the poet's juxtaposition of it with the formal shape.

In spite of such difficulties, the strophic convention in solo song was very strong in the seventeenth century. There *are* through-composed songs, but they appear to be settings of poems that are not stanzaic to begin with; I do not know of any songs from the period that set a balladlike text as a through-composed song, and, in fact, composers sometimes *created* a strophic song out of a poem with a continuous structure, as Lawes did with "Weepe not."

Musical setting, as we have seen throughout these two chapters, necessarily acts as a formal poetic structure in many significant ways. This formalizing effect is especially apparent in the strophic song, because the setting forces the succeeding stanzas to conform to all the elements of formal organization that have been fixed in musical notation for the first stanza. But many of these formalizing elements affect the listener's perception of meaning in the poem as well as its

organization and surface texture. And, of course, musical settings have other dimensions and other, less mechanical, means of interpreting poetry as well. In the chapters that follow we shall consider some of the other ways in which musical setting can represent meaning in poetry and thus overcome some of the restrictions imposed by the representation of the organizational principles of texts.

Part II English Songs and Their Poetry

Prologue

The musical development that is the primary focus of this study is the shift from the lute song to the continuo song as the favored type of secular, solo vocal music in England. The most obvious alterations in musical style involve melody and texture. The lute song of the first quarter of the seventeenth century often had a polyphonic accompaniment and contrapuntal interplay between voice and accompaniment; the melodic character in such songs is similar in all voices, including those of the accompaniment. The continuo song of the second quarter of the century features a treble melody setting the text, supported by a relatively homophonic accompaniment derived from an unfigured but clearly functional bass line. The change in musical taste is particularly interesting, coming as it does on the heels of the Elizabethan and Jacobean periods so noted for musico-textual harmony. A desire to maintain that harmony accompanies the movement toward the continuo song, and although the major shift in musical style is not pronounced until the third decade of the century, the beginnings of the attitudes that would shape the change are visible in songs from before 1600.

At the beginning of the seventeenth century, the polyphonic madrigal was extremely popular in England. The union of music and poetry in both the madrigal and the lute song is celebrated. As we have seen earlier, lyrics written for music from the 1580s through about 1620,[1] the fruits of the Petrarchan movement in English poetry, derive much of their excellence from precisely those linguistic conventions that make them good candidates for musical setting.

Whether writing for one voice or several, composers of the period were able to respond to those linguistic characteristics without obscuring the attractiveness of the poems or sacrificing purely musical significance. Many madrigals, however, derive from attitudes toward the text substantially different from those toward the solo songs—attitudes that in some instances were, by opposition, the focus of the development of the solo song style, not only in England but on the continent—and we should briefly consider what those attitudes entailed.

The madrigal is a secular composition for several voices in which all voices sing the same text. The home of the madrigal, of course, was Italy, and in that country, several sophisticated lines of development of the genre emphasized various means of presenting the text through music. But of the madrigal types that flourished in England, the most popular (perhaps excepting the dance-related, largely homophonic ballett or "fa-la") was that in which musical structure was derived from versification. The characteristic method of handling the text was to set each line of the poem as a unit with its own contrapuntal treatment. The composer might divide the line into phrases or might single out individual words, repeating those words or phrases to the same or new musical motives, imitated perhaps in other voices, sung by contrasting pairs of voices, and so on, creating a unit of musical structure that grows out of but is not confined by the line of verse. The musical structure of the entire song is built from the linking of these units,[2] and the poem is thus presented not as one continuous statement but as a series of related ones, each of which has been independently interpreted. This is an important point, for the madrigal composer cannot have intended to provide a continuous reading of the poem. Although this method of composition is used in many lute songs written around 1600, composers of solo songs during the next 50 years wrote songs that tended increasingly to be notated recitations of poetry, treating the text not so much as a starting point but as the primary objective of a song and deriving musical structure from a consecutive, uninterrupted reading of the poem.

A musical structure that builds on poetic structure rather than merely following it might well have been a cause for objection in a humanistic reconsideration of appropriate musico-poetic relationships. But whereas this change in structural principles is striking to us, it was the contrapuntal texture of the madrigal that was the

object of the strongest arguments in favor of solo songs in the late Renaissance. Each phrase of the text in a madrigal is sung by all voices, often imitating each other. Each voice line usually provides good accentuation, but the words are rarely sung simultaneously by all voices so that even good declamation is all but lost to the listener. An important feature of this declamation in the madrigal was word-painting, the conventionally established representation of words or phrases of the text with musical images, especially appropriate to the decorative Petrarchan lyric. But of course these musical images, like the words they accompany, do not occur in all voices simultaneously but are the threads of a contrapuntal musical texture. The polyphonic style thus demanded that a listener (who could not be expected to follow the text in all voices) either focus on one part alone, trying to follow the textual continuity and catch the interpretive nuances of the musical symbolism, or concentrate on the total musical expression, thereby very likely losing an appreciable amount of the textual interpretation. Later critics have emphasized that the madrigal was not designed for the listener but rather for the pleasure of singers, and there is certainly good evidence for this distinction. Nevertheless, the polyphonic nature of madrigal composition and its effect on the listener's ability to understand the text drew sharp criticism in its own day, particularly in Italy and in England, as the influence of musical humanism came to the fore.

The goal of musical humanism was the re-creation of the fabled powers of music to affect the soul; the effect of the words was to be enhanced through the union of music and poetry. The representation of the text accomplished in the madrigal through word-painting was derived from the humanist interpretation of these powers in the early sixteenth century, but to all the musical humanists of the late sixteenth and seventeenth centuries, the search for effect meant primarily an insistence that the words of the text be fully intelligible; to many, it involved a more direct relationship between the singer and the text. For two important reasons, the composition of solo songs became increasingly fashionable around the turn of the century.

The first lute songs, or airs, appeared in 1597 (probably known and circulated in manuscript some years before this printing date). The solo medium was certainly not new. Sixteenth-century manuscript sources contain solo songs, often associated with the choir-school plays, and usually accompanied by a consort of instruments.[3]

William Byrd wrote a good number of these "consort songs" and in the later printed versions underlaid the instrumental parts with text to conform to the then-current popularity of the madrigal and part song. It is likely that madrigals too were at least occasionally sung as accompanied solos, if only because of the inconvenience of having to gather a group of singers to perform them polyphonically. But these solo songs were quite different from what we usually think of as the solo art song, for the primary musical conception of the consort song was contrapuntal, and the text seems to have been regarded not as a verbal statement to be interpreted but as a vehicle for the construction of a musical work. Although in performance the consort of instruments might be very light, allowing the singer to project well above it, the nature of the accompaniment (typically a dense polyphonic web related to the musical style of the sacred motet or the more "learned" kind of madrigal) and the rhythmic and melodic style of the voice line (usually slow-moving and with little rhythmic or melodic activity) virtually ruled out specifically musical interpretation of the text in this kind of song.[4] Furthermore, composers of consort songs—especially Byrd—seem to have been moving away from this solo style toward the more balanced polyphony of the madrigal.

The lute song, when it appeared, was a gesture in the direction of the humanistic ideal of personal statement, though by no means a full realization of it. The lute song still carried with it the polyphonic accompaniment of the consort song, reduced to what a single instrumentalist (often supported by a viola da gamba) could perform, and frequently bearing interpretive techniques borrowed from the madrigal. Most of the lute songs also appeared in part song versions, allowing them to become part of the after-dinner-singing repertoire along with the madrigal.

Some features of the lute song, however, were new. These songs were courtly entertainment, performer's art, and not the amateur art of the madrigal, where the declamation of individual voice lines is primarily for the pleasure and understanding of the singer. Some of the most important composers of lute songs were also professional performers, John Dowland being among the most famous, and that most of these airs seem to have been played and sung by professional musicians for the pleasure of others suggests they had features that depart from the style of the madrigal. First and most important was

Prologue to Part II 79

the predominantly solo medium with the vocal part almost always written for a treble voice. The text, in line with humanistic beliefs as well as performance requirements, is intended not only to be heard and understood, but given an interpretive context in its musical setting. One of the most characteristic features of the lute song is greater reliance on syllabic declamation in the solo vocal line, contrasted to the frequently melismatic lines of the madrigal. The text is set without adornment, except for occasional figures of word-painting, and in rhythms that usually conform to the natural accentuation of the words.

It has been argued convincingly that many of the lute songs that appeared in part song as well as solo versions are essentially arrangements of solo songs, the lower parts usually being drawn from the lute accompaniment.[5] Such arrangements often have awkward vocal writing and text underlay in the lower voices, and only the treble gives the clear reading of the text that became the hallmark of the lute song. The arguments in favor of an originally solo conception for these songs are similar to those maintaining that Byrd's part songs, and some madrigals as well, originally were thought of as solos.[6] In most airs written as part songs, however, the musical texture is more nearly homophonic than in consort songs or polyphonic madrigals, sometimes resembling the ballett. Declamation is at least close to being simultaneous in all voices (rather than strung out through imitative entries and textual repetitions), and individual lines of the text usually are delineated in all parts (as opposed to the polyphonic dovetailing of lines in the madrigal or the continuous contrapuntal understructure of the accompaniment in the consort song). Thus whether solo or part song, the lute song comes closer than the polyphonic madrigal to providing a reading of the poem that is intact, proceeding from one end to the other without pausing to "discuss" every line musically.

Another major facet of the lute song that will deserve some attention is its characteristically strophic setting of a text. The polyphonic madrigal is by definition through-composed. It treats individual lines of the text as independent units, but the composer never has to consider whether a very specific treatment of one line will also be appropriate in tone, or rhythmically accurate, as a setting for the comparable line in a succeeding stanza. Poets who were writing with the understanding that their verses would be set as lute songs some-

times tried to arrange the stanzas of their poems so that they would all fit the same music;[7] composers of lute songs, on their part, sometimes provided settings that were not as specifically detailed representations of their texts as the madrigals, being more judicious, for instance, in their use of word-painting or highly interpretive declamation. Yet even these precautions are not always present in the lute songs. Although by far the greatest number of both lute songs and continuo songs are strophic, it is usually only in the setting of the first stanza that the care with declamation and expression is apparent.[8]

The songs of John Dowland are the best-known examples of lute songs to present-day listeners, and the familiar ones by other lutenists tend to be rather like his lightly polyphonic, expressive style. Other types of lute songs, however, emphasize the necessity of viewing changes in musical style as the result of not one but several attitudes whose perspective was altered during the first quarter of the century. One of the most important of these subtypes is the "plain" style of Thomas Campion. Some of Campion's best-known songs (such as "Follow thy fair sun," or "Author of light") are similar to Dowland's, but many of his songs have apparently little contact with the speech rhythms and interpretive musical representation of the text that seem so characteristic of the lute song. These remarkably simple, hymnlike settings often have been passed over by modern-day commentators, or have been the subject of reproof, and support for the contention that Campion's was an inferior musical imagination. Without claiming equal musical status for Campion and Dowland, I shall suggest below that such criticism misses the point of Campion's style. I think it can be convincingly argued that such settings are representative of a different attitude toward the text from that governing Dowland's style—one that gives a clear reading of the poem, as is the general aim of the lute song, but with an emphasis on different elements of the text.

A facet of the lute song sometimes overlooked is represented by versions of some airs that appear in manuscript sources of the period with the treble voice, highly ornamented, and only a viola da gamba accompaniment. These arrangements are often in "tutors" or commonplace books that seem to be primarily instructional material,[9] and though the gamba accompaniment may be a household convenience, the soloistic nature of the vocal line seems to indicate a

performance style that was an accepted goal of instruction. Whether originally solo songs or not, many of the lute songs adapted very well to this truly solo, even virtuoso, medium and show a tendency in the direction opposite to Campion's homophonic style. Though their basis in the lute song is still quite apparent, these are gestures toward the continuo song, showing an awareness of the treble-dominated style that signals the change. Interestingly enough, even Campion was a herald of this new musical conception, for his treatise on counterpoint (*A New Way of Making Fowre Parts in Counter-point,* c. 1614) suggests an understanding of harmonic thinking upwards from the bass — an essential requirement for the continuo style of accompaniment that would distinguish the new songs musically from the old. Yet Campion's attitude toward the text was not forward-looking, and that of the ornamented manuscript versions of lute songs shows an understanding of the isolation of the solo voice and quasidramatic presentation of the text that also were essential to the new style.

It is difficult to say just when the first continuo songs appeared in England. Since none were printed before 1651, no precise means of dating the earliest examples is available. But we can assume from other evidence (such as dates in the manuscripts, or performance dates of masques containing some of the songs) that they were being written by 1625. Earlier than 1625, though songs of a style similar to continuo songs exist, they are still most often accompanied with a lute tablature, or, in manuscript sources, with a viola da gamba line that is obviously not a continuo bass line but intended either to supplement a contrapuntal lute accompaniment or to be a duet with the voice. Like the lute songs, the airs of the second quarter of the seventeenth century are syllabic solo songs and definitely suggest a performer's art; some of the more declamatory indeed are difficult to perform.

Within the category of continuo song we must identify two distinct types: those songs that are "musically oriented" (primarily dance and dance-related songs, sometimes called "tuneful airs" or "ballads," in which the purely musical impulse predominates over the humanistic goal of textual interpretation), and those that are "textually oriented" (the "declamatory airs" in which a concern with text is preeminent, turning sharply from the tuneful style to a dramatic, occasionally recitative style).[10] Many of the lute songs were also dance-related, but the distinction in musical style between these and

the textually oriented lute songs was, at the start of the century, relatively slight. By the 1630s, the distinction is pronounced; in fact, it becomes meaningless to discuss the tuneful songs and the declamatory, textually oriented ones as a single group. The common features, by which they are all known as continuo songs, are the defining dominance of the treble voice, the relatively inactive and harmonically designed bass line, and the probable accompaniment on lute or theorbo with viola da gamba (like the lute songs), or perhaps keyboard, always intended to be improvised from the bass line, essentially as chords.[11] The two types of continuo song differ markedly in musical style: The vocal line is typically conjunct in the musically oriented songs, with narrow melodic range and restricted rhythmic variety; in contrast, in the textually oriented songs, it is broad, disjunct, and dramatic, with great rhythmic variety. The bass line tends to be more active in the musically oriented songs than in the textually oriented ones.[12]

As the distinction between musically and textually oriented songs becomes increasingly apparent with the change in musical style from the lute song to continuo song, a change also takes place in the predominant modes of textual interpretation. We shall see a gradual shift, beginning before 1610, from an attitude (related to French neoclassicism) that emphasizes elements of verisification and is highly characteristic of the early lute songs, to one (derived from the principles of Italian musical humanism) that emphasizes narrative or thematic structure and is especially notable in the textually oriented continuo songs. The parallel to the changing poetic taste — from the Elizabethan style that emphasizes surface details such as metrics and decorative language to the metaphysical and Cavalier styles that feature argument and irony — should be clear. But the earlier musical stance continued to be influential in the musically oriented continuo songs and may even be seen in some aspects of the declamatory air (particularly in the setting of strophic texts or those in which thematic structure is closely related to versification), whereas elements of the declamatory approach are sometimes present in the lute songs. Representation of the meaning of the text, both the literal meaning of the words and the rhetoric of emotional content, was a goal throughout the period. Here too, however, we can see a change in mode, from an attitude that seeks a musical symbolism to correspond to poetic imagery, to one that attempts rather to en-

hance the poet's own presentation of the words through oratorical means. But again the change is not decisive, for word-painting—the musical symbolism in the lute song and madrigal—continued to be present in all types of continuo song, and the techniques of interpretive declamation that predominate in these later songs are clearly inherent in the rhythms of earlier song styles. Thus the reevaluation of interpretive stances and of the means of achieving appropriate joining of music and poetry, as important as it is to the understanding of the evolution of English song, is not sudden. Nonetheless, evidence that English composers in the first half of the seventeenth century *did* readjust their methods of interpreting poetry in response to literary taste lies in the songs themselves.

Chapter 3
Measured Music

The influence of humanism is one of the most important factors in the development of musico-textual relationships in the early seventeenth century. The interpretation of the Classical union of words and music adopted by French humanists gives a clear statement of a particular attitude toward a text. The movement affected English poets and musicians too, but its influence in England seems to have been less concentrated, and far less unified, than on the continent. The English were not as consistent as their continental counterparts in putting their beliefs about music and poetry into practice, and those beliefs themselves shifted during the first quarter of the century. But especially in the early years of the seventeenth century, the joining of music and poetry in England seems to have been guided, at least in part, by attitudes similar to those so carefully developed by the French humanists. In this chapter we shall examine various features of English song in the light of the attitudes—and in some instances, direct influences—of the philosophy and practice of musical humanism in France.

The basis of the French attitude lay in the doctrine of the affective powers of music that was the principal belief of musical humanists all over Europe. Descriptions of music and poetry in ancient Greece seemed to stress two main elements: First, music and poetry were closely united, lyric poetry in particular being inseparable from its musical notation, and second, the combination of words and music could produce miraculous effects.[1] Stories of wonderful cures

wrought by music, of rapid emotional changes brought on by changes in musical character, and of moral and pedagogical aims realized with the aid of music were no doubt appealing to the neo-Platonists of the sixteenth century. Although they probably did not anticipate literal cures or moral benefits, the musical humanists took as their goal the re-creation of these magical effects that were attributed to music in ancient sources. Their interpretations of how these effects were to be accomplished, however, differed, with varying opinions expressed as to which effects were most desirable. In France, where pedagogical and moral aims seem to have been paramount, the attitude toward the text seems to be related to a prevailing frame of mind and national goals. In practice, the French tried to revive what was believed to be the precise union of music and poetry in the ancient Greek lyric on the premise that such a union would make the words clear, and at the same time would infuse the words with the supposed power of music to enter the soul.

Musical neoclassicism is first clearly apparent in France in the work of Ronsard. His belief in the union of music and poetry[2] is founded on a knowledge of the writings of some of the lyric poets of antiquity. Ronsard's favored instrument was the lute, but his statements concerning the necessary union of music and poetry merely insist on the presence of instrumental accompaniment for the singing voice:

> car la poésie, sans les instruments, ou sans la grâce d'une seule ou plusieurs voix, n'est nullement agréable, non plus que les instruments sans être animés de la melodie d'une plaisante voix.[3]

The fabled effects of music were important to Ronsard, as he shows in his recounting of the traditional stories about the powers of music in the Dedication of his *Livre des mélanges*.[4] Here too he manifests his belief in the moral possibilities of music's effects:

> He is unworthy to behold the sweet light of the sun who does not honor music as being a small part of that which, as Plato says, so harmoniously animates the whole great universe. Contrariwise, he who does honor and reverence music is commonly a man of worth, sound of soul, by nature loving things lofty, philosophy, the conduct of affairs of state, the tasks of war, and in brief, in all honorable offices he ever shows the sparks of his virtue.[5]

Apparent throughout the dedication, and as we shall see, prominent

in other writings of the musical humanists in France, is an insistence that "all things [the implication here being that this includes music] as well in the heavens and in the sea as on the earth, are composed of *accords, measures, and proportions.*"[6] Order and balance are high on the list of effects desired by French humanists, in the state and daily life as well as in music and poetry, and these goals have a decided influence on the way the humanists set about re-creating the musical effects of Antiquity.

Ronsard makes no specific recommendations as to how the effects of music are to be obtained in setting his verse to music. His main contribution was to regulate the external forms of his verse to make it more conformable to the musical forms a composer would be likely to use. The two rules Ronsard formulated are (1) that succeeding stanzas (or *couplets*) are to conform to the pattern of the first, and (2) that masculine rhymes must alternate with feminine rhymes in verse intended to be set to music "afin que les musiciens les puissent plus facilement accorder."[7] These rules were designed to impose order and balance on poetic structure, thereby helping the composer not only to accommodate musical structures to those of the poetry — which conceivably could be done in a disorderly fashion as well — but also to further the desired effect of controlled statement.

Both of Ronsard's requirements have the additional effect of making verse structure more audible, even without musical setting. His "Mignonne, allons voir si la rose" is most famous in its lovely polyphonic setting by Guillaume Costeley; but the metric regularity of its verse structure is much more strictly represented in a monophonic, *voix de ville* setting by Jehan Chardavoine. The combined moderating effect of a regular syllabic linear structure and a rhythmically repetitive musical structure delineating lines of verse imposes order, reduces the purely musical interest, and makes the text fully intelligible. Chardavoine's setting is based on a popular style, and its musical structure is formulary, but the technique of emphasizing the external verse structure with musical structure is basic to the French humanist attitude toward the text. (See example 3.1.)

I have dwelt at some length on Ronsard not because he or his songs are of direct concern to this investigation, but because we can see at work not only what I believe to be the goals and attitudes generating the musical style of French humanism but some scholarly misconceptions as well. D. P. Walker, for instance, takes Ronsard

Example 3.1.

Jehan Chardavoine, "Mignonne." From *Le Recueil des plus belles et excellentes chansons* (1576); *La Fleur des musiciens de P. de Ronsard*, p. 74. Ed. M. Henry Expert, Repr., 1965. Reproduced by permission of Broude Bros., Ltd., New York.

to task for allowing such generalized musical realizations of his verse as he did. Walker says of settings like the long strophic hymns set by Goudimel, or the "Air pour chanter tous sonets" by Fabrice Marin Caietain:

> La musique n'est plus qu'un accompagnement indéterminé du texte, dont elle rehausse automatiquement l'effet affectif, quel qu'il soit; elle met l'auditeur dans un état propre à être ému—et c'est tout.
>
> . . . Une poésie inspirée de toutes les fureurs, c'est-a-dire sérieuse, intellectuelle, souvent très longue, et qui doit produire de puissants effets sur les moeurs et les émotions, requiert une musique d'une sorte spéciale. Cette musique doit conserver le mètre et le rythme du texte, puisque ceux-ci sont des éléments essentiels dans sa puissance affective; elle doit exprimer puissamment l'éthos du texte, et elle ne doit pas distraire l'auditeur par des traits d'un intérêt purement musical; elle doit donc être très simple, surtout si elle est employée d'une façon strophique; finalement, il ne faut pas qu'elle empêche l'auditeur d'entendre et de comprendre chaque mot.[8]

Such reasoning assumes that Ronsard's opinion of the appropriate role for music was the arousal of emotions or "fureurs." The power of music to restrain and control passion is also a part of the ancient claims that humanists revered, and it seems equally plausible that Ronsard, and those who followed him, sought to represent the

formal features of their verse—the meter and rhyme scheme—for these, after all, are under control.

With Baïf, founder of the *Académie de poésie et de Musique,* Ronsard's concern with verse form takes a more Classical turn in an attempt to adapt French poetry to the quantitative meters of Greek verse, and with a strict interpretation of these meters in musical rhythms. Baïf, too, was a firm believer in the effects of music, and like Ronsard's, his method of achieving the union of words and music that would produce those effects involves poetic meter and the controlling restrictions that a rigorously imposed meter provides. Moral and pedagogical aims are even more decisively at work here, as spelled out in the Letters Patent granting the formation of the Académie:

> Et que l'opinion de plusieurs grands Personnages, tant Législateurs que Philosophes anciens ne soit a mépriser, a sçauoir qu'il importe grandement pour les moeurs des Citoyens d'une Ville que la Musique courante & visitée au Pays soit retenué sous certaines loix, dautant que la pluspart des esprits des hommes se conforment & comportent, selon qu'elle est; de façon que où la Musique est désordonée, la volontiers les moeurs sont déprauez, & où elle est bien ordonnée, la sont les hommes bien moriginez.[9]

Though the statement refers specifically only to the order of music, a later passage in the same document implies that Baïf and Thibault de Courville had already achieved the same effect in poetry during the previous three years of study.

Baïf's *vers mesurés à l'antique* were an imposition of quantitative meters onto French verse.[10] We have seen that, at least according to one theory, it was never a requisite of quantitative meters that the metric pattern be audible. Nevertheless, Baïf seems not to have recognized this, or to have ignored the possibility, for he was most anxious that his meters be heard; if the meters were not audible, then part of the controlling effect on the listeners would be lost. To this end Baïf, and his principal collaborator, the composer Jacques Mauduit, sought in musical notation a means of defining the metric units and fixing them in a clear and audible rhythmic relationship to one another. *Musique mesurée* did just this, going so far as to dictate that the long syllable must be twice the duration of the short.

An example by Mauduit will demonstrate most of the musical conventions associated with musique mesurée:

Example 3.2.

Puis que tu as dans tes yeux Ie ne sçay quoy

qui me peut Fai - re vi - vre et mou-rir.

Fay que je soys, ou ne soys plus.

Jacques Mauduit, "Puisque tu as dans tes yeux." From *Chansonettes mesurées de Ian-Antoine de Baïf* (1586); *Les Maîtres musiciens de la renaissance française*, Vol. X, pp. 36-37. Ed. M. Henry Expert. Repr., n.d. Reproduced by permission of Broude Bros., Ltd., New York.

The typical characteristics are the homophonic texture (often more austere than in this example), relatively narrow, conjunct and smoothly flowing melodic lines, restricted rhythmic values, and unmetered rhythmic flow. The only bar lines used are at the ends of lines of verse, thus graphically delineating versification, while cadences provide an aural conclusion to each line.

Claude le Jeune, the only composer other than Mauduit to write a significant amount of musique mesurée, found ways to soften the rather austere musical style of Mauduit's settings. Le Jeune occasionally indulged in word-painting, and tempered the strict homophonic declamation with nonharmonic tones more consistently than Mauduit,

adding more purely musical interest without sacrificing the essential features of measuring syllables in two-to-one proportion and pronouncing syllables simultaneously in all voices.

Example 3.3.

Claude le Jeune, "Voicy le verd et beau May." From *Le Printemps* (Ier Fascicule) (1603); *Les Maîtres musiciens de la renaissance française,* Vol. XII, p. 70. Ed. M. Henry Expert. Repr., n.d. Reproduced by permission of Broude Bros., Ltd., New York.

Some of the conventions of musique mesurée we shall find in English songs, too; what is most important, however, is an understanding of the attitude toward the text that generates the conventions. To reiterate one of the essential precepts of musical humanism, the words must determine the music. Smooth melodic writing is designed in conformity with the nonaccentual character of the French language and thus furthers intelligibility. Strict homophonic texture is a concession that musique mesurée makes to modernity: It allows for the clear and audible declamation of the words that polyphony obscures, without giving up what were thought to be the musical advances Renaissance composers had made in the use of harmony.[11] It is rhythm, however, that most clearly sets the musical style of musique mesurée apart. And the source of its distinctive rhythmic style is poetic meter—not the normal syllabic meter of French verse, but the mechanically contrived quantitative meter, imposing an artificial structure formalized through musical notation. The composer's attitude toward the text becomes one of subservience to surface detail; he does not interpret the poem, except insofar as his setting aids in placing the poem in a controlled and ordered atmosphere, making audible the effect implied by the poet's use of strict and regular meter.

In England, the movement toward classicizing of poetry appeared a little later and did not seem to have the moral objectives nor the

fervency of application found in the French academies. Yet the writings of Sir Philip Sidney and the group of poets sometimes known as the Areopagus illustrate the broad dissemination of this aspect of humanism. Sidney's work has many parallels to that of both Ronsard and Baïf, and though Sidney was not himself a musician, he seems to have been well aware of connections between music and poetry. Sidney's greatest contributions to versification were in broadening the spectrum of rhythm, meter, and even rhyme for English verse; but he also had a great concern with stanza forms, and, like Ronsard, he insisted that the structural details of the first stanza of a poem be repeated in succeeding stanzas. Such a concern has obvious relevance to strophic musical setting, especially in view of recent convincing arguments that some of his verses were written to metric patterns of Italian songs.[12] Though the technique is the opposite of fitting musical notation to poetic meter, the attitude determining the relationship between words and music is similar. Music can in no sense be thought of as an expression of particular emotions in the text, yet the controlling influence of metric pattern is certainly part of the effect Sidney desired, whether or not he envisioned the poems actually sung to those tunes. Poetic meter is externally imposed, just as quantitative meter is in a nonquantitative language.

Sidney wrote some quantitative verse, particularly in the Old Arcadia (where the context indicates that the verses were sung to instrumental accompaniment, most likely improvised). He also wrote in prose (in the *Defense of Poesie* and, at greater length, in early versions of the First Eclogues) of the relationship between quantitative poetic meter and music:

> Dicus said that since verses had ther chefe ornament, if not eand, [sic] in musike, those which were just appropriated to musicke did best obtaine ther ende, or at lest were the most adorned; but those must needs most agree with musicke, since musike standing principally upon the sound and the quantitie, to answere the sound they brought wordes, and to answer the quantity they brought measure. . . . Lalus on the other side would have denied his first proposition, and sayd that since musike brought a measured quantity with it, therfor the wordes lesse needed it, but as musicke brought tune and measure so thes verses brought wordes and rime, which wer foure beawties for the other three. And yet to denye further the streng[t]h of his speach, he sayd Dicus did much abuse the dignitie of poetry to apply it to musicke, since rather musicke is a ser-

vaunt to poetry, for by [the one] the eare only, by the other the mind was pleased.[13]

Yet, despite an interest in the relationship, Sidney does not seem to have had his quantitative verses set to music, and most of his other verse that was set did not appear with music until after his death.

In contrast to vers mesurés, hardly any of the English experiments in quantitative meters actually were set to music. The first two lines of Sidney's "O sweet woods" were used by both Dowland and Henry Lawes[14] in settings that do not reflect poetic meter to any substantial degree. William Byrd set to music the anonymous quantitative lines, "Constant Penelope sends to thee, careless Ulysses" in what is a most interesting compromise. The superius sings the text in the correct quantitative scansion, while the other voices fill in, madrigal-like, with Byrd's flowing polyphony. The meter, though accurately rendered, would be apparent only if the performance were by a solo voice,[15] with instruments taking the other voice parts in the manner of Byrd's consort songs. Yet some very nice touches of madrigalesque interplay occur among the voices. It seems, thus, that the attitude toward the text that promotes poetic meter through musical notation is only partly in operation here, and Byrd's lovely song is one of those unclassifiable pieces that represent primarily an interesting and creative musical mind.

Had the Classical revival followed the same course in England that it did in France, the union of music and poetry through musical scanning of poetic meter might logically have occurred with Sidney or one of his circle; but this interaction between the two arts was delayed another twenty-five years, until Thomas Campion somewhat belatedly took up the cause of classicizing English poetry. Campion's "Come let us sound with melody" is a genuine experiment along the lines of the Académie's ventures and is the only extant example of English quantitative verse set to music according to the principles of musique mesurée. It was not followed by others of its kind, and one might conclude that the attitude toward the text fostered in musique mesurée in France found no better home in England than it did in Italy. I do not believe this to be the case, however, and in the remainder of this chapter we shall explore what I suggest were the main lines of development, first, of the attitude toward musico-textual relationships, and second, of the musical style originally associated with this attitude.

The early lutenists were familiar with songs like Byrd's, and although relatively little French vocal music seems to have been current in England around 1600,[16] both Dowland and Campion had visited France and would have been familiar with airs de cour, and possibly even with some pieces of musique mesurée. Early lute songs often resemble the French songs in musical style[17] and in fidelity to the versification of the text (a feature that is easy to see in the airs de cour), and they show some attempt to use rhythmic quantities to declaim the text in what might logically be assumed to be the French manner. But the representation of poetic meter (as opposed to the representation of poetic rhythm), which originally generated the French rhythmic style, is not present in these songs to any great degree.

The development of the lute song in England seems to take two courses with respect to the attitudes and musical style of French humanism. Thomas Campion, himself the poet of his lyrics and obviously interested in versification, comes progressively closer to the original attitude behind the French style, realizing that an English accentual meter cannot be accurately represented by duration, and therefore departing from the musical style of musique mesurée in an effort to adapt its philosophy to the needs of English verse. This course of development, bringing to the English air the attitude toward the text of French humanism, becomes generalized, and the attention to poetic meter expands to include all the formal elements of poetic composition. As such, we can see indications of its continuation in the songs of Henry Lawes; but in the main, this particular form of musical humanism could not survive the lute song and its characteristic poetry.

The other course, concentrating upon the musical style of musique measurée and airs de cour, can be seen through Dowland, who continued to favor the musical style, and later in the light, popular airs of the continuo composers. This development is what I shall call the trivialization of the style (without any intent to denigrate the musical results, which are often quite pleasing), for it makes a simple, tuneful musical style of what was originally a textually dominated one, and ultimately loses the close relationship to the text that was its original source and strength.

Campion is the only English composer of his period who consistently shared the philosophy of French humanism. The important

aspect of Campion's song style that sets him apart from his musical contemporaries is the tendency to give precedence in his musical settings to details of formal verse structure and the texture of the language over narrative structure or emotional content. Such precedence bespeaks a fundamentally different attitude toward the text from that of Dowland and the more dramatic song writers, and from the Italianate attitude that largely superseded the French in Caroline song. Campion's attitude comes in part from his dual role as poet and composer, and in part from a neoclassical approach (similar to that of the French humanists) to the appropriate correspondence between words and music.

There are several external indications that Campion was familiar with the work of French humanists. It has been reasonably well established that Campion spent three years in France, from 1602 to 1605, attending medical school in Caen. His literary and musical activity both before and after his sojourn in Caen makes it unlikely that he would not at least have been interested in the activities of poets and composers in France during this time, and we can probably assume some first-hand knowledge of the airs de cour popular at the time. Furthermore, we can be reasonably certain that Campion was familiar, even before going to France, with the principles, if not actual pieces, of vers mesurés and musique mesurée; his own treatise, *Observations in the Art of English Poesie,* already an anachronism when it was published in 1602, is a plea for quantitative verse in English, including rules, similar to Baïf's, for determining syllable length, as well as examples of various metric forms in English. And his song, "Come let us sound with melody," is the only serious attempt to equate English quantitative verse with musical notation in the manner of musique mesurée.

Campion's work with quantitative verse has one significant difference from that of either the members of the Académie or of Sidney and the other poets of his group: Campion recognized the accentual nature of the English language and the consequent inconsistency of artificially imposing a metric system that did not work with the natural rhythms of the language; he therefore tried to align quantity with stress in his experimental quantitative verse. But the bulk of Campion's poetry has nothing to do with quantitative meter, and the attention paid to stress patterns and details of pronunciation of English syllables in the *Observations* has more bearing on his attitude

toward music and poetry than does his interest in quantitative meters per se.

Campion's songs cover a fairly narrow spectrum, from a few that have been claimed to have declamatory elements,[18] to the rhythmically varied, typical lute songs comparable to Dowland's simpler songs, engaging the voice and lute in decorative contrapuntalizing over an essentially homophonic framework, and finally to a large group of homophonic, almost hymnlike songs that call to mind the restricted musical language of *musique mesurée*. The songs of this last group have no parallel in the works of Dowland, and very few likenesses to the works of other contemporaries; but they form a sizeable proportion of Campion's canon. These are not Campion's more memorable songs musically, their style being what may aptly be described as "plain";[19] even critics who set out to be comprehensive in their coverage of Campion's work are content with a paragraph listing some of the "hymnlike" songs, typically concluding that "Such melodies, as may be expected, are not among Campion's most interesting, unless they are distinguished by other factors."[20] But their number, their increase in the later song books,[21] and Campion's demonstrable interest in rhythms, meters, and other details of versification, should make one question the dismissal of these songs as merely the product of an inferior musical mind. Campion was not, like most of the other lute song composers, a professional musician; but also involved, I think, is Campion's inherently neoclassical approach to the relationship between music and text.

One of Campion's most important observations is that the only "feet" that will work in English verse are those of two syllables, the iambic and the trochaic:

> Let us now then examine the property of these two feete, and try if they consent with the nature of English sillables. And first for the *Iambicks,* they fall out so naturally in our toong, that, if we examine our owne writers, we shall find they unawares hit oftentimes upon the true *Iambick* numbers, but alwayes ayme at them as far as their eare without the guidance of arte can attain unto. . . . The *Trochaick* foote, which is but an *Iambick* turn'd over and over, must of force in like manner accord in proportion with our British sillables, and so produce an English *Trochaicall* verse.[22]

This recognition has a direct influence not only on his accentual poetic meters, which are generally regular iambic or trochaic lines of

equal length, either through the whole poem or in pairs, but also on his most common kinds of musical setting, which often represent poetic meter with musical meter.

In a song using the plain style, we can see this sort of correlation at work. "Tune thy Musicke to thy hart" seems a particularly appropriate example because of the conventional humanistic reference to

Example 3.4.

Thomas Campion, "Tune thy Musicke." Excerpt from *The Works of Thomas Campion,* p. 67. Ed. and with Introduction by Walter R. Davis. Copyright © 1967 by Doubleday and Co., Inc. and Faber and Faber, Ltd. Reprinted by permission of the publishers.

the relation of well-tuned music and human emotions. The meter of the poem is a very regular trochaic pattern, and Campion has used the "musical" effect of word sounds to reinforce the metric pattern

("*Túne* thy *Músicke tó* thy hárt," the stressed syllables suggesting aurally the musical accord of which the poem speaks) so that, even though syntactical phrase rhythm demands "tõ thỹ hárt," the strength of the meter prevails. The musical setting further supports the meter of the verse. Campion's recognition of the predominance of the two-syllable units in English verse, coupled with his knowledge that word stress in English is accentual rather than durational, dictates that, to realize poetic meter accurately in musical notation, the syllables must be set in equal rhythmic duration and word stress must be correlated with musical accent. This correlation results in a homorhythmic style, invariably in duple meter.[23] Such is, essentially, the style of "Tune thy Musicke," and the duple meter, with its alternation of stressed and unstressed beats, is strengthened by the harmonic rhythm, changing chord only on every stressed syllable.

The accentual pattern just described is broken only at the end of the last line, and I think the alternation may be seen as support, rather than contradiction, of my argument. The line[24] speaks of a seeming paradox—that the rich (i.e., the complex, the "curious") may borrow (an attitude) from the poor (the simple, concordant)—and the setting, by departing finally from the strict regularity of the poem's meter and emphasizing the enigmatic "may" with an agogic accent, points up the epigrammatic twist Campion so enjoyed.

Campion wrote many songs in this essentially homorhythmic style, usually associating it in this way with a regular poetic meter. "When the god of merry love." (*Songs from Rosseter's Book of Airs/* 15), "Why presumes thy pride" (Third Book/6), "Awake thou spring" (Third Book/13), and "I must complain" (Fourth Book/17) are but a few examples in which the technique is rigorously applied; some others use a slightly modified approach, but with the same metric effect. Inasmuch as "to meter" means "to measure," these songs of Campion's are certainly as much "measured music" as is musique mesurée; the difference lies merely in what is measured. Mauduit and le Jeune measured duration; Campion is measuring intensity and coordinating the imposed pattern of poetic meter with the pattern of changing intensity implied in a musical meter.

My insistence on Campion's musically accentual approach to poetic meter may seem strange in view of his early championing of the cause of quantitative meters for English poetry. That aspect of his treatise seems more an exercise than a practical suggestion, especially

since, except for the examples in the treatise, his own verse shows no traces of attempts to work with quantity. Yet in a sense, these plain settings are concerned with quantity and the duration of English syllables, and an early indication of that interest is also to be found in the *Observations.* In Chapter Ten, where he discusses the rules for determining syllable length, Campion states:

> we must esteeme our sillables as we speake, not as we write, for the sound of them in a verse is to be valued, and not their letters.[25]

This is a telling comment, for, in spite of a few inconsistencies, Campion's rules generally do concur with pronunciation. But beyond that, the rules indicate a careful study of enunciation, particularly of the consonants and consonantal clusters, as in his observation that "when silent and melting consonants meete together" the syllable is short, even though position should make it long (e.g., the first syllable of "oprest.")[26] Even the rule of position (that when a vowel is followed by two or more consonants, the syllable is long) has a certain amount of justification in terms of consonantal clusters, for the longer duration makes possible the enunciation of both consonants (e.g., "setled love," where the second syllable of "setled" is counted long).

These are only suggestions of his concern with enunciation; by the time of publication of his *Two Bookes of Ayres* (c. 1613), in an introduction, "To the Reader," he is much more specific:

> In these *English* Ayres, I have chiefly aymed to couple my Words and Notes lovingly together, which will be much for him to doe that hath not power over both. The light of this will best appeare to him who hath pays'd our Monasyllables and Syllables combined, both which are so loaded with Consonants, as that they will hardly keepe company with swift Notes, or give the Vowell convenient liberty.[27]

The specification of "*English* Ayres" is significant, for a few lines earlier he had mentioned the great popularity of French and Italian airs, and the implication seems to be that his airs, unlike others, are decidedly English in their musico-textual relationship. Campion certainly suggests here that, since he *does* have power over both words and notes, he can weigh the syllables and give each one "convenient liberty." This is the attitude of the poet, who works consciously and carefully with the *sounds* of his words, who weighs and measures every sound to make certain it fits into the texture he is seeking.

Several writers have noted the tendency in Campion "to use sound as a means of organization,"[28] and although "sound" seems to suggest rhythm and meter to some, assonance, alliteration, and rhyme to others, and phonetic patterning to still others, it is unquestionable that all the auditory qualities of poetry were important to Campion.

I believe that the plain, metric musical style that Campion used with greater and greater frequency is closely related to the enunciation of syllables and the leisurely articulation of the sounds of verse, as well as to the accentual representation of poetic meter. Even as far back as the Rosseter Book, Campion had the aural characteristics of his poetry in mind in setting it to music. "Follow thy fair sun" is one of Campion's most successful songs, and one that repays analysis from almost any angle. Wilfrid Mellers has explored it thoroughly from the point of view of word-painting,[29] but although the song is one of Campion's best efforts at textual illustration, its style is not narrative; a description of the illustrative techniques does not explain why the song is pleasing to the ear.

> Followe thy faire sunne, unhappy shaddowe:
> Though thou be blacke as night,
> And she made all of light,
> Yet follow thy faire sunne, unhappie shaddowe.
>
> Follow her whose light thy light depriveth:
> Though here thou liv'st disgrac't,
> And she in heaven is plac't,
> Yet follow her whose light the world reviveth.
>
> Follow those pure beames whose beautie burneth,
> That so have scorched thee,
> As thou still blacke must bee,
> Til her kind beames thy black to brightnes turneth.
>
> Follow her while yet her glorie shineth:
> There comes a luckles night,
> That will dim all her light;
> And this the black unhappie shade devineth,
>
> Follow still since so thy fates ordained:
> The Sunne must have his shade,
> Till both at once doe fade,
> The Sun still prov'd, the shadow still disdained.[30]

The arrangement of word sounds in "Follow thy fair sun" is care-

fully done, not only to produce a pleasing sound but to explicate the text as well. The first line begins with "Follow" and ends with "shadow," an obvious echo effect that indicates aurally the relationship of the shadow to the sun. The effect is augmented by the repetition of line 1 in line 4, and it is even possible to read the shadow's eventual disappearance in the gradual lessening of the repetitive element from stanza to stanza. The heavy alliteration of line 2, "loaded with consonants" to use Campion's own phrase, and the lighter effect of line 3, where there are few initial consonants, none of them double, form a kind of phonetic word-painting. But Campion's purely aesthetic desire for pleasing word sounds is also apparent. In the first line, a combination of alliteration and assonance links almost every syllable in the line to another syllable; and this linking process is prominent in the first line of each stanza. "Though thou" at the start of the second line apparently pleased Campion a great deal too, for the musical setting, uncharacteristically for Campion, repeats these words.

The music for "Follow thy fair sun" parallels the structure of the verse, and well over half the song proceeds in the even note values we have associated with Campion's plain style. The effect of the neutral rhythmic character is a lingering over every syllable, allowing time for clear enunciation of each. Even more important is the equalization of syllables like "sun, un-," which would not be rhythmically equal in speech rhythm or in a durational representation of poetic meter. This effect is exaggerated on "Though thou," where both syllables are given twice as much duration as the surrounding syllables. To make certain that these sound links are heard, Campion makes all syllables so joined of equal duration, using musical meter to sustain the meter of the verse.

Of the later songs that use this technique, one of the nicest is "Now winter nights." The poem is as follows:

> Now winter nights enlarge
>   The number of their houres,
> And clouds their stormes discharge
>   Upon the ayrie towres;
> Let now the chimneys blaze
>   And cups o'erflow with wine,
> Let well-tun'd words amaze
>   With harmonie divine.

Example 3.5.

Fol - low thy fair sun, un - hap - py sha-dow.

Though thou, though thou be black as night And she made all of

light, Yet fol - low thy fair sun, un - hap - py — sha - dow.

Thomas Campian, "Follow thy fair sun." From *The Songs from Rosseter's Book of Airs* (1601); *The English Lute-Songs*, Series I, Vol. 4/13, p. 34. Ed. Edmund H. Fellowes. Rev. Thurston Dart, 1969. Reproduced by permission of Stainer and Bell, Ltd. and Galaxy Music Corp.

> Now yellow waxen lights
> > Shall waite on hunny Love,
> While youthfull Revels, Masks, and Courtly sights,
> > Sleepes leaden spels remove.
>
> This time doth well dispence
> > With lovers long discourse;
> Much speech hath some defence,
> > Though beauty no remorse.
> All doe not all things well:

> Some measures comely tread,
>   Some knotted Ridles tell,
>   Some poems smoothly read.
> The Summer hath his joyes,
>   And Winter his delights;
> Though Love and all his pleasures are but toyes,
>   They shorten tedious nights.[31]

The interlocking rhymes, linking pairs of run-on lines, suggest the possibility that internal rhymes are intended instead of separate lines,

> Now winter nights enlarge the number of their houres,
>   And clouds their stormes discharge upon the ayrie towres;

and the possibility is supported not only by Campion's setting (which comes to a cadence only after every second line, representing the formal structure of versification), but by the sound patterns as well. The phonetic patterning inherent in the diction of this poem is striking.[32] The first two lines, for instance, explore the possibilities of vowels in combination with *n*; the next two lines work with *r* combinations; and the last four lines of the first stanza work with *l*. Throughout the poem the language illustrates aurally the richness of the scene and the expansive, almost timeless enjoyment of it as announced in the first lines: "Now winter nights enlarge The number of their houres." To accomplish this languor, Campion writes successions of long syllables, full of consonants (see especially lines 3 and 11) that require careful enunciation.

The same sensation is achieved musically with a strict homophonic texture, softened and expanded with nonharmonic tones. None of these extra notes is set to a separate syllable; all are expendable as far as declamation of text is concerned. But they do give a languorous quality to the setting without disturbing the steady, accentual declamation of poetic meter. With this method of word setting, Campion allows every syllable equal time to resound and all of the consonantal clusters time to be articulated as they would in a careful, deliberate reading, with a slight metric accent on every other syllable. As certain sections of "Follow thy fair sun" were evened out, in this song nearly every syllable is given equal duration. We can hear the chime through the first four lines of "Now . . . houres . . . clouds . . . tow'rs" even though they are not all stressed metrically and do not appear at regular metrical intervals; and the *l*s on un-

Example 3.6.

Now—win - ter nights en - large The num - ber — of — their hours,
This—time doth well dis-pense With lov-ers' — long — dis - course;

Thomas Campian, "Now winter nights." From *Third Booke of Ayres* (c. 1617); *The English Lute-Songs*, Series II, Vol. 10, p. 22. Ed. Edmund H. Fellowes. Rev. Thurston Dart, 1969. Reproduced by permission of Stainer and Bell, Ltd. and Galaxy Music Corp.

stressed syllables in "While youthful revels" are made prominent enough to be remembered in the next line, "Sleepes leaden spels remove."[33]

What began a half-century earlier as a neoclassical desire to re-create the fabled effects of music, has with Campion become a definite form of interpretation. The attitude toward the text the French humanists promoted was one almost of nonintervention; in strict musique measurée it is only the meter of the text that is the concern of the composer in his setting. Campion shows an early awareness of this austere attitude, and indeed some of the simpler examples of even his later plain settings cannot be said to make any specific musical interpretation beyond the representation of poetic meter. But in many of these settings, the concept of poetic meter is broadened to include most other details of formal organization, within the context of a simple, controlled, and regular musical style. Campion himself said, as if in echo of the French moral ideals supporting musique measurée:

> The world is made by Simmetry and proportion, and is in that respect compared to Musick, and Musick to Poetry.[34]

His settings interpret his poetry, in a manner that is ultimately that of the poet rather than the musician, by reaffirming the importance of its formal organization.

But poetry was not to remain so based in symmetry and proportion. John Donne was already active when Campion wrote those

words in 1601, and there was no conceivable way a plain, homorhythmic setting could do justice to his rough rhythms and irregular
meters. Campion himself, some of whose poetry shows traces of the
newer style, had some difficulties suiting his outmoded musical style
to his own verse.[35]

Plain metric settings such as Campion's could no longer represent
poetic meter, except in the very simplest verse, and we shall see
hardly any of this type in the textually oriented songs of the next
generation. A few will be found among the dance-derived songs, but
more often these are in triple meter and use duration rather than
musical accent to reinforce word stress. Attention to surface structure in songs of this type did not die with Campion, however, but
found a new expression in the works of Henry Lawes. Lawes's textually oriented songs are declamatory, and many more features of their
style resemble the Italian interpretation of humanistic goals than the
French. The combination of the two attitudes will be taken up in
Chapter 6, but it seems appropriate here to isolate some of the
features in Lawes's songs that are definitely related to his interest in
the formal organization and texture of words, a concept that plays
little part in the Italian style.

Like the metric songs of Campion, Lawes's textually oriented
songs are invariably in duple meter. Lawes rarely provides a strict
musical representation of poetic meter in his textually oriented songs,
yet his rhythmic style is not entirely based on speech rhythms either.
The accentual iambic (or trochaic) nature of the language seems to
have been as apparent to Lawes as to Campion, but his declamation
of it tends to be through musical rhythm rather than musical meter,
setting the alternating stressed and unstressed syllables to strings of
sharp dotted rhythms:

Example 3.7.

Henry Lawes, "If I freely may discover." From *Henry Lawes Autograph Manuscript;*
Additional MS 53723, f. 7. Reprinted with permission of The British Library, Department of Manuscripts.

Because he varies the actual note values, the effect is not as regular

and orderly as Campion's, nor even as controlled as those that use the two-to-one ratio of note values. But in later chapters we shall see that this realization of accentual language patterns is not usual in Lawes' contemporaries and is no doubt one of the primary reasons Lawes was praised for his "just note and accent."

Equally indicative of Lawes' attention to surface texture is his treatment of assonance and rhyme. The phrase structure in the declamatory songs usually coincides with the grammatical structure of the text rather than the verse form, yet Lawes is usually careful to set off the end rhymes with the same rhythms or with longer note values, sometimes followed by a rest, so that the poetic lines are audible.[36] Assonance and alliteration are not frequent in the poetry Lawes set to music, but when they do occur, he often singles out the syllables involved by setting them off from the prevailing rhythm, typically with longer note values. In this example the assonant "all . . . false" pair is promoted not only with rhythm, but with large melodic leaps:[37]

Example 3.8.

Whi-ther are all _____ her false _____ oathes blown?

Henry Lawes, "Whither are all her false oathes blown?" From *English Songs 1625-1660; Musica Britannica*, Vol. XXXIII, p. 78. Ed. Ian Spink. Reproduced by permission of Stainer and Bell, Ltd., on behalf of the Musica Britannica Trust, and by permission of Galaxy Music Corp.

Lawes also seems to have been aware of the problem of consonantal clusters in English verse. In the above example, for instance, the only place where declamation is not strictly syllabic is where there is a particularly difficult consonantal group: ♫ ♩ The slide

oathes blown
through a nonharmonic tone is an aid to articulation. Not all the continuo composers were so attentive to the enunciation of individual syllables in their settings; in fact, Lawes has been criticized for being too "detailed."[38] But his attention to the problems peculiar to the language and the verse that he is setting are indications of an attitude that is textually derived, not musically—the attitude, as we saw in Campion, of the poet or in this case the friend of poets.

We have gone a little astray from the specific conventions of

French humanism and musique mesurée, yet not too far, I think, for we are still concerned with an attitude that looks on features of versification—whether meter, rhyme, or phonetics—as the province of music. This attitude is reasonable, linking the physical properties of the two arts, but, like any other rigorously applied approach, it can quickly degenerate into facile and stereotyped musical convention. Even Lawes could not sustain the attention to formal conventions that distinguished the attitude of the French humanists toward the text. In textually oriented songs, he was increasingly faced with rhythms and verse forms too complex to be convincingly represented through music; poetic structures regular enough to be accommodated in musical notation came more and more to be associated with the simple, musically oriented songs. The air de cour shows the effect of this sort of trivialization, and in the corresponding English song, we can see both the adoption of musical characteristics of the air de cour and the tendency, in this emphasis on versification, toward reduction of the musical style to the simplicity of the "popular song." Interesting as are the definitely humanist-inspired experiments of Baïf and his Académie, and later of Campion in England, it is the adoption of the principles, typically in conjunction with a deterioration of the basis in humanism, that forms the most far-reaching link with the development of the air and song style in England. The air de cour, which existed simultaneously with and subsequent to the musique mesurée of the Académie, forms a fascinating study in the trivialization of a style, and provides some interesting insights into the process of transfer of ideas.

Baïf's poetry was measured (quantitative) and unrhymed, in imitation of the ancients. But of course much verse was written in the old style, syllabic verse, often rhymed, owing to the influence of Ronsard. Furthermore, all composers were not as systematic as Mauduit and le Jeune, nor were they always writing for as exacting an audience as the members of the Académie. Yet the musical style of musique mesurée seems to have gained a certain amount of popularity, for many of the airs de cour written in the following decades are patterned after this specialized style without the humanist basis of musique mesurée. The airs de cour are characterized by the same freedom from musical meter, with bar-lines used only at the ends of lines of poetry, by the same restricted rhythmic language, with only two or three note values, by melodies of narrow range and generally

smooth, conjunct voice leading, and by a greater reliance on homophonic texture than in the *chansons* of the period.

The air de cour is thus in many ways the descendant of musique mesurée; in some instances the musical style is so similar that, if one did not know the text, it would be difficult to tell the difference, for it is the text that makes the crucial difference. Since the texts of airs de cour are not quantitative, whatever rhythmic or musical similarities the airs de cour have to musique mesurée are imitation of the musical style and have little or nothing to do with the philosophy behind the humanist songs.

Of interest with regard to correlation with the English lute song is the appearance of many airs de cour—and even some musique mesurée—in solo form with lute tablature after the turn of the century. It would appear that demand, whether humanistic or pragmatic in origin, was the impetus, for most of these arrangements were made by the publishers rather than the composers.[39] Since they are transcriptions of essentially homophonic songs, the lute parts tend to be fairly simple, chordal accompaniments, similar to those in many of Campion's and Rosseter's songs, and present, too, in songs by Dowland, Pilkington, Jones, and others in which there are other elements in common with the musical style of the air de cour.

The airs de cour fall into two general categories[40] with regard to their musico-textual relationship, the first group representing an adaptation of the metrical attitude toward poetry, and the second derived primarily from the musical style of musique mesurée. In one group of airs the rhythmic style of musique mesurée seems to be adapted to represent the syllabic metric structure of French verse, with longer note values indicating the caesura, or coupe, and the end of each line. The example often given of airs of this type is this:

Example 3.9.

C'est un a-mant, ou-vrez la por - te,   Il est plein d'a-mour et de foy

[M.], "C'est un amant." From *Airs de cour pour voix et luth (1603-1643)*, p. 24. Ed. André Verchaly, 1961. Reproduced by permission of the Société Française de Musicologie.

This song certainly illustrates the technique, but it perhaps gives an

overly rigid impression of its use. Actually rather few songs exist in which the two-to-one ratio of note values and the reservation of the longer notes for the structural points of the line are so rigorously enforced. A more typical example is the following, where the long notes at the coupe and the rhymed line endings are definitely apparent but are not the only long notes in the line. The effect could be described as a general slowing down at the structural points, making them more apparent aurally.

Example 3.10.

Pres - sé   d'en - nuis,   af - fli - gé   de   dou - leurs

[Guillaume Tessier], "Pressé d'ennuis." From *Airs de cour pour voix et luth (1603-1643)*, p. 20. Ed. André Verchaly, 1961. Reproduced by permission of the Société Française de Musicologie.

The rhythmic style used thus to delineate verse structure is borrowed from musique mesurée; there is no inherent reason this kind of meter could not be as well represented in the rhythms typical of another style, such as that of Italian monody. It seems obvious that the restricted rhythms and unmetered flow were liked for their own sake. Because of the lack of accent in French, settings like these can be imposed for any desired purpose—including the representation of poetic meter—without seriously distorting the declamation of the text.[41]

That some Englishmen were aware, albeit somewhat confusedly, of this characteristic of the French language is demonstrated in an English publication of airs de cour that appeared in 1629 (*French Court Airs, with their Ditties Englished.*) The publisher, "Ed. Filmer, Gent," has this to say about musical settings:

> the *French* when they compose to a ditty in their owne Language being led rather by their free Fant'sie of Aire (wherein many of them do naturally excell) then by any strict and artificial scanning of the Line, by which they build, doe often, by disproportion'd musical Quantities, invert the naturell Stroke of a Verse, applying to the place of an *Iambicke* Foot, such modulation as Iumps rather with a *Trochey*. And this without much violence to their *Poems*, since the disorder and confusion of *metricall* Feet

in their Verse is as Inoffensive as Indiscernable, by reason of the Even Pronunciation of their Tongue.[42]

In practice, English recognition of the nonaccentual nature of the relationship between words and music in French is not consistent. We shall see below that in several ways, the airs of Dowland, in particular, among the English lutenists, used techniques related to those of the first group of airs de cour, usually with a good understanding

Example 3.11.

John Dowland, "A shepherd in a shade." From *The Second Book of Songs* (1600); *The English Lute-Songs*, Series I, Vol. 5/6, p. 36. Ed. Edmund H. Fellowes. Rev. Thurston Dart, 1969. Reproduced by permission of Stainer and Bell, Ltd. and Galaxy Music Corp.

of what the style can and cannot do with respect to English verse. One example, however, in which his judgment seems to have failed him, is this obvious imitation of the musical style of the air de cour (though without the rhythmic articulation of versification typical of the first group), which nicely demonstrates that its rhythms cannot be imposed with disregard for accent in English as they can in French as seen in example 3.11.

The setting does not work well for a number of reasons. The musical rhythms do not coincide regularly with either the accentual meter or the phrase rhythms of the poem. Perhaps more important are the length and shape of the musical phrases. The melodic lines resemble those characteristic of the air de cour, and their structure is firmly reinforced by the bass line and harmonic rhythm of the piece. But as units of textual representation they fail to do justice to the poem's interplay of rhyme scheme, varying line lengths, and syntax.

A song by Robert Jones, interesting in particular because of the allusions in the first line of the text, is still more obviously patterned after the airs of the first group. The rhythmic style is limited, the texture is homophonic, the musical meter is irregular, and the versification is very precisely represented, with either rests or long notes at every caesura and line ending. Accentuation of the text, however, is again not well done, particularly at two crucial points where it corresponds neither to speech rhythm nor to its implied metrical structure as shown in example 3.12. The start of the first line should read, "When lóve on tíme" and the second "Tíme thăt mŭst énd." Jones could easily have improved accentuation without appreciably altering the music (see example 3.13).

It should be stressed that in the airs de cour of the first group, poetic meter—the syllabic meter characteristic of French poetry—is, in fact, being set, just as much as in musique mesurée. Music is still in the service of formal verse structure. The attitude toward the text is no different from that of the musical humanists, even though the verse structure that originally inspired the relationship is no longer present and the moral and pedagogical aims are no longer spelled out. The procedure, however, would seem to owe much more to the influence of Ronsard than of Baïf, for it will be recalled that the thrust of Ronsard's recommendations was toward regularizing and making audible the normal metric structure of French verse. In terms of attitude toward the text, the composers of airs de cour of this first type

Example 3.12.

Robert Jones, "When love on time." From *The First Booke of Songes and Ayres* (1600); *The English Lute-Songs*, Series II, Vol. 4, p. 18. Ed. Edmund H. Fellowes. Rev. Thurston Dart, 1959. Reproduced by permission of Stainer and Bell, Ltd. and Galaxy Music Corp.

Example 3.13.

are close to Campion who, as we have seen, looked for ways to make music correspond to elements of versification in vernacular poetry. But in adoption of the *musical* style, it is Dowland among the lutenists who, despite an occasional lapse like "A shepherd in a shade," most consistently used the rhythmic conventions of the air de cour, with their emphasis on the external linear structure of the poetry (even though, for Dowland, and English accentual poetry, this is *not* poetic meter, as it was for the French.)

Dowland's handling of the linear structure of poetry shows the most affinity with the French convention in his settings of verse of eight or ten syllables to the line. In lines of this length, a natural pause, or caesura, occurs, and Dowland's settings typically indicate this pause and the end of each line with a long note, a rest, or both. "Daphne was not so chaste," and "It was a time when silly bees," both from the Third Book (1603), are good illustrations:

Example 3.14.

John Dowland, "It was a time." From *The Third Booke of Songs* (1603); *The English Lute-Songs*, Series I, Vol. 10/11, p. 36. Ed. Edmund H. Fellowes. Rev. Thurston Dart and David Scott, 1970. Reproduced by permission of Stainer and Bell, Ltd. and Galaxy Music Corp.

These lines are accentual iambics, ten syllables to the line; but Dow-

land's setting has shaped each line as it would be were it French verse, with the coupe clearly indicated at the fourth syllable of each line. Yet the setting works for a number of reasons. First, the syntax provides a natural pause after the fourth syllable; second, the effect of the pause is reinforced by the recurrent word "time" on the fourth syllable, and Dowland's setting of "time" to long notes stresses the intended play on words as well as the shape of the line. Finally, Dowland manages to do all this without the stilted and obvious manipulation of rhythms that accompanies less felicitous attempts to indicate versification in the French manner, largely because his rhythms do not fail to take into account the accentuation of the line.

Even with shorter lines (less common in Dowland's songs than the eight- or ten-syllable lines), the individual lines usually are carefully set off with rests:

Example 3.15.

John Dowland, "Come again." From *The First Book of Ayres* (1597); *The English Lute-Songs*, Series I, Vol. 1/2, p. 34. Ed. Edmund H. Fellowes. Rev. Thurston Dart, 1965. Reproduced by permission of Stainer and Bell, Ltd. and Galaxy Music Corp.

Examples of this kind of breaking up of the musical line in response to textual demands are frequent in Dowland's songs; here the technique serves primarily to make the verse structure audible, but in

some of his later songs, the pauses in the voice line become longer and the intervals are filled up with complex lute parts. He seems to be using a feature of his style, which grew out of a particular kind of fidelity to the text, to expand the more exclusively musical aspects of song writing, sometimes in the service of the text and sometimes for their own sake.[43]

It should be pointed out, since this will be a major consideration in later chapters, that the respect Dowland shows for the lines of poetry is partly dictated by the nature of the verse he set; most of the lines are endstopped, and in the one instance in the First Book where enjambment occurs, he follows the grammatical structure rather than the verse structure:

Example 3.16.

Think'st thou then by thy feign - ing Sleep with a proud __ dis - dain - ing,

John Dowland, "Think'st thou then." From *The First Book of Ayres* (1597); *The English Lute-Songs*, Series I, Vol. 1/2, p. 20. Ed. Edmund H. Fellowes. Rev. Thurston Dart, 1965. Reproduced by permission of Stainer and Bell, Ltd. and Galaxy Music Corp.

Yet the strength of the musical enjambment is not like what we shall see later in the century, and the example is such a rarity, especially in the books before *A Pilgrimes Solace,* that it is justifiable to cite fidelity to versification of the poetry as one of Dowland's characteristic features.

Campion's approach to the musical representation of linear structure follows quite a different path. In the Rosseter Book (1601), and less often in the later books, Campion sometimes uses a technique similar to Dowland's for separating the lines, though he more often uses a long note for the last syllable than a rest between lines.[44] But even in the early book, he seems to show a liking for a continuous musical texture, and a steady declamation of the text without un-

necessary pauses, as seen in example 3.17. This preference is most apparent in the early songs that tend toward the plain, metric style (such as "Follow thy fair sun"); in the later books, the settings in the plain style typically end each line with one solid chord or make

Example 3.17.

Thomas Campian, "Your fair looks." From *The Songs from Rosseter's Book of Airs* (1601); *The English Lute-Songs*, Series I, Vol. 4/13, pp. 32-33. Ed. Edmund H. Fellowes. Rev. Thurston Dart, 1969. Reproduced by permission of Stainer and Bell, Ltd. and Galaxy Music Corp.

no rhythmic distinction at all at the ends of lines, presumably relying on the audibility of the poetic meter and the rhyme scheme to indicate the linear structure.

Almost never with Campion do we find the long pauses between lines of the text as in Dowland; such pauses as do occur usually are

set with one sustained chord rather than the musical interludes that became common with Dowland. Campion's interest in poetic meter, with its regularly recurrent pattern, is again apparent—whether or not the setting is of the strictly metric type—in his unwillingness to delay the continued declamation for musical reasons.

Example 3.18.

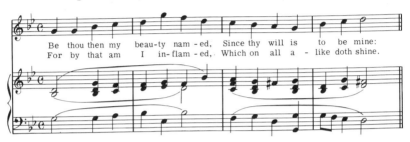

Be thou then my beau-ty nam - ed, Since thy will is to be mine:
For by that am I in-flam - ed, Which on all a - like doth shine.

Thomas Campian, "Be thou then." From *The Third Booke of Ayres* (c. 1617); *The English Lute-Songs*, Series II, Vol. 10, p. 35. Ed. Edmund H. Fellowes. Rev. Thurston Dart, 1969. Reproduced by permission of Stainer and Bell, Ltd. and Galaxy Music Corp.

He again shows a greater doctrinal, if not musical, affinity with the French style.

In general, it is typical of the lutenists to be faithful to the linear structure of the verse they set, whether they tend, like Campion, to favor a continuous declamation of the poem or, like Dowland, a fragmented style, breaking the verse with musical interludes between the lines. The continuo composers are less consistently respectful of external verse structure, especially in songs that are textually oriented. Purely musical considerations are not prominent in these songs, and insofar as verse structure is a factor, its musical representation is more like Campion's uninterrupted reading than Dowland's more musical interpretation. Henry Lawes, as we have seen above, often provides a rhythmic reinforcement of the rhyming words, which functions as a reminder of the lines of verse. Once again, however, the poetry he sets is apt to have more run-on lines than that set by the lutenists, and considerations of syntax usually take precedence over those of verse structure. Furthermore, the rhythmic language in these songs is not that of the air de cour, and a musical re-

lationship to the French style is apparent in only a few continuo songs that are definitely textually oriented.

It is in the musically oriented, tuneful airs of the continuo composers that the musical conventions of the air de cour are preserved. These light, popular airs result, at least in part, from the process of trivialization of the musico-textual relationship of certain kinds of lute song, much as the second group of airs de cour result from erosion of the principles of musique mesurée.

The airs de cour of the first group, it will be recalled, use the rhythmic and musical conventions of musique mesurée, adapted to represent the syllabic meter of French poetry. The airs of the second group have the same musical style as those of the first, but with no discernible correlation between the musical rhythm and the external structure of the poetry. In songs like the following, it is apparent that the musical style has now been taken over entirely for its own appeal, with little concern as to how it suits the text:

Example 3.19.

[Pierre Guédron], "Cette Princesse." From *Airs de cour pour voix et luth (1603-1643)*, p. 60. Ed. André Verchaly, 1961. Reproduced by permission of the Société Française de Musicologie.

It should be noted again, however, that such a setting does no violence to declamation, since its French text is not accented and long notes do not have to correspond to word stress; it is merely a rhythmic pattern superimposed on the text.

Once the principle that music should represent certain features of the text has been left behind, as in these airs of the second group, the process of trivialization has begun. Musical considerations have assumed control of the style, and in this period there is a strong tendency for such musically oriented songs to become stereotyped. In the airs de cour of both groups musical meter begins to be im-

posed, and because of the two-to-one ratio of note values characterizing the style, that musical meter is usually triple. At first the
metric organization is not regular, and, as pointed out by Walker,
especially at the ends of lines of verse, the triple meter turns to
duple as shown in example 3.20.

Eventually the airs de cour, at this level of distance from the text,
merged with the dance. The regular musical meters of the dance became predominant, and the rhythmic repetitiveness, standard in the
text-related airs because of the representation of the recurrent
feature of poetic meter, fit right in with the necessary rhythmic re-

Example 3.20.

Je___ne scay s'il vous sou - vient   De   nostre a - mi - tié   pas - sé - e,

Mais,   he-las!   el-le   re - vient   Tou-jours de - dans ma   pen-sé - e.

[Gabriel Bataille], "Je ne scay s'il vous souvient." From *Airs de cour pour voix et
lutb (1603-1643),* p. 40. Ed. André Verchaly, 1961. Reproduced by permission of
the Société Française de Musicologie.

currence of dance music. The resultant dance-song, musically oriented,
light, rhythmic and tuneful, gained rapidly in popularity over the
précieux airs de cour of the textually oriented type during the early
decades of the seventeenth century.

Among the lute songs are, as we have already seen, some instances
of the application of the rhythmic conventions of musique mesurée
in which, as in the airs de cour of the second group, there seems to
be no correlation between the musical rhythms and the rhythm or
meter of the text. But these instances are rather infrequent. Most of
the lutenists were consistent in adopting a rhythmic language that
either declaims the text metrically, such as Campion's plain style, or
equates duration with word stress. Although I think we have established that the former convention is closer to the philosophy of the
humanists, the latter will be seen to bear the strongest musical affinity with the style of the airs de cour, though the association of
length with accent was never a part of its origin. This correlation of
moderately varied rhythmic values, like those of the air de cour, with
stress patterns of the text—particularly interpretive stress patterns—

gives the most typical lute songs their characteristic smooth and supple rhythms and accounts in part for their fidelity to the text.

Of course the equation of musical rhythm with textual rhythm was not new in England, nor was the unmetered declamation of individual lines of a text. Both are present in the madrigal; only the use of this rhythmic declamation in a solo or homophonic setting, where its correlation with the textual rhythms may be clearly heard, was new at the beginning of the century. Yet, given these conditions, the sound of some of these lute songs is remarkably similar to the airs de cour of the same period. Francis Pilkington, one of the few composers of the time who wrote both madrigals and lute songs, writes these lines, which in another setting could be characteristic of the madrigal, but are here, with alternative four-part harmony or chordal lute accompaniment, very much akin to the French style.

Example 3.21.

Francis Pilkington, "With fragrant flow'rs." From *The First Booke of Songs* (1605); *The English Lute-Songs*, Series I, Vol. 7/15, p. 44. Ed. Edmund H. Fellowes. Rev. Thurston Dart and David Scott, 1971. Reproduced by permission of Stainer and Bell, Ltd. and Galaxy Music Corp.

Pilkington's fidelity to textual rhythm is noteworthy. He obviously has not given a simple translation of the iambic meter of the poem into notes of short and long duration, but has used the limited

rhythmic values interpretively to promote "we" in the first line and "chief" in the second. This technique is used regularly by Dowland in his settings of this type. Except in some of his dance-songs, Dowland never sets the meter of his text, but uses musical rhythm to provide an approximation of speech rhythms, reserving the longer note values for interpretive stresses.

It is apparent that Dowland is not interested in setting the meter of poetry. Perhaps we may see an early indication of his attitude in the Dedication to Sir George Cary of his *First Book of Ayres*, in which he states the expected humanist doctrine that music's power to affect the minds of the hearers will be enhanced by the presence of "the lively voice of man, expressing *some worthy sentence* or excellent Poeme."[45] This statement could have no place in the French humanists' interpretation of the doctrine of the effects; so strong was their belief in the union of music and *poetry* — not music and "some worthy sentence" — that it was the formal features of verse, and not its own "sentence," that they sought to represent. But although Dowland's attitude was never that of the French humanists, his speech rhythms, smoothly declaimed at first, in the air de cour-like rhythms, unmetered through the textual phrase, do have the smooth and subtle musical rhythms of the French style.

Example 3.22.

John Dowland, "In darkness let me dwell." From *The First Book of Ayres* (1597); *The English Lute-Songs*, Series I, Vol. 1/2, p. 40. Ed. Edmund H. Fellowes. Rev. Thurston Dart, 1965. Reproduced by permission of Stainer and Bell, Ltd. and Galaxy Music Corp.

The long notes on "heart," "Sor-row," and "cries" are obviously interpretive, dwelling on the dolor that was Dowland's trademark. Occasionally Dowland's interpretive use of duration takes him

beyond the limited rhythmic range we have associated with this style. As early as 1600 we see instances like the one shown in example 3.23. But what was exceptional interpretive rhythm in 1600 becomes common in *A Pilgrimes Solace* (1612). Lines such as those seen in example 3.24 are the rule rather than the exception.

Example 3.23.

All   my   plea - - - sures best be - lov-ed.

John Dowland, "Woeful heart." From *The Second Book of Songs* (1600); *The English Lute-Songs*, Series I, Vol. 5/6, p. 35. Ed. Edmund H. Fellowes. Rev. Thurston Dart, 1969. Reproduced by permission of Stainer and Bell, Ltd. and Galaxy Music Corp.

Dowland's exaggeration of the interpretive element in the speech rhythms led him eventually to a rhythmic style that was much more varied than the rhythmic conventions of airs de cour. In the later songs, these rhythms begin to assume the dramatic character of the Italian style. Thus for Dowland, who had used the supple French conventions with lyrical smoothness and sensitivity, the style was dead. To continue in the direction of his emotional speech declamation was to leave the French conventions behind and move toward those associated with Italian musical humanism.

The course of development of the French musical style in Campion's songs is naturally quite different. Although there are some instances similar to Dowland's early use of this style, Campion is generally less inclined to use duration for interpretive stress and tends, even in his songs that are not in the plain style, to work with the meter of his text. "I care not for these ladies" is a simple, rustic text with a fairly regular iambic meter, changing to trochaic for the third line of the stanza and making a nice variety without creating irregularities within the lines. A strong caesura is present in every line but the last of each stanza, as seen in example 3.25.

Example 3.24.

John Dowland, "In this trembling shadow cast." From *A Pilgrimes Solace* (1612);
The English Lute-Songs, Series I, Vol. 12/14, pp. 37-38. Ed. Edmund H. Fellowes.
Rev. Thurston Dart, 1969. Reproduced by permission of Stainer and Bell, Ltd. and
Galaxy Music Corp.

Campion's setting is based strictly on the use of duration as the
equivalent of metric stress, with either lengthened notes or, in line
four, a rest to mark the metric break of the caesura. The rhythms are
restricted to two or three note values, the melodic writing is smooth,
the texture is homophonic, and the musical structure corresponds
exactly to both the metric structure and the linear structure of the
verse. If words could describe a piece accurately, these sentences
would lead one to expect "I care not for these ladies" to be similar to
musique mesurée in both musical style and attitude toward the text.
But the one factor that my description has ignored is what happens
to musical rhythm and meter when an English accentual iambic line
is set strictly to long and short note values: The song will inevitably
be in a triple meter, and the regular alternation of stressed and unstressed (long and short) syllables will produce a rhythmic style not
only ultimately tedious, but also, as we shall see in the next chapter,
inherently unsubtle, even awkward in its declamation of poetry in
the English language. The setting of the most common meters of

Example 3.25.

Thomas Campian, "I care not for these ladies." From *The Songs from Rosseter's Book of Airs* (1601); *The English Lute-Songs*, Series I, Vol. 4/13, pp. 6-7. Ed. Edmund H. Fellowes. Rev. Thurston Dart, 1969. Reproduced by permission of Stainer and Bell, Ltd. and Galaxy Music Corp.

English lyric poetry to a musical style that equates duration with word stress will thus quickly degenerate into a simple, popular style. "I care not for these ladies" works very well in such a style, for its text is hardly more subtle than its music, but the setting cannot in any real sense approach the ideals of musical humanism.

If to proceed in the direction of Dowland's speech rhythms meant to leave the musical style of the air de cour, to continue in the direction of poetic meter, with musical duration aligned with word stress, could only mean more songs like "I care not for these ladies." With English iambic or trochaic verse, they would be triple meter songs; the facile equation of rhythm with poetic meter would invite a trivialization of the technique into stereotyped, dancelike songs, just as it did with the air de cour.

Examples of simple, metric songs of this type abound in the sources of continuo songs; the following one is typical. It is by Henry Lawes, with text by Robert Herrick—a frequent combination in these light songs—and the rhythmic pattern, beginning like a galliard, then falling back to a rhythmic declamation of the poetic meter, becomes a cliché as it appears in song after song of the Caroline period.

Example 3.26.

A Wil-low Gar-land thou didst send last day Per-fum'd to mee, which did but one-ly this por-tend. I was for - sook of thee.

Henry Lawes, "A Willow Garland." From *The Treasury of Musick, Containing Ayres and Dialogues, Book I*, p. 19. London: John Playford, 1669. Facsimile ed. Ridgewood, N.J.: Gregg Press, Inc. 1966.

Another feature that becomes frequently associated with this

triple-meter style is the shift to duple declamatory rhythm in the context of the broadened triple meter of hemiola. Many of these songs, like their French cousins, have obviously become related also to the dance, and the use of hemiola is often attributed to the influence of the dance. The effect, however, is remarkably similar to the shifting to duple meter at the ends of lines or couplets in the triple-time airs de cour; thus it seems conceivable that this convention grew as much out of adaptation of the French style to English meters as it did from the influence of the dance. Given the unwillingness to subdivide the beat in a triple musical meter that was characteristic of the period, the typical iambic meter, with masculine ending, could be declaimed thus in a triple meter:

But if a change to duple declamation in imitation of the air de cour

Example 3.27.

[Anonymous], "Ask me no more." Oxford Bodleian MS Don c. 57, f. 70. Reprinted with permission of the Bodleian Library, Oxford.

was desired, the rhythmic pattern would have to be like the following, adding an extra beat to the conventional French rhythm:

English air

Air de cour

Whatever the derivation, the hemiola became a standard rhythmic counterpart to the subtle shifting rhythms of the air de cour, and was featured, often with charming results, in many of the tuneful and dance-related songs by the continuo composers, such as the lyrical anonymous setting of Thomas Carew's "Ask me no more," as seen in example 3.27.

Like the trivialized air de cour, this song is evidently more musically than textually oriented; and by the 1630s its type is so distinct from that of the textually oriented songs that these tuneful airs must be considered as a separate category in the next chapter.

Chapter 4
Dance Songs and Tuneful Airs

And since it is so stored with variety, I hope it will and may please most Ears, though, I fear, not all; for our new *A la mode* Gallants will Object, They are old, and after the *English* Mode; had I fill'd it with the light Ayres of the *French,* or the wanton Songs of the Stage, it would have liked their Humour much better.[1]

Thus did John Playford introduce the Second Book of *"Select Ayres and Dialogues* . . . Composed by Mr. Henry Lawes . . . And other Excellent Masters," in 1669. The implication is clear: that "light Ayres" do not appear in this collection, nor are they to be found in the works of "English" masters (like Henry Lawes). Such, of course, is not the case in this book or in any other of Playford's collections, and though Lawes adopted a peculiarly English form of the air de cour, the label of "light Ayres" must certainly be applied to a considerable number of his songs. The songs of Lawes that are not declamatory have been referred to as his "tuneful airs." Perhaps this label will do as well as anything as a designation for all such light songs that do not give predominance to the text over purely musical values. The tuneful songs tend to follow a musical rather than a textual logic, in that the smooth, continuous melodies and regular, engaging rhythms are not altered by textual concerns, and I have called them musically oriented because their strongest appeal is the toe-tapping, physically musical impulse of the popular song and dance.[2]

The tuneful airs of the Lawes generation, as we have seen in the previous chapter, are in many ways closely related to the court airs of the French. The process of reduction of musical features to the lowest common denominator created, in both countries, a smooth,

facile musical language, often in triple meter, with limited rhythmic variety and frequent use of such conventions as hemiola. The predictability of the musical language makes it suitable for setting only the most generalized sentiments and the most regular features of versification; the texts chosen thus tend to be the less serious, as well as the less interesting ones. But although the tuneful continuo airs have a definite relation to the trivialization of the air de cour in England, and may therefore be justifiably classed with the "light Ayres of the *French*," they derive also from the dance songs of the lutenists. Whereas the musical style of the air de cour and its generating principle of representing poetic meter in musical notation suggest musical features of the tuneful airs, many of the conventions of textual interpretation in these songs are peculiar to the English language. These conventions are present in the dance songs and dance-derived songs of the lutenists in which another impulse altogether is the source of attitudes toward the text. The dances themselves are closely related to French musical styles, and many of the specific dances also are present in the French song repertoire. But the problems that arise in setting English texts in this musical style produce a stance toward textual interpretation in the English dance song somewhat different from that in the French air.

It is the purpose of this chapter to trace, through the dances of the lutenists and the disintegration of the ideals of the air de cour, the conventions of word-setting that give the tuneful airs a characteristic flatness. At the same time, we shall consider their occasionally delightful nuances of declamation. The great popularity of the tuneful airs seems baffling in the light of Lawes' celebrated relationship with poets of his own day. Were these songs included in the acclamations of both poets and public? And if they were, how do they manage to rise above the pleasant but slight efforts that, on the surface, they seem to be? The renown enjoyed by Dowland and Campion, as well as Lawes, for care in joining music with poetry cannot have been held without regard for such large numbers of songs; we shall try to see not only where the composers gave in to the force of musical conventions, but how they worked with the conventions, establishing an attitude toward the text at once casual and attentive.

Although some of the lute songs are obviously of a lighter nature than others, no major differences are apparent between the lighter songs and the more serious ones in the handling of declamation and

phrasing. The differences are more in the nature of musical aims, and the conventions imposed by those aims.

The lighter lute songs appear to have two sources: the simpler madrigals (such as the ballett, canzonet, and "light madrigal")[3] adapted for solo presentation and the more formal court dances such as the pavane, galliard, coranto, branle, and almain. The madrigal types, very frequent in the lute songs of Morley, Pilkington, Cavendish, Bartlet, Corkine, and Jones, are characterized by points of imitation with the accompaniment, repetition of phrases of the text, and sequential treatment of short, parallel phrases of the text. They are typically very responsive settings of their texts, using the smooth, flexible declamatory rhythms we saw in the last chapter as common to both French and English songs of this period, and featuring the devices of word-painting characteristic of the polyphonic madrigal. These madrigal-like songs are often attractive pieces, but they are not a radical departure from the Renaissance polyphonic ideals, and they seem to have been as much on the wane as the genuine madrigals by the second decade of the seventeenth century. Most of the features that distinguish the declamation in these songs, as well as their purely musical characteristics, virtually disappear from the light songs of the next generation. Some of the conventions appear in the more serious declamatory songs in a new guise, and we shall have to look more carefully at these songs as textually oriented airs in Chapter 5; but the future of the musically oriented, tuneful air lay definitely with the dance song.

In the early books of lute songs, particularly those by Dowland and Campion, a large proportion of the airs are based on the French courtly dances. These, of course, were quite unlike the madrigals, having a musical point of departure. The dance basis of the early lute songs was a prominent enough feature for them to be first known outside England as dances, rather than as songs.[4] Yet they are in general tasteful settings of their texts in addition to being pieces of great musical charm, and it seems likely that the dance song was looked on as a new medium for relating music and poetry.

Dowland's *First Book of Ayres* includes many dances underlaid with text. Some of these appear elsewhere without texts, in some instances as instrumental dances in sources antedating any texted versions. However, the question of whether instrumental or vocal versions were written first is largely immaterial in these songs, for the

presence of the dance governs the musical characteristics; the setting of the texts generally follows conventions that do not differ essentially from one to the next. The dance format involves preestablished metric and rhythmic patterns (and often a harmonic pattern as well), whether or not the association with a text was inherent in the original conception of the piece. For Dowland, the presence of a formulary structure does not dictate that all galliards, for instance, will be identical, for his musical imagination was fecund enough to compensate for, perhaps even to be stimulated by, the restrictions of a preexistent form. But the possibility of stereotyped musical structures and strongly conventional handling of texts in songs like these certainly exists.

Campion does not work as directly as Dowland with the dance tradition. Very few of his songs can be labeled as specific dances. Nevertheless, the rhythms associated with dances are present in some of his songs, and certain features of his handling of textual rhythms in those songs can be shown to be related to impulses ultimately derived from a basis in dance rhythms. The relation to dance rhythms is most apparent in Campion's songs in triple meters, most of which occur in the early Rosseter Book. Although Campion, as we have seen in the previous chapter, tended away from songs in this style in his later books in favor of his particular fidelity to the text, this combination of elements related to the dance, without strict adherence to the dance forms, and the trivialization of the characteristic rhythms and approach to the text of the air de cour, determined the course of the tuneful air of the next generation.

For both Campion and Dowland, the presence of dance conventions does not necessarily imply a light popular style, nor the use of a less serious text, nor a careless attitude toward the text. We shall see, for instance, that in a galliard song, Dowland's rhythmic handling of the text usually is not essentially different from what we saw in the last chapter. But the presence of the dance basis, with its requisite regular meter and conventional rhythmic patterns, has significance for the ultimate relationship between music and text, and brings with it some conventions of declamation that will carry over to the dance-related continuo songs.

Curiously, the overt presence of dance meters diminishes notably in the lute song books after about 1605. Lute songs, following various humanistic pursuits, went in other directions: in the strongly

metric direction of Campion's songs, or in more Italianate, textually oriented directions like Dowland's. But the dance song impulse obviously did not die, for it reemerges full strength in the continuo songs. It is likely that the dances were primarily associated with the masque during the second and third decades of the century; dancing was the essence of the masque, and some of the surviving masque songs are dance-related.

When the dance song does reappear, however, it is as a distinct genre. Henry Lawes' songs, in contrast to the lute songs, fall into two remarkably disparate catetories: the declamatory, textually oriented songs, which are invariably in duple meter, and the light, dancelike songs, sometimes almost frivolous in their simplicity, which are almost as invariably in triple meter; whereas the dichotomy is not so striking in the works of the other continuo composers, the general characteristics of the two kinds of song are apparent in their airs as well. In the tuneful airs of all the continuo composers, the relation to the dance, and to the dance songs of the lutenists, is important, though the dance basis is rarely so formally laid out as it is in Dowland's songs. But what is most immediately evident is the degree of homogeneity in the tuneful airs. They are predictable and conventional in the extreme, and the relationship of music and text shows little variety, little subtlety in the use of word-setting conventions derived from the dance songs and from the air de cour. Yet the tuneful airs were obviously among Henry Lawes' most popular songs. They appear throughout the autograph manuscript of his songs, becoming more frequent in the later part of the volume and forming a large proportion of the songs that Playford chose to anthologize — despite the publisher's pronouncements on the degeneracy of taste that would favor such "light Ayres" — and they can probably be considered his most likeable songs today.

Several features of musical style are common to the dance-related and musically oriented songs, both lute songs and continuo songs, setting them apart from the more textually oriented continuo songs. All of the songs of this type have the restricted rhythmic language associated with the air de cour in the previous chapter that was sometimes characteristic as well of the English madrigal. This factor does not distinguish the lute songs of this type from other lute songs, but the tendency to associate rhythms of this kind with the simpler, dance-related or tuneful airs increases, beginning with Dowland's

growing use of exaggerated speech rhythms in the songs of *A Pil-grimes Solace* and culminating with the vast difference in rhythmic language between the tuneful airs and the monodic songs of Henry Lawes. The tuneful airs are very simple rhythmically, dotted rhythms are scarce, and the typical song uses not more than three or four note values.

A similar situation exists with the narrow, conjunct voice lines and the homophonic texture in both the air de cour and the early lute songs. Virtually all of the dance songs of the lutenists, and most other lute songs as well, feature smooth voice leading, but in the continuo songs only the tuneful airs have this kind of melodic line. The declamatory songs often have wide ranging melodies and many leaps, whereas in the lighter songs the melodies are smooth, mostly conjunct, and the leaps that do occur are rarely large or affective. The melodic lines in the tuneful airs are usually continuous from beginning to end, and harmonic pauses tend to come at regular intervals corresponding to the ends of the poetic lines, in contrast to those of the declamatory airs, which punctuate nearly every phrase of the text with a rest or a fermata.

Since Dowland is the most familiar of the lute song writers, we tend to think of his madrigal-related, lightly polyphonic style as the norm for lute songs. Polyphonic texture clearly predominates in Dowland's nondance songs and in those of John Danyel and other composers working close to the madrigal tradition. But in most of the early lute songs—including Dowland's dance songs—and many of the later ones by Campion and some lesser-known composers, a homophonic texture is the rule. The vocal line is supported by a chordal accompaniment, or by other voices in part song renditions, and any polyphony is merely decorative.

The continuo songs, as they appear in manuscript or printed sources, are neither polyphonic nor homophonic but monophonic. Yet the tuneful airs preserve the homophonic style of the dance song and other chordal lute song traditions. The tuneful airs typically have more active bass lines than their declamatory relatives, implying a chord on each bass note and therefore a homophonic texture (in contrast to the declamatory and monodic styles, which have much slower harmonic rhythm and a true polarity between an active treble and a static bass). Furthermore, many of the tuneful airs appeared, like their lute song predecessors, in part-song arrangements in Play-

ford's editions (though, for the most part, not in the original manuscript sources), and of course such arrangements could not easily be made of the less homophonic styles.

Some musical characteristics common to the songs under consideration here are more specifically pertinent to the relation of the tuneful airs to the dance songs, rather than to the general category of lute songs. The dance impulse dictates that one of the criteria for determining a musically oriented song in this period is the presence of a strong, regular musical meter. It is true that the bar-line gained metrical significance only gradually during the period, but the sense of regularly recurring metrical accent nonetheless had been a necessary feature of dance music for some time, and its presence is implied in the rhythms of all the dance-related songs.

Because of the formality of dance structures, two other characteristic features are precisely balanced musical phrasing and much repetition of musical material. It is extremely common in Dowland's dance songs, for example, for the first and second lines of the text (or sometimes the first and second couplets) to be set to the same music, and for the remaining lines to be exactly as long in musical duration as the first, though rhythmically changed; Campion, in a dance-related song such as "Though you are young," sets every line to the same rhythmic pattern, while the melodic line changes.[5] The regularity obviously is designed to fit the standardized patterns of dance steps. Insofar as it derives at all from consideration of the text, it is necessarily related to the external structure of the poem, whether poetic meter or simply line length. This musical regularity is prominent for Dowland only in the musically oriented dance songs; in more textually oriented songs, he often manipulates the duration of his lines, as though to counter the regularity implied by the poetic meter.[6] With Campion the impulse is somewhat different, for, as we have seen in the last chapter, he espouses this attitude in his more serious songs as well. Nonetheless, it is generally characteristic of the lute song dances to feature equal phrases and musical or rhythmic repetition, and a similarly balanced and repetitive character is typical of the tuneful continuo airs.

Predictably balanced phrases and repetition will tend to impart a musical similarity to the dance and dance-derived songs; and the standardized rhythmic patterns associated with the various dances augment their tendency to sound alike. We have noted that Dowland

managed to introduce a considerable amount of variety into his dance songs, but the reduction to convention and cliché is as inevitable with these regular rhythms as it was with the rhythms of the air de cour, and when the dance rhythms reappear in the tuneful continuo air, they tend often toward stereotyped patterns.

Although some of Dowland's most famous songs were duple meter dances, it is generally the triple meter dances that are associated with the light, tuneful style in the lute song; that association becomes solidified with the amalgamation of these dances with the air de cour in its eroded, and by this time frequently triple meter, form. Thus the continuo songs in this tuneful manner are preponderantly triple meter songs, and it is here that we shall begin investigating how standardized musical conventions dictated by the influence of the dance and the air de cour style affect declamation of a text.

As I have already suggested, declamation in the tuneful airs is not without problems; usually it is assumed that these were not songs in which interpretation of the text was a primary goal. But that the musically oriented style and its somewhat casual approach to declamation of text is linked with the predominance of musical triple meters in this style suggests that it is perhaps the triple meter itself that presents difficulties, rather than a careless attitude toward the text. If we recall some points already made concerning the correlation of musical and poetic meter, we may begin to focus on the problems.

First, the triple metric organization, perhaps through association with the dance, makes its presence more strongly felt than a duple meter. This effect is particularly apparent in the songs of this period because it seems to have been uncharacteristic to subdivide the beat for purposes of declamation in a triple meter, and what we hear is the three beats, not two-plus-two-plus-two. Occasionally the beat is subdivided with nonharmonic tones, but the subdivision is merely musical ornament and does not alter the declamation of one syllable to each beat of the musical meter; nor do the smaller note values of the polyphonic lute accompaniments affect declamation. In both the dance songs of the lutenists and the tuneful airs of the continuo composers, the triple meter usually is clearly outlined in the declamatory rhythms.[7]

Second is the nature of poetic rhythm and meter in English verse. To repeat, briefly, a few points from Chapter 1: The most common

metric structure in English poetry (accentual iambics) is made up of units of two syllables, primarily because that is the prevailing (though not the exclusive) rhythm of the language. An iambic meter can be set to music in one of two ways: If musical accent is used to represent word stress, then the musical meter will be duple and the syllables will be essentially all of one duration (as in the Campion plain settings); but if duration is made to represent stress, the musical meter will be triple and the stressed syllables will be twice the length of the unstressed. Or — to view the problem from the other direction, as we shall in this chapter — if the musical meter is to be triple, whether because the composer intends the song as a dance or as an air de cour-like song, it will be nearly impossible for him to do anything other than equate the poetic meter with long and short note values. The strength of the triple metric organization will impose an accent every third beat — an accentual pattern inherently incompatible with either the usual metric structure of English poetry or the natural speech rhythms of the language.

This description sounds as though the triple meter should put a strait jacket on the composer. Yet possibilities for manipulation of rhythm do exist, and the triple meter, dance-related songs are obviously not so rigidly conceived as such restrictions might suggest. Though in most songs composers choose an interpretation essentially either accentual or durational, by combining the use of accent and duration in representing the rhythms of the text, they can achieve considerable variety. The rhythmic patterns of the dances themselves prevent a completely metric approach to textual declamation, and although these patterns sometimes seem to impose new restrictions, composers found ways of circumventing difficulties in setting texts to these musically attractive rhythms. Thus we shall find in these songs a pleasing balance between attempts to master the correlation of music and text, and occasions for surrendering to the purely musical appeal of the dance.

The two most common triple-time dances in this period were the galliard, one of the favorite dances in the *Fitzwilliam Virginal Book*, and the most often used by the lutenists, and the coranto, which gained in popularity during the course of the century and is often suggested by rhythmic patterns of the continuo songs. Both the galliard and the coranto have sources in France and Italy, but it seems to be the French form that is most often used in the English dance

songs. Early in the seventeenth century, the galliard and the coranto are sometimes indistinguishable, as they appear in *The Fitzwilliam Virginal Book:*

Example 4.1a.

William Byrd, "Galiarda." From *The Fitzwilliam Virginal Book,* Vol. II, p. 207. Ed. J. A. Fuller Maitland and W. Barclay Squire. New York: Dover Publications, 1963. Reprinted with permission of Dover Publications.

Example 4.1b.

[Anonymous], "Coranto." From *The Fitzwilliam Virginal Book,* Vol. II, p. 308. Ed. J. A. Fuller Maitland and W. Barclay Squire. New York: Dover Publications, 1963. Reprinted with permission of Dover Publications.

The long note on the fourth and fifth beats, however, is particularly characteristic of the galliard; it provided for the leap that is one of the main features of the dance. The coranto, as its rhythmic characteristics develop during the century, often has an upbeat, and a "running" rhythm takes the place of the galliard's leap. Example 4.2 is nearer to the typical coranto. The two types of dances will not always be specifically identifiable in the songs, but their basic rhythms and harmonic structure can be seen underlying many of them.

John Dowland's first song book (1597) contains a relatively high proportion of dance songs. Eight of the twenty-one songs are in a triple meter, and of these most are galliards, several of the tunes appearing elsewhere as instrumental dances. It seems apparent in these

Example 4.2.

William Byrd, "Coranto." From *The Fitzwilliam Virginal Book*, Vol. II, p. 305. Ed. J. A. Fuller Maitland and W. Barclay Squire. New York: Dover Publications, 1963. Reprinted with permission of Dover Publications.

songs that whether or not he had the instrumental versions before him, Dowland conceived of the pieces as galliards and merely arranged the distribution of syllables in the poem to fit a galliard rhythm. The standard rhythmic pattern for the first line of a galliard can be seen from the example below:

It should be obvious that the iambic poetic meter common in English poetry normally cannot fit this rhythmic scheme, whether accent or duration is the basis of correlation. Dowland's most frequent means of accommodating the text to the musical rhythm is to work with interpretive phrase rhythms of the text. In some instances the results are excellent. In "Captain Digorie Piper's Galliard," for instance, metric scansion of the line is abandoned; the formulaic galliard pattern puts an interpretive emphasis on the conditional "If":

Example 4.3.

John Dowland, "Captain Digorie Piper's Galliard." From *The First Book of Ayres* (1587); *The English Lute-Songs*, Series I, Vol. 1/2, p. 8. Ed. Edmund H. Fellowes. Rev. Thurston Dart, 1965. Reproduced by permission of Stainer and Bell, Ltd. and Galaxy Music Corp.

The resultant textual rhythm makes perfectly good syntactical sense. But in "The Earl of Essex's Galliard," the scansion imposed by the galliard rhythm is less logical. The first three words fall reasonably well, but there can be no interpretation that would deny the necessity for stresses on "wrongs" and "Vír-tue's."[8]

Example 4.4.

John Dowland, "The Earl of Essex's Galliard." From *The First Book of Ayres* (1597); *The English Lute-Songs*, Series I, Vol. 1/2, p. 10. Ed. Edmund H. Fellowes. Rev. Thurston Dart, 1965. Reproduced by permission of Stainer and Bell, Ltd. and Galaxy Music Corp.

Dowland has allowed the dance rhythm here to take precedence over the declamation of textual rhythm or meter. It may be noted that a hemiola shift of accent would accommodate this text:

But, though the hemiola is common in these songs, and often seems to be required by the declamation, it does not conform with the dance structure at this point and is far more likely to occur at the end of the second line. The harmonic patterns characteristic of the dances are perhaps even more standardized than the rhythmic patterns. The galliard is made up of repeated strains of eight "measures" of three beats each. There is usually what we would call a dominant or half cadence at the end of the first four measures and a full or authentic cadence at the eighth measure. This second cadence is the occasion for hemiola, extending the cadence formula rhythmically to give greater closure to the strain:

Thus, in "If my complaints," where the rhythmic pattern of the first line is repeated for most of the other lines, the shift in accentuation is not only more appropriate in the second line, but is indicated in the bass—and therefore the harmonic rhythm—as well:

Example 4.5.

John Dowland, "Captain Digorie Piper's Galliard." From *The First Book of Ayres* (1597); *The English Lute-Songs*, Series I, Vol. 1/2, p. 8. Ed. Edmund H. Fellowes. Rev. Thurston Dart, 1965. Reproduced by permission of Stainer and Bell, Ltd. and Galaxy Music Corp.

If awkwardnesses like those in "Can she excuse my wrongs" occur in the galliards because of the superimposition of a dance rhythm and harmonic formula on a text, then theoretically they should not appear in the settings that are not specifically dances and that should be more flexible rhythmically. "Sleep, wayward thoughts" is in a triple meter, but although it begins rhythmically like a galliard, the length of the first line rules out the actual dance format: The line encompasses the equivalent of five triple measures, and the galliard requires the measures to be in groups of two.[9] As a setting for the text, however, the line is perfect. Dowland has fitted the syllables to the rhythmic pattern in an accentual interpretation of the textual rhythm (the grammatical importance of predicate and subject, "Sleep" and "thoughts," taking precedence over the adjective "wayward"). But this interpretation takes durational differences in English syllables into account as well as differences in stress. The caesura after "thoughts" makes the longer note a necessity. The re-

Example 4.6.

Sleep, way-ward thoughts, and rest you with my love: Let not my

John Dowland, "Sleep, wayward thoughts." From *The First Book of Ayres* (1597);
The English Lute-Songs, Series I, Vol. 1/2, p. 26. Ed. Edmund H. Fellowes. Rev.
Thurston Dart, 1965. Reproduced by permission of Stainer and Bell, Ltd. and
Galaxy Music Corp.

mainder of the line, "and rest you with my love," is one of those
troublesome strings of monosyllables that account for many of the
difficulties composers had with English verse, but Dowland's interpretation, again in speechlike rhythms, is accurate and musically
tasteful. The short, unaccented "and" is set as an upbeat; "rest" is
obviously accented; but unless the setting is going to represent only
poetic meter, "you" must also receive an emphasis, since it is the
subject of the clause. In accordance with phrase stress, "with" and
"my" are unaccented, and "love" must finish the line on a strong
beat. The resultant textual rhythm is ⌣ / / ⌣ ⌣ / for this second half
of the line; and this is nearly impossible to set to a triple meter if
both ictus and length are taken into consideration.

Of course, Dowland does not set the clause to a triple meter. The
setting, by lengthening both "rest" and "you," puts them both on
strong beats in a duple meter, a musical hemiola supported by the
harmonic rhythm. But our memory of the underlying triple meter
prevents too much emphasis from thus being placed on "with," and
"love" falls on the strong beat whether we are thinking in twos or
threes. The resulting cross-rhythm might be clearer if diagrammed:

Because the rhythmic pattern is only dance-related, and not a genuine

galliard, such rhythmic manipulation is possible here, where its use would have violated the standard dance rhythm in "Can she excuse"; and I think it will be agreed that this setting serves the text ideally. But after such a pleasing beginning, Dowland's musical logic, which seems to have held particular sway in the early books, did not allow him to continue to work so specifically with the text. Instead, as so often in the real galliards, he sets the next three lines to the identical rhythm, in the second and fourth lines placing an undue stress on "with," in the last line a stress on "But," and in general giving precedence to musical structures.

Example 4.7.

John Dowland, "Sleep, wayward thoughts," p. 26.

The most successful of Dowland's dance songs, at least from the standpoint of the musical handling of the accentuation of the text, is "Now, O Now, I needs must part." This piece is sometimes known as the "Frog Galliard," although as Thurston Dart notes, it is actually closer to the rhythmic pattern of the coranto.[10] As in "Sleep wayward thoughts," the first line establishes the pattern that will be the basis of the musical rhythms of the piece (see example 4.8). In this setting duration reinforces the stresses of the poetic meter, and the syllables of the first line certainly invite such an interpretation: The first three stressed syllables are either diphthongs ("Now") or double vowels ("needs,") both of which demand more time to articulate than single vowel sounds. The poet, of course, does not keep up this coincidence of length and stress (the first syllable of "absent" in the second line, for instance, is a particularly "short" but stressed syllable); however, the meter of the poem is very regular, and the rhythmic pattern of the first line, which appears five times in each stanza, never distorts the accentual pattern of the text.

Such strict adherence to poetic meter, coupled with so much musi-

Example 4.8.

Now,   O   now,   I   needs   must   part,

John Dowland, "The Frog Galliard." From *The First Book of Ayres* (1597); *The English Lute-Songs*, Series I, Vol. 1/2, p. 12. Ed. Edmund H. Fellowes. Rev. Thurston Dart, 1965. Reproduced by permission of Stainer and Bell, Ltd. and Galaxy Music Corp.

cal repetition would in most circumstances lead to a dull, trite song; but this song is saved from tedium by a shift to an accentual interpretation of lines 4, 8, 10, and 12 of the poem. The accentual interpretation of line 4, the first to be so treated, seems to take into account the near equality of the first three words, all monosyllables, whereas a durational rhythmic interpretation here would tend to swallow up "once" and lose some of the punch of the line.

Example 4.9.

Joy   once   fled   can-not   re - turn.

John Dowland, "The Frog Galliard," p. 12.

This, however, is a small detail, for the poem continues its regular meter *ad nauseam,* and the hemiola seems here to be more of musical than textual inspiration, dependent again on the cadential formula of the dance. Dowland also upset the regularity of the dance structure, however, for the hemiola appears too early, in effect shortening the lines; only by extending the last note of each of these lines through

two whole measures does he fill out the required number of beats for the dance.

That Dowland sometimes gave in to the musical demands of the dance measures at the expense of declamation of the text is understandable, for Dowland was first and foremost a musician, a lutenist to whom the dances were probably second nature. With Campion, on the other hand, we might expect a somewhat different attitude toward the relationship of music and text, in view of his leanings toward the poetic side of the balance. However, the triple meter problem and the force of musical convention had an effect on Campion's dance-related settings too.

Campion's "Blame not my cheeks," although it is a serious song and not of the frivolous character later associated with the triple meter, is based, like Dowland's "Sleep wayard thoughts," on a galliard rhythm and the harmonic structure of the dance; it again demonstrates the kind of textual difficulties encountered with a triple meter. The first phrase scans well in an accentual triple (dactylic)

Example 4.10.

Thomas Campian, "Blame not my cheeks." From *The Songs from Rosseter's Book of Airs* (1601); *The English Lute-Songs*, Series I, Vol. 4/13, p. 26. Ed. Edmund H. Fellowes. Rev. Thurston Dart, 1969. Reproduced by permission of Stainer and Bell, Ltd. and Galaxy Music Corp.

beat, putting stress on "Blame" and "cheeks." But from that point on, the scansion of the poem is at odds with the demands of the dance pattern and its triple meter. The first line should read

Bláme nŏt mȳ chéeks, thŏugh pále wĭth lóve thĕy bé

If the composer were to use musical accent to represent word stress (as Campion often does), he would have to shift to duple meter:

Blame not   my   cheeks, though   pale with   love they   be

This is clearly not possible in the dance song. Another alternative would be to shift to a durational interpretation of the iambic part of the line, thus maintaining the triple meter:

Blame not   my   cheeks, though   pale   with   love   they   be.

But this interpretation gives us five measures to the phrase. Campion was quite capable of adding a measure or even of inserting extra beats in an established metrical pattern if there were not enough beats to fit the syllables he wanted to set. But the rhythmic and harmonic patterns in this song are clearly those of the galliard, not simply an imitation of its style, and such additions are not possible if it is to be a real dance. As we have seen, the hemiola expected in the dance often helps out in the declamation of the text. Unfortunately, even that solution does not work well with this text. In the first line, the hemiola adjustment would add stress to "pale" but remove it from "love" (mitigated, it is true, by the agogic accent on this word), and in the second, the hemiola serves nicely for "heart," but gives us an ungainly accentuation of "untó."

   I do not know of the existence of this tune anywhere else, but the setting does have the look of a contrafactum. If the reader will imagine the piece instrumentally performed, he will find it smooth and convincing as a dance. One wonders whether Campion was not induced by the opening dactyl of his poem to set it to that characteristic galliard rhythm and perhaps even to a preexistent tune, regardless of what happened to the rest of his verse in the triple meter.

A similar problem seems to arise for Campion in other songs in which the opening syllables have suggested an accentual triple-time interpretation. "When thou must home" (Rosseter Book/20) requires an adjustment of the metric accent before the end of the first line; so does "Thou art not fair" (Rosseter Book/12). All of these songs move progressively further from the triple meter as they continue to declaim the text accentually. Only two of the seven triple time songs from the Rosseter Book are not essentially accentual. One is "I care not for these Ladies" (Rosseter Book/3). The other, "Follow your Saint" (Rosseter Book/10), though not perfect in its declamation, does succeed in maintaining the triple meter because Campion is more flexible than usual in switching from accentual to durational declamation.

It is perhaps significant that in Campion's *Third Booke of Ayres* (c. 1617), containing some of his best songs, only one song is in triple meter throughout, "So Quick, So Hot, So Mad" (No. 28). It is rather a strange song, not altogether typical of Campion's usually smooth and undramatic style; even the poem is unusually sardonic, providing a clear demonstration that the lutenists did not necessarily associate triple meter with lightheartedness. But Campion has not really given us a dancelike triple either. In fact, he seems determined not to write a straightforward triple meter, for the text does not always demand the alterations he makes. The poem is essentially iambic. In choosing to set an iambic line to a triple meter, Campion would, at least to some degree, have been thinking in terms of syllable

Example 4.11.

Thomas Campian, "So quick, so hot, so mad." From *The Third Booke of Ayres* (c. 1617); *The English Lute-Songs*, Second Series, Vol. 10, p. 52. Ed. Edmund H. Fellowes. Rev. Thurston Dart, 1969. Reproduced by permission of Stainer and Bell, Ltd. and Galaxy Music Corp.

lengths. The first line, as usual, is set very well on this basis, as seen in example 4.11. The ornamental flourishes (which do not affect the declamation of the text on the primary units of the meter and thus do not function as subdivisions of the beat) merely add an urgency to the melodic line but do not alter the durational setting of the syllables. So careful has Campion been with this line that the rhythmic reversal on "thy fond," placing the decorated long note on "fond," gives a convincing emphasis to "fond." The next line begins like the first, but concludes with a hemiola demanded by the music, not by the text:

Example 4.12.

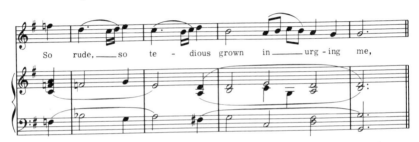

Thomas Campian, "So quick, so hot, so mad," p. 52.

We shall see below that when Lawes switches to a hemiola, it often involves a definite shift to accentual declamation. But that technique does not work here, because Campion has only four syllables to set to the six beats. The broadened triple of the hemiola would provide an accent only on "grown" and omit the necessary stress on "urging":

But if Campion has used the hemiola to avail himself of the duple division of the beat, his setting puts an unnecessary emphasis on "in." The eighth-note flourish on this word helps the singer lighten up on it but has the curious counter-effect of drawing attention to it.

It is unlike Campion to distort the declamation of his text for purely musical reasons, but I think we must consider the possibility that he has done so in some of his triple-time songs. "So Quick, So Hot, So Mad" is rhythmically very repetitious. The ornamental rhythmic motive ♩. ♫♩ is striking and effective the first few times we hear it. But it becomes tedious as we hear it eleven times in the first stanza alone, and because the motive is so striking, the musical repeat that links lines 1-2 and lines 3-4 in many of Campion's songs seems ill-chosen here. One reason for the difficulties Campion encountered in this song is the very fact that he chose to write it in triple meter, against his usual preference for duple meter. The features I have just mentioned—the shift to hemiola, the repetition not only of rhythmic motives but of whole sections—seem to be very common in triple meter songs of this period, in fact so common as to be almost clichés, at least to our ears. But these features probably were not clichés to seventeenth-century ears, but were instead the expected norms for triple meter dances set as songs. Campion seems to have been trying to write the standard popular type of triple meter, dance-related song. That he did not find it easy is apparent from the foregoing, but if further proof is required, we need only look at the last two lines of "So Quick" where he almost abandons the attempt altogether (example 4.13). Here he has essentially left the triple meter behind, although no actual change in time signature occurs. He has also changed from what was basically a durational interpretation to an accentual interpretation of the text. Fellowes, in his edition of the song, has tried to remedy some of the accentual problems with irregular bar lines, but the actual meter, as governed by the verse, is duple, with an extra beat (as a bit of word-painting?) on "counted." Musically, of course, the lines flow as well in the triple meter, but do so in a way that would turn the poetic iambs into dactyls and distort the verse beyond recognition. I have suggested elsewhere that Campion is the archetype of the composer to whom music was indeed the "handmaiden of poetry." "So Quick, So Hot, So Mad" is surely an unsuccessful attempt to reverse the balance.

Two conventions in the use of triple meter in Dowland's and in Campion's dance-related songs should be reiterated, for they become almost formulas in the triple time songs for the next fifty years. First is the obvious choice of an interpretive basis, and thus a rhythmic pattern, from the first line of the poem. Campion chose an accentual

Example 4.13.

An hour__ with thee I care not to con - verse: For

I would not be count - ed too per - verse.

Thomas Campian, "So quick, so hot, so mad," p. 53.

interpretation in "Blame not my cheeks" because of the dactylic structure of the opening words; Dowland chose a durational setting in "Now, O now" because the coranto rhythm fit the longer stressed syllables of the first line well; and we shall see that Henry Lawes establishes the overall character of a triple-time song on the basis of the first line as well. None of these songs, of course, is strictly durational or accentual, but in any one song, one or the other approach seems to prevail and set the character of the piece.

The second feature is the tendency to shift to hemiola towards the end of a poetic line or a musical unit (usually made up of two lines of verse), reflecting an inability to maintain a triple meter in setting English verse. Interestingly, the keyboard treatment of the dances is often much freer than the songs, especially by the second decade of the century. The hemiola convention does not appear to have been so popular in the keyboard galliards of the period, although it becomes increasingly apparent in the coranto. Perhaps this feature is simply one more indication of the degree to which composers felt musically confined in their attempts to set a text to a triple meter. Although in "Now, O now" the hemiola accompanies a shift to an

accentual metric interpretation, this is not always the case. In Campion's songs the hemiola is usually an admission that the original accentual triple does not work, but the hemiola does not always work either. If the metric structure of the poem changes, as it often does in the poetry that Lawes sets, then the hemiola serves to reinforce the poem's structure, not merely to compensate for accentual problems. But over and above these textual considerations, there appears to be a purely musical convention at work, most obvious in Dowland's galliard songs, but frequent in the other composers' works and especially apparent in songs whose phrase structure has been allowed to exceed that of the dance. Although the hemiola clearly has its origin in the harmonic patterns of the dances, at this point it is also related to the musical style of the trivialized, popular air de cour, which seems to me to represent the same genre as the tuneful airs of this generation and the next.

Campion, finding it more and more difficult to accommodate his metric approach to declamation to a triple meter style, by his last song books had almost given up the effort. His attitude toward the text was tending toward the representation of versification in the duple meter songs. Dowland's attitude in the early galliard songs is polite, but hardly deferential. Declamation is rarely truly awkward, but it provides little interpretation of the poem. Yet in his duple meter songs, particularly the emotional airs of A *Pilgrimes Solace* (1612), Dowland was leaning toward the exaggerated interpretive rhythms that would become a part of the declamatory style, and it might be expected that his manner of working with rhythm would change in the triple meter dance songs too.

It is instructive at this point to look at how Dowland used a triple meter in A *Pilgrimes Solace*, his last book of songs. Four of the twenty-one songs in this remarkable book are in triple meter (Nos. 5, 6, 7, and 18). Two of the four, Nos. 7 and 18, show the same kind of textual difficulties as in the earlier books, although No. 18 is at least freer of the repetitive quality. No. 6, "Were every thought an eye," though it is a dance-song, is also free of the continual rhythmic repetitions of the earlier galliards, and has the additional interest of a new setting for each of the three stanzas (part of the dance structure), melodically and rhythmically related but allowing for accentual differences (for example, where "And *all those* eyes could see" is set to a hemiola to refer "those" back to the "thoughts" of the first line,

the comparable line of the second stanza is not forced into a hemiola as it would have been in the earlier songs).

But No. 5, "Shall I strive with words to move," particularly catches our attention, for this song seems to alter the conventional framework of the triple time song, and has, like the duple time songs of this book, much greater rhythmic variety than any of the earlier

Example 4.14.

John Dowland, "Shall I strive." From *A Pilgrimes Solace* (1612); *The English Lute-Songs*, Series I, Vol. 12/14, p. 10. Ed. Edmund H. Fellowes. Rev. Thurston Dart, 1969. Reproduced by permission of Stainer and Bell, Ltd. and Galaxy Music Corp.

triple time songs. The most obvious change is that the three beats are subdivided, which means that the iambic feet can now be accentual even though the primary musical rhythm is in threes. The subdivisions have the further virtue of increasing the number of note values available, thereby avoiding the monotony of the earlier triple meter songs. Except for the sectional repeats, which are common even in Dowland's duple songs, "Shall I strive" also is free of the repetitious rhythmic motives and phrases that seemed to be stock material before. These relaxations of the formulas should make it

much more possible for the composer to interpret the text as he chooses or to set it in something approaching a speech rhythm.

"Shall I strive with words to move" is another galliard, and from the foregoing possibilities we might expect that here Dowland has found a way to work as expressively with the text as he does in the duple time dances, that perhaps he is headed toward a declamatory style in a triple meter. Yet if Dowland felt any freedom from the strictures of the triple meter in this song, he did little to exploit it. The setting is basically accentual but does not seem to place the accents with any particular care (the metric and agogic accents on "*nei*ther," for instance, would make more sense if the preceding lines had given us two possible recipients for the poet's speech), nor is it a very convincing speech rhythm, as some of Dowland's duple songs are. When we come to the second section, the new-found rhythmic freedom is laid aside and Dowland falls once again into the hemiola of the earlier triple songs. "Shall I strive" appears in other sources as a lute solo, and Diana Poulton suggests that "it is possible that Dowland reverted to the earlier practice of setting words to preexisting dance measures."[11] Although she goes on to speculate that, instead, it was written earlier as a song, I think the former explanation is likely, since it also explains the presence of the metric subdivisions: They are lute figuration, underlaid with text. And we must conclude that the conventional attitude toward the text, which is a part of all the other triple meter dance-related songs, the musical, dance structure taking precedence over the text, is still in effect for Dowland, even after experimenting with much more expressive rhythms in the duple-meter songs.

It seems, thus, that in Dowland's mature works the disparity between a serious, expressive, duple meter song and a more light-hearted, triple meter song was increasing. The presence of the triple time dance acts as an automatic deterrent to the development of declamatory means of expression; and it is presumably the meter, not the dance structure, that does so. The famous "Lachrimae," a serious song, also is a dance, but it is in duple meter. In Henry Lawes' songs, the disparity between light and serious styles is considerably more pronounced than in the lute songs, the serious songs going much farther than Dowland's in the direction of declamatory rhythms, and the tuneful airs being reduced to the utmost simplicity of ex-

pression. But the disparity has as its point of departure the same distinction between a triple and a duple musical meter.

Two songs by Lawes that seem to represent the epitome of the rhythmic monotony that is the greatest pitfall of the triple meter style are "Love's Drollery" and "To his Forsaken Mistresse." These songs are little better than nursery rhymes in their almost sing-song reading of the poems. In both songs, not only are lines or pairs of lines set to the same rhythmic pattern (as we saw in the lutenists) but a prevailing rhythmic foot is established and repeated over and over, giving the whole piece a sameness that seems to be a purely musical—and not very imaginative—kind of organization. Yet even in these simple, repetitive songs, Lawes reveals a certain amount of attention to the text, especially in attention to details often lacking in the lute songs (particularly after the first line). In "Love's Drollery" we might

Example 4.15.

I Love thee for thy Fick-le - ness, and great In-con-stan-cy; _____ for

had'st thou been a con-stant Lass, then thou had'st ne'r lov'd mee. _____

Henry Lawes, "I Love thee for thy Fickleness." From *The Treasury of Musick, Containing Ayres and Dialogues, Book I*, p. 22. London: John Playford, 1669. Facsimile ed. Ridgewood, N.J.: Gregg Press, Inc., 1966.

note the rhythmic reversal of "Fickleness": ♩ ♩ ♩♩ As an instance of Lawes' awareness of the subtleties of syllable duration, this reversal breaks the established metric pattern. But the only other such reversal in the song is not so obviously right. Lawes' musical sense apparently has told him that another reversal is necessary to balance the first, so he sets "thou had'st ne'r" to the same rhythm. In isolation, the declamation seems wrong, throwing the accent off the subject of the clause and onto an auxiliary verb; it does, however, reinforce the

parallel with the conditional clause of the previous line where subject
and verb are in reverse order:

Presumably Lawes felt that the necessity of pointing out the paradox
of the last two lines of the first stanza (which is indeed the main idea
of the poem,) and/or balancing the rhythmic pattern introduced on
"fickle-" overruled a natural speech rhythm. Interestingly enough,
the poet does not seem to have thought of this kind of musical interpretation, for though he has preserved the paradox in the last two
lines of each of the five stanzas,[12] the syntax is not the same, so
Lawes' little rhythmic nuance is lost on the remaining stanzas.

Example 4.16.

Henry Lawes, "I do confess." From *The Treasury of Musick, Containing Ayres and
Dialogues, Book I*, p. 24. London: John Playford, 1669. Facsimile ed. Ridgewood,
N.J.: Gregg Press, Inc., 1966.

"Love's Drollery" is set in a completely durational representation of the iambic verse, in the manner we have related in Chapter 3 to the air de cour; the majority of Lawes' triple meter songs use this durational approach. The other of the very simple songs mentioned above, "To his Forsaken Mistresse," shows us one of Lawes' common devices for introducing variety into these iambic settings (see example 4.16). The first measure gives us three even beats, although the bulk of the song is to proceed in the long-short pattern that dominates so many of the triple time songs. In this song, the accentual first measure works well with the text, putting an added emphasis on the subject, "I":

I   do   con-fess   th'art   smooth   and   fair

But Lawes often uses this pattern whether it fits or not, as in these two of Herrick's poems that Lawes set:

Amidst   the   Mir - tles

A   Wil-low   Gar - land

The number of Lawes' triple time songs that begin this way is considerable, and again I think this practice has to do with the discomfort of setting English verse to a triple meter. Much of this lyric verse is essentially iambic, but the iamb has to be rearranged musically because, in spite of the recent emergence of the accentual barline in Lawes' time, there can be no question that a stress was felt at the start of each group of three. Therefore the feet of iambic verse cannot correspond literally with the measures, even if the intent is to interpret the stresses with duration. Lawes begins with an upbeat in some songs, such as "Love's Drollery," making musical and poetic stress correspond. But more often he prefers to start on a down beat, squeezing the first foot-and-a-half into one measure, so that the second accented syllable falls on a musical accent. If we looked only at songs like "To his Forsaken Mistresse" (and quite a few fit this pattern), we might conclude that Lawes was truly sensitive to the metric variety of English verse. Unfortunately, too many examples

are like the Herrick settings mentioned above to justify such a contention, and we must conclude instead that Lawes, like Dowland and
Campion, worked more with preestablished rhythms in his triple
meter songs. In fact, this rhythmic pattern is reminiscent of the
galliard rhythm that Dowland used so often, but like Dowland's
"Sleep, wayward thoughts," Lawes' songs that start this way are not
real galliards either. The rhythmic pattern is catchy and familiar,
setting the mood of the piece. But often it leads the composer into a
hemiola alternation of duple and triple that as in Campion's "So
Quick, So Hot, So Mad," with Lawes seems to be a musical idea
rather than one imposed by the rhythm of the text.

An extreme example is "On a Bleeding Lover." The poem reads
as follows:

> A Lover once I did espy,
> With bleeding heart and weeping eye;
> He wept and cry'd, How great's his pain,
> That lives in love, and loves in vain.

A perfect example of the trivial verse Lawes found for his triple
songs, and an ideal candidate for a monotonous, plodding, durational interpretation. But Lawes resists that temptation, only to fall
into a repetitive hemiola pattern that occasionally plays havoc with
the accentuation of even so simple a meter, as shown in example 4.17.
The first three syllables of each line are the worst offenders, because
of the accent on the first beat; also a little clumsy is the lengthening
of "and" in lines 2 and 4, presumably satisfying a pattern of musical
organization, but in the process giving undue emphasis to the conjunction. Once again, however, some touches suggest that the musical
choice was at least partly dictated by the text. The first hemiola unit
gives an added strength to the frame of the poem by lengthening "I,"
the poet's persona; and in the third line Lawes rightly avoids the
hemiola pattern, because "great's" of "How great's the pain" would
have fallen on the third and weakest unit of the hemiola (and, after
all, we are aware of the broader triple meter in a hemiola in spite of
its duple subdivision). With a song like this, in spite of the textual
niceties just described, musical organization still seems to dominate,
but the text does seem to have been a factor in determining the
shape of the ultimately musical structure.

"Love's Drollery" and "To his Forsaken Mistresse" both remain

Example 4.17.

A Lov-er once I did es-py, with bleed-ing heart and weep-ing eye; he wept and cry'd. How great's his— pain, that lives in love, and loves in vain

Henry Lawes, "On a Bleeding Lover." From *The Treasury of Musick, Containing Ayres and Diaglogues, Book I*, p. 25. London: John Playford, 1669. Facsimile ed. Ridgewood, N.J.: Gregg Press, Inc., 1966.

steadfastly in the triple meter (unusually so for Lawes), in the first instance because no major irregularities occur in the meter of the poem; in the second instance, triple meter prevails in spite of roughness in the second line, which appears to have been smoothed over so the same music can be used to set lines 1-2, and the enjambed lines 3-4. And in "On a Bleeding Lover" we saw an almost slavish alternation of duple and triple. But Lawes was not always this inflexible, and his duple insertions into a triple meter are sometimes unequivocally in response to the accentuation of the text, sometimes to aid the expressive purpose of the setting. One of his best known songs is the setting of Herrick's "A strife betwixt two CUPIDS reconciled," better known by its first line, "About the sweet Bag of a Bee," (see example 4.18). Herrick's poem has a structure that is one of Lawes' favorites for triple meter; each stanza is really two effectual fourteeners, and the alternating lines of eight and six syllables gave Lawes a good opportunity to add variety to a triple setting. The method used in "About the Sweet Bag of a Bee" is his usual one, the eight-syllable line set to a real triple, the six-syllable line to a hemiola. Assuming the verse is basically iambic (which this one is), the eight-syllable line is

Example 4.18.

Henry Lawes, "A strife betwixt two Cupids reconciled." From *The Treasury of Musick Containing Ayres and Dialogues, Book I*, p. 3. London: John Playford, 1669. Facsimile ed. Ridgewood, N.J.: 1966.

thus set with duration, and the six-syllable line accentually. This procedure has the effect of exaggerating the difference in line lengths, because the accentual setting, in assigning a syllable to every beat, instead of two beats out of three, moves the declamation faster. In this poem, the effect is particularly appropriate, for Herrick has arranged the verse in such a way that the short lines in the first two stanzas all deal with action: The two Cupids, in the first stanza, fall at odds in line two and vow to ask the gods in line four; Venus strips them in line six and whips them in line eight. And the hemiola of Lawes' setting gives an appropriate brusqueness to the lines. The situation is changed in the third stanza where Venus' principal action, kissing and drying the Cupids' eyes, is pacifying rather than punishing, and the slower pace of the rhythmic setting seems appropriate.

Before we leave this song, we should note that a galliard-like rhythm begins lines 1, 3, 5, and 7. That this rhythm was by this time purely conventional seems apparent here. The first line of the poem has an irregular rhythm, drawing attention to the unusual nature of the object of the Cupid's strife. Except for the first three syllables, the accentuation of lines 1 and 5, which are melodically alike, is carefully handled, and we cannot conclude that Lawes was oblivious to the accentuation of his text. Yet those first three syllables are set to the familiar galliard rhythm, regardless of declamation. "About the sweet Bag of a Bee" is definitely of the lighthearted triple type, and, like most of the triple songs, does have some cumbersome spots in the declamation. Further, as we have seen throughout this chapter, Lawes does not seem content to remain in a real triple meter. But at least this song shows Lawes working directly with the poem in a triple meter and not simply applying a preestablished dancelike pattern.

I would like to conclude this discussion of the dance-related triple meter songs on a positive note. Most of the discussion in the preceding pages has centered on the difficulties that English composers had in working with a musical triple meter, but a few genuine triple meter songs from this period really work, both musically and as settings of their texts. Campion's "I care not for these ladies" is a durational representation of the poetic meter in triple meter throughout, and Lawes' "Sufferance," a setting of a poem by Aurelian Townshend, is an accentual triple meter.

Campion's song, as we have already seen in Chapter 3, is a strict

and regular rendition of the poetic meter, using the rhythmic language we associated there with the air de cour. The use of duration as the musical equivalent to word stress, in conjunction with Campion's regular iambic poetic meter, makes the triple meter here as inevitable as it is appropriate to the rustic simplicity of the text.

Lawes' "Sufferance" works in quite the opposite way. Townshend's poem reads as follows:

> Delicate Beauty, why should you disdain
> With pity at least, to lessen my pain?
> Yet if you purpose to render no cause,
> Will, and not Reason, is judge of those laws.

For once, here is an English poem that is not iambic, but dactylic, and the two remaining stanzas are as convincingly so as the first. With a little manipulation, Lawes makes this poem fit beautifully into a genuine accentual triple meter. "Delicate" is a natural dactyl; by putting the emphasis on the conditional "should," Lawes makes "beauty, why" another dactyl; and he is not afraid (as Campion apparently was in the second line of "Blame not my Cheeks") to begin

Example 4.19.

Henry Lawes, "Sufferance." From *Select Ayres and Dialogues, The Second Book*, p. 41. London: John Playford, 1669. Facsimile ed. Ridgewood, N.J.: 1966.

the second line on an upbeat and to lengthen one note (on "least") to keep to the actual rhythm of the poem.[13] Neither poem nor music could be classified as great art, but they do work together to create the poised delicacy of which the poem speaks. The primary reason for this ideal balance, of course, lies in the poem, which, unlike most English verse, is not iambic. But also involved is Lawes' decision to write a light, rhythmic song that treats the text accentually. If he had used duration to represent the dactylic meter, we would get

de-li-cate

But we do not say the word that way, and to impose such a reading on the words with musical notation would be to add a deliberate heaviness that belies the language of the poem.

Both songs I have singled out as successfully using a triple meter are of the sort I have termed "lighthearted," and both poems have fairly regular meters. The primary difficulty with the triple time songs, especially those of Henry Lawes, but present to a lesser degree in the lutenists' songs, is the metrical sameness that the triple meter seems to force onto the rhythmic interpretation of the text. The small but very real differences in length of English syllables, whether accented or unaccented, which appear to be taken into consideration in the duple-time settings, especially those of Dowland and Lawes, are hardly possible in the limited rhythmic vocabulary of the triple songs. Thus, in spite of some nice rhythmic touches in Lawes' songs, I think we must conclude that the triple-time songs usually are not as successful in their interpretation of the text as are the duple time songs. This no doubt explains, at least in part, why so many of Lawes' triple meter songs treat such simple texts. An extremely regular poetic meter tends to trivialize the subject of a poem; but, as we have seen, only verse with very regular, uninteresting meter of its own is suitable for the undivided triple beats favored in this period. The triple songs typically establish their own rhythm and, except in occasional instances, they impose this rhythm on the text. In the more declamatory duple time songs, the reverse is true; it is the rhythm of the text (and usually not a strict "metric" rhythm) that imposes itself on the music. That a duple meter could theoretically be infinitely subdivided without destroying its basic nature made the

duple songs a much more suitable vehicle for the recitation of texts that were more interesting and varied metrically and that expressed complex emotional states. The triple time songs became, with Lawes, a definite contrast to the seriousness of the duple, poetically dominated songs—an outlet for the real song-impulse of composer, singer, and audience alike.

When we leave the triple meter dances, the clear distinction in declamatory techniques begins to break down. We can still distinguish the dance-derived songs of the lutenists, and some of the duple-meter songs by both the lutenists and the continuo composers are definitely of a lighter nature, but real differences in musical style and differences in attitude toward the text are harder to pinpoint. The most famous of the duple-meter texted dances is of course Dowland's "Flow my tears." We have noted in Chapter 1 a few instances where the declamation in this beautiful song suffers because of the metric strictures of the pavane, but in general the text underlay is so well done here that it has been suggested that Dowland himself must have written the text specifically for this musical setting.[14] But this is hardly a tuneful or light-hearted song, and it may be more appropriately discussed in Chapter 6.

Some duple meter, dance-related songs, however, do fit the category under consideration here, the tuneful airs. Features of the triple meter dance songs that will also distinguish the lighter of the duple meter songs are the tendency to musical repetitions and regular phrase lengths, and the presence of a strong and regular musical meter. These are features associated with the dance basis of the forms, but, as with the triple meter songs, they also have an effect on the declamation of the text.

Dowland's "Now cease my wand'ring eyes," shown in example 4.20, is an almain.[15] The music consists of two phrases repeated to different lines of text, and although the relatively slow pace of the almain keeps the musical meter from exerting the force it does in some of the triple dances, the piece nonetheless falls into quite regular duple meter phrases with little rhythmic variety in the setting, though good declamation requires some accentual adjustments in the last lines. Length is used infrequently, and in a restrained manner, to reinforce the accentuation of the text, which otherwise is achieved almost solely with the metric accents of the music. The poem is an unusual one to find set to a dance measure, for its last four lines have not only greatly

Example 4.20.

John Dowland, "Now cease my wand'ring eyes." From *The Second Book of Songs* (1600); *The English Lute-Songs*, Series I, Vol. 5/6, pp. 28-29. Ed. Edmund H. Fellowes. Rev. Thurston Dart, 1969. Reproduced by permission of Stainer and Bell, Ltd. and Galaxy Music Corp.

varied numbers of syllables but are departures from the typical iambic line usually set to the regular dance meters. The first four lines are set adequately, though without any apparent gesture toward interpretation (except for the dotted note on "*long* desire," which may be nothing more than a happy coincidence, since the identical musical phrase sets "*to* admire" above). Lines 5 and 7, both lines of four monosyllables, remind us that this is Dowland, for his setting each syllable to a half note takes into account the shortness of the line, and sets the poetic rhythm in such a way that we—quite properly—hear the four words as four stresses. But the next lines (6 and 8) seem to be merely crowded into the remaining beats, with a gesture toward good declamation in the lengthening of "*plea*sures" but little else to suggest a concern with the text.

But Dowland does not often write like this in a duple meter. Most of his duple meter dance songs are pavanes, for which he seems to have had a much greater affinity. In fact, his pavanes are among his

most carefully declaimed songs, and as such belong only nominally in this chapter. The very slow pace of the pavane reduces the pervading sense of regular musical meter that sometimes seemed to have hindered Dowland's imagination in matters of declamation.

Of the faster, more metric duple time songs, Dowland's best known is surely "Fine knacks for ladies." This is not a dance song in the strict sense of the word, nor does it have many of the features we have pointed out as characterizing the dance-derived songs; in particular, it lacks the repetitive element that was undoubtedly also a hindrance to good declamation. It does, however, have a steady duple meter and very regular phrases coinciding with the lines of the poem, which are also regular, at least in length. The meter of the poem, on the other hand, is quite irregular. Here Dowland has demonstrated the interplay of metric accent and agogic accent that usually makes his settings true to the accentuation of the text, whether or not it is a regular iambic pattern, without sacrificing the variety that makes the piece interesting musically as well. The second half of the first line is a notable instance:

Example 4.21.

John Dowland, "Fine knacks for ladies." From *The Second Book of Songs* (1600); *The English Lute-Songs*, Series I, Vol. 5/6, p. 26. Ed. Edmund H. Fellowes. Rev. Thurston Dart, 1969. Reproduced by permission of Stainer and Bell, Ltd. and Galaxy Music Corp.

"Cheap," "choice," "brave," and "new" are all accented. Dowland could have accomplished that within his duple meter thus:

Cheap, choice, brave and new[16]

But this setting would not only have been very ordinary musically, it

also would have lost the boldness suggested by bringing in "brave" a-head of time; "cheap," "choice," and "new" are stressed with musical accent, but "brave" derives its stress from the longer note value and the effect of syncopation.

The last line of the song is Dowland's only departure from the structure of the poem: Here he divides the line at the grammatical caesura, repeating the second half in the manner of the madrigal. This is, of course, outside the character of the dance song, making this one something of a hybrid. In fact, Dowland wrote very few duple meter songs as rigidly structured as the triple meter dances. His second and third books contain a fair number of duple meter songs in a light vein in which repetition of the music for the first two lines with the second two is frequent. This repetition is also common in Campion. But in neither Dowland nor Campion is it indicative of actual dance meters so much as a convention in the lighter songs.

Among Dowland's freer, light duple time songs, should be mentioned "Say love if ever thou didst find," apparently a complimentary poem to the Queen. This poem is disarmingly regular in metric structure, except for the short third line and the surprising feminine ending on the last line of each stanza. The regular iambics make it possible for the melody to move rapidly along in consistent quarter notes, the divisions of the musical duple meter taking care of the accentuation of the text. Dowland's only moment of declamatory interpretation is in the half note on "*only* she" in the next to last line, striking in the context of so many even quarter notes.

Example 4.22.

John Dowland, "Say love if ever thou didst find." From *The Third Booke of Songs* (1603); *The English Lute-Songs*, Series I, Vol. 10/11, pp. 14-15. Ed. Edmund H. Fellowes. Rev. Thurston Dart and David Scott, 1970. Reproduced by permission of Stainer and Bell, Ltd. and Galaxy Music Corp.

Campion's songs in duple meter are virtually all of the sort discussed in Chapter 3, whether light or serious, in their regular equa-

tion of poetic meter with musical meter. Though with Campion I think the technique represents a definite attitude towards the musico-textual relationship, and not a giving-in to musical dictates in the lighter song styles, this treatment of poetic meter is also a typical feature of most of the duple meter, tuneful continuo songs.

John Wilson's "In the merry month of May" is such a song. The poem is by Nicholas Breton and was written for the Entertainment at Elvetham for Elizabeth in 1591. The original setting is difficult to date. It is found in Wilson's autograph manuscript (Oxford, Bodleian Library, MS Mus. b. 1), which Ian Spink dates around 1656,[17] and in several printed sources after that date; but the song may have been written much earlier, for Wilson was active in the music of the court as early as the 1620s.

The song is much like a Campion song. No musical repetition occurs, but the musical phrases, which correspond faithfully to the

Example 4.23.

John Wilson, "In the merry month of May." From *English Songs 1625-1660; Musica Britannica,* Vol. XXXIII, p. 54. Ed. Ian Spink, 1971. Reproduced by permission of Stainer and Bell, Ltd. on behalf of the Musica Britannica Trust, and by permission of Galaxy Music Corp.

lines of the poem, are equal in length, and almost equal in rhythmic and harmonic shape. The declamation is simple, in keeping with the

regular alternation of stressed and unstressed syllables that make up the poetic meter. Wilson uses nothing but the alternation of the duple musical meter to express the poetic meter. The declamation is in almost uninterrupted quarter notes, with the typical half note to mark the end of each line of the poem. The eighth-note runs are, again as in Campion, purely decorative and have no effect on declamation. (Those on "merry" could be said to have a pictorial function, but since the others do not seem to have any such function, this is unlikely.) Thus no interpretation of the poem is made through declamation beyond the placement of poetic meter in the musical meter so as not to violate normal word accentuation.

Wilson was not always this disarmingly simple, even in his light songs. "In a maiden time profess'd" is almost as simple, but here the rhythms are a little freer and note length is used to emphasize some syllables. Thus, in line 4, Wilson compresses the first two syllables so that the third is lengthened:

Example 4.24a.

John Wilson, "In a maiden time profess'd." From *English Songs 1625-1660; Musica Britannica*, Vol. XXXIII, p. 45. Ed. Ian Spink, 1971. Reproduced by permission of Stainer and Bell, Ltd. on behalf of the Musica Britannica Trust, and by permission of Galaxy Music Corp.

And in the last line, the most important syllable is lengthened even more:

Example 4.24b.

John Wilson, "In a maiden time profess'd," p. 45.

This technique will be common in Henry Lawes' songs, though far less frequent in the lighter songs than in the more declamatory ones.

But Wilson hardly ever becomes as monodic as Lawes, and this and most of his other tuneful songs incorporate some features from all styles, rather than distinguish the styles so clearly as Lawes.

Henry Lawes' works include rather few tuneful songs in duple meter. The ones that are may be distinguished by a more active bass line than the more declamatory songs and by a much smoother, less varied melodic line. His setting of Suckling's "Out upon it, I have lov'd" is a good instance. The song, like all of Lawes' tuneful songs, is very short. The bass line, although obviously harmonically con-

Example 4.25.

Henry Lawes, "Out upon it, I have lov'd." From *English Songs 1625-1660; Musica Britannica*, Vol. XXXIII, p. 67. Ed. Ian Spink, 1971. Reproduced by permission of Stainer and Bell, Ltd. on behalf of the Musica Britannica Trust, and by permission of Galaxy Music Corp.

ceived (no chromaticism, many leaps of fourths and fifths, clear movement within the key), has a little more shape than we shall see in the declamatory songs, where the bass is only a support for the declamation in the treble. Here, though it does support the harmonies of the song, it also has a musical melodic function, such as might be interesting for a violist to play. The treble, by contrast, is far less active than we shall see in the declamatory songs. There are no leaps larger than a third; the entire melody is so simple in conception that it appears to be merely a slightly decorated scale, descending the octave from c″ to c′ and then back up again. As in Wilson's "In the merry month of May," the declamation is not at all adventurous: The poetic meter is a regular alternation of stressed

and unstressed syllables, and the musical setting aligns the stresses with the metric pulses. The musical phrases are clearly shaped to the lines of the poem, and the only interesting feature is the extension of the feminine endings of lines 2 and 4 to make the musical phrases correspond in length with lines 1 and 3. But then, Suckling's text is certainly not one that invites a complex or highly emotional interpretation.

But, like Dowland, Lawes did not write many duple meter songs as simple as the triple meter ones. Even with lighter texts, in a duple meter he usually introduces declamatory elements. His setting of "Beauty and love once fell at odds," from *Wit and Drollery* (1655), shows us this hybrid style: The first line could well be taken for the simple technique of the triple meter dance songs:

Example 4.26.

Henry Lawes, "Beauty and love once fell at odds." From *English Songs 1625-1660; Musica Britannica*, Vol. XXXIII, p. 91. Ed. Ian Spink, 1971. Reproduced by permission of Stainer and Bell, Ltd. on behalf of the Musica Britannica Trust, and by permission of Galaxy Music Corp.

The declamation falls easily within the metrical structure of the music, accentuation is correct without being in any way exaggerated, and the poetic line is represented by the musical phrase—even to a pause at the caesura. With the second line, we begin to see some evidence that this mode is not to prevail. The line starts off the beat and moves quickly to the fourth syllable ("*revil'd*") where a long note draws attention to the word. From here on, the quality of vilification will dominate the declamation: The mood becomes brusque and abrupt in comparison to the lyrical tone suggested by the first line and "Beauty and love," so abrupt that the division between lines 5 and 6 is eliminated altogether in the portrayal of anger and spite. But these techniques belong to another style, to be considered in the next two chapters. The musically oriented style, giving precedence to musical factors over those of declamation, is no longer in operation.

Chapter 5
English Monody

One of the most interesting features of solo song in England during the first half of the seventeenth century is its tendency to split into markedly different types. The songs cover a broad spectrum in musical style and attitude toward the text—from light, musically conceived dance songs, and textually oriented songs in the French vein (whose musical style tends to be simple and structured in a manner similar to the dance songs), to more obviously textually oriented types of strophic song and the first tentative experiments with recitative: the English monody. At the latter end of the spectrum is the declamatory air. The term usually includes both strophic and through-composed songs in which a more or less passionate declamation of the text is the goal of the musical style; it would probably describe at least half of the songs by Caroline composers. Declamatory air is thus a useful general category, but within it is still a broad divergence in selection and treatment of the texts, and a further division seems in order if we are to understand the complex dissolution of the celebrated cooperation of music and poetry in England.

The monodic style is essentially textually oriented. The music exists to facilitate or enhance a recitation of the text. The songs we shall consider English monody are strictly through-composed and usually have no audible element of musical cohesion except tonality (and even that is not always stable in this period). The formal structure of the song is likely to be dependent on the narrative structure of the text (not, as in the songs considered in earlier chapters, on the verse structure). The rhythms, too, are dependent on the textual rhythms, typically derived from some conception of speech rhythm

(again not, as in some of the French-inspired songs, dependent on the meter alone), although the particular rhythmic style is determined also by other factors, such as Italian influence and the affective goal of the setting. Both are elements we shall take up below.

The epitome of this declamatory technique is, of course, the recitative of opera. The period with which we are dealing is of particular interest in this respect, since it saw the introduction of the recitative style in Italy and its spread throughout Europe during the next half-century. England did not develop a native opera at this point, however, and there is no recitative in the true sense of the word in England until after mid-century.[1] The songs of English monody are not true recitative, but what McDonald Emslie has termed "recitative songs."[2] The musical style is derived from the approach to declamation that characterized recitative, but the songs are self-contained rather than a part of a larger work, as we think of recitative. A few Jacobean songs seem to contain attempts to use the new monodic kind of declamation, but most of the English monodies are from the continuo song corpus of the Caroline period.

The "recitative musick" that began to appear in England, probably sometime before 1620, has several sources, both native and foreign. The setting of the kind of melancholy and pathetic texts associated with the monodic style in England has a long insular precedent in the dramatic laments sung in the choir-boy plays. The lament is a rhetorical set piece, didactic in function and assigned a specific place in the drama, and was a stock feature in English drama of the latter half of the sixteenth century. These set speeches would no doubt sometimes be spoken, but since we have both stage directions and extant musical sources for some,[3] we know that they were often sung in the context of the plays. The melancholy nature of the text is a feature that accompanies all phases of the declamatory song, but several features of these dramatic laments are relevant specifically to the development of English monody.

The lament texts originally were part of the drama, but because they were rhetorical set pieces, they took on a formulary structure that was easily imitated and easily dissociated from the play. Typically spoken by a woman who has lost her husband or lover, either through desertion or through death, the laments almost always begin with an invocation to the gods, often include a call to the forces of Nature (the sea, the wind, etc.), and conclude with the speaker's

desire for death. In its elemental adherence to this structural pattern, this early lament by Richard Farrant is typical:

> (Ah, ah), alas, you salt sea gods!
> Bow down your ears divine
> Lend ladies here warm water springs
> To moist their crystal eyne,
> That they may weep and wail
> And wring their hands with me
> For death of lord and husband mine:
> Alas, (Alas, alas alas), lo this is he!
> You gods! that guide the ghosts
> And souls of them that fled
> Send sobs, send sighs, send grievous groans,
> And strike poor Panthea dead.
> Abradad. Abradad.
> Ah, ah, alas poor Abradad!
> My sprite with thine shall lie.
> Come, death, alas, O death most sweet,
> For now I crave to die, (to die, to die, to die, to die).[4]

It is difficult to determine just how or when the laments became autonomous enough to have a separate identity, but their inclusion in manuscript song books from the Elizabethan and Jacobean periods attests to the possibility of their existence in isolation from the original source, and their typical structural pattern appears in other poems not associated with particular plays. As separate poems, the laments became more elaborate, building in some instances an integral dramatic structure on the rhetorical formulas. These poems are related to the more generalized Elizabethan genre of the complaint poem in which the victim, often feminine, recites her tragedy; they are, in addition, often linked to the Ovidian subject material popular at the turn of the century.[5] But most important here, although these pieces grow through the accretion of nondramatic poetic tendencies and lose their association with staged drama, the laments continue to be standard text material for a dramatic kind of solo vocal setting— so much so that the two most significant Caroline monodies, Nicholas Lanier's *Hero and Leander* and Henry Lawes' *Ariadne*, have elaborate, Ovidian lament texts following the structural formula outlined above. Furthermore, both texts probably were written specifically to be set to music. Monteverdi's famous *Lamento d'Arianna* is often

cited as the inspiration for these two Caroline monodies, but more probable is that they all have a common ancestor. With Monteverdi's lament we know of its dramatic origin and eventual separation from that context. In the Lanier and Lawes examples, the dissociation from the drama is a prior condition; they are clearly autonomous pieces.

Yet it is not unlikely that a lament text, set to solo vocal music, would retain some association with the drama in the minds of the courtly audience that heard it. This is another crucial point of contact between the earlier dramatic laments and Caroline monody. The revolution in musical style occurring in Italy at the turn of the seventeenth century was inherently related to the drama; the ultimate goal of the musical declamation was a dramatic presentation of the text, and the ultimate result in Italy was recitative. English composers had at their disposal the highly rhetorical convention of the musically declaimed lament, originally associated with drama and therefore expected to be in some measure dramatic, but self-contained and conventional enough that it could be removed from the context of the play. Unwilling or unable to create a music drama in English (perhaps because of the enormous strength of spoken drama after the turn of the century), composers seized upon a musical and rhetorical convention, related to the drama, as a vehicle for the development of an English dramatic musical language along the lines of what they knew to be developing in Italy.

It has been argued that the special performing conditions of the drama, and particularly of the masque, provide the source for the declamatory musical style in England.[6] The association with the stage is unquestionably an important factor in the growth of English monody, but not in so direct a manner. The songs that are the clearest examples of English monody are, as we saw above, once removed from their connection with the drama, and because they are once removed, they must create their own dramatic situation to have a suitable context for the emotional declamation that is their essential musical feature. Their texts become, in fact, like cantata texts, with the entire dramatic framework worked into the narration, except that, like their forebears, they are still first-person complaints with all the conventional invocations and rhetorical gestures. These are chamber pieces, not staged drama, though their roots are easily traceable to dramatic sources.

Musically, the earlier dramatic laments have little in common with monody, except insofar as they are sung by a solo voice. As in these lines from the Farrant lament cited above, the declamation of the text is typically very clear and direct, almost always syllabic, and with very little rhythmic variety. Interpretation of the text seems to

Example 5.1.

Richard Farrant, "Ah, ah, alas, you salt sea gods." From *Consort Songs; Musica Britannica*, Vol. XXII, p. 15. Ed. Philip Brett, 1967. Reproduced by permission of Stainer and Bell, Ltd. on behalf of the Musica Britannica Trust, and by permission of Galaxy Music Corp.

be left to the dramatic abilities of the singer. The accompaniment to these laments is usually a consort of viols (although some appear in manuscript with lute tablatures, and in at least one instance a stage direction indicates regals).[7] It is the relationship between the vocal

line and the accompaniment that sets them apart from monodic developments, for although the lines of the text are clearly and individually declaimed, the intervals between lines are filled up by the continuous polyphony of the accompaniment. A continuous texture will, at the least, impart to the piece the kind of distance from the text that the polyphonic motet has. John Stevens comments that "The peculiar effect of music in this type of play . . . is to intensify the emotional climaxes—moments of parting, of death, of utter misery."[8] But such effects can have been achieved only by setting these moments apart from the dialogue of the play; the music itself is not vividly dramatic or emotional—certainly not in comparison with the contemporary Italian style nor with the musical style of the Caroline monodies.

There is thus a plausible native line of development for the general type of piece and choice of texts for the English monodies. The musical style, on the other hand, must be seen as an English reaction to the development of recitative and monody in Italy. Actually very little monody of the Italian sort occurs in England, but to deny the influence of the new Italian style on English song at the turn of the century, as some writers have done,[9] seems unjustifiable. Some songs from the lute song collections bear definite indications of familiarity with Italian recitative, and Caroline monody presents us with various attempts to graft Italian conventions on an English tradition.

Italian monody was essentially a musical revolution; it does not seem to have accompanied a major upheaval in literary taste in the way that the new musical ideals in France did. As a new musical style, Italian monody was definitely known in England, whether or not the English were aware of its goals and implications. The books of English lute songs published around 1610, for instance, show a number of signs of at least a superficial awareness of Italian musical styles. Several Italian songs are to be found in printed and manuscript sources of this period, some by Italian composers like Caccini, some by English composers like Ferrabosco, Coperario, and even John Dowland. There are manuscript versions of English lute songs from this period that omit the lute tablature, giving the piece at least the appearance of the treble-bass polarity that was current in Italy and soon to dominate England too, and in which the treble is often lavishly embellished in the Italian manner. Most important of all, however, is the evidence in English songs of various attempts to grasp the significance of Italian monody.

The monodic style of writing for the voice, which swept Italy around the turn of the seventeenth century, had its roots—like those of musique mesurée in France—in the humanists' desire to return to the ancient conception of lyric in which music and poetry were interdependent, if not virtually inseparable. The ultimate goal was the re-creation of the storied effects, by making music subservient to text. But whereas the French approach to the re-creation of this ideal union of music and text was to fuse the rhythm and meter of the two, thus making music an extension of the verse structure, the Italian approach was much more concerned with the projection of the "affetti" or the emotions of the text through its narrative structure and ultimately with the dramatic possibilities of such a union.[10]

The Italians most strongly influenced by humanism, and in particular those associated with the Florentine Camerata, believed that all ancient Greek music was monodic, and deduced from this the further belief that it was through the words that the ethical powers of Greek music were effective.[11] This point cannot be too strongly urged, for it is here that we find the most significant break with the past. In the sixteenth century, *musica reservata,* as well as the techniques of the madrigalists, had sought to represent the words musically.[12] The quarrel was not that earlier composers were oblivious of the text, but that in representing the text through music, they lost the text itself.[13] For this reason the primary doctrine of the Camerata and its successors was that music be in the service of the text, and not vice versa. There is ample evidence for this position in the writings of the members of the Camerata,[14] and even composers of the stature of Caccini and Monteverdi, both of whom brought a great deal of the purely musical to their actual composition, were active verbal defenders of the doctrine of supremacy of text over music.[15]

Italian monodists, therefore, had two main goals: intelligibility of the text, and the rhetorical function of portrayal of the emotions in the text. These two goals were related in practice, for intelligibility was accomplished through a declamation that heightened the emotions, not through strictly musical means but dramatically, in such a way that the singer assumes the character of the poet's persona.[16] Given these two goals, monody was the logical medium. The homophony of musique mesurée, although it did provide intelligibility, was not so amenable to a dramatic portrayal of emotion. The detailed way in which monodic declamation was used in the service of

these goals in Italy is discussed more specifically below; for the moment I wish only to emphasize the dual nature of the monodists' aim, for the English reaction to the humanist monody is a groping for the real significance of the style through piecemeal adoption of its various facets—its technical approach to declamation, its emphasis on intelligibility, and its complementary emphasis on emotional rhetoric.

Monody first began to appear in Italy—if we can credit Caccini's claim in his *Nuove musiche*[17] —sometime in the 1580s. "Perfidissimo volto," a solo madrigal, is one of the songs Caccini lists as having been performed for the members of the Camerata as representative of the new expressive medium. In it we can see techniques that made the recitative style a radical departure from the polyphonic madrigal, techniques obviously devised to facilitate the understanding of the text: the many repeated notes and narrow conjunct melodies that re-place flowing melodic lines in the madrigals; the clear cadences at the ends of lines of verse, breaking the whole into small units markedly different from the continuous web of polyphony; the placement (as Caccini indicates in his preface)[18] of chords on stressed syllables; and most important, the strict polarity of the melodic, rhythmically active treble over a rather stable and slow-moving bass line. These features are all designed to allow for intelligibility of the text and were to be used, even exaggerated, in the development of operatic recitative and the dramatic monodies that became popular in the first quarter of the seventeenth century.

Caccini himself did not often utilize such a spare style of musical speech in his later songs, but worked more with the other humanistic aspect of the new style, the portrayal of the emotions. But Jacopo Peri, credited with the composition of the first real opera, established his reputation on a kind of declamation that was barely melodic in its strict imitation of speech. Pietro de' Bardi, son of the patron of the Camerata, would recollect of these two composers, "Peri had more science, and having found a way of imitating speech by using few sounds and by meticulous exactness in other respects, he won great fame. Giulio's [Caccini's] inventions had more elegance."[19] The sparse speaking style did engender some notable examples and set a standard for absolute clarity of declamation. Monteverdi did not essay the recitative style for some years after it was introduced, but when he did, he showed himself to be fully aware of its aims and

implications. Though a little outside the framework of this study because its text is (most unusually) prose, Monteverdi's *lettera amorosa*
"Se i languidi miei sguardi" is an example of the purest monody outside the context of opera.[20] It is a virtual case study in the techniques
of declamation that were conventions of the Italian style, and, as
such, were imitated by English composers. This, and his "Lamento
d'Arianna," will illustrate the conventions and their source in the service of the text.

As in Caccini's "Perfidissimo volto," one of the most immediately
apparent features in "Se i languidi" is the large number of word
phrases that are set to the same note, or to narrow, conjunct melodic
lines that usually include repeated notes. Pitch accent is not commonly featured within the phrase, although pitch is regularly used to
delineate the ends of phrases, always in a manner that reflects the
structure of the Italian language and indicates the extent to which
the conventions of declamation were evolved in the service of intelligibility of the text. The inflectional character of the language makes
for many polysyllabic words, which are more often than not accented
on the penultimate syllable; phrases and clauses therefore will close
with a feminine cadence. Monteverdi's method of signalling the
phrase endings is to drop the pitch of the antepenultimate syllable,
raising it back to the prevailing pitch for the final two syllables. In
this way the stress that seems to be naturally felt with a rise in pitch
is placed on the accented penultimate syllable, without losing the
nonmelodic quality achieved by setting the phrase to a single note:[21]

Example 5.2.

Se i lan - gui - di miei sguar - di   se i sos -pir in-ter-rot - ti

Claudio Monteverdi, "Lettera amorosa." From *Arie, canzonette et recitativi, p. 7.*
Ed. G. Grancesco Malipiero. Copyright © 1953. By kind permission of G. Ricordi
& C. S. p. A., Milano (Italy).

Since his text is prose, Monteverdi does not have the breaks provided
by the lines of poetry and often has long grammatical constructions
to work with. These he shapes in the same manner, dropping the
pitch on the syllable before the one he wants to be particularly accented, as in the first line of the following example at "scorgerete"

and "pensieri." An alternative method, when the text is moving to some climactic point, is to raise the pitch slowly, by stepwise progression, towards the end of the phrase:

Example 5.3.

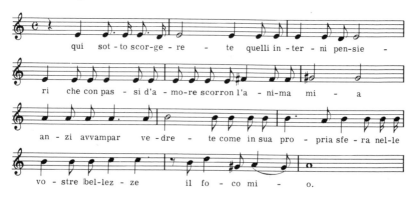

Claudio Monteverdi, "Lettera amorosa," p. 8.

In any of these examples it is obvious that pitch changes are in the service of textual clarity, not of musical melodiousness. The vocal line has a static, nonmelodic quality that is reinforced by an even more static bass line, which stays on the same pitch for five or six measures at a time. Against this static pitch background the rhythmic values assigned to the syllables assume almost complete authority in declamation. Here, too, certain patterns are particularly important in the development of English monody.

First is the large number of phrases that begin as musical upbeats. The upbeat entrance figure appears as early as 1600 in the recitative of Jacopo Peri,[22] although it does not seem to have been so popular as to be a mannerism until the second decade of the century. Only moderately used in Caccini's songs, the figure became so prominent in the recitative style that a piece like the *"Lamento d'Arianna"* could make an expressive feature of the reverse. By the 1620s the upbeat had become a convention, and by the 1630s, especially in the three-note form we shall examine below, it was so much of a cliché in both Italy and England that a present-day commentator can refer to the "odd-rest group" as the defining characteristic of the declamatory song.[23]

Monteverdi uses the upbeat figure often and skillfully. In the

Lettera amorosa most of the phrases begin on an upbeat; in the lament, all but five. Yet Monteverdi avoids monotony by using the figure in a natural and varied manner, conforming precisely with the rhythm of the text. The natural rhythm in Italian is directed much more strongly toward the phrase accent than in English, where individual word accents are felt. When Monteverdi uses the three-note upbeat, it is usually to set a prepositional or adverbial phrase, sweeping through initial, unstressed syllables to the more crucial syllable of the phrase accent.

In Italian, the frequent combination of a monosyllabic preposition and an inflected (and therefore often bisyllabic) adjective or adverb leading to the noun or important adjective provides many opportunities to use the three-note upbeat to set the natural rhythm; and the large number of vowels, particularly at the ends of words (again because they are inflected), facilitates this naturally swinging phrase rhythm in the language. We shall find that English, on the contrary, has relatively few naturally occurring opportunities to use this rhythmic figure.

A corollary of the increasing use made of upbeat phrasing is the special effect gained from a downbeat. Musical meter is not always clearly defined in a monodic style; a regular metric accent cannot be assumed in any songs of this period except the dance-derived songs. Nevertheless, there are metric pulses that imply a certain amount of stress. In the songs with basso continuo (or with any harmonically directed bass line, as the bass viol parts accompanying the lute songs often are) the bass line will play a large part in defining metric stress. In the Arianna lament, for instance, the bass line proceeds in units that the ear perceives as regular beats, in this case the smallest perceptible unit being the half note.[24] The harmonies implied by the bass line will have some effect on whether one particular beat gets more stress than another, as will the rate of harmonic rhythm. But Monteverdi works on the level of the beat itself as well. Of the many phrase beginnings in the lament, only five begin directly on one of the half note pulses, that is, in conjunction with a note of the bass

line and therefore directly with a chord of the accompaniment. Two of these phrases are emphatic, angry questions; two are exclamations ("Ahi, che pur non respondi"); and the last is the wonderfully understated pathos of "Misera" opening the final section of the piece. Because individual word accent is not a significant factor in Italian, the composer can shape the phrase to suit his interpretation without distorting declamation. These verbal phrases all begin with relatively stressed syllables, but so do others in the piece; Monteverdi has singled these out for particular emphasis by beginning them on strong beats.

The second rhythmic convention the English borrowed from the recitative style in Italy governs the overall shape of longer phrases, whether they begin on or off the beat. Many of the phrases in "Se i languidi" begin on a relatively long note value, speed up in the middle, and come to rest again on longer notes; if the phrase is very long, it will have median points of stress/length, but will have typically a rapid swing from one phrase-stress/long-note-value to the next. The polarity of treble and bass is an important factor, for the bass (defining the harmonic rhythm) reinforces the points of stress and thus emphasizes the unaccented swing between stresses. This pattern, like the others, is derived from the characteristic stress patterns of Italian.

Monteverdi is setting prose in the *Lettera amorosa*, but the pattern is even clearer in Italian poetry. The meter of Italian verse is syllabic— that is, the element of organization is the number of syllables, not the placement of accents as in accentual English verse. Because the Italian language has so many words with the stress on the penultimate syllable, a line of Italian verse invariably has a feminine ending. The resultant penultimate stress is the only accent requisite in the line; one or two others may occur, depending on the length of the line, but their placement is irregular, and the rhythm of the line is decidedly not the jog-trot iambic accentuation that characterizes English verse. The musical rhythmic pattern described above, sometimes referred to as "festooning," is therefore quite in keeping with the stress pattern of the line of Italian verse with two or three stressed syllables, and a swing in smooth, steady declamation in between stresses.

Monteverdi's musical rendering of the pattern has considerable rhythmic variety within this conventional context, note values varying freely from whole note to sixteenth. There are, however,

relatively few dotted rhythms (Example 5.3 above is typical); his music is, in fact, notable for the large number of undifferentiated eighth-notes sometimes strung together—four or six being very common—in a "festoon" between phrase stresses. The relative lack of individual word stress in Italian means that a rhythmically undifferentiated sweep through the middle of a phrase will not distort its pronunciation or syntactical clarity. The sense of the words is not affected by a declamation that avoids articulation of stressed and unstressed syllables for long stretches. Furthermore, the supposed mellifluousness of Italian, attributable at least in part to the number, quality, and placement of vowels, makes it possible to pronounce every syllable as fully as in spoken language, in rapid, even note values.

In English, of course, the situation is quite different. We shall turn now to some early English attempts at a monodic style, the question before us being whether particular features are superficial imitation of detail, or whether they have the same goal as Italian monody, working with the characteristics of the English language.

One of the earliest English imitators of the Italian monodic style was Giovanni Coperario. As John Cooper he may have been to Italy in the early years of the century and may even have sung in one of the first Italian operas.[25] He is certainly one of the few English composers of the earlier part of the period who had direct contact with the Italian style, though the extent of his Italian-ness has been the subject of debate. Coperario is known primarily as a composer of music for viol consort and some masque songs, most of which are in a light vein, decidedly not Italianate. He also wrote two sets of threnodies, one on the death of the Earl of Mountjoy (*Funeral Teares,* 1606) and one, with texts by Thomas Campion, on the death of Prince Henry *(Songs of Mourning,* 1613), both of which seem to contain highly derivative attempts at monodic declamation. Although they have a much greater polarity between treble and bass than most of the songs of this period, these songs do not sound much like Monteverdi or Caccini: Coperario's melodies are much freer ranging and have little if any word-painting, and his bass line is generally like the lute-song bass, more active than the Italian continuo bass line. But the declamation in these songs, the rhythmic articulation of syllables, is unlike anything in England before this period, and quite like the rhythmic conventions of early Italian recitative.

"How like a golden dream," the fifth of the *Songs of Mourning*, is a good example. The musical rhythms of the first line are typical of this entire set of songs—starting on a long note, rushing through the middle of the line with shorter note values moving faster than the harmonic rhythm or the bass line (often in even eighth notes), and coming to rest at the end of the line with a long note again—in effect, "festooning" the line in the same manner as Monteverdi.

Example 5.4.

How   like a   gol-den dream you met and part - ed

John Coprario, "How like a golden dream." From *Songs of Mourning* (1613); *The English Lute-Songs*, Series I, Vol. 17, p. 30. Transcribed and ed. Gerald Hendrie and Thurston Dart, 1959. Reproduced by permission of Stainer and Bell, Ltd. and Galaxy Music Corp.

Coperario has not followed the Italian melodic conventions but has tried to go Monteverdi one better with a melodic "festoon" as well, his melody sweeping down the octave and then back up, rather than hovering around one pitch as Monteverdi's phrases of this sort do.[26] The effect, of course, in Coperario's case is purely musical, and, if anything, distorts the text rather than making it more intelligible through a musical rendering of speech rhythms. The even declamation has instead the effect of preventing any kind of interpretive emphasis on particular syllables, and smooths out the natural accentual pattern of the verse.[27] Campion surely cannot have intended that first line to be read without articulation after "dream" and "met." In the second line, Coperario's desire to festoon has led to a rhythmic misinterpretation, as shown in example 5.5. A comma after "pleasing" might have helped the composer; as it stands the singer must rush through "pleasing straight," making nonsense of the line.

This kind of syntactic awkwardness is surprisingly common in an age renowned for the cooperation of musicians and poets, but it seems to be most common in songs, like this one, whose rhythms follow a pattern similar to the conventional rhythms of the new Italian recitative style. The purpose of Coperario's declamatory

Example 5.5.

That   pleas-ing straight doth va-nish:

John Coprario, "How like a golden dream," p. 30.

rhythms here is apparently the imitation of impassioned, grief-stricken speech in keeping with his subject (and it is worth pointing out that the threnody is a nondramatic form of lament); but the song is not successful because it fails to take into account the necessarily accentual nature of the English language. One can only infer that Coperario really did not know the Italian language well enough to understand the relationship of the musical rhythms to the rhythm of the language, and that his imitation of the style was therefore based on only part of the humanist doctrine, the rhetorical and ethical function of music. The musical language of these threnodies does establish a mood of uncontrolled and uncontrollable grief. The broad, almost reckless sweeps of the melodic line are, in fact, baroque in their extravagant portrayal of passion. But the passion is musical, and does not come through the words themselves, as was advocated by the proponents of monody.

The use of these rhythmic conventions, however, was prevalent among English composers around 1610, most often in setting texts of a doleful nature. John Danyel's songs (1606), especially the three-section threnody ("Grief keep within") and the three-section plaint ("Can doleful notes"), contain many upbeat phrase beginnings and strings of undifferentiated eighth notes.

Example 5.6.

And   sor -row none that is   her   own

John Danyel, "Grief keep within." From *Songs for the Lute, Viol and Voice* (1606); *The English Lute-Songs*, Series II, Vol. 8, p. 29. Ed. Edmund H. Fellowes. Rev. Thurston Dart, and David Scott, 1970. Reproduced by permission of Stainer and Bell, Ltd. and Galaxy Music Corp.

Alfonso Ferrabosco the Younger uses similar rhythmic patterns both in setting Italian, where he shows his familiarity with the style of Monteverdi, and in setting English, where he sometimes falls into the same awkward declamation as Coperario:

Example 5.7.

Con _____ quel-la in si-di - o - sa

Alfonso Ferrabosco II, "O Crudel' Amarilli." From *Manuscript Songs; The English Lute-Songs*, Series II, Vol. 19, p. 33. Ed. Ian Spink, 1966. Reproduced by permission of Stainer and Bell, Ltd. and Galaxy Music Corp.

Example 5.8.

could   I sus - pect that thine

Alfonso Ferrabosco II, "Was I to blame?" From *Manuscript Songs; The English Lute-Songs*, Series II, Vol. 19, p. 7. Ed. Ian Spink, 1966. Reproduced by permission of Stainer and Bell, Ltd. and Galaxy Music Corp.

Even John Dowland fell under the spell of the new rhythmic style, though he seems to have been more selective than his contemporaries. The upbeat rhythmic motive is frequent in Dowland's later songs and is used to good effect in such songs as "Far from triumphing court," and "In darkness let me dwell" (though Dowland's devotion to strophic texts reduces the effectiveness somewhat). However, the groups of undifferentiated notes that do not coincide with the bass line, which we have seen to be the cause of declamatory awkwardness in setting English, are almost entirely absent from Dowland's works.[28] Other examples of Italian rhythmic mannerisms may be found in the lute-songs of almost every composer active in the second decade of the century (with the notable exception of Thomas Campion, whose use of them is infrequent).

This rhythmic style is quite different from anything found in the first decade of lute-songs, where there is often a strong relationship to dance rhythms. In these lamentlike songs the rhythms obviously are not devised to fit a musical pattern, but rather to express the

text. It is noteworthy that none of the songs just mentioned (except those by Dowland) is strophic, and the composers seem to have been trying to work closely with the rhythms of their texts. But these songs are still a long way from monody. The rhythmic motives usually are merely gestures at monodic declamation in the context of the more musically derived rhythms of the lute-song. We do not have monody until the rhythmic style of the entire piece is derived from the rhythms of impassioned or dramatic speech.

Because of the dramatic function of Italian monody and the development of opera along with the recitative style, it would seem reasonable to expect that the nearest English approaches to recitative also would be in connection with the drama, or perhaps with that hybrid Jacobean entertainment, the masque. Ian Spink, who argues that the declamatory style took hold because of the new performance requirements that solo songs be presented from the stage rather than among friends, goes so far as to deny any Italian influence, claiming for the masque the raison d'être for the monodic tendency in England:

> It was the special requirements of the masque-song that brought about the origins of the English declamatory style. . . . In the masque, a ceremonial, heroic rather pretentious type of song (and singing) was called for and this is what Ben Jonson provided in association first with Ferrabosco, then Lanier. Lanier's song 'Bring away this sacred tree' [which is from Campion's *Squire's Masque*] is really the earliest ayre that is clearly of the same type as that which flourished towards the middle of the century. It is almost impossible to attribute circumstantial evidence of Italian influence.[29]

Lanier's "Bring away this sacred tree" does have a definitely declamatory musical style, and we shall look at it in a moment. But first it should be pointed out that most of the surviving masque songs are far less declamatory than this one; in fact, many of them have a tuneful simplicity comparable to the dance songs. Coperario, who was interested enough in passionate declamation to try it in another context, wrote in a very different, more frankly "songlike" style in his masque music. Ferrabosco wrote some slightly declamatory masque songs, but was also capable of a dance tune like this one for Jonson's *Oberon* (1611):

Example 5.9.

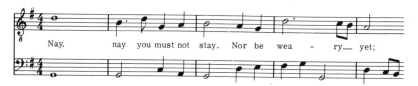

Alfonso Ferrabosco II, "Nay, nay, you must not stay." From *Four Hundred Songs and Dances from the Stuart Masque*, p. 62, by Andrew J. Sabol. Brown University Press, 1978. ©1978 by Brown University.

Lanier's "Bring away this sacred tree" has features in common with the monodic style and has been called justifiably "Our earliest dateable declamatory ayre."[30] But an unprovable suspicion leads me to discount even this song as evidence that the conditions of the masque led to the particular musical style used. Our earliest source for this song is Campion's masque of 1613, but shortly thereafter, and in most later sources, Lanier's music was known with the words "Weep no more my wearied eyes." Emslie makes note of this, saying that "the declamatory setting is so rudimentary and unsubtle that it could easily be fitted to other lyrics having a similar stanza-form."[31] I suggest that it may be Campion's text that is the contrafactum, for though the monodic style is indeed rudimentary, it is not really unsubtle when fitted to the alternate text. And the doleful character of "Weep no more" makes it much more the kind of text set in a declamatory style in this period.

The declamatory rhythms, although not exactly wrong in the Campion version, are more convincingly placed in "Weep no more," with regard not only to correct accentuation but also to interpretive emphasis. The first four lines of the latter text contain many references to weariness and grief: "wearied eyes," "sad lamenting," "Mournful cries"; and their cause: "my tormenting." These Lanier has carefully underlined musically by dwelling on them. The same long notes that outline a pattern of sorrow in "Weep no more," with Campion's text give us a declamation that is at best unsubtle, and at worst awkward, as shown in example 5.10. The only conventional monodic rhythms in this half of the song are the upbeat entrances, or "odd-rest groups" as Emslie calls them, [32] but in the second half of the song Lanier makes increased use of the even speech rhythms in the Italian examples and in Coperario. Here

Example 5.10.

Nicholas Lanier, "Bring away this sacred tree." From *Four Hundred Songs and Dances from the Stuart Masque*, p. 76-77, by Andrew J. Sabol. Brown University Press, 1978. ©1978 by Brown University.

again the declamation falls more comfortably with the anonymous lines than with Campion's, especially when Lanier's use of melodic shaping as an aid to articulation is taken into account (e.g., the three-note scale to set "endlessly" rather than "any sup-," the leap emphasizing "to her," and the ornament on "I" rather than "a"):

Example 5.11.

Nicholas Lanier, "Weep no more my wearied eyes." From *English Songs 1625-1660; Musica Britannica*, Vol. XXXIII, p. 1. Ed. Ian Spink, 1971. Reproduced by permission of Stainer and Bell, Ltd. on behalf of the Musica Britannica Trust, and by permission of Galaxy Music Corp. "Bring away this sacred tree." From *Four Hundred Songs and Dances from the Stuart Masque*, pp. 76-77, by Andrew J. Sabol. Brown University Press, 1978. ©1978 by Brown University.

If Lanier wrote the music for the text "Weep no more," then we can discount Campion's masque as the source of his desire to write in a dramatic, declamatory style. But whichever version we take as the first, the song is not in any case a monody or a recitative song, for in its most common form it is strophic. This kind of song, the strophic song in a quasimonodic style, I take to be the real declamatory air and will discuss it in the next chapter. Lanier's song is of particular interest to us here, however, because it is one of the first sustained attempts to adapt the Italian style to the English language. The style

is at times reminiscent of Coperario's abortive attempt, but generally reflects a better grasp of the purpose: to allow the text to express its emotions. Dowland worked well with the speech rhythms of the English language, but musically his songs are more closely related to the English madrigal than to Italian monody. Lanier's song has the treble-bass polarity, the upbeat entrances and varied rhythms directed by the rhythms of the text, and the lack of external musical organization that, taken together, characterize the recitative style. But, more important, Lanier was one of the few English composers of the century to write a real monody in the Italian manner, adapting the style to the English language.

Hero and Leander, although its early history is curiously obscure, seems to have been one of the most celebrated and popular pieces of the century. Playford published it in his *Choice Ayres and Songs* of 1683, and it is also extant in several manuscript sources, though all date from late in the century.[33] Roger North praises it repeatedly in his retrospective writings, and Samuel Pepys thought enough of it to have it copied out for his own use. Emslie has surveyed the references to *Hero and Leander,* again mainly from the second half of the century, and concludes that Lanier wrote the piece sometime after 1628, when he returned from a trip to Italy.[34] This seems to be as close as we can come to a dating, but whatever its date *Hero and Leander* is an obvious imitation of the recitative style of Italian monody. An imitation it must be called, for it is demonstrably dependent on Italian models. Nonetheless, it is of importance, for Lanier, in his grasp of the significance of the style, has come a long way from the superficial imitations of the first two decades of the seventeenth century.

Our discussion thus far has been concerned primarily with that facet of Italian monody that leads to the clearest intelligibility of the text. We have seen how the melodic and rhythmic conventions of Italian monody are derived from the natural rhythms of the language and how these conventional rhythms might be borrowed wholesale and forced onto the English language. But of course the musical language of Italian monody is also highly emotional. The rhythms of the upbeat phrase beginnings and "festooning" of lines fit the rhythms of the language and allow the emotion expressed in the text to be understood, but they also add to the emotional content in the same way that a dramatic reading adds to the effect of a text. Declamation

per se is Lanier's most strikingly Italianate feature. In discussing *Hero and Leander* we shall look first at Lanier's obvious borrowings of rhythmic conventions, but it will soon be clear that he uses the conventions in very specific responses to the emotional content of his text. Although the rhythmic figures do not always set the text with the most natural English accentuation, they are not the general kind of imitation that Coperario attempted but reflect a direct concern that the text be clearly and emotionally expressed.

The rhythmic conventions of Italian monody are everywhere apparent in *Hero and Leander*. The opening phrase contains the three-note upbeat figure, awkwardly fitted to an English mouthful of consonants that would normally be pronounced in something much closer to an iambic rhythm: "Nor com'st thou yet?" The figure sometimes fits the phrase rhythm of the text (e.g., "to be thy guide," or "and even now,") but more often than not it imparts a rhythm that is not natural to English poetry:

Example 5.12.

Nicholas Lanier, "Hero and Leander." From *English Songs 1625-1660; Musica Britannica*, Vol. XXXIII, p. 13. Ed. Ian Spink, 1971. Reproduced by permission of Stainer and Bell, Ltd. on behalf of the Musica Britannica Trust, and by permission of Galaxy Music Corp.

Yet Lanier uses the three-note upbeat at least thirty times in the course of the piece, and other upbeat configurations begin many of the phrases. Similarly, the strings of undifferentiated eighth notes, which worked so smoothly in setting the unaccented sections of the line of Italian poetry, find an uneasy match with Lanier's English text:

Example 5.13.

Nicholas Lanier, "Hero and Leander," p. 18.

Yet this kind of parlando declamation dominates entire sections of *Hero and Leander* and almost as few dotted rhythms are present here as in Monteverdi. Lanier is guilty of the same kind of literal borrowing of rhythmic patterns that Coperario and Danyel tried, with hardly better rhythmic justification for his attempt. Lanier's justification lay in a much deeper grasp of the emotional goal of Italian monody, and to see the depth of his understanding we must look at his text in some detail.

> Nor com'st thou yet, my slothful love, nor yet;
> Leander! O my Leander! can'st thou forget
> Thy Hero? Leander! Why dost thou stay?
> Who holds thee, cruel! What hath begot delay?
> Too soon, alas, the rosy-finger'd morn
> Will chase the darksome night, Ah me! I burn,
> And die in these my languishing desires.
> See, see the taper wastes in his own fires,
> Like me, and will be spent before you come;
> Make haste then, my Leander, prithee come.　　　　10
> Behold the winds and seas, deaf and enrag'd,
> My imprecations have in part assuag'd;
> Their fury's past, but thou more deaf than they
> More merciless, torment'st me with delay.
>
> If far from hence upon thy native shore
> Such high delights thou tak'st, why did'st thou more
> Incite my hot desires with faithless lines,
> Flattering me with promise that when the winds
> Became less high, and shores had some repose,
> If I did but the friendly torch expose　　　　20
> To be thy guide, thou would'st not fail to come.
>
> The shores have peace, the winds and seas are dumb;
> Thy Hero here attends thee, and the light
> Invades the horror of the sable night.
> Come quickly then, and in these arms appear.
> That have been oft thy chiefest calm, thy sphere.
>
> Wretch that I am! 'tis so! ye gods, 'tis so!
> Whilst here I vent to heav'n and seas my woe,
> He at Abydos in a newer flame,
> Forgets that e'er he heard poor Hero's name.　　　　30
> Ah! lighter than blossoms, or the fleeting air

That sheds them; How, oh how can'st thou repair
Thy broken faith? Is this the dear respect
Thou bear'st to oaths and vows, thus to neglect
Both Citherea and her nun? Is this
The inviolable band of Hymen! this
The knot before the sacred altar made
Of sea-born Venus? Heav'ns lend your aid
And arm yourselves in thunder.

Oh! but stay!
What vain thoughts transport thee, Hero? Away   40
With jealous fury! Leander's thine, thou his;
And the poor youth at home lamenting is
The wary eyes of his old parents. Now
Steals from them apace unto the shore; now
With hasty hand doth fling his robes from him,
And even now, bold boy, attempts to swim,
Parting the swelling waves with iv'ry arms,
Borne up alone by love's all-pow'rful charms.

You gentle, peaceful winds; if ever love
Had pow'r in you, if ever you did prove   50
Least spark of Cupid's flame, for pity's sake,
With softest gales more smooth and easy make
The troubled floods unto my soul's delight.
You show'rs! you storms and tempests black as night,
Retire your fury till my love appear,
And bless these shores in safety, and I here
Within my arms enfold my only treasure.
Then all enrag'd with horror, send at pleasure
The frothy billows high as heav'n that he
May here for e'er be forc'd to dwell with me.   60

But hark! O wonder! What sudden storm is this?
Seas menace heav'ns, and the winds do hiss
In scorn of this my just request. Retire!
Retire my too too vent'rous love, retire!
Tempt not the angry seas! Ah me! Ah me! the light,
The light's blown out. O Gods! O deadly night!

Neptune! Aeolus! Ye pow'rful deities!
Spare, O spare my jewel; pity the cries
And tears of wretched Hero. 'Tis Leander,
Trusts you with his love and life; fair Leander,   70

Beauty of those shores. See! see the bashful morn,
For sorrow of my great laments, hath torn
Through cloudly night a passage to my aid.
And here beneath, amidst the horrid shade,
By her faint light, something methinks I spy
Resembling my soul's joy.
Woe's me!
'Tis he,
Drown'd by th'impetuous floods. O dismal hour!
Curst be the seas, these shores, this light, this tow'r.
In spite of fate, dear love, to thee I come;
Leander's bosom shall be Hero's tomb.[35]   80

The *Hero and Leander* story is from Ovid's *Heroides* and is of the genre of the brief epic. Ovidian tales were extremely popular source material for Elizabethan and Jacobean poets. Christopher Marlowe's lengthy *Hero and Leander* is one of the best known examples of the cult. Lanier's text is not from Marlowe—in fact, I have not been able to trace it in any source other than Lanier's setting—but is an obvious imitation of the genre,[36] using not only the same story as Marlowe's but sometimes imitating the language as well. It differs from poems like Marlowe's, however, in its relation to the complaint poem. Marlowe's tale is complete (with the continuation by George Chapman), and it is narrated by a third person. In Lanier's text the narration is all Hero's; we get only so much of the story as she can realistically give us without losing the dramatic tension of the situation. The relationship to the laments discussed earlier should be apparent, and for this reason I suspect that the text was written specifically for a musical setting, perhaps specifically for Lanier's setting.[37]

The poem falls into several clear-cut sections. The four sections to be described here are broad divisions, based on overall emotional content. Lanier's setting divides the sections further, as indicated by my divisions of the text and the subgrouping of lines below. All the sections are spoken by Hero, but give us enough of the story to make a dramatic situation. Whereas in the Farrant lament (see p. 172 above) we see only one dimension, one incident from the story, and one emotional reaction, in this one we share the anxiety of waiting, doubting, and fearing with Hero, not simply her grief.

The first section (lines 1-26) shows us an eager, impatient, and lusty Hero. The impatience manifests itself in the first six lines in the many short phrases that make up the poetic lines. Throughout the section, Hero's desires form the central theme. Though her prayers are all to Leander, the word "love" is not used once in this section. The suggestions that Leander might have betrayed her (lines 15-21) are, in this section, almost enticements to her lust, as well as a means of giving the poet a framework for telling us the details of their plan: Leander will come to her when the sea is calm, if she will put out a torch to guide him. Throughout this first section of the poem Hero obviously expects Leander to come to her. The last five lines (22-26) are her happy expectation that their tryst will go as planned.

The second section (lines 27-39) is Hero's rage scene. Now it suddenly occurs to her that Leander may truly have betrayed her. And again we start off with short, piercing phrases, the first line of the section breaking into three units. Hero here calls upon the gods, not for help but as witnesses. From line 31 to the end of the section, Hero's anger is carried vigorously forward by a succession of enjambed lines, ending with what appears to be a short line: "Heav'ns lend your aid / And arm yourselves in thunder." A powerful climax to her fury, which we know in retrospect (as the line goes on "Oh! but stay!") is brought up short by Hero's better judgment and the return of her loving thoughts.

The third section (lines 39-60) is a lyrical interlude. The emotion Hero expresses is no longer lust, but love; the language changes, including more terms of endearment ("love," "treasure"). Here (lines 39-48) Hero pictures her lover stealing out into the night and swimming to her. This is the only part of the poem that is pictorial. Now (lines 49-60) she calls upon the elements not as deities, but as themselves ("You gentle, peaceful winds," "You show'rs! you storms and tempests black") to help Leander come safely to her.

But she calls in vain, for section four (lines 61-80) portrays the storm that Hero quite rightly fears will claim her lover's life. In contrast with the lyrical third section, we again hear short, dramatic phrases. The language is now violent, the first two lines hissing like the winds they describe. Now the elements are invoked as deities: "O Gods! O deadly night! / Neptune! Aeolus! Ye pow'rful deities!" It is Leander, dead; Hero, lamenting her fate, chooses to die with him as Panthea chose to die with Abradad.

The poem is ideally suited for the kind of musical experiment Lanier had in mind. *Hero and Leander* is far more than the rhetorical set piece of the boys' company plays. A broad range of emotion is given here, a dramatic situation to be resolved; one might even say that there is a characterization of the persona, for we have seen Hero in greatly varied responses to her situation. This text gives the composer fully as much to work with as an opera text, but in shortened, monologue form. The first-person narration makes it an ideal vehicle for a musical setting that will express dramatically the emotions of the speaker.

Before we consider how Lanier responded to this dramatic text, we need to look at its language and prosody, for a large part of Lanier's effectiveness is achieved through declamation. The poem is in heroic couplets throughout, but the regularity implied by the couplets is constantly being compromised by the short phrases that occasionally punctuate its texture and by an extraordinary number of run-on lines, often bridging the normal relaxation at the ends of couplets. The rhythm of the poem is thus active and interesting. It varies widely between stopping the motion in mid-line (lines 2 and 3) and providing continuation through several lines at a time (lines 15-21). Syntax is obviously one of the poet's devices for preventing his couplet rhythm from taking over the narrative of the poem.

Syntax is the element Lanier is most careful of in his setting. In fact, he apparently pays no attention whatsoever to the verse structure, concentrating so exclusively on the proselike sentence structure that it is often difficult for the ear even to pick up the rhymes. Lanier pays scrupulous attention to punctuation, giving nearly every punctuation mark a rest,[38] or at least a long note to provide a pause for inflection, and wherever the lines are broken into definite phrases, his musical texture breaks too. The only exceptions are in sections

Example 5.14.

Wretch that I am!   'tis so!   ye gods, 'tis so!

Nicholas Lanier, *Hero and Leander, Musica Britannica*, vol. XXXIII, p. 15.

where longer phrasing is used for rhetorical purpose, and here gram-

matical articulation is provided by pitch. Conversely, run-on lines are usually run on musically as well:

Example 5.15.

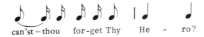

can'st — thou   for-get Thy   He - ro?

Nicholas Lanier, *Hero and Leander, Musica Britannica*, vol. XXXIII, p. 12

This concern with syntax is obviously Lanier's response to the humanists' demand for intelligibility of the text. The solo voice-basso continuo texture plus the shaping of musical phrases to coincide with grammatical phrases ensure that the actual words of Hero's emotional outbursts will be heard and understood. We have already seen, however, that Lanier's rhythmic style sometimes does violence to the natural accentuation of the words. Lanier has something more than intelligibility in mind when he uses the conventional rhythmic patterns of Italian monody. Here we must turn to musical rhetoric, for Lanier's handling of rhythmic patterns clearly is geared to interpretation of emotional content, and thus to the art of persuasion, or rhetoric.

Let us return to the opening phrase:

Example 5.16.

Nor com'st thou yet

Nicholas Lanier, "Hero and Leander, " p. 12.

By surging over the iambic rhythm implied by the text, setting it to the three-note upbeat figure, Lanier puts particular stress on "yet," emphasizing the urgency that we have seen is the central emotion of the first section of the poem. Hero is not really worried that Leander will not come, but that he hasn't come *yet.* The second phrase repeats the device, but expanded to a five-note upbeat:

Example 5.17.

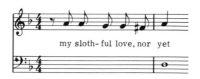

my sloth- ful love, nor yet

Nicholas Lanier, "Hero and Leander," p. 12.

Further on, the figure serves again to bring out the element of time, which seems to be Hero's greatest concern, as shown in example 5.18. The first section has the greatest number of three-note upbeat phrase

Example 5.18.

in these my lan   -   guish-ing   de- sires.

Nicholas Lanier, "Hero and Leander," p. 12.

entrances, returning to the figure after the moment of serenity on "The shores have peace, the winds and seas are dumb."

In the context of so many phrases beginning with an upbeat, the downbeat phrase beginning "Wretch that I am!" (p. 195 above) that opens the second section of the piece is particularly striking, recalling Monteverdi's technique of setting off such phrases as "Ahi, che pur non respondi." Here Hero seems to be jumping in ahead of time in her anger, contrasting with the more hesitant upbeats.

The three-note upbeat figure also has the effect of portraying Hero's breathless passion by accentuating rhythmically the short, choppy phrasing of the text. But we should notice that Lanier by no means always uses the three-note form of the upbeat figure. In fact, the length of the rhythmical phrasing seems to be one of the main devices by which he indicates the alterations in Hero's emotions that delineate the sections of the poem. One can almost judge her passion by the number of eighth-notes in a string, before a long note finally signals the primary (interpretive) phrase stress. The three-note upbeat

is less prominent in section two, but returns whenever Hero thinks of Leander with longing, as in section three ("Leander's thine," etc.) and in the last two lines of the piece.

In contrast, Hero's first real indication of jealousy (lines 15-21) elicits a long musical phrase leading to "hot desires" (again to the urgent lust of this first section). These long phrases are similar to the "festooning" rhythms in Monteverdi, aiming at interpretive phrase stress, but without the metric justification provided by the Italian language. In the "rage" section, such long, recitativelike figures predominate; this passage comes at the height of Hero's anger; as shown in example 5.19. She is no longer breathlessly passionate but enraged, and her anger pours forth in rapid-fire declamation. Fewer rests occur

Example 5.19.

Nicholas Lanier, "Hero and Leander," pp. 15-16.

and more phrases begin on a strong beat. The bass line in this section (and in lines 15-21) becomes almost completely inactive, and the

melodic line relies more and more upon repeated notes, moving slowly up by step in the nonmelodic way we saw in Monteverdi, as though whatever musical interest may have existed in less fiercely emotional passages (lines 22-26, for instance) must give way to the dramatic enunciation of Hero's rage.

We may note once more that Lanier's use of these Italianate rhythms occasionally produces cumbersome declamation, especially when combined with his determination to set the grammatical structure rather than the lines of poetry. The last phrase above ("this the knot before the sacred altar made / Of seaborn Venus?"), for instance, is syntactically too complex to be clear without some kind of rhythmic aid to articulation. Lanier tries to add this articulation with pitch, much in the manner that Monteverdi uses pitch changes to indicate phrasing. Here Lanier makes the melodic line move by step, connecting "made" with "knot," but more important, setting "of seaborn Venus" off from "made." The method works better in a less troublesome grammatical construction:

Example 5.20.

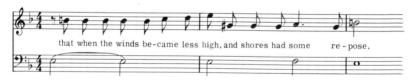

that when the winds be-came less high, and shores had some re - pose,

Nicholas Lanier, "Hero and Leander," p. 14.

Although no rhythmic break occurs, the melodic leap seems designed to set off the phrases of the text. But in either instance, it must be admitted that Lanier has had to sacrifice the natural rhythms not only of the words, but of the phrases, to achieve the rhetorical effect of the longer phrasing. The depiction of Hero's emotional state has taken precedence over the natural rhythms of the language.

The tone of the third section of the text becomes the inspiration for the most musically lyrical and melodious section of the piece. An abrupt change is indicated harmonically by a shift up a major third, and rhythmically by a drastic slowing down of the pace of declamation. Lines 40-48 continue the recitativelike declamation, but the melodic line is much more active than in the preceding

section, and the bass line (and therefore the harmonic rhythm) is more active as well. The length of the phrases is cut back to the shorter phrases associated with Hero's longing in the first section. Lines 49-60, Hero's supplication to the elements, continue the lyrical tone with a supple melodic line and relatively active bass. Lanier maintains the mood by avoiding the coincidence of a long note (implying phrase accent) with the harmonic rhythm, and the agogic accent on *"pi-*ty" is reduced by the leap up a fifth in the bass, implying a suspended $^6_4$ chord, and the accent on *"soft-*est" by a move from a root position to a sixth chord. Most of the accents thus are not as strong as in other sections, and the declamation is not as forceful, as seen in example 5.21.

The contrast is made clear once more by the fourth section

Example 5.21.

for pi - ty's sake, with soft - est gales more smooth and ea-sy make

Nicholas Lanier, "Hero and Leander," p. 18.

(Hero's anxiety and eventually her grief), where melodic motion is again curtailed by a large number of repeated notes, the bass line becomes static once again, and the pace of declamation is speeded up by the use of sixteenth notes. Hero's agitation suggests phrases that are longer than those associated with mere longing, but not so long as those associated with her uncontrollable anger:

Example 5.22.

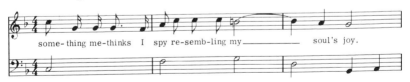

some-thing me-thinks I spy re-sem-bling my_____ soul's joy.

Nicholas Lanier, "Hero and Leander," p. 21.

Thus we can see that the emotional states suggested by the various

sections of the text have provided the justification for Lanier's use of rhythmic and melodic conventions. Lanier unquestionably came closer to the Italian style with *Hero and Leander* than other English composers would for many years. North's praise of it is probably an accurate reflection of contemporary response to the piece as an imitation; but imitation it still must be. Lanier has successfully used music to express the "affetti," but whereas Italian composers had done so while working with the rhythms of the language, Lanier's setting produces awkward declamation in English. The effort is certainly an improvement over the superficial imitations by Coperario, but the reluctance of other composers to continue in this direction is perhaps attributable to a feeling that the Italianate rhythms could not do justice to an English text. If the composers were going to pursue the new baroque sensitivity to the emotions in the text, it seemed they would have to do so at the expense of the rhythmic union of poetry and music so prized by Elizabethan and Jacobean poets and composers.

Henry Lawes made a valiant effort to combine the old with the new. Lawes' *Ariadne* is another piece in the tradition of the dramatic lament. It was no doubt inspired by Lanier's *Hero and Leander* and by Monteverdi's *Arianna*, but it is not so derivative as it has sometimes been claimed to be. *Ariadne* is the "story" Milton singled out as a setting by Lawes deserving of particular praise; present day commentators, however, tend to disparage it, especially in comparison with Monteverdi's lament. *Ariadne* is not like *Arianna*, nor is it like *Hero and Leander*, although it is obviously another attempt to write in recitative style for an English text. But the differences arise first of all from Lawes' approach to declamation, which is entirely different from Lanier's and far less dependent on Italian models; second, the text itself is also very different from Lanier's and in some ways less suitable for the dramatically oriented kind of musical setting.

The text of Lawes' *Ariadne* is by William Cartwright. From its placement in the Lawes MS, it is thought that Lawes composed the piece between 1637 and 1643. It is generally assumed that the poem dates from about the same time and that possibly it was written as a collaborative effort. Like Lanier's text, *Ariadne* combines an Ovidian tale with the complaint genre in the form of a dramatic monologue, and it has the same apparent relationship to the earlier dramatic laments. But that is about the extent of their similarities.

Theseus, O Theseus, hark! but yet in vain;
Alas deserted I complain;
It was some neighboring Rock, more soft than he,
Whose hollow bowels pity'd me,
And beating back that false and cruel name,
Did comfort and revenge my flame,
Then faithless whither wilt thou fly?
Stones dare not harbour cruelty;

Tell me ye gods, who e're ye are,
Why, O why, made ye him so fair?   10
And tell me wretch why thou
Mad'st not thyself more true?

Beauty from him might copies take,
And more majestic heroes make,
And falsehood learn a while
From him too, to beguile:
Restore my clue:
'Tis here most due,
For 'tis a labrinth of more subtle art,
To have so faire a face, so foul a heart: 20

The rav'nous Vulture tear his breast,
The rowling stone disturbe his rest;
Let him next feel
Ixion's wheel,
And add one fable more
To cursing poets store
And then yet rather let him live and twine
His woof of days with some thread stoln from mine;
But if you'l torture him, how e're
Torture my heart. You'l find him there.   30

Till mine eyes drank up his,
And his drank mine,
I ne'r thought souls might kiss,
And spirits joyn:
Pictures till then
Took me as much as men
Nature and Art
Moving alike my heart;
But his fair visage made me find
Pleasures and fears,   40
Hopes, sighs and tears,

As several seasons of the mind.
Should thine eyes Venus on him dwell,
Thou would'st invite him to thy shell,
And caught by that live jet,
Venture a second net,
And after all thy dangers faithless he;
Should'st thou but slumber, would forsake ev'n thee.

The streams so court the yielding banks,
And gliding thence ne're pay their thanks,   50
The winds so woo the flowers,
Whispering among fresh bowers,
And having rob'd them of their smels,
Fly thence perfum'd to other cells;
This is familiar hate, to smile and kill,
Though nothing please thee, yet my ruin will:

Death hover, hover, o'er me then,
Waves let your christall womb,
Be both my fate and tomb,
I'll sooner trust the sea then men.   60

Yet for revenge to heav'n I'll call
And breath one curse before I fall;
Proud of two conquests Minotaure and me,
That by my faith, this by thy perjurie.
May'st thou forget to wing thy ships with white,
That the black sails may to the longing sight
Of thy gray father tell thy fate, and he
Bequeth that sea his name, falling like me,
Nature and love thus brand thee, whil'st I dye,
'Cause thou forsak'st Aegeus 'cause thou draw'st nigh.   70

And ye O nymphs below, who sit
In whose swift floods his vows he writ,
Snatch a sharp Diamond from your richer Mines,
And in some Mirror grave these sadder lines;
Which let some god convey
To him, that so he may
In that both read at once, and see,
Those looks that caus'd my destiney.

Her Epitaph

In Thetis arms, I Ariadne sleep,
Drown'd; First in mine own tears, then in the deep: 80

Twice banish'd first by love, and then by hate,
The life that I preserv'd became my fate
Who leaving all was by him left alone.
That from a monster free'd, himself prov'd one:

Thus then I F _____ but looke,
O mine eyes:
Be now true spies,
Yonder, yonder comes my dear,
Now my wonder, once my fear;
See Satyrs dance along
In a confused throng,   90
Whilst horns and pipes rude noise,
Do mad their lusty joys;
Roses his forehead crown,
And that recrown the flowers;
Where he walks up and down,
He makes the Desarts bowers;
The Ivy and the Grape
Hide not, adorne his shape,
And green leaves cloath his waving Rod,
'Tis he, 'tis either Theseus or some God.[39]   100

The single most important difference between *Ariadne* and *Hero and Leander* is that though Hero's plight unfolds with the poem, and details of the story are narrated as unfulfilled promises that might still be made good (Leander said he would come if she set out the light), the only parts of Ariadne's lament that imply any possibility of action in the present are her call for revenge and, in the final section of the poem, the approach of Bacchus, whom she momentarily mistakes for Theseus. This is not, like *Hero and Leander*, a miniature drama in monologue form nor, like *Arianna,* a part of a complete drama; it is a narrative poem, even though it takes the form of a first-person lament.

Because the poem is a narrative, not only are the dramatic possibilities fewer, but the emotional range also is considerably restricted. Ariadne's emotional fluctuations are much less extreme in recollection than Hero's had been in the course of her vigil. The emotional tone of the entire text (with the possible exception of the final 16 lines, where she thinks her lover has returned) is a mixture of love and hate that cannot be separated. Lines 21-30, for instance, which contain some vicious curses, are hardly allowed to get going before

we are reminded that Ariadne still loves Theseus. Likewise, the next section of the poem (lines 31-46), where Ariadne describes her falling in love with Theseus, is tinged with bitterness; we know she is narrating what is past—not because we have prior knowledge of the story but because of what Ariadne herself has already told us.

All of this probably makes for a better, more unified poem than *Hero and Leander,* but it does not provide the substitute opera libretto that Lanier had to work with, and Lawes' setting of it is correspondingly less dramatic. The sections of the poem (as indicated by the divisions in the text) Lawes separates with clear cadences, but no appreciable distinction is made in musical language from one section to another. The harmonic structure shows the most variety, but it does not appear to be directly reflective of varying emotions in the text.[40] Rather, Lawes uses a fluctuating tonal center (there are cadences in g, d, c, B♭, F, e, B, and G!) to suggest a general state of uncertainty. This device occurs in other Lawes settings of texts dealing with uncertainty or inconstancy (e.g., "O tell me love! O tell me fate!"), but any specific assignation of keys or modes to emotions does not hold up. The device is not a dramatic one, but it might be called rhetorical since it does establish a tone of uncertainty for the entire piece, just as Cartwright set up the tense emotional mixture of love and hate to govern the tone of the entire text.

To this extent, then, Lawes is concerned with the expression of the "affetti" in music, in a general rather than a specific manner. In this case at least, his method is derived from the nature of the text. But Lawes is primarily concerned with intelligibility, letting the specific emotions of the text speak for themselves. Declamation is therefore a primary objective of his rhythmic style.

Lawes' rhythms are not, like Lanier's, derived from the rhythms of Italian monody but come rather from an attempt to reflect the rhythms of the English language. *Ariadne* does not have the many repeated notes and long strings of undifferentiated note values that we found in *Hero and Leander;* it does not have nearly so many upbeat phrase entrances; and where upbeats or long phrases do occur, they produce a quite different effect because Lawes' rhythmic language includes a great many dotted rhythms. Phrases like this one are common in this and Lawes' other monodic songs, showing his realization of the essentially iambic rhythms of English by making length coincident with stress.[41]

Yet this phrase alone might give an overly rigid, metric notion of

Example 5.23.

A-las de-ser-ted I com-plain

Henry Lawes, "Ariadne Deserted." From *Ayres and Dialogues*, p. 1. London: John Playford, 1653. Reprinted with permission of the Folger Shakespeare Library, Washington, D.C.

Lawes' setting of the rhythms of English poetry. We have defined poetic meter in Chapter 1 as a recurrent pattern that uses some feature of the language to give form to lines of verse. Cartwright's poem is dependent on a recurrent pattern of iambic accentuation for its external structure. The poem is quite strictly conceived in couplets and quatrains that share not only framing rhymes but metric regularity as well. Although the couplets, as units, are of varying lengths, within the couplets any irregularities (such as missing or added syllables) are definitely felt in reading the poem, because the meter is for the most part so regular. But poetic meter is not an important factor in Lawes' monodic style; he seems almost to go out of his way to deny a literal recurrence of declamatory rhythms in setting lines of the same metric pattern. Couplets like this are fairly typical in the poem: "The streams so court the yielding banks / And gliding thence ne're pay their thanks"; Lawes' setting, while preserving the naturally iambic rhythm of the words with *relatively* short and long notes on each pair of syllables (except on "ne're," a special case we shall discuss below), prevents metric regularity by introducing a variety of note values as seen in example 5.24.

Another way in which Lawes indicates a care for the pronunciation of his text is his attention to the difficulties of enunciating the consonantal clusters that are so common in English. We may recall that Lanier chose to rush through the groups of consonants in Italianate rhythmic patterns, patterns designed for a language that has many more vowel sounds, especially at the ends of words and syllables. Lawes, on the other hand, is willing to give up a prevailing iambic rhythm to make the articulation of every syllable possible for the singer. The couplet "And ye O nymphs below, who sit / In whose swift floods his vows he writ," is set in such a way that the singer has

Example 5.24.

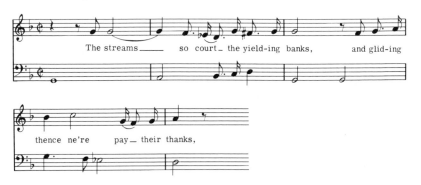

Henry Lawes, "Ariadne Deserted," p. 4.

plenty of time to enunciate the consonants of "in whose swift floods"; the rest after "nymphs" has the same purpose: to allow time for full articulation. This procedure is frequent in Lawes' other monodic and declamatory settings too. In fact, so careful is Lawes with the rhythms of the language that it is possible to account for the rhythmic value assigned to virtually every note he sets in the monodic style, either as part of a prevailing iambic rhythm, or as a deviation from it for reasons of articulation.

But even within this context, Lawes' rhythmic language has considerable variety. The long note/accent of any particular iamb may be anything from a dotted eighth note to a dotted half note. Often the reason behind such choices seems to be interpretation, the musical rhetoric observed in Lanier's monodic style. For instance, the declamation seen in example 5.26 puts the most emphasis on "revenge." No metric reason can be adduced for "revenge" to receive more stress than "comfort"; in the context of the sentence, the "neighboring Rock" has done as much to comfort her as to revenge. But

Example 5.25.

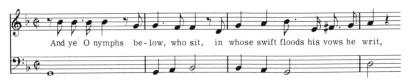

Henry Lawes, "Ariadne Deserted," p. 5.

Example 5.26.

Did   com-fort and re-venge   my flame,

Henry Lawes, "Ariadne Deserted," p. 1.

revenge is one of the most important elements in the tone of the entire text, so Lawes helps establish that tone right away by drawing attention to the word. Interpretation can also interrupt the iambic flow, as in the case of "The streams so court the yielding bank / And gliding thence *ne're* pay their thanks." (See example 5.24) Normally "ne're" would be set to a short note value, but the half note helps emphasize the similarity to Theseus.

Like Lanier, Lawes generally chooses to follow the grammatical structure of his text in a monodic setting, but unlike Lanier, in *Ariadne* Lawes never lets his listener forget that the text is poetry, not prose. In the Ariadne lament, few instances occur in which this creates any difficulties, because Cartwright's poem has a formal structure much better designed for monodic setting than *Hero and Leander*. Almost every line of *Ariadne* is end-stopped, and what enjambments there are do not run from one couplet to another but merely solidify the couplet. If the poem were constructed in heroic couplets as *Hero and Leander* is, the musical effect would be deadly dull. But the poet has avoided monotony by making his couplets of varying lengths. Thus Cartwright has relieved Lawes of the necessity of avoiding verse structure to be faithful to syntax or to create an interesting variety of phrase lengths.

Nevertheless, Lawes takes pains, in the few instances that do occur, to cover himself on both counts. Rhyme seems to be the defining feature of verse structure for him. The rhyming words in *Ariadne* are almost all long note values, providing not only the stress that accompanies a long note, but time for the rhyming sounds to be heard; and most of the couplets and quatrains end with a harmonic progression by fifth, giving a sense of cadence to each rhymed group of lines and setting off verse structure even more.[42] Where an enjambment does occur, Lawes relies on the strength of the rhyming

Example 5.27.

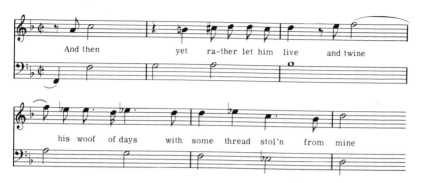

And then   yet   ra-ther let him live   and twine

his woof   of days   with some thread stol'n from mine

Henry Lawes, "Ariadne Deserted," pp. 2-3.

words and the pattern of reinforcement he has established to make the verse structure apparent; the rhyming word is set to a long note, even though the phrase break, indicated by a rest, occurs elsewhere (see example 5.27).

This kind of respect for the poet's lines was a hallmark of the lute-song, and in general it was a tradition Lawes continued. He took care here to preserve verse structure, even where the monodic goals of intelligibility and dramatic delivery of the text demanded a more flexible attitude towards the poem. In addition to *Ariadne*, Lawes composed a number of other songs, shorter than *Ariadne*, many of them with texts by Thomas Carew, that must be classified as English monodies: Their musico-textual relationship is characterized by techniques of declamation emphasizing speech rhythms and interpretive stress patterns, and they are through-composed rather than strophic. The settings of Carew mark an important step in the dissolution of the union of music and poetry, for when faced with the strong enjambments used by a poet like Carew, Lawes was forced to abandon his concern with verse structure. His settings of some of Carew's poems, while preserving the iambic English rhythms for which he was beloved of poets, are as grammatically structured as was Lanier's *Hero and Leander*. In the setting shown in example 5.28 it is nearly impossible to hear the rhyme scheme.

The lutenists had no such lines to work with. It was relatively simple to preserve the verse structure of the text when to do so did not cause a serious syntactical break, but a text like Carew's leaves

Example 5.28.

when thou, poor ex-com-mu-ni-cate From all the joys____ of
love, shalt see The full re-ward and glo - - rious
fate Which my strong faith hath pur-chas'd me,

Henry Lawes, "When thou poor excommunicate." Text by Thomas Carew. From *English Songs 1625-1660; Musica Britannica*, Vol. XXXIII, p. 87. Ed. Ian Spink, 1971. Reproduced by permission of Stainer and Bell, Ltd. on behalf of the Musica Britannica Trust, and by permission of Galaxy Music Corp.

the composer little choice. He must sacrifice either verse structure or grammatical structure. It seems clear that, given the kind of poetry that was the composer's stock by the second quarter of the century, there was no conceivable way in which the kind of cooperation of music and poetry so cherished in the lute-song could be maintained.

Another of these shorter monodic songs provides an excellent example for some final points about Lawes' monodic style. It is usual for commentators to concentrate on the melodic line in discussing relationships between music and text, since this is obviously where the closest connection lies. But Lawes' monodic songs have definite links between the bass line, the harmonic rhythm, and the placement of stressed syllables. This use of the bass line is apparent in most of the songs, but it is made very clear in the songs that Lawes revised, for the two elements that he changed most often in his revisions were the placement of bar lines and the coincidence of notes of the bass line with notes of the melody. "Break heart in twain!" is one of the monodic songs that Lawes revised in the manuscript, and since the manuscript is thought to be roughly chronological,[43] we can assume

that the version found on f. 31 was intended to be an improvement over that on f. 14v.

Most of the changes in the later version involve rhythm and meter, not melody, and thus declamation. Lawes' barring in both versions of the song is regular, and his normal procedure is to have a note of the bass line struck on the first beat of the measure. Without claiming any unjustified accentual importance for the bar line,[44] I think it can be shown that Lawes felt that the bar line implied some kind of ictus and worked with this possibility. Thus, when he makes a change like this

Example 5.29.

Henry Lawes, "Break heart in twain!" From *English Songs 1625-1660; Musica Britannica,* Vol. XXXIII, p. 63. Ed. Ian Spink, 1971. Reproduced by permission of Stainer and Bell, Ltd. on behalf of the Musica Britannica Trust, and by permission of Galaxy Music Corp.

it has the effect of removing some of the accent on "Wert," making the phrase head more strongly toward "dead," and adding the emotional effect of the off-beat entrance. Conversely, when he changes this line

Example 5.30.

Henry Lawes, "Break heart in twain," p. 63.

the coincidence of the bass note with the treble note on "Not" gives added stress to the word, reducing the petulancy that may be felt with the pre-beat entrance, and is thus an aid to interpretive rhythm.

Example 5.31.

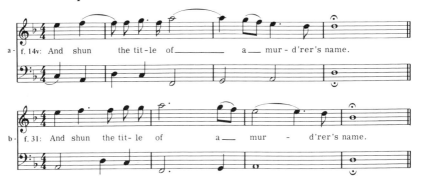

Henry Lawes, "Break heart in twain," p. 64.

In the final line, again by rearranging the barring, not only does he make the climatic "murd'rer" fall on the ictus of the bar line, but, to end with the masculine ending demanded by the text also extends the duration of "Murd'rer's." Although in a number of places the declamation seems to be smoother in the original version, in every instance of a change, there is an explanation in interpretation; Lawes makes the most effective—perhaps even affective—use of the ictus implied by the bar line and by the bass note and its implied chord that almost invariably falls immediately after the bar line. In the long run, of course, this kind of reliance on the regular ictus of musical meter would prove inimical to the free declamation of the monodic style.

In many of his shorter monodic songs, Lawes' careful concern with textual rhythm and poetic structure shows up to best advantage. Here the emotional changes and dramatic situations that may be developed in a longer text are not possible, and the music consequently has less need to create sustained emotional or dramatic stances. Lawes' ability to set the text clearly and precisely lets the text speak for itself, and because the pieces are not so long, his jerky speech rhythms do not lose force through constant repetition. Furthermore, the external structure of the poem—the rhyme scheme, the line lengths, and the presence or absence of enjambment—which was also important to Lawes, is more interesting if it is not repeated 40 times. Finally, thematic structure, especially progression to a climax, which cannot be represented musically over a long time span without major changes in musical language, can be reflected convincingly in a shorter work through control of melodic range or harmonic progression.

Looking again at "Break heart in twain!" we find that Lawes rather significantly altered the melodic line in his revision of the song. In the first version, melody climbs to a'' half-way through the song on "laughter they from her, not pity win," and again in the climactic last line where the extent of the lady's cruelty is revealed. The revised version omits the first a'', saving this climactic pitch, which is indeed high even for these continuo songs that lie rather high, for the climax of the poem. (See example 5.31 above: "And shun the title of a murd'rer's name.") The overall musical shape has been improved and made to coincide better with the thematic structure of the text.

Lawes' monodic settings were extremely popular in his own day. The commendations of poets and musicians alike and the frequency with which Playford reprinted his songs, including the monodies, attest to the contemporary belief that Henry Lawes was England's answer to humanist demands for clarity and passion in setting a text to music. Lanier had been able to bring the passion of the Italian style to a setting of English, but his music was derivative—it was famous *as an imitation*—and could not sustain a musical expression of emotion without losing fidelity to the rhythms of the text. Lawes tried to work from the other direction, creating a solo style from the rhythms of the text. But this method was not successful either. The very nature of the language worked against him, for the highly accentual rhythms of English, if carefully followed in musical rhythms, create a rough, jerky, and often monotonous rhythmic language, precluding any sustained musical interpretation of emotion in the manner of Monteverdi. Composers of the next generation adopted a much more melismatic style, borrowing again from the floridity popular in Italian opera, perhaps in an effort to add a sustained musical line to the choppy effect of Lawes' strictly syllabic settings. But in doing so, they lost completely the close relationship to the rhythm, meter and structure of the original text that embodied the neoclassical cooperation between musicians and poets. The intensely emotional representation of a text through clear and forceful declamation—so much desired by baroque sensibilities—seems not to have been compatible with the physical properties of English poetry. The songs of English monody, when they are the most successfully declamatory, when they represent most accurately the speech rhythms of the text, fail to create a rhetorical stance and fall instead into what might best be described as a narrative stance, letting the text tell its own story but adding little musical embellishment.

Chapter 6
Pathetic Airs

The last three chapters concerned three categories of solo song in Jacobean and Caroline England, clearly definable through their choice of conventions of setting a text, and representative of three particular attitudes toward which aspects of a poem might be represented in music. Each of the three types established a set of conventions for such elements as rhythmic declamation, phrase structure, and interpretive techniques, and each type had its own conventional relationship to the text; and although these conventions were handled somewhat differently in each group as we moved from the first quarter of the century to the second, and indeed from composer to composer, enough continuity existed to allow us to trace the attitudes embodied in each category throughout the period.

But such categorization has left virtually untouched a large body of songs, including many of the best and perhaps the most characteristic songs of the period. These are the emotionally expressive lute songs (such as Dowland's "In darkness let me dwell") and the declamatory airs of the continuo composers (such as Henry Lawes' songs for Milton's "Comus" or Nicholas Lanier's setting of Thomas Carew's "Mark how the blushful morn"), which are neither as rigorously metrical as those considered in Chapters 3 and 4, nor as explicitly declamatory as those in Chapter 5. More important, whereas the attitudes directing the choice of conventions in the categories discussed in the last three chapters were largely concerned with the mechanical features of versification, they dealt only peripherally with thematic content or the rhetoric of emotions (the *pathos*), an important aspect of humanistic interpretation. In this final chapter

I shall try to fill in both gaps through a group of songs—somewhat less homogeneous than the others, but sharing a middle ground in declamatory technique and a consistent emphasis on expressiveness—which I have grouped under the heading of "pathetic air."

The pathetic airs are perhaps more easily defined by what they are not than by what they are, for songs of several different musical styles must be so classified. We may exclude settings that give precedence to musical structures (such as the dance songs) and those that emphasize poetic meter over considerations of poetic rhythm. Such songs are generally not specifically musical representations of the pathos—the emotional contours—of the text, nor, in most cases, of the organization of words in a meaningful order, whereas the pathetic airs, though usually working within the context of the poem's versification, are more expressive of its content. On the other side, the pathetic airs may be distinguished from monody by the designation "air," which should convey some connotation of songs as opposed to narrative or speech. The pathetic airs operate in a more inherently musical context than the strict examples of monody; most of them are strophic, implying that at some level the musical expression is expected to carry its relevance from one stanza to the next. The texts set as pathetic airs are lyric poetry—often melancholy, especially in the lute songs—and do not go as far toward narrative as those used for monody. The settings likewise do not generally follow a narrative structure in the poem as closely as a monodic setting, but seem to represent a compromise between fidelity to the external structure of verse and the syntactic structure of the words.

All the songs I shall consider pathetic airs work with poetic rhythms in one way or another, and a reasonably careful declamation of the text, at least of the first stanza, is an identifying feature. But these songs are an amalgamation of styles and attitudes, and they do not have any one of the mechanical features of versification as an external goal. The representation of subject matter is therefore not only more feasible (because the composer is less confined by strict adherence to a set of rhythmic conventions) but more necessary to give the song thrust or to add some new interpretive dimension. Where in the other categories we saw sacrifices made to good declamation out of respect for meter (poetic or musical), or sacrifices to sustained musical expressivity out of respect for poetic rhythms,

or concessions to poetic structure for the sake of grammatical or narrative structure, in these airs consideration of any of these aspects of the temporal organization of words is sometimes sacrificed to the musical representation of meaning. Effect, in other words, is placed above fidelity to verse structure or even above declamatory accuracy, as the determinant in the choice of conventions of setting.

Instances of this kind of interpretation, of course, occur in all the other kinds of song. In the last chapter, although we were concerned primarily with intelligibility and declamation of speech rhythms of the text, we began to see—especially with Lanier's *Hero and Leander*—that some of the conventions were also capable of forming a set of techniques for representing the meaning and the pathos·of the words, as well as their temporal organization in poetic meter, poetic rhythm, or the progressively more exaggerated rhythms of speech or drama. Here we shall try to relate the sustained and effective use of the representation of meaning and pathos—which is most consistently operative in this group of songs—to the similar uses of the conventions of language in the poetry, the control of syntax and word choice, and the figurative or symbolic uses of language that are as integral a part of poetry as the control of sound patterns (indeed, a far more important part to poets of some periods). The tradition of rhetoric and elocution in the organization of words for purposes of emphasis and persuasion may also be a part of a composer's interpretive attitude toward his text. We shall thus be defining the conventions of a rhetoric of music in English song of the early seventeenth century.

Rhetoric is the art of persuasion. The idea that words can be organized according to established principles to be more persuasive— a concept known from the writings of Classical Greeks and Romans (especially those of Aristotle, Quintilian and Cicero) and enjoying the renewed interest that the Renaissance fostered in all phases of ancient knowledge—formed the basis of numerous treatises on the construction and criticism of poetry during the Renaissance.[1] But writers in sixteenth-century England were not in complete agreement as to what was included in a system of rhetoric. Classical tradition had divided the art into invention, disposition or arrangement, style or elocution, memory, and delivery; but following the lead of Petrus Ramus, some theorists sought to treat only elocution and delivery as rhetoric, considering the other four areas as the province of logic.[2]

Thus two definitions of rhetoric were current to which we might relate a rhetoric of music: The first defines an integrated system that treats all aspects of the organization of words, prescribing a set of conventions through which the writer's work will appear clearly and logically presented, and that will appeal to the emotions as well as the intellect of the audience through the force of elocution; the second describes only a system of conventions of style that seeks to add persuasive force to words through ornament, and to make the words effective through beauty and an appeal to the emotions.[3]

The second definition would seem at first glance to be the closest to music, since it appears to deal with the surface texture of words; it would be possible to view such a rhetorical system as a means of approaching the emotions through the decorative arrangement of words, much as the humanists thought of the addition of music to a text as a means of reaching the soul. But the rhetoricians are very clear in their insistence that ornament[4] in rhetoric is inherently related to meaning; and elocution, although it may provide beauty and grace in speaking, also must be seen not merely as an adjunct, but as an integral part of the thematic content of a poem. Thus a facile equation of music with the rhetoric of elocution will not suffice; ultimately we shall find that music is capable of functioning on several planes in the representation of emotion and meaning in the text.

For all Renaissance rhetoricians, whichever definition of rhetoric they espoused, the use of language was ordered by a set of conventions, or figures of speech, covering grammar, elocution, and sometimes logic, which were listed and described in treatises and handbooks on poetry. Cicero had defined a figure of speech as "any deviation, either in thought or expression, from the ordinary and simple method of speaking."[5] George Puttenham's description in *The Arte of English Poesie* (1589) of the use of figures is indicative of the power and breadth of effect attributed to them in the sixteenth century. He begins his chapter "Of Figures and Figurative Speaches" with a warning:

> As figures be the instruments of ornament in every language, so be they also in a sorte abuses or rather trespasses in speach, because they passe the ordinary limits of common utterance, and be occupied of purpose to deceive the eare and also the minde, drawing it from plainnesse and simplicitie to a certaine doublenesse, whereby our talke is the more guilefull and abusing.[6]

But he later concedes that in the hands of the poet the figures are less dangerous than they are pleasing:

> but in this case, because our maker or Poet is appointed not for a iudge, but rather for a pleader, and that of pleasant & louely causes and nothing perillous, such as be those for the triall of life, limme, or liuelyhood, and before iudges neither sower nor seuere, but in the eare of princely dames, yong ladies, gentlewomen, and courtiers, beyng all for the most part either meeke of nature, or of pleasant humour, and that all his abuses tende but to dispose the hearers to mirth and sollace by pleasant conueyance and efficacy of speach, they are not in truth to be accompted vices but for vertues in the poetical science very commendable.[7]

Further on he describes how the figures affect the use of language:

> Figurative speech is a noueltie of language euidently (and yet not absurdly) estranged from the ordinarie habite and manner of our dayly talke and writing, and figure it selfe is a certain liuely or good grace set vpon wordes, speaches, and sentences to some purpose and not in vaine, giuing them ornament or efficacie by many maner of alterations in shape, in sounde, and also in sence, sometime by way of surplusage, sometime by defect, sometime by disorder, or mutation, & also by putting into our speaches more pithe and substance, subtilitie, quicknesse, efficacie, or moderation, in this or that sort tuning and tempring them, by amplification, abridgement, opening, closing, enforcing, meekening, or otherwise disposing them to the best purpose:[8]

In more modern terms, the following summary of the functions of the Renaissance figures of speech will give an idea of the extent to which an Elizabethan poet was expected to be in control of his words:

> The Renaissance figures . . . deal with words, in the figures of orthography; with grammar, in such matters as interrogation, exclamation, the unfinished sentence, the periodic sentence, ellipsis, rhythm, and the means of varying through them; with coherence, through figures of conjunction and transition; with emphasis, through word order and the figures of repetition; with clarity and obscurity; with amplification and condensation; with beauty, through exergasia and all the figures of exornation; with force, through vehemence *(pathos)*; with proof, through *logos*; with *ethos*; even with gesture (mimesis and mycterismus), and voice (pathopopoeia and tasis).[9]

The figures of speech, then, are conventions of writing designed to

influence the way in which words are perceived, whether on the surface level of embellishment of thematic content, or on the deeper level of the arrangement of terms in argument. The relationship of such a system of conventions to the conventions of setting a text to music should be obvious, for we have already seen that a musical interpretation will also influence the listener's perception of the words. Musical rhetoric can work in a number of ways: As an aid to elocution, music can emphasize rhetorical conventions in the words, it can supply its own conventions or "figures," or it can add significance not inherent in the words to a conceit or a figure of speech in the text; as a representation of thematic content or pathos, music can help to establish the *ethos* of the speaker, it can add vividness to descriptive passages or metaphors, or it can emphasize figures of comparison or contrast; and finally, music may be used as an aid to delivery in the form of rhetorical declamation.

In some instances musical conventions are analgous to particular figures of speech. The figures of repetition, for instance, may easily be related to music, and musical conventions can be used in conjunction with figures of emphasis and those dealing with clarity and obscurity, beauty, amplification, and condensation. In a larger sense, however, such analogies are less important than the conception of musical conventions as another set of figures performing a function in the persuasion of the listener that is similar—but not identical—to that of the rhetorical devices in the poem. The very act of setting the words to music removes them from "the ordinary and simple method of speaking" and is thus a form of rhetorical gesture. The predominant rhythmic style of declamation in any setting—the distance of the rhythmic language from the rhythms of normal speech—establishes the degree of distance between singer and text, as well as a conventionally accepted emotional tone, and may be compared to the establishment of the ethos or moral character of the speaker that is the purpose of one set of rhetorical figures. Campion's songs in the "plain" style are a deviation from ordinary speech in the direction of noninterpretation; insofar as they are deviant, however, their particular rhythmic character may be considered a rhetorical gesture, though it is very limited in its intrinsic ability to further elocution or to convey additional meaning. Monodic songs, on the other hand, are deviant in the other direction and often seem to stress exaggerated speech rhythms. The effect of such rhythms is

a strong identification of the singer with the persona of the poem, and the rhythmic style thus has a direct bearing on the speaker's credibility.

In the pathetic airs we shall find a less clearly defined musical ethos, but more flexibility in developing other means of expression. Beyond the initial gesture of setting a text to music, a rhetoric of music must ultimately be concerned with the meaning and the inherent emotional effect of the text, for the rhetoricians were explicit in the requirement that ornament be used for a purpose, not for its own sake. The function of music in these songs is to make the words more forceful, more persuasive, and more pathetic through musical means as much as through the words themselves. The setting should add a dimension to the text that the words alone could not convey, just as the manipulation of language can imply dimensions of meaning that normal speech does not.

If musical conventions are to be used as a set of rhetorical figures, some agreement must exist as to their effect; unfortunately, there are not catalogues of devices for music as there are for words.[10] Nevertheless, if techniques for representing meaning with music are used repeatedly, or if the association of musical figures with particular aspects of a text is sufficiently striking, I think we may assume that conventions have been established. Any of the techniques described in Chapter 1 may be used as rhetorical devices, and many of the rhythmic conventions that have been discussed in earlier chapters—particularly those used for intepretation—will reappear as figures in the rhetoric of music. But in the previous contexts they have not usually been pushed beyond the "normal," at least after the essentially rhetorical function of setting a text at all is taken into account. We shall consider them rhetorical only when they are exaggerated beyond the needs of interpretation or are demonstrably used for a particular effect. Musical elements that are not used for declamation (that is, such nonrhythmic elements as chord choice, dissonance, chromaticism, melodic intervals or melodic figuration, or musical texture) are more clearly available for use as rhetorical gesture than rhythm,[11] but they too must be used in a manner significantly out of the ordinary as defined by the context of the song in which they appear, to be considered conventions of rhetoric.

It is my belief that a change in the rhetorical stance, and a concomitant change in the conventions used as a rhetoric of music, most

clearly define the drastic change in musical style of solo song that occurred in England shortly before the start of the second quarter of the century. And it is mainly in the pathetic airs that changes in poetic style required finding new methods of interpreting the thematic content and the rhetoric of emotions and adopting a fundamentally different rhetorical stance. I have suggested that certain kinds of musical representation are more appropriate than others to particular kinds of poetry. With respect to Elizabethan lyric poetry, which depends greatly upon the precise, even minute, manipulation of words according to the figures of Classical rhetoric, a setting that represents individual images or emotional states, rhetorical repetitions, or the figures of paradox or comparison, through a musical language capable of multiple and rapidly shifting gestures, is responding in kind to the rhetorical organization of the text. Jacobean and Caroline verse, on the other hand, is much less dependent on the conventions of elocution, much less decorative in its use of language, than Elizabethan verse, and more dependent on argument (following Donne) or decorum (following Jonson). In either case, a musical style that is highly emotional or decorative in its own right would not be representative of the rhetorical stance of the text. Further, the use of imagery, conceits, and metaphors in metaphysical and Cavalier poetry is notably less conventional. It was a characteristic of the age to search for fresh images, so a musical language that is conventional in its representation of images would clearly be inappropriate. We shall look first at the rhetorical conventions established in the lute song; but I will point out as we proceed why some of these conventions could not be appropriate to the continuo song and its particular kind of text.

The pathetic airs have two points of departure in the lute songs: the madrigal-related airs, which have polyphonic accompaniments, and the homophonic, unmetered songs similar in musical style to the air de cour. Both types are notable for their fidelity to textual rhythms in declamation, but whereas this feature is prominent in the expressive language of the latter kind of song, in the madrigal type the purely musical devices of word-painting and the musical effect of the polyphonic texture itself are more central to a listener's perception of the piece.[12] Although the reduced textural interest of the homophonic style was to surpass the polyphonic style in the continuo song, the influence of the madrigal remained particularly

strong in the emotionally expressive songs of John Dowland, and it is evident in those of John Danyel and some of the less important lutenists as well.

Elizabethan lyric poetry, on one level of organization, is built on the careful and purposeful use of figures of speech. But just as the reader was not expected to scan quantitative meters, he (or she, since the majority are love lyrics addressed to a woman) certainly was not expected to analyze the conventions of rhetoric, but rather to be moved by them in their total effect as a poem; and it is again important to remember that elocution is not an ultimate goal but a means of making the entire lyric persuasive. Nevertheless, if we analyze the multiple figures that make up such a poem, it is easy to see that a musical representation that works in a similar manner—by combining many small elements into an integrated whole—will be representative of the composition of the verse.

There are significant ways in which the madrigal does just this. The representation of the meaning of words was an essential principle of the madrigal, based on one interpretation of the humanistic goal of obtaining the "effects" of music; and if it were not for the requirement that the text be fully understood as well as represented through music, the madrigal might have become a more important literary medium in England than it did. As it was, many of the elements of the madrigal that may be called rhetorical were incorporated into the lute songs.

Some of these elements can be related to particular figures of speech. The devices of word-painting come first to mind as characteristic of the madrigal, and although they are not as consistently used in the lute songs, they do appear often enough to be notable. Word-painting, I think, may be most aptly related to the figures of description and the use of imagery. In example 6.1, the descriptive function is certainly obvious; we might relate it to the figure of speech known as pragmatographia: "the vivid description of an action or event."[13] But Danyel could use word-painting in somewhat subtler ways that are suggestive of the use of metaphor, as seen in example 6.2. The conventional running figure, rather than occurring on the word "run," is set to the words "days" and "years" to suggest by association the rapid passage of time. The ordinary uses of word-painting, in which a conventional device is associated with the word it represents, is in a sense the equivalent of the epithet; Danyel's procedure

Example 6.1.

John Danyel, "Grief keep within." From *Songs for the Lute, Viol and Voice* (1606); *The English Lute-Songs*, Series II, Vol. 8, p. 26. Ed. Edmund H. Fellowes. Rev. Thurston Dart and David Scott, 1970. Reproduced by permission of Stainer and Bell, Ltd. and Galaxy Music Corp.

here, on the other hand, where the device—which already has its conventionally assigned meaning in association with "run"—is used in conjunction with other words, is the equivalent of the metaphorical use of language. The displacement of the figure brings together musically two elements of the text: time and its passing.[14]

Although word-painting continues to be present in the continuo songs, it does not seem to be as significant as an expressive, rhetorical device as it was in the lute songs (and would be again in the songs of Purcell and his contemporaries). In the continuo song, word-

painting usually is confined to the small gestures on particular words, such as William Lawes' "breathless" rhythm on the word "breathles," (example 6.3), John Wilson's long note to represent "slowness," (example 6.4), or Henry Lawes' pathetic minor third on "mournes," (example 6.5).

Example 6.2.

al-though she makes no steem Of days____ nor years. but lets them run in vain.

John Danyel, "Time, Cruel Time." From *Songs for the Lute, Viol and Voice* (1606); *The English Lute-Songs*, Series II, Vol. 8, p. 23. Ed. Edmund H. Fellowes. Rev. Thurston Dart and David Scott, 1970. Reproduced by permission of Stainer and Bell, Ltd. and Galaxy Music Corp.

Example 6.3.

when _____ thou art growne breath-les and hast

William Lawes, "God of winds." From *William Lawes Autograph Manuscript*; Additional MS 31432, f. 31. Reprinted with permission of The British Library, Department of Manuscripts.

In the continuo song, word-painting typically does not function in the organization of whole passages nor add a new dimension of meaning as it did in examples 6.1 and 6.2 from lute songs. Two reasons for the difference in approach to word-painting may be found in characteristics of the musical style of the period: the syllabic setting with lack of melisma, and the derivation of the melodic line from a straight reading of the poem without repetition of words.

The figures of word-painting, like the figures of speech, are by de-

Example 6.4.

to chide   me for slow - ness in her pride,

John Wilson, "Goe happy hart." From Oxford Bodleian MS Mus. b 1, f. 27v. Reprinted with permission of the Bodleian Library, Oxford.

Example 6.5.

he sub-mits,   A-dores,   and mournes,

Henry Lawes, "The Chyldish God of Love." Text by Richard Lovelace. From *Henry Lawes Autograph Manuscript;* Additional MS 53723, f. 145. Reprinted with permission of the British Library, Department of Manuscripts.

finition a highly conventional, agreed-upon set; they can function effectively when there is also an agreed-upon and conventional set of poetic images that they can be assumed to represent, as there is in much of the Petrarchan verse of Elizabethan lyricists. But the uses of language in Jacobean and Caroline lyric poetry are less formulaic than in Elizabethan poetry; many poets, following Donne, sought new and changing images and metaphors to give their verse a spontaneity and direct appeal that the older poetry no longer had. The older devices of word-painting were no longer as appropriate to the new uses of language, and to use them in more than an ornamental manner might detract from the images and conceits of the verse. Caroline composers do use the traditional figures of word-painting when the poem contains a conventional image. Since such images are less frequent, however, word-painting is rarer in continuo songs than in lute songs. Furthermore, these musical figures in continuo songs are momentary images, appearing only with a specific word and not repeated throughout the musical texture as is common in the lute song. Thus their effect is ornamental and no more substantive musically than the words they represent are substantive in the poem.

One of the most characteristic features of the madrigal is the re-iteration of words or phrases of the text, and again, many of the lute songs adopt this practice. Such repetitions may be related to the figures of speech in at least three ways. Figures of repetition are among the most frequent embellishments in elocution, and though the figures themselves deal with repetition in particular arrangements (such as the use of the same word at the beginning and end of a clause), the emphasis that a reiteration provides is a function of any of the figures, whether of speech or of music.

The kind of textual repetitions derived from the madrigal style may also serve a function similar to those of figures of division and amplification. The repetition of "enjoy" broadens its importance in the line, and at the same time puts a specific connotation on Dow-

Example 6.6.

John Dowland, "I must complain." From *The Third Booke of Songs* (1603); *The English Lute-Songs*, Series I, Vol. 10/11, p. 34. Ed. Edmund H. Fellowes. Rev. Thurston Dart and David Scott, 1970. Reproduced by permission of Stainer and Bell, Ltd. and Galaxy Music Corp.

land's interpretation of it. The device may be likened to the rhetorical figure of epandos: "repeating the terms of the general proposition in the amplification which particularizes it."[15] A similar use is made of repetition in the following song by Francis Pilkington, seen in example 6.7, where the general rhetorical function of persuasion is surely apparent.

Repetition of parts of the text is almost entirely absent from the songs of the continuo composers. The direct and unembellished language of Jacobean verse does not invite the amplifications and divisions that musical repetition can accomplish, and the function of

Example 6.7.

Francis Pilkington, "Look mistress mine." From *The First Booke of Songs* (1605); *The English Lute-Songs*, Series I, Vol. 7/15, p. 27. Ed. Edmund H. Fellowes. Rev. Thurston Dart and David Soctt, 1971. Reproduced by permission of Stainer and Bell, Ltd. and Galaxy Music Corp.

emphasis, as we have seen in preceding chapters, is almost always provided through rhythm and meter in songs of this period.

Figures of comparison also may have equivalents in musical conventions. In example 6.8 by John Danyel, the gradation from bad to worse in the afflictions the speaker has to bear is represented by an ascending sequence, suggesting musically the figure of auxesis: "advances from less to greater by arranging words or clauses in a sequence of increasing force."[16] And figures of opposition or contradiction may be represented as in the apparent paradox seen in example 6.9 that Dowland strengthens by building up the first term with repetition, sequence, and rising pitch, and abruptly releasing the tension as he presents the second term.

Some musical conventions of both the madrigal and the lute song cannot be so easily related to particular figures of speech, but are nonetheless musically rhetorical elements in their conventional sug-

Example 6.8.

John Danyel, "Eyes, look no more." From *Songs for the Lute, Viol and Voice* (1606); *The English Lute-Songs*, Series II, Vol. 8, p. 47. Ed. Edmund H. Fellowes. Rev. Thurston Dart and David Scott, 1970. Reproduced by permission of Stainer and Bell, Ltd. and Galaxy Music Corp.

gestion of emotional states. Particular chords and the introduction of dissonance are commonly used as devices of word-painting to indicate anguish. In example 6.10 by John Danyel, the momentary sound of an augmented traid (on "keep") helps to convey the speaker's struggle with his own emotions.

Chromaticism often is associated with pathos, particularly in the Italian madrigal. Although its use is much less common in England, Danyel makes the association explicit in his "Can doleful notes" in example 6.11. Danyel's text in this song is surely a plea for a musical style in the Italian vein rather than the "measured" and largely diatonic style of the French air or of the simpler lute songs like Campion's:

> Can doleful notes to measur'd accents set,
> Express unmeasur'd griefs which time forget?
> No, let Chromatic tunes, harsh without ground,
> Be sullen music for a tuneless heart,

Example 6.9.

John Dowland, "Cease these false sports." From *A Pilgrimes Solace* (1612); *The English Lute-Songs*, Series I, Vol. 12/14, pp. 69-70. Ed. Edmund H. Fellowes. Rev. Thurston Dart, 1969. Reproduced by permission of Stainer and Bell, Ltd. and Galaxy Music Corp.

> Chromatic tunes most like my passions sound,
> As if combin'd to bear their falling part.
> Uncertain certain turns, of thoughts forecast,
> Bring back the same, then die, and dying, last.[17]

His use of chromaticism in this instance is thus a part of the rhetoric of his argument, as well as a figurative representation of pathos. Elsewhere Danyel uses both chromaticism and progression by whole tones to suggest the irony that tears can accompany joys as well as sorrows, perhaps playing not only on the conventional connotation of grief or despair, but also on the uncertain harmonic implications of such passages as seen in example 6.12.

John Danyel's songs have been cited a number of times in the last few pages because Danyel is, at least on the surface, a composer who relied rather heavily on conventions of musical rhetoric in his interpretations of poetry. But Danyel's musical language is ultimately too conventional to be satisfying. Although his vocal lines and accompa-

Example 6.10.

And keep out sor - row from this—room—with - in,

John Danyel, "If I could shut the gate." From *Songs for the Lute, Viol and Voice* (1606); *The English Lute-Songs*, Series II, Vol. 8, p. 48. Ed. Edmund H. Fellowes. Rev. Thurston Dart and David Scott, 1970. Reproduced by permission of Stainer and Bell, Ltd. and Galaxy Music Corp.

Example 6.11.

Chro - ma - tic tunes most

like my pas - sions sound.

John Danyel, "Can doleful notes." From *Songs for the Lute, Viol and Voice* (1606); *The English Lute-Songs*, Series II, Vol. 8, pp. 39-40. Ed. Edmund H. Fellowes. Rev. Thurston Dart and David Scott, 1970. Reproduced by permission of Stainer and Bell, Ltd. and Galaxy Music Corp.

niments are at times complex, they do not seem to grow from a per-vasive interpretive goal so much as from the amalgamation of small

Example 6.12a.

John Danyel, "Grief keep within." From *Songs for the Lute, Viol and Voice* (1606); *The English Lute-Songs*, Series II, Vol. 8, p. 24. Ed. Edmund H. Fellowes. Rev. Thurston Dart and David Scott, 1970. Reproduced by permission of Stainer and Bell, Ltd. Galaxy Music Corp.

Example 6.12b.

John Danyel, "Grief keep within," pp. 27-28.

figures of musical rhetoric, put together as they are suggested to him more by figures of speech in the poem than by the purpose for which the poet has used them. Eloquence or ornament becomes its own excuse for being, and the persuasive purpose is thereby diminished.

Dowland, however, in his best songs, was able to use the conventions of musical rhetoric to form an integrated interpretation of the poetry he set. Examples of Dowland's expressive use of a musical rhetoric abound, especially in the songs from *A Musicall Banquet* (1610) and *A Pilgrimes Solace* (1612), but I think we can best understand this aspect of his art by comparing his justly famous "In darkness let me dwell" with Coperario's two-voice setting of the same text.

In his air Dowland uses some of the devices indicated above as a

musical rhetoric. Repetition of words and phrases is frequent, though significantly Dowland's textual repetitions are almost never literal (from a musical point of view) but provide the repeated words with a new musical context. Thus, in the following example, the music is "jarring" the first time, through startling textual accentuation and a harmonic cross-relation, and the second time, through suddenly increased rhythmic activity and the dissonance of the major seventh between melody (suspended, of course, from the previous chord) and bass:

Example 6.13.

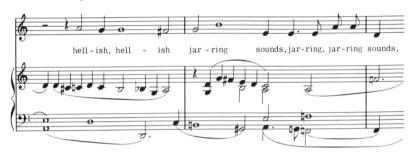

John Dowland, "In darkness let me dwell." From *A Pilgrimes Solace* (1612); *The English Lute-Songs*, Series I, Vol. 12/14, p. 82. Ed. Edmund H. Fellowes. Rev. Thurston Dart, 1969. Reproduced by permission of Stainer and Bell, Ltd. and Galaxy Music Corp.

Coperario uses very few textual repetitions in his setting, as shown in example 6.14, and those that do occur are not likely to add any new dimension of meaning, but are primarily decorative.[18]

One of Dowland's most fruitful techniques is his fully integrated use of the accompaniment, his inheritance from the polyphonic style of the madrigal and consort song. Specific rhetorical conventions, derived from the text, are made a part of the polyphony, and the accompaniment thus takes on a role in the representation of the poem. Although Coperario's setting is also polyphonic, he does not use the texture in a rhetorical way. The irony of the clauses "wedded to my woes" and "bedded to my tomb" does not seem to have had much effect on Coperario, for he merely shows their parallel construction with sequential melodic phrases in the upper voice; the lower voice and the accompaniment have no tangible relationship to either aspect of the text.

Example 6.14.

John Coprario, "In darkness let me dwell." From *Funeral Teares* (1606); *The English Lute-Songs*, Series I, Vol. 17, p. 9. Transcribed and ed. Gerald Hendrie and Thurston Dart, 1959. Reproduced by permission of Stainer and Bell, Ltd. and Galaxy Music Corp.

Dowland, on the other hand, (in example 6.16) sets the "wedded and bedded" clauses to similar—but not identical—phrases, with a cross-relation in the accompaniment at the moment of irony in each instance; realizing the cliché, Dowland puts the dissonance not only on the pathetic "woes," but on the unaccented "my," throwing a somewhat different light on the conjugal images of "wedded" and "bedded" in a manner we might relate to the rhetorical figure of hypallage, "the changeling," in which "the application of words is perverted and sometimes made absurd."[19]

Similarly, the image of the weeping walls calls forth little pathos from Coperario, whereas in Dowland's setting, the small chromatic gesture at depicting weeping is picked up in the accompaniment and extended beyond the textual phrase into a completely musical, polyphonic expression of the emotional state suggested by the textual image, seen in examples 6.17 and 6.18.

This kind of expressiveness—the creation of a musical texture from conventions of textual representation—is, of course, not available to the composer of continuo songs; the accompanist may elaborate figures from the melodic line in his realization of the bass line, but unless it is indicated in the bass (which it seldom is), such elaboration cannot be part of the composer's expressive goals because of the greatly reduced texture of solo voice line and unfigured bass.

Dowland's greatest achievement in "In darkness" is the organiza-

Example 6.15.

John Coprario, "In darkness let me dwell," p. 10.

tion of conventions like those described above into a musical structure that is rhetorical itself on a larger scale and that uses the ornaments of rhetoric, as a good Elizabethan lyric does, for the purpose of creating a single, persuasive entity. His method of working his own set of rhetorical conventions through the entire texture is of great importance in the integrated effect of the setting. Equally important is the establishment of a predominant mood or pathos, putting the listener in an appropriate frame of mind. This Dowland accomplishes with a unified conception of the musical elements to be used in his song, introduced in the opening bars by the lute, not by the voice, as seen in example 6.19. This introductory section sets forth the unusually long, slow-moving contrapuntal lines that will, when set to lines of text, amplify the words; it gives us, in the top line, a melodic shape

Example 6.16.

John Dowland, "In darkness let me dwell," p. 83.

(a leap upwards followed by a gradual descent) that will recur through-out the piece in either vocal line or accompaniment. In the alto range, we hear the melody with which the voice will begin and end the piece, making the singer's first words sound as though they have literally

Example 6.17.

John Coprario, "In darkness let me dwell," p. 9.

Example 6.18.

John Dowland, "In darkness let me dwell," pp. 81-82.

emerged from burial in the musical texture. The impassioned out-bursts at "O, let me living die" thus take on particular rhetorical force in the otherwise emotionally unified musical context.

Dowland is without question the major figure among the com-posers of lute songs in the rhetorical use of musical conventions. Most of the other lutenists, with Campion in the lead, moved toward simplicity of both vocal line and musical texture; Dowland moved instead toward the rhythmic complexity that in the vocal line at any rate, is a necessary ingredient of the declamatory style. In Chap-ter 3 we noted that in his later song books Dowland began to exag-gerate the rhythmic variety in his normally smooth melodic style and to add some embellishments in the manner of the monodic writing of Caccini; some of these features are even evident in "In darkness let me dwell." I have purposely avoided pointing out the use of declama-tory rhythms as rhetorical gesture, however, since so much of the preceding chapters has discussed rhythmic interpretation. But as we approach the declamatory style, rhythm becomes increasingly pro-minent as an expressive element, and in these later songs Dowland,

Example 6.19.

John Dowland, "In darkness let me dwell," p. 80.

Example 6.20.

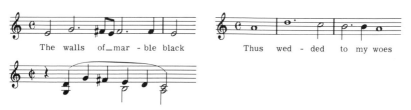

John Dowland, "In darkness let me dwell," pp. 81-83.

too, often exaggerates rhythmic variety beyond the "normal" to the point where it must be taken into account. Yet no matter how exuberant Dowland's declamatory rhythms became, he did not achieve a truly declamatory style, because of his fundamentally musical conception of the representation of meaning, rooted in his practical experience as a lutenist and in his adherence to Renaissance ideals of musical expressiveness.

"Tell me true love," from Dowland's last book of airs, features the rhythmic variety that would characterize the declamatory air in the next generation. The voice line of the song might well be taken for a monodic line by Caccini (examples 6.21a and 6.21b). And even the accompaniment to this first line is quite homophonic, as the realized bass line of a declamatory song would be. It is apparent in this and a few other songs that Dowland knew the conventions of the declamatory style, and could use the rhetorical figures implied by that style. But with the second line of this song, Dowland begins to introduce the polyphonic accompaniment that typically bears a substantial amount of his musical rhetoric, and his interest in developing what Jerome Mazzaro has termed a "fully self-expressive form"[20] seems to outweigh his commitment to the interest in expressive declamation, borrowed from the Italian musical style that was fashionable in England around 1610. Thus the conventions of declamation—used for rhetorical effects in the ways we shall find characteristic of the declamatory air—become, along with other rhetorical devices, part of the fabric of a musical texture, just as the devices of word-painting do in the madrigal or the melodic and harmonic conventions do in the more typical lute song.

The extent of Dowland's dependence on the resources of musical texture for expressiveness, even in as rhythmically declamatory a

Examples 6.21a and 6.21b.

John Dowland, "Tell me true love." From *A Pilgrimes Solace* (1612); *The English Lute-Songs*, Series I, Vol. 12/14, p. 18. Ed. Edmund H. Fellowes. Rev. Thurston Dart, 1969. Reproduced by permission of Stainer and Bell, Ltd. and Galaxy Music Corp.

Giulio Caccini, "Aria Terza." From *Le Nuove Musiche*, p. 122. Ed. H. Wiley Hitchcock, 1970. Reproduced by permission of A-R Editions, Inc., Madison, Wisconsin.

song as "Tell me true love," is apparent in the use of contrasting textures for different lines of the poem: Polyphony accompanies "In thoughts or words, in vows or promise-making, / In reasons, looks, or passions never seeing, / In men on earth, or women's minds partaking"; but a homophonic texture is used to introduce the syllogistic final couplet,[21] as shown in example 6.22.

Like many of the songs in the category of pathetic air, "Tell me true love," for all its declamatory rhythms and rhetorical figures directed specifically at the interpretation of the text, is strophic; and like all the other strophic settings, it does not work convincingly with the rhythms of stanzas other than the first. But Dowland's particular handling of musical expression, the organization of rhetorical conventions into a purely musical texture, becomes more evident the further he gets from a simple, metrical rendition that could suit all stanzas equally well. In "Tell me true love," as in "In darkness let me dwell," Dowland uses similar musical motives in the accompaniment throughout the piece to give it cohesiveness. Thus, although the individual declamatory rhythms or the specific conventions of rhetoric may not fit succeeding stanzas, the strength of their organization into a musical whole, and the reciprocal derivation of that unity from the rhetorical representation of the text, make the setting appropriate for the poem as a whole.

Dowland's attitude in songs like "In darkness let me dwell," or even "Tell me true love," is eminently appropriate to a verse form

Example 6.22.

John Dowland, "Tell me true love," p. 19.

that creates its effect not through single, striking images but through a carefully controlled interweaving of conventions of language; he constructs a musical organization that is parallel to that of the poem. To return to the two definitions given to rhetoric in the Renaissance,[22] I think it can be said that Dowland's stance would correspond to the first, more inclusive definition, for it is apparent that he has taken much more than merely elocution or delivery into account. His conventions of setting include means comparable even to the figures of invention and the construction of arguments. The most remarkable aspect of Dowland's genius is that his settings are responsive to their texts in multiple layers; not only do they interpret poetry rhythmically and through rhetorical gesture, but on a larger scale, they represent the whole poem in what is ultimately a purely musical expression.

This, of course, is the point at which instrumental music must enter the picture, for if Dowland's songs are "fully self-expressive" musically, they will be just as coherent without a text as with one; and as many writers have pointed out, this is precisely the period in which instrumental music began to assume a life of its own. But the

rise of instrumental music, often cited as a cause for the decline of vocal music (particularly in England), might better be seen as the result of the full development of a rhetorical stance in musico-poetic relationships, in correspondence with the systematically elaborate poetry of the late Renaissance. The coincidence of Elizabethan verse, humanistic ideals of textual representation, and a musical imagination like Dowland's produced as democratic and as successful an alliance of music and poetry as could be desired. That it did not survive beyond Dowland's lifetime, however, was owing not so much to the rise of instrumental music as to the decline of poetic styles to which such musical elaboration was appropriate.

In the poetry set as declamatory airs, the influences of John Donne and Ben Jonson are prominent. Donne is responsible for more naturalistic diction than was characteristic of Elizabethan verse, turning from the artifices of formal elocution to language and syntax derived from "normal" speech. The example of Jonson's emphasis on taste and decorum made much Cavalier poetry as suitable in external structure for song as the Elizabethan lyric, but his characteristic restraint kept his use of language as far from the formulaic conventions of Classical rhetoric as was Donne's. And whereas the Elizabethan lyric had been impersonally complimentary in its persuasion, the typical Cavalier lyric used the force of argument to persuade and had little use for the decorative language of compliment. Thus where conventions of rhetoric appear in Cavalier poetry, they are more likely to be used for the purpose of furthering an argument than as ornament in the creation of a finely wrought work of art.

In this change we can see an alteration in the function of rhetoric in song as well. If words are no longer used conventionally as ornament, then music cannot appropriately be so used either. There can no longer be an agreed-upon set of referents for the figures of a musical rhetoric; for the musical language to add its own decorative plane of expression to the poetry would be out of keeping with what was inherent in the verse. A rhetoric of music, to be effectively joined to this new kind of poetry, must be used not to make the language of the poem more colorful but to make its arguments more forceful. The strength of an argument for the Jacobean or Caroline poet lay partly in the logic of its terms, and partly in the ability of the speaker to create the necessary emotional tone. The problem for the Jacobean composer thus was to find a musical language that

could suitably represent these aspects of the text without being decorative in the way the madrigal and the lute song had been.[23]

Another important feature that set the Cavalier lyric apart from the Elizabethan was its more personal tone. This, too, indicated a change in rhetorical stance. In the earlier lyric style, the poet's role was that of singer;[24] poets sang about love, or about people in love, but not about their own experiences with love. The identification of the poet with the poem's persona was apparent as early as the 1570s in the work of Sidney, but seems not to have affected the song verse until the early seventeenth century. Once it invaded the song lyrics, this personal stance made musical settings like Dowland's less suitable, for a setting that cushioned the poem in a "fully self-expressive" musical context inevitably removed some of the force of personal statement from the poem's presentation. Another challenge to the Jacobean composer then was to develop a musical language that would sustain the sense that the poet was speaking directly to an audience, presenting personal thoughts and emotions.

The Italians seemed to have found a way to represent at least the pathos of the text with recitative and monody, and the English made several attempts to follow their example. Dowland's "Tell me true Love" was certainly a step in that direction, but its polyphonic texture, used for expressive purpose of its own, provided too much embellishment that was external to the logic and the pathos of the text. Not all Jacobean composers shared Dowland's commitment to the ideals of Renaissance polyphony, however, and it must have become clear to some that one of the reasons the Italian style could be so effective as a representation of the rhetoric of emotions in the text was its greatly reduced musical texture.

The humanists' position on intelligibility of the text is again relevant here, for not only did it suggest a fundamental change in musical texture so that the words could be understood by an audience, but it seems also to have spelled out a musico-textual relationship that would comply more effectively with the characteristics of the new kind of poetry. Argument is best represented through its own words; the best way to set it to music is in a style that will make it fully intelligible and not detract from its force with ornament. Personal emotions also will be most emphatically represented through the speaker's words, for the translation of the rhetoric of emotions into a musical rhetoric generalizes its terms into those of

convention. Thus, in line with both the humanistic ideal and the reduction of artifice in poetry, the next step in the search for a suitable
musical rhetoric had to be the elimination of the polyphonic accompaniment that had borne so much of Dowland's expressiveness.

The lute songs with a superficial resemblance to the musical style
of the air de cour (with unmetered declamation of textual rhythms
by the voice over a homophonic accompaniment) provide a sounder
basis for this development than the madrigal-related airs, for in such
songs the declamatory rhythms are expressive in their own right
rather than as part of a polyphonic texture. During the second
decade of the century, as composers began to set poetry with more
complex rhythms and meters evolving from the influence of Donne,
the rhythmic character of the vocal line became comparably more
complex, while the accompaniment—if it was not to emerge as the
polyphony of Dowland—necessarily became simpler. Musical texture in the declamatory air was thus pared to the minimum of solo
voice and unfigured bass line. What remained was a kind of song in
which, if the attitude of the composer involved the representation
of the emotions and meaning of the text, it must be through the
words themselves and not through any conventionally meaningful
set of figures. Declamatory rhythm, in the service of intelligible and
forceful presentation of the text, was necessarily the primary basis
for a musical rhetoric.

The devices of rhetoric used in the continuo song are not generally capable of carrying any significance in their own right, but only
in their particular attachment to words; there will thus be no appreciable plane of musical meaning added to the text in a continuo
song, but only a reinforcement of the meanings inherent in the
poem. But, of course, this is true also of figures of speech. The
rhetorical conventions of the declamatory air are no more nor less
"self-expressive" than the conventions of language, but they are
capable of aiding the exposition of thematic content and the development of elements of persuasion in ways that are comparable to
linguistic conventions. Since many devices of declamatory interpretation have been presented in Chapter 1 and referred to repeatedly throughout this study, to spell them out again here would be
redundant. Instead we shall look at a few instances in the declamatory airs where these conventions are used as specifically rhetorical
gesture, as opposed to "normal" use as interpretation of textual
rhythms.

The nature of the conventions of rhetoric appropriate to the style of Cavalier verse is such that they are probably more nearly comparable to the schemes of grammar than to ornament or invention, not by way of specific correlation but in general function. One of the primary functions of the declamatory rhythms in the continuo song is the articulation of grammatical constructions; and there is written evidence that by the 1630s "grammar" had assumed a place along with poetry as an "art" to be joined to music. Charles Butler, in the Dedication of his *Principles of Musik* (1636) says:

> Meerly to Speak and to Sing, ar of Nature: and therefore the rudest Swains of the most barbarous Nations doe make this dubble use of their articulate voices: but to speak well, and to sing well, ar of Art: so that among the best Wits of the most civilized people, none may attain unto perfection in either faculty, without the Rules and Precepts of Art, confirmed by the practice of approved Authors.
>
> I have been induced, (My GRACIOVS LORD) for the furtherance of the studious, to set forth the Principles of both these vocall Arts, [*Grammar* and *Musik*].[25]

The rhetorical use of grammatical structure can be seen in examples like 6.23a and b from William Lawes' highly declamatory "Amarillis tear thy hair," where melodic shape articulates the syntactical structure and rests punctuate the phrases of the text.[26]

The technique of setting strongly enjambed lines with musical lines overriding the linear structure of the verse becomes a rhetorical convention when to pause at the end of a line would destroy a segment of the argument in the poem, as seen in example 6.24.

One of the most frequent and effective conventions of rhythmic—and rhetorical—interpretation in the declamatory air is the agogic accent. In Henry Lawes' setting of the eighth sonnet from Spenser's *Amoretti*, for instance, (see example 6.25) the agogic accent on "More" has two functions: First is the interpretation of poetic rhythm, ensuring that the dactyl of the first three syllables is heard. But although the rhythm of the second line is the same, Lawes gives it a far less emphatic setting, as shown in example 6.26. The agogic accent on "More" is thus a deviation from what is necessary for "normal" interpretive accentuation and its second function is rhetorical. The strength of the speaker's appeal to the lady lies in his comparisons—always in her favor, as Lawes' setting establishes with its very first note.

And of course the rugged melodic lines and wide leaps that are characteristic of the declamatory airs may also be part of the con-

Example 6.23.

[William Lawes], "Amarillis tear thy hair." From *Select Ayres and Dialogues, The Second Book*, p. 25. (Ascribed there to Henry Lawes.) London: John Playford, 1669. Facsimile ed. Ridgewood, N.J.: Gregg Press, Inc., 1966.

Example 6.24.

Henry Lawes, "The Chyldish God of Love." Text by Richard Lovelace. From *Henry Lawes Autograph Manuscript;* Additional MS 53723, f. 145. Reprinted with permission of The British Library, Department of Manuscripts.

Example 6.25.

Henry Lawes, "More than most fayre." Text by Edmund Spenser. From *Henry Lawes Autograph Manuscript;* Additional MS 53723, f. 17. Reprinted with permission of The British Library, Department of Manuscripts.

Example 6.26.

Henry Lawes, "More than most fayre," f. 17.

ventions of rhetoric. In example 6.27 William Lawes builds intensity by increasing the size of the leaps (minor third, major third, fourth, fifth and finally seventh). The final leap of a major seventh emphasizes the irony that the tyranny of "men and gods" will destroy itself. Any of the conventions of interpretive declamation, if they are exaggerated enough to be prominent in the musical language, and particularly if they are used with obvious reference to rhetorical devices in the text, may be considered elements in the musical rhetoric of the pathetic airs of the continuo song.

Finally, we must consider what effect the declamatory rhetoric has on the composer's ability to set a strophic text. With Dowland, it will be recalled, the creation of a musical expression that was *generally* comparable to the rhetorical structure of the poem made the setting appropriate at least on that level for all the stanzas. If, however, the rhetorical conventions of the declamatory air do not carry conventionally accepted meaning and must therefore be correlated with particular words to be effective, or are not used in the construction of a musically integrated whole, it would appear that in this respect—as in the difficulty posed by increasingly complex rhythms that cannot be maintained from one stanza to the next—the declamatory style was not likely to be acceptable for strophic song.

Example 6.27.

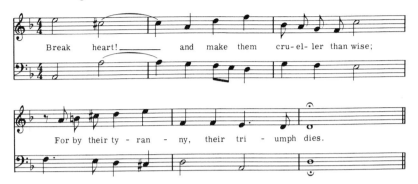

Break   heart!_____   and   make   them   cru-el-ler than wise;

For by their ty - ran - ny,   their tri - umph dies.

William Lawes, "To whom shall I complain; to men or gods?" From *English Songs 1625-1660; Musica Britannica*, Vol. XXXIII, p. 133. Ed. Ian Spink, 1971. Reproduced by permission of Stainer and Bell, Ltd. on behalf of the Musica Britannica Trust, and by permission of Galaxy Music Corp.

Nonetheless, a good number of the pathetic, declamatory airs are strophic, and an interesting comparison is afforded in settings of Sir John Suckling's "No, no fair heretic," one anonymous and one by Henry Lawes.

> No, no, fair heretic, it needs must be
>   But an ill love in me,
>   And worse for thee.
> For were it in my power
> To love thee now this hour
>   More than I did the last,
> 'Twould then so fall
>   I might not love at all.
> Love that can flow, and can admit increase,
> Admits as well an ebb, and may grow less.
>
> True love is still the same; the torrid zones
>   And those more frigid ones,
>   It must not know;
> For love, grown cold or hot,
> Is lust or friendship, not
>   The thing we have;
> For that's a flame would die,
>   Held down or up too high.

Then think I love more than I can express,
And would love more, could I but love thee less.[27]

Typical of its period, Suckling's lyric is not the ornamental compliment of the Elizabethan style, but a reasoned argument on the va-
garies of love: The first stanza argues that if the lady wants a love
that can increase, she must accept that it might just as easily decrease;
the second stanza counters that *true* love (with the implication
that this is the speaker's love) will do neither, but will remain con-
stant. In each stanza, the final couplet sums up the argument of the
stanza with the figures of testimony: the adage and the maxim.

The anonymous song is a melodious, strophic setting, using declamatory rhythms only as representation of textual rhythm—and
this not very emphatically. The up-beat figures, which in the last
chapter were shown to characterize attempts at the Italian style, are
frequent, giving the setting some of the urgency of a declamatory air,
but without particularized interpretation of words or phrases. Thus,
the setting shown in example 6.28, is rhythmically acceptable for
both stanzas of the text. But there is hardly a sense in which this
setting can be called rhetorical. If it is a pleasing musical entity, it is
so in spite of the text, not through its interpretation of the text as
Dowland's settings were; its general relationship to the theme of the
poem is equally innocuous for both stanzas. The rhythmic style, too,
avoids rhetorical conventions and is therefore appropriate to both
stanzas only in its refusal to deviate from the "normal" in interpreting textual rhythms.

Henry Lawes' setting, as by now should be expected, takes a definite rhetorical stance toward the poem, with clearly interpretive
rhythms and a shift to triple meter for the final couplet, which (given
the associations of the triple-meter convention as we have described
them in Chapter 3) has the interesting effect of setting off the adage
as common or popular knowledge.[28] The rhetorical conventions of
the declamatory air make the setting of the first stanza an emphatic
statement of the poet's argument. The musical phrasing, set off by
rests and melodic shape, corresponds to the grammatical structure and
to the logical presentation of the argument (see example 6.29). The
conditional clause is a long, ascending phrase, and its consequent
falls back down to a middle range. Agogic accents emphasize "now"

Example 6.28.

No,   no, fair he - re-tic,   it needs must be But an ill love in me,

[Anonymous] , "No, no, fair heretic." From Drexel MS 4041, f. 8v. Reproduced with permission of the Music Division, The New York Public Library, Astor, Lenox, and Tilden Foundations.

and its reinforcing appostive "this hour," adding the immediacy characteristic of Cavalier verse to the argument.

In the printed sources of Henry Lawes' setting,[29] it is given as an ordinary strophic song, with the second stanza printed at the bottom of the page. But in the Henry Lawes Manuscript, the composer has written out a variant setting for the second stanza, its rhythmic changes indicative of Lawes' understanding of the rhetorical nature of his setting. In the first line, for instance, though the meter of the poem would have made the first interpretation acceptable, the rhythm is altered for the second stanza to put emphasis on "True," since that is the key word in the speaker's argument in this stanza (see example 6.30). The variant setting of the lines corresponding to those quoted in example 6.29 ("For were it in my pow'r") are even more pointedly changed for rhetorical purpose. I have given the passage shown in examples 6.31a and b first as it would be in the ordinary strophic setting, and second as Lawes sets it in the manuscript version.[30] The crucial point, of course, is the handling of the grammatical structure, particularly the setting of the strong enjambment of lines 15-16. But the second version is also more emphatic in its accentuation of the words important to the argument, such as the parallel rhythms aligning "cold or hot" with "lust or friendship." We would fail to do justice to Lawes' reading of the poem if we did not notice the slight rearrangement of the melody to place a chromatic line, unusual for Lawes, on "Is lust or friendship."

The conclusion should be obvious: Strophic settings cannot possibly succeed when the composer's attitude toward the text includes the representation of the rhetoric of argument. Yet if we consider the interpretive possibilities of the typical Cavalier lyric—like Suckling's poem—there seems to be little else in it that music could re-

Example 6.29.

For were it in my pow'r, To love thee now____
____ this hour More than I did the last, 'twould then so
fall. I might not love at all. ℭ Love that can flow,

Henry Lawes, "No, no, fair heretic." From *Henry Lawes Autograph Manuscript;*
Additional MS 53723, ff. 52v-53. Reprinted with permission of The British Library,
Department of Manuscripts.

present. The conditions set by the poetry made it impossible, on the
one hand, to continue using a musically self-expressive language like
Dowland's that could at least sustain strophic repetition, and on the
other hand equally impossible to use the kind of musical rhetoric
appropriate to it for more than one set of words. Henry Lawes'
solution was to widen the gap between the tuneful, strophic airs and
the declamatory airs, which he tended more and more to set as
through-composed songs rather than strophic, particularly in his set-

Example 6.30.

No. no. fair__ he - re-tic
True love is still the same;

Henry Lawes, "No, no, fair heretic," ff. 52v-53.

Example 6.31a.

For love, grown cold or hot,   Is lust or friend - ship, not

The thing we have; For that's   a flame would die,   Held down or   up   too high;

Example 6.31b.

For love   grown_ cold   or hot   Is   lust   or friend-ship,

not The thing we have.   for that's a flame would die Held down, or___   up   too   high;

Henry Lawes, "No, no, fair heretic," ff. 52v-53.

tings of the poetry of Thomas Carew. Ultimately the strophic, declamatory air could not survive, and in the next generation, songs in which the composer adopted a rhetorical stance, or sought to represent the pathos of the text, were usually strophic variations or some other form in which exact repetition was obviated.

A gradual change is apparent in the contents of the Playford volumes from 1651 onwards, as the declamatory strophic song fell more and more into oblivion in England. The dichotomy between the light, homophonic dance songs and the through-composed, monodic airs was increasing, with the result that the hybrid style — our "pathetic air"—virtually disappeared. Its history was rather brief, but not without significance, for during this half-century composers of art songs to English texts tried, and found the limits of, radically different methods of representing meaning in song. Succeeding ages have preferred the earlier method in the songs of Dowland, but the declamatory method, though it could not sustain a reciprocal bond between the two arts, seems to have been as firmly rooted in a consideration of the poetry as the lute song. In the final analysis, the continuo composers had to confront what composers of

art song to the present day have had to face: that from the beginning of the seventeenth century on, English poetry has not, in truth, been designed for song. The kind of careful representation attempted by the composers of declamatory airs could not, without doing violence to the poetry, generate a significant musical style.

Conclusion

The purpose of this study has been to look at the development of English solo song during the first half of the seventeenth century from the standpoint of varying attitudes toward what the musical half of the partnership will represent. Now we must try to draw together what happened to the various attitudes discussed in Chapters 3-6 to see whether they form a coherent picture of the reasons behind changing musical fashions and the dissolution of the union of music and poetry. If, as I believe, the particular development in English is inherently related to changes in poetic style, then we should see some continuity in the way musical styles, derived from any of the attitudes, evolved.

Let us consider once again, in very general terms, which elements of English poetry may be represented with music. On the most mechanical level is the re-creation of the accentual-syllabic poetic meter through musical notation. One step in the direction of non-interpretation of text would take us to songs in which poetic meter is merely a convenient correlative for musical rhythms, while one step in the other direction takes us to songs in which the syllabic versification is preserved, but musical rhythm tends toward speech rhythms rather than toward poetic meter. A further step in this direction leads toward a representation of speech rhythms within their syntactic contexts rather than within the context of the line of poetry. Superimposed on the rendition of these elements of temporal organization is the more subjective representation of the meaning of the poem.

Every one of these elements changed in the poetry itself during the first quarter of the century, and my aim has been to relate any changes in musical style to these alterations in poetic taste. In the

early lute song style, a composer might choose to represent either poetic meter or poetic rhythm without significantly changing his musical conventions, since in the Elizabethan lyric poetic meter and rhythm usually are not far apart. Similarly, a tuneful dance-related style, such as is frequent in the early lute songs, can be successfully correlated with a typical Elizabethan lyric, since the poem will probably have well-balanced lines, often of equal length, that will coincide with the balanced phrasing of the dance. But as poetic styles changed, it became increasingly difficult to maintain anything like a homogeneous song style, and composers had to adopt a definite attitude regarding which aspect of the text they were going to represent in any given setting.

The representation of poetic meter—what I have called the French attitude because it is so clearly and unequivocally present in musique mesurée and certain airs de cour—was a serious goal for some lutenists, and the songs of Thomas Campion show a sustained effort to represent the vernacular poetic meters—English accentual meters—with music. But whereas the coordination of music with poetic meter in either French or Italian allowed a great deal of rhythmic freedom since their syllabic meters do not involve accentuation, such correlation with English accentual meters inevitably produced rather monotonous musical rhythms, and greatly restricted the possibility of any other kind of interpretation of the text. Furthermore, as poetic rhythm and meter became more disparate in the poetry of John Donne and poets following him, the representation of poetic meter put a strain on declamation, making the musical setting more often a distortion of natural pronunciation than it had been with the smoother poetic rhythms of Elizabethan lyrics. Therefore, from the point of view of the representation of poetic meter, songs had to take one of two courses with respect to their texts: Either they would be trivialized, tuneful songs in which the composer has not taken the interpretation of the text as a goal, or they would have to abandon the representation of poetic meter.

A similar situation was inevitable with regard to the representation of versification. The dance-related lute songs and those that followed the style of the air de cour in meticulously setting off the individual lines of a poem were also pushed to their limits by new poetic tendencies to override the lines, as with Donne, or to avoid lines of such regular lengths as the dance structure could accommodate. And again

we find that song styles of necessity diverged into the tuneful and dance-related types, which could set only the very regular (and by this time the less serious or interesting) poetry, and those whose more attentive attitude toward the text determined that they must leave the dance tradition and assume the more flexible approach to rhythm and phrasing that were characteristic of monodic song.

Thus, before the second quarter of the century, two distinct types of solo song are apparent in England: simple, tuneful airs, often related to the dance, which continue at least superficially to represent the meter and versification of their texts, and those songs in which, because representation of some aspect of the text remains a serious goal, composers found it necessary to abandon poetic meter, and sometimes versification as well. The simple, tuneful airs were popular far into the century; but for our purposes they may now be dismissed, for, in spite of some interesting and sometimes clever points of reference to the text, they are generally not serious interpretations of poetry, and the development of their musical style from this point on is not significantly related to poetic styles. For the composer who wished to provide a serious interpretation of the text, with poetic meter and versification no longer viable referents, there remained declamatory rhythm and rhetoric. These, of course, were not new elements for song writers; madrigal technique included the representation of both, and many of the early lute songs involve the setting of poetic rhythm and the representation of meaning much more than of poetic meter. But because of the greater emphasis on irregular rhythms, on syntactical rather than linear construction, and on rough diction in Jacobean poetry, declamation seems to have been the only practicable approach to textual interpretation after the decline of Elizabethan lyrics as song texts.

Dowland worked almost exclusively with speech-like rhythms in his settings of English poetry. But although his musical rhythms were derived from those of the text, they were typically smooth and musical, like the normal rhythms of the Elizabethan lyric. Recognizing the need for a more variable and vigorous rhythmic style to correspond to the rougher rhythms of Jacobean poetry, composers from about 1610 on (including Dowland) tried to follow the Italian lead in developing a musical language that would correspond more precisely with the rhythms of the text. The early English attempts to imitate the Italian monodic style were based on the musical style

itself, and because they failed to take into account the differences between the stress patterns characteristic of the two languages, they were generally not successful. Lanier, with *Hero and Leander,* came closest to making the Italian style work with an English text, but this was primarily because he achieved a fully rhetorical relationship between music and poetry, not because his setting was appreciably better than any of the other Italianate attempts at representing the rhythms of the English language. Most of the composers who adopt the Italian musical style are no more accurate in their representation of the rough diction and rhythms of Jacobean poetry than were the earlier lutenists with their smooth declamation.

Henry Lawes did seem to recognize the highly accentual nature of the English language, and in his settings we can see the most sustained effort of the period to represent the actual rhythms of English poetry with a varied enough rhythmic vocabulary to accommodate the less predictable stress patterns of Jacobean and Caroline poetry. Unfortunately, in developing this style, Lawes seems to have invited a kind of monotony comparable to what developed earlier in the representation of poetic meter. There are, I think, two fundamental reasons for this: First, the rhythmic language Lawes adopted was not very pleasing musically and was not capable of generating its own interest; second, because even Jacobean poetry was by no means *always* rough in its rhythmic character, and because the normally occurring rhythm of English is iambic, Lawes' interpretation of the syllables intervening between striking poetic rhythms falls into jerky, repetitive patterns, no more capable of forming a significant song style than were the plain, metrical settings of Campion.

Lawes' style—and that of most continuo composers—was best when it combined speech rhythms with a consistently rhetorical attitude. This, too, was an approach to textual representation that was prominent in the lute song. Dowland and Danyel were the most consistently rhetorical of the lutenists, borrowing many techniques from the madrigal (word-painting, text repetitions, sequential repetitions, coloristic harmony, dissonance, chromaticism, textural contrast) to represent the meaning and the emotional context of the poem. But once again, the changes in poetic style—with a more argumentative tone and a less formulaic approach to rhetoric in poetry—made continuation with the same rhetorical conventions inappropriate; the continuo composers expressed their interpretation of pathos pri-

marily through exaggeration of the conventions of declamation (the agogic accent, the accentual effect of a leap, the use of rests and melodic articulation to reinforce syntactical construction). However, these rhetorical conventions, although they were suitable to the poetry and effective for the task, had two major drawbacks: First, they were not a separate set of conventions, but were shared with simple declamation of the text; and second, they had no inherent musical significance, as most of the rhetorical conventions of the lute song did. Thus, the rhetorical attitude also failed—largely because the demands of poetry were far less amenable to musical representation—to produce a substantial song form.

This combination of developments in poetic style made it necessary, by the second quarter of the seventeenth century, that music be the servant of poetry if it was to represent the poetry in any significant way; and ultimately it made the composer's position necessarily subservient too. The union of music and poetry in the lute song was one in which the composer's role was equal to that of the poet; his music, while taking its inspiration from the poem, was in the best songs, as capable of standing on its own as the poem was. But the continuo song could not produce such a union. The poetry, in its striking originality, was too strong to permit an equally self-sustaining musical style.

It is significant in this respect that it was Henry Lawes who received such lavish praise from poets. Our knowledge of Dowland's relationship with poets can be nothing but conjecture. He did not name the poets of his songs, and many of the poems in his song books still remain unidentified. Dowland received no accolades from poets, though he was widely renowned in his own day; except for one short poem by Campion (mainly commending Dowland's putting his songs into print!), the song books do not have the flattering poems that accompanied song books in the second half of the century. Playford's editions of Lawes' songs, on the other hand, almost all have two or three commendatory verses, and several of the better-known poets—whose authorship of the poetry Lawes set was advertised by Playford—wrote laudatory poems. Milton's famous sonnet, which unquestionably refers to Lawes' declamatory airs rather than the tuneful ones, is typical of the many poems that praise Lawes' settings not for their musical worth, but for their fidelity to the verse.

The lack of written praise of Dowland's songs is not necessarily an indication that poets were not happy with his settings; it may instead be indicative that his works spoke for themselves and were not *merely* settings of their verse. There was no need for poets to justify his work. With the continuo song, there obviously was such a need, and perhaps it was Playford, in his entrepreneurial role as publisher, who sought out the support of poets. The union of music and poetry, the partnership of musicians and poets had to be publicly proclaimed, because, although the humanistic ideal of joining the two arts continued to be proclaimed in poetry and treatises well into the second half of the century, in actual practice, with English poetry it had become impossible to accomplish.

Notes

Introduction

1. Thomas Campion, "To the Reader," *Two Bookes of Ayres* c. 1613, in *The Works of Thomas Campion*, ed. Walter R. Davis (New York: Doubleday and Co., 1967, and Faber and Faber, Ltd., 1967), p. 55.

2. It is, of course, almost impossible to discuss English song of the late Renaissance without reference to its poetry. Mention should be made, however, of some of the more important studies in which the two art forms have been correlated. Among the earlier works Miles Kastendieck's *England's Musical Poet, Thomas Campion* (New York: Russell and Russell, 1963), though now largely outdated, was a pioneering study. In this category, too, belong Willa McClung Evan's *Ben Jonson and Elizabethan Music* (New York: DaCapo Press, 1965) and *Henry Lawes. Musician and Friend of Poets* (New York: Kraus Reprint Corp., 1966). Bruce Pattison's *Music and Poetry of the English Renaissance*, second edition (London: Methuen, 1970) covers the earlier part of the period investigated here. Joseph Kerman's *The Elizabethan Madrigal* (New York: American Musicological Society, 1962) is a valuable genre study. Approaching the alliance from the literary side, John Hollander's *The Untuning of the Sky* (Princeton, N.J.: Princeton Univ. Press, 1961; repr. New York: W. W. Norton, 1970) considers the transfer of ideas between the two arts, while two more recent books — Paula Johnson's *Form and Transformation in Music and Poetry of the English Renaissance* (New Haven: Yale Univ. Press, 1972) and Jerome Mazzaro's *Transformations in the Renaissance English Lyric* (Ithaca, N.Y.: Cornell Univ. Press, 1970) — are more concerned with the similarities in constructional principles. Finally, Ian Spink's *English Song, Dowland to Purcell* (London: B. T. Batsford, 1974) takes account of the poetry in its survey of the songs of the period.

In addition, sections of other books and numerous articles (many of which are cited in the Bibliography) offer insight into the union of music and poetry in late Renaissance England.

Mention also must be made of the editors who have made large numbers of the songs from this period available to the modern scholar and the public. The work of Edmund H. Fellowes is monumental; his editions of the madrigals and the lute songs (now mostly available in new editions, revised by Thurston Dart and others) revived a whole generation of song. The continuo songs have been less completely edited, though the work of Ian Spink in his *English Songs 1625-1660; Musica Britannica*, Vol. XXXIII (London: Stainer and Bell, 1971) is a valuable contribution.

3. See, for instance, the discussion in Kerman, *Elizabethan Madrigal*, pp. 21-37.

4. Solo song, of course, was not new in England in the seventeenth century. Sixteenth-century manuscript sources contain solo songs, often associated with the choir-school plays,

and usually accompanied by a consort of instruments. (See Philip Brett, "The English Consort Song, 1560-1625," *Proceedings of the Royal Musical Association,* LXXXVIII [1962], 73-88.) William Byrd wrote a large number of consort songs and in the later printed versions underlaid the instrumental parts with text to conform to the then current popularity of the madrigal and part song. However, like the madrigals of the period, these songs usually are not settings of the better poetry. Furthermore, though some aspects of Byrd's approach to the text are carried on in the songs of Campion and other lutenist composers, these solo songs represent the end of an older tradition rather than the emergence of the lute song. (See the discussion of Byrd's *Psalms, Sonnets and Songs* of 1588 in Kerman, *Elizabethan Madrigal,* pp. 102-8, and Philip Brett, "Word-Setting in the Songs of Byrd," *Proceedings of the Royal Musical Association,* XCVIII [1971-72], 47-64.)

It is likely that madrigals too were sung at least occasionally as accompanied solos, if only because of the inconvenience of having to gather a group of singers to perform them polyphonically; but the approach to the text, as well as the nature of the texts themselves, is still that of the madrigal and in most instances differs from that of the lute song, as will be shown in Chapter 1.

5. One of the most puzzling features of solo song during the second quarter of the seventeenth century is the complete lack of printed sources. The lute songs of the first quarter of the century were printed, and a collection of madrigals and part songs by Walter Porter appeared in print in 1632, but although it is obvious that solo songs continued to be written and sung during this period, for nearly thirty years (from the last book of lute songs in 1622 to Playford's first anthology in 1651) no secular solo songs were printed in England.

6. Playford's three-volume *Treasury of Music* published in 1669 is, in fact, composed of reprints of his own earlier publications: Book I is a reprint of his *Select Ayres and Dialogues* of 1659; Book II is probably a reprint of his *Select Ayres and Dialogues* of 1663 (of which there are no extant copies); and Book III is a reprint of Book III of the *Ayres and Dialogues* of Henry Lawes, first published in 1658. Thus, although some songs will be cited from Playford volumes as late as 1669, they are all of earlier composition.

7. A problem peculiar to the interdisciplinary nature of this study is the repeated frustration of identifying and defining terms and concepts that have markedly different meanings in the two disciplines. This section of Part I will clarify my use of such terms in succeeding chapters.

Prologue to Part I

1. The notable exception to this is the vocal music of the twentieth century. Contemporary composers have been thoroughly eclectic in their selection of texts, choosing poetry — and sometimes prose — from all periods and cultures.

2. Other writers have described various aspects of this poetry. I should like particularly to refer the reader to Jerome Mazzaro *Transformations in the Renaissance English Lyric* (Ithaca, N.Y.: Cornell Univ. Press, 1970), especially Chapter IV, where the use of rhetorical conventions and the function of the persona in Elizabethan song lyrics are dealt with in some detail.

3. John Hollander, "Donne and the Limits of Lyric," *John Donne: Essays in Celebration,* ed. A. J. Smith (London: Methuen, 1972), p. 261.

Chapter 1: Music for Meter and Rhythm

1. Perceptual differences in the arts, of course, raise complex aesthetic and psychological issues that cannot be of prime concern here. It should be noted, however, that some of

my statements concerning the perception of organizational principles consider them only from the point of view of the auditor, thus ignoring the possibility of structural perception by a reader. Since it is more likely that a poem will be read than heard, and the reader can refer back if he chooses, and since a piece of music will more likely be heard than read, the necessity for perception in process is much greater in music than in poetry. In spite of these reservations, I am going to discuss such problems as identical in the two arts for the simple reason that we shall not generally be considering the poems as literary phenomena per se, but rather as the texts of songs and therefore subject to the same perceptual criteria as the music that accompanies them. Some problems of perception of complex poetic structures are discussed in Chapter 2.

2. Curt Sachs, in *Rhythm and Tempo* (New York: W.W. Norton, 1953), gives an account of this confusion. Current musical dictionaries continue to have considerable variety in their definitions of rhythm and meter. Grosvenor Cooper and Leonard Meyer offer clear and useful definitions of pulse, meter, and rhythm in music in *The Rhythmic Structure of Music* (Chicago: Univ. of Chicago Press, 1960). Their definition of rhythm, however, deals more with accent than with duration. My definition below isolates the durational characteristics of rhythm for purposes that should be clear in my discussion of certain aspects of the relationship of music and poetry.

3. "Semantic" is admittedly a somewhat problematic choice as a descriptive term. My ad hoc definition is rather broader than the usual definitions (themselves by no means always consistent) by linguistic theorists (e.g., Edward Stankiewicz: "the *subject matter*, that is, the thing spoken about, the referent, or . . . the 'semantic dimension,'" in "Linguistics and the Study of Poetic Language," *Style in Language*, ed. Thomas A. Sebeok [New York: Wiley, 1960], p. 71). I take "semantic" to mean not only "the thing spoken about" but the relationship of verbal symbols to their meanings—that is, the way in which the elements of language and their organization into recognizable patterns affects perception of them as meaningful symbols. Thus, where John Hollander has used "formal" and "semantic" with reference to meter and ("since English has phonemic stress") rhythm, and in discussion of enjambment ("The Metrical Frame," *Vision and Resonance* [New York: Oxford Univ. Press, 1975], pp.145-46), I have expanded the distinction to include all dimensions of the organization of words in poetry. A similar (though not identical) distinction is made, using the terms "formal" and "semantic," in David Crystal, *Prosodic Systems and Intonation in English* (Cambridge: Cambridge Univ. Press, 1969), a linguistic study of the effects of patterns of sound in the establishment of (formal) prosodic systems. In Chapter 7, "The semantics of intonation," Crystal says, "The view of semantics underlying the approach used in this chapter is strictly intra-linguistic: I am concerned in the first instance with the establishment of meaning-relationships between formal contrasts in language, and not with the relationships which exist between language and extra-linguistic 'reality' or 'experience'"(p. 282).

4. A recent study of rhythm in the English language is D. W. Harding, *Words into Rhythm* (Cambridge: Cambridge Univ. Press, 1976). Harding probes the effects of the simultaneous perception of rhythm and meter in English much more thoroughly than I can here. See especially Chapters 2-4: "Speech and the rhythm of verse," "Metrical set and rhythmical variation," and "Effects of deviation from metre."

5. Some aspects of the relationship of the English language to music are considered in a brief essay by Monroe C. Beardsley: "Verse and Music," *Versification: Major Language Types*, ed. W. K. Wimsatt (New York: New York Univ. Press, 1972), pp. 238-52. Other essays in this volume also are relevant to this study in that they concern the relationship of systems of versification to the characteristic features of their languages.

6. D. P. Walker, in an important five-part article, presents a thorough account of the theoretical and practical effect of humanistic studies on music in the late Renaissance.

"Musical Humanism in the Sixteenth and Early Seventeenth Centuries," *Music Review*, II (1941), 1-13; 111-21; 220-27; 288-308; III (1942), 55-71.

7. As Walker points out, most musical humanists seem either to have forgotten that the Greeks did not exclude instrumental music from their discussions or to have distorted this information to support their own claims. "Musical Humanism," 226-27.

8. For an excellent account of this transfer and its subsequent, misunderstood adoption by Elizabethan poets, see G. L. Hendrickson, "Elizabethan Quantitative Hexameters," *Philological Quarterly*, XXVIII (1949), 237-60.

9. *Ibid.*, 243.

10. In this song, as in other French *airs* to be cited, the time signature, when there is one, is largely without significance. The tactus is nonetheless always evident from the notation.

11. It is this characteristic of the French language that is involved in a correspondence between Richard Strauss and Romain Rolland three centuries later. Strauss, for example, questions Debussy's setting of "cheveux" as "chĕ-véux," "cĥe-véux," and "ché-veux" in three different places, to which Rolland replies that many French words "are fluid and Protean; they obey [in accentuation] and yield to circumstances which are logical, psychological, etc." Richard Strauss and Romain Rolland, *Correspondence*, ed. Rollo Myers (Berkeley and Los Angeles: Univ. of California Press, 1968), pp. 43-45.

12. A recent study of this movement is Derek Attridge, *Well-Weighed Syllables: Elizabethan Verse in Classical Metres* (Cambridge: Cambridge Univ. Press, 1975).

13. Henrickson, "Elizabethan Quantitative Hexameters," 242.

14. Thomas Campion, *Observations in the Art of English Poesie,* in *The Works of Thomas Campion,* ed. Walter R. Davis (New York: Doubleday and Co., 1967 and Faber and Faber, Ltd., 1967), p. 313.

15. All the examples in this study are given as notated in the source cited; I have, however, added the convention of slurs to indicate syllabification, with slashes where the slurs are not in the cited source.

16. Walker, "Musical Humanism," 298.

17. [Anon.] , "The silver swan," quoted from *Elizabethan Lyrics from the Original Texts,* ed. Normal Ault (New York: Capricorn Books, 1949; repr. 1960), p. 441.

18. Sir Philip Sidney, "Fourth song," from "Astrophil and Stella," *The Poems of Sir Philip Sidney,* ed. W. A. Ringler (London: Oxford Univ. Press, 1962), p. 210. The last couplet, being all monosyllables, has a delightfully ambiguous metric pattern, hovering between the trochaics of the first four lines and the iambics suggested by the prepositional phrases "to thee" and "to me."

This particular poem was set to music by Henry Youll in his *Canzonets* of 1608, and apparently was also known to the tune of "Shall I wasting in despair" (See Bruce Pattison, *Music and Poetry of the English Renaissance,* second edition [London: Methuen, 1970], pp. 175-76). The association of Sidney's trochaic meters with music is hinted at by Ringler (p. xliii) and developed more fully by Frank Fabry, "Sidney's Poetry and Italian Song-Form," *English Literary Renaissance,* III (1973), 233-48. It seems likely that Sidney's first experiments with English trochaics were occasioned by his writing *contrafacta* to Italian tunes.

Another point that should be made about this and most other English trochaic poems (which became quite popular in the 1590s and the early years of the seventeenth century) is that they are often truncated. Though Sidney himself did use the feminine ending rather frequently, it is much less common in English verse than in continental poetry; the use of both trochaics and the infrequent dactylics is often characterized in English, because of the tendency of the language to masculine endings, by the lack of the final unaccented syllable or syllables.

19. This kind of musical interpretation of certain features of poetic rhythm is discussed

by John Hollander in "Donne and the Limits of Lyric," *John Donne: Essays in Celebration*, ed. A. J. Smith (London: Methuen, 1972), pp. 259-72. See especially pp. 266-67.

20. It should be noted here that the rhythmic breaking up of the quarter notes into eighths does not affect the regular declamation of syllables within the musical meter.

21. This is particularly apparent in the triple meter songs of seventeenth-century England, for the beat is hardly ever subdivided; but I think the generalization will hold for music in triple meter that does have subdivision too. We are still consciously aware of the ternary organization.

22. There are, of course, exceptions; but they are not without difficulties in maintaining both the triple meter and the serious manner of handling the text. See, for example, the discussion of Campion's triple meter songs in Chapter 4.

23. See also the discussion in Chapter 4 of Campion's "Blame not my cheeks" and Henry Lawes' "About the sweet Bag of a Bee."

24. Ault, ed., *Elizabethan Lyrics*, p. 437.

25. Thomas Campion, "I must complain," *Works*, p. 184.

26. See, for example, the discussion of Campion's "Now winter nights," in Chapter 3.

27. It has been suggested to me that the musical organization of the piece falls into measures of $\frac{8}{4}$ (beginning with a half-measure). Even if $\frac{8}{4}$ measures are implied, however, the rhythm and the chord changes in combination with the text produce a clear pattern of emphasis on the words.

28. Thomas Campion, *Observations in the Art of English Poesie, Works*, p. 298.

29. This song has the added interest of being almost certainly a *contrafactum*; instrumental versions are known from sources considerably earlier than the song book in which this version first appeared. So well are words and music matched that Diana Poulton has conjectured that Dowland himself wrote the text: *John Dowland* (London: Faber and Faber, 1972), pp. 254-55.

Chapter 2: Music for Lines and Stanzas

1. As has been well demonstrated by John Stevens, *Music and Poetry in the Early Tudor Court* (Cambridge: Cambridge Univ. Press, 1961; repr. 1979) and Philip Brett, "Word-Setting in the Songs of Byrd," *Proceedings of the Royal Musical Association*, XCVIII (1972), 47-64, it was customary far back into the sixteenth century for musical setting to correspond to the formal division of a poem into lines. Indeed, even in the madrigal and the sacred motet or anthem, one usually finds the ends of lines of verse clearly indicated with a change in musical phrase, if not with rests. Whether musical or poetic conventions came first is an academic, and for this study irrelevant question, the essential fact being that at the start of the seventeenth century the well-established traditions of accentual-syllabic, end-stopped lines, and musical settings that would predictably represent those lines, existed side by side.

2. One of the difficulties of a study of this kind is the overlapping of terminology. We have encountered the failure of "rhythm" and "meter" to fit music and poetry in the same way. "Linear" is another troublesome term, meaning horizontal or melodic organization (as opposed to vertical or harmonic) in music, but referring in poetry to organization in lines, i.e., versification; "thematic" refers in music to the melodic idea, but in poetry to the presentation of the "story" or argument of the poem. "Syllabic" has perhaps even more disparate meanings, referring in poetry to meter based on syllable count, and in music to declamation with one note per syllable. I shall try to avoid ambiguities in the contexts in which such terms are used.

3. Anonymous, "God of winds," *William Lawes Autograph* (London: British Library Add. MS 31432), f. 31.

4. Thomas Carew, *The Poems of Thomas Carew*, ed. Rhodes Dunlap (Oxford: Clarendon Press, 1949), pp. 48-49. Dunlap prints the poem as a single stanza, following the 1640 edition of Carew's works.

5. The text used here is from Henry Lawes, *Select Ayres and Dialogues, The Second Book* (London: John Playford, 1669; facsimile edition, Ridgewood, N.J.: Gregg Press, 1966), p. 40. The song, however, is an early one and appears also in the *Henry Lawes Autograph MS* (London: British Library Add. MS 53723), f. 19v. In the manuscript version, the text is more nearly that found in the 1640 edition of Carew's works; the punctuation in the MS version makes somewhat more sense than in this version, and the omitted lines are included (lines 11 and 12). The setting, however, is the same except for a few minor rhythmic differences. The text is given in four-line stanzas as it is in the printed source, and the two extra lines — in this case lines 13 and 14 — are given simply as an additional couplet for which Lawes provides no music at all. It is quite possible that some of the alterations to the text were done by the publisher, John Playford. But the alterations are all, as I hope will be clear, fully in keeping with the kind of havoc Lawes' setting wreaks on this poem.

6. These are the songs referred to by Murray Lefkowitz as "bipartite." *William Lawes* (New York: Dover Publicatons, 1960). As pointed out in the paragraphs that follow in the text, the musical division can reinforce thematic as well as formal divisions in the poem, or, as will be demonstrated elsewhere, the connotations of the difference in musical style between the duple-meter declamatory song and the triple-meter dancelike song can bear interpretive significance of its own.

7. Carew, "Admit, thou Darling of mine Eyes," in Henry Lawes, *Select Ayres and Dialogues, Book I* (London: John Playford, 1653), p. 66. Copy in Folger Shakespeare Library. Carew, *Poems*, p. 110.

8. Carew, *Poems*, p. 18.

9. Henry Lawes, "Hee that loves a Rosie cheeke," *Select Ayres and Dialogues* (1653), p. 12; Walter Porter, "He that loves a Rosie cheeke," *Madrigales and Ayres* (1632), No. III.

10. Carew, *Poems*, p. 16.

11. Anonymous, "Break heart in twain!" in *Henry Lawes Autograph* (London: British Library Add. MS 53723), f. 31. Lawes actually wrote two versions of this song, the first on f. 14v of the MS and that on f. 31 apparently a revision. The climactic shape described here is much more forcefully done in the second version which reserves the high a'' for the last line whereas the first version had introduced it earlier as well.

12. The obvious exception, of course, is a song like Lawes' "Weep not, my deare," which appears to have divided arbitrarily and incorrectly a continuous structure into a stanzaic one. I have not taken the space here to describe any of the longer, through-composed songs of the period since their *principles* of organization are dependent on conventions as easily described with shorter examples.

13. Quoted from Edward Doughtie, ed., *Lyrics from English Airs 1596-1622* (Cambridge, Massachusetts: Harvard Univ. Press, 1970), pp. 156-57. The text, which appeared in numerous late sixteenth-century sources including *The Phoenix Nest, England's Helicon, A Poetical Rhapsody*, and various manuscripts, is given here from the setting by Robert Jones (1601). It has sometimes been attributed to Sir Walter Raleigh. See Doughtie, *Lyrics*, pp. 505-6.

14. See Doughtie, *Lyrics*, pp. 506-7.

15. Edward Doughtie uses this term in describing this characteristic of the poems, linking it to the rhetorical device of exergasia. (*Lyrics*, p. 37.) He goes on to point out that "The repeated music discourages the poets from allowing later stanzas to move too far away from the atmosphere and ideas of the first." Doughtie's Introduction and Paula Johnson's *Form and Transformation in Music and Poetry of the English Renaissance* (New Haven: Yale Univ.

Press, 1972) (where the terms "associative" and "climactic" are used much as I shall use them below) have influenced my thinking in this section.

16. From the number of times I have cited this poem it might be assumed to be an ideal song text—and indeed it does seem to have all the *technical* characteristics of the "classic" songs. I do not, however, think Dowland's setting of it is among his more inspired songs, and I might take this occasion to recall that a *good* setting of a poem involves a great deal more than the representation of its means of organization, and that a song—no matter how technically accurate its representation of rhythm, meter, versification, syntax, and so on—may still be a bad song.

17. Quoted from Doughtie, *Lyrics*, p. 363 (Jones, 1610). This poem, like "Disdain me still," has many additional elements that make it a "classic" song text of the period. Of note are the grammatical independence of individual lines, the regularity of the accentual meter, and even the identical placement of the caesura in each line (with only one exception in the third stanza).

18. I think this is probably the kind of structure Doughtie means by "spiral" (*Lyrics*, p. 37) although he does not seem to distinguish between "circular, spiral, or cumulative."

19. Quoted from Doughtie, *Lyrics*, p. 180 (Dowland, 1603).

20. Thomas Campion, *The Works of Thomas Campion*, ed., Walter R. Davis (New York: Doubleday and Co., 1967, and Faber and Faber, Ltd., 1967), p. 31.

21. Campion, *Works*, p. 46.

Prologue to Part II

1. It should be noted that this is by no means all of the poetry of the period and in fact includes relatively little by the major Elizabethan poets—Sidney, Spenser, Shakespeare, Donne; even Ben Jonson is not very well represented in the song books.

2. Paula Johnson, in *Form and Transformation in Music and Poetry of the English Renaissance* (New Haven: Yale Univ. Press, 1972), discusses formal structures in such terms rather than as genres.

3. See Philip Brett, "The English Consort Song, 1570-1625," *Proceedings of the Royal Musical Association*, LXXXVIII (1962), 73-88.

4. See Chapter 5, p. 174 (example 5.1).

5. See David Greer, "The Part-Songs of the English Lutenists," *Proceedings of the Royal Musical Association*, XCIV (1967-68), 97-110; see especially 99.

6. See, for example, Joseph Kerman's discussion of some of the madrigals of Orlando Gibbons, *The Elizabethan Madrigal* (New York: American Musicological Society, 1962), pp. 122ff.

7. This point has been made often by previous writers. Cf. Edward Doughtie, *Lyrics from English Airs* (Cambridge, Mass.: Harvard Univ. Press, 1970), pp. 30-41; Bruce Pattison, *Music and Poetry of the English Renaissance*, second edition (London: Methuen, 1970), p. 148; Catherine Ing, *Elizabethan Lyrics* (London: 1951; repr. New York: Barnes and Noble, 1969), pp. 133 ff. For my discussions of strophic composition, see Chapter 2.

8. Campion is perhaps an exception because of his particular approach to the text. See Chapter 3.

9. For instance, British Library Add. MS 24,665, "Giles Earle his Booke," contains an ornamented rendition of Campion's "Silly boy it is full Moone," from his *Third Book of Ayres* (c. 1617), a highly ornamented version of Daniel Batchelar's "To plead my faith" which was published in much simpler form in Robert Dowland's *Musicall Banquet* (1610), and so on.

10. For lack of better general terms I have adopted "musically oriented" and "textually oriented" despite some objections. The designation "tuneful air" was not—for my pur-

poses—sufficiently descriptive of the conceptual basis of the songs, whereas "ballad" seemed wrong because of its technical use with regard to folk song (where it means specifically a song with narrative text, which most of these do not have). "Declamatory air," on the other hand, I wished to retain for a particular kind of song within the textually oriented category (see Chapter 6). Furthermore, both terms should be taken as indicative of broadly conceived attitudes towards the musico-textual relationship, and although these attitudes are most clearly distinguished in the "tuneful airs" and "declamatory songs," they are present also in the lute songs and other types of continuo songs. I hope, therefore, that as descriptive terms "musically oriented" and "textually oriented" will prove more useful than cumbersome.

11. The few sources that provide tablatures for these songs indicate rather little polyphony in the accompanying instrument or instruments.

12. These points are considered in more detail in Chapter 4.

Chapter 3: Measured Music

1. See Frances Yates, *The French Academies of the Sixteenth Century* (London, 1947; repr. Nendeln, Liechtenstein: Kraus Reprints, 1968), pp. 36, 46, and Chapter III, *passim.*

2. For a more thorough discussion of Ronsard's convictions regarding music and poetry, see Raymond Lebègue, "Ronsard et la musique," *Musique et poésie au XVIe siècle* (Paris: Centre National de la Recherche Scientifique, 1954), pp. 105-19; Frances Yates, *The French Academies,* pp. 44-50, and D. P. Walker, "Le Chant orphique de Marsile Ficin," *Musique et poésie au XVIe siècle* (Paris: Centre National de la Recherche Scientifique, 1954), pp. 25-28 are also useful. Other important studies by Walker are listed in the Bibliography.

3. Quoted from Lebègue, "Ronsard et la musique," p. 109. The quotation is from Ronsard's *Abrégé de l'art poétique* (1565).

4. The dedication is printed in translation in Oliver Strunk, *Source Readings in Music History* (New York: W. W. Norton, 1950), pp. 286-89.

5. Quoted from Strunk, *Source Readings,* p. 287.

6. Quoted from Strunk, *Source Readings,* p. 287. Italics mine.

7. Quoted from Lebègue, "Ronsard et la musique," p. 111.

8. Walker, "Le Chant orphique," p. 27.

9. Quoted from Yates, *The French Academies,* p. 319.

10. The derivation of Renaissance quantitative meters from the Latin adaptation of Greek poetic meters is explained more fully in Chapter 1.

11. Le Jeune makes this clear in the Preface to *Le Printemps:* "Car l'Harmonique seulle avec ses agréables consonances peut bien arrester en admiration vraye les esprits pl' subtils." Claude le Jeune, *Le Printemps* (Ier Fascicule) (1603); *Les Maîtres musiciens de la renaissance française,* Vol. XII, ed. Henry Expert (New York: Broude Bros. repr. n.d.), p. 3.

12. Frank J. Fabry, "Sidney's Poetry and Italian Song-Form," *English Literary Renaissance,* III (1973), 233-48.

13. William A. Ringler, Jr., ed., *The Poems of Sir Philip Sidney* (London: Oxford Univ. Press, 1962), pp. 389-90.

14. Dowland's and Lawes' settings of the first two lines are as follows:

Example a.

O   how   much do I love your   so - li - tar - ri-ness

John Dowland, "O sweet woods." From *The Second Book of Songs* (1600); *The English Lute-Songs*, Series I, Vol. 5/6, p. 22. Ed. Edmund H. Fellowes. Rev. Thurston Dart, 1969. Reproduced by permission of Stainer and Bell, Ltd. and Galaxy Music Corp.

Example b.

O   sweet   woods   the de-light   of   sol- i-tar   -   i-ness

O   how I like   your sol - i - tar - i - ness

Henry Lawes, "O sweet woods." From *Henry Lawes Autograph Manuscript;* Additional MS 53723, f. 11v. Reprinted with permission of The British Library, Department of Manuscripts.

The remaining lines are not Sidney's and do not maintain the quantitative meter of Sidney's poem.

15. Joseph Kerman believes that all the songs from Byrd's 1588 set were intended to be performed this way. *The Elizabethan Madrigal* (New York: American Musicological Society, 1962), p. 102.

16. Only two books of French vocal music were published in England in this period. They are Tessier's *Le premier livre de chansons* in 1597 (containing Italian as well as French songs), and a collection entitled *French Court Airs, with their Ditties Englished*, collected, translated, and published by Edward Filmer in 1629.

17. The extent to which the musical resemblances between airs de cour and lute songs are evident may be indicated by Thurston Dart's remark on the subject: "L'air anglais était un rejeton vigoureux de l'air de cour français," perhaps overzealous, but, as we shall see, not altogether without basis. "Rôle de la danse dans l' 'ayre' anglais," *Musique et poésie au XVIe siècle* (Paris: Centre National de la Recherche Scientifique, 1954), p. 205.

18. Edward Lowbury, Timothy Salter, and Alison Young, *Thomas Campion, Poet, Composer, Physician* (London: Chatto and Windus, 1970), pp. 162ff.

19. Walter Davis, whose edition of Campion's poetry has been used in this study, refers thus to the later poetic style. See *The Works of Thomas Campion* (New York: Doubleday, 1967 and Faber and Faber, Ltd., 1967), p. xxii, which follows the Renaissance use of the term "plain" to refer to a poetic style in which content is more important than expression, matter more important than manner.

20. Lowbury, Salter, and Young, *Thomas Campion*, pp. 157-58.

21. Thurston Dart's very plausible suggestion that Philip Rosseter at least helped Campion arrange the lute accompaniments in the early Rosseter Book is much less likely in the later books, Revisor's Note to Thomas Campion, *The Songs from Rosseter's Book of Airs*

(1601); *The English Lute-Songs,* Series I, Vol. 4/13, ed. Edmund H. Fellowes, rev. Thurston Dart (London: Stainer and Bell, Ltd., 1968), p. v.

22.Thomas Campion, *Observations in the Arte of English Poesie,* quoted in *Works,* p. 297.

23.My argument here, I realize, seems to fly in the face of frequently voiced opinion that no regular musical meter occurs in the lute song. It should be stressed that I am not talking about bar lines, but about the unquestionably metric sense implied by harmonic rhythm, by the ratio of melodic notes to accompaniment, and even by the reciprocal correlation with textual rhythm and meter.

24.This seems an appropriate place to reiterate my belief that none of the composers of this period, including Campion, were much concerned with setting anything beyond the first stanza of the text in any detail. Of course, this entire poem may be read as an argument in favor of the "concordant" as opposed to the "curious," and in that sense, too, Campion's setting is illustrative of his opinion of the function of art.

25.Campion, *Works,* p. 314.

26.*Ibid*.

27.*Ibid*., pp. 55-56.

28.Davis, ed., *The Works of Thomas Campion,* p. xv. See also Catherine Ing, *Elizabethan Lyrics* (London: 1951; repr. New York: Barnes and Noble, 1969) and John T. Irwin, "Thomas Campion and the Musical Emblem," *Studies in English Literature,* X (1970), 121-41.

29.Wilfrid Mellers, *Harmonious Meeting* (London: Dennis Dobson, 1963), pp. 75-77.

30.Campion, *Works,* p. 24.

31.*Ibid*., p. 147.

32.For a thorough exploration of the phonetics of this poem, see Irwin, "Thomas Campion and the Musical Emblem."

33.Campion used this technique for expanding his steady, accentual declamation in many of his songs. See, for example, "The peacefull westerne winde" (Book II/12), "Thrice toss these oaken ashes" (Book III/18), or "To his sweet lute" (Book IV/8).

34.Thomas Campion, *Observations in the Arte of English Poesie,* quoted in *Works,* p. 293.

35.See, for example, "Think'st thou to seduce me then" (Book IV/18).

36.For a particularly striking example, see Chapter 5, p. 209 (example 5.23).

37.The "false fourth" on the word "false" is, of course, an instance of word-painting

38.Ian Spink, *English Song, Dowland to Purcell* (London: B. T. Batsford, Ltd., 1974), p. 105.

39.A modern collection of these airs, from which many of my examples of airs de cour are taken to facilitate comparison with solo song in England, is André Verchaly, ed., *Airs de cour pour voix et luth* (Paris: Société Française de Musicologie, 1961).

40.My discussion of the musical characteristics of airs de cour is based primarily on the work of D. P. Walker, "The Influence of *musique mesurée à l'antique,* particularly on the *airs de cour* of the Early Seventeenth Century," *Musica Disciplina* (1948), 141-63; "Some Aspects and Problems of *musique mesurée à l'antique,"* *Musica Disciplina* (1950), 163-86. The division of airs de cour into two groups is from Walker's "The Influence of *musique mesurée*." Also consulted were Kenneth Jay Levy, "Vaudeville, vers mesurés et airs de cour," *Musique et poésie au XVIe siècle* (Paris: Centre National de la Recherche Scientifique, 1954), 185-201; André Verchaly, "Poésie et air de cour en France jusqu'à 1620," *Musique et poésie au XVIe siècle,* 211-24; and André Verchaly, *Airs de cour pour voix et luth,* Introduction.

41.D. P. Walker, and others who have written about the air de cour, seem to be under

the impression that natural rhythms *are* violated in these settings. (Cf. Walker, "Influence of *musique mesurée*"; Verchaly, *Airs de Cour*, Introduction: see especially p. ix; Nigel Fortune, "Solo Song and Cantata," *The New Oxford History of Music*, Vol. IV, ed. Gerald Abraham [London: Oxford Univ. Press, 1968] , pp. 192-93; and James R. Anthony, *French Baroque Music from Beaujoyeulx to Rameau* [New York: W. W. Norton Co., 1974] , pp. 338-39.) I would be interested to know more specifically what is meant by accent in Walker's statement; perhaps he is referring to speech inflection, which is somewhat different, being first of all variable with syntax. Inflection is sometimes awkwardly represented (if at all) in these songs, but it is occasionally very nicely represented with melodic shaping.

42. *French Court Airs, with their Ditties Englished, Of fourre and five Parts. Together with that of the Lute*. Collected, Translated, Published by Ed. Filmer Gent, London, 1629. Quoted in Walker, "Influence of *musique mesurée*," 158 and note, 159. James R. Anthony quotes this passage in arguing that textual accent *is* distorted in the air de cour, but, significantly, leaves out the last sentence (*French Baroque Music*, p. 338).

43. See Chapter 6 for further discussion of this characteristic of Dowland's song style. The relationship of this continuous polyphony to the style of the madrigal should be obvious.

44. The singer, of course, will have to pause to breathe. But the psychological suggestion of the notation is that no large break should occur between lines.

45. John Dowland, *The First Book of Ayres: The English Lute-Songs*, Series I, Vol. 1/2, ed. E. H. Fellowes, rev. Thurston Dart (London: Stainer and Bell, 1965), p. iv. Italics mine.

Chapter 4: Dance Songs and Tuneful Airs

1. John Playford, "To all UNDERSTANDERS   and LOVERS of Vocal MUSICK," *Select Ayres and Dialogues, The Second Book*. (London: John Playford, 1669; facsimile edition, Ridgewood, N.J.: Gregg Press, Inc., 1966), p. A2.

2. The designation "musically oriented" is not, however, intended to imply that they are—or that their composers thought they were—profound pieces of music. Many of them are very simple musically. It is primarily in their casual, sometimes even careless handling of the text that they differ from the textually oriented songs.

3. See Joseph Kerman, *The Elizabethan Madrigal* (New York: American Musicological Society, 1962), Chapter Five; note especially pp. 172-74 on the attitude of the composer which distinguishes the "light" from the "serious" madrigals.

4. Thurston Dart, "Rôle de la danse dans l'‘ayre’ anglais," *Musique et poésie au XVIe siècle* (Paris: Centre National de la Recherche Scientifique, 1954), p. 207.

5. This, of course, is essentially what a strophic setting does with respect to the whole text.

6. See Chapter 2, Example 2.10.

7. A curious exception is this little tune by Henry Lawes:

Footnote 7.

Though Cu - pid   be a   God,   A - las,   he's but a   boye,   And

Ve - nus who he mo- ther   calls,   we   all   know   for___   a   toye.

Henry Lawes, "Though Cupid be a God." From *Henry Lawes Autograph Manuscript;* Additional MS 53723, f. 35. Reprinted with permission of The British Library, Department of Manuscripts.

Lawes has subdivided the beat here, but he seems uncomfortable with the rhythms that result.

8. Unless perhaps, as is sometimes apparent with a poet like Donne or Carew, it is used contrastively. Had the text gone something like this:

> Can she excuse my wrongs with Virtue's cloak?
> Without it, she might excuse e'er I spoke.

then Dowland's imposed accentuation might be presumed to have a thematic justification. If musical notation italicizes for a syntactical reason, the apparent misplacement of accent can be assumed to be intentional.

9. Thoinot Arbeau, *Orchesography*, translated by Mary Stewart Evans (New York: Dover Publications, 1967), p. 98.

10. Thurston Dart, "Rôle de la danse," p. 207.

11. Diana Poulton, *John Dowland* (London: Faber and Faber, 1972), p. 295.

12. I Love thee for thy Fickleness,
> And great Inconstancy;
> For had'st thou been a constant Lass,
> Then thou had'st ne'r lov'd mee.

> I love thee for thy Wantonesse,
> And for thy Drollerie;
> For if thou had'st not lov'd to sport,
> Then thou had'st ne're lov'd mee.

> I love thee for thy poverty,
> And for thy want of Coyne;
> For if thou had'st been worth a Groat,
> Then thou had'st ne'r been mine.

> I love thee for thy Uglynesse,
> And for thy foolerie;
> For if thou had'st been fair or wise,
> Then thou had'st ne'r lov'd mee.

> Then let me have thy heart a while,
> And thou shalt have my mony;
> Ile part with all the wealth I have,
> T'enjoy a Lass so Bonny.

13. It is, of course, possible that the rhythms would be dotted in performance, reinforcing even more the dactylic meter.

14. Poulton, *John Dowland,* p. 255.

15. *Ibid.*, p. 266.

16. This rhythm would suggest that the metrical scheme of the poem for these lines was

two accentual lines of four stresses; in fact, the meter is a rather ambiguous iambic pentameter, and the strength of Dowland's interpretation lies in his recognition of the "sprung" rhythm quality of the line.

17. Ian Spink, ed., *English Songs, 1625-1660; Musica Britannica*, Vol. XXXIII (London: Stainer and Bell, Ltd., 1971), p. 189.

Chapter 5: English Monody

1. This appears to be true despite Ben Jonson's claim that his masque, "Lovers Made Men," was sung *"Stylo recitativo"* in 1617. See McDonald Emslie, "Nicholas Lanier's Innovations in English Song," *Music and Letters*, XLI (1960), 13-14, for the argument that, since Jonson's claims appear only in the 1640 folio of the masque, it must not be taken as literal evidence of recitative in Jacobean England. The only extant piece from the first half of the century that approaches a true recitative style is Lanier's *Hero and Leander*, which will be discussed below. This piece has, with some justification, been called a cantata (e.g., J. A. Fuller Maitland, "Lanier (4)," *Grove's Dictionary of Music and Musicians*, fifth edition, ed. Eric Blom [New York: St. Martin's Press, 1954], p. 51), and does contain some passages that can be described as recitative. However, since the date of its composition is so uncertain (see Emslie, "Nicholas Lanier" and Ian Spink, *English Songs, 1625-1660; Musica Britannica*, Vol. XXXIII, [London: Stainer and Bell, Ltd., 1971], pp. 193-94), and it was so long in being followed, the above statement must stand. The Italians did use the word *recitativo* to describe any of the monodic types of composition in which the declamation of the text was a prime concern, and I shall use the word as descriptive of a style. To avoid confusion with later usage, "monody" will be used as the generic term for these songs.

2. Emslie, "Nicholas Lanier," 19.

3. See Philip Brett, "The English Consort Song, 1570-1625," *Publications of the Royal Musical Association*, LXXXVIII (1962), 79-80.

4. Published in *Consort Songs; Musica Britannica*, Vol. XXII, ed. Philip Brett (London: Stainer and Bell, Ltd., 1967), pp. 15ff. Richard Farrant was choirmaster at Windsor from 1564 to his death in 1580. He is thought to be the author of the play *Warres of Cyrus* of which this lament may be a part (see Brett, "Consort Song," 80). The piece is ascribed to Farrant in a Christ Church, Oxford MS of 1581, although E. K. Chambers notes that Robert Parsons is given as composer in another manuscript source for the song. Chambers, *The Elizabethan Stage*, Vol. II (London: Oxford Univ. Press, 1967; first printed, London: 1923), p. 63n.

5. See Hallett Smith, *Elizabethan Poetry* (Cambridge, Mass.: Harvard Univ. Press, 1966), especially Chapter II.

6. Ian Spink, "English Cavalier Songs, 1620-1660," *Publications of the Royal Musical Association*, LXXXVI (1960), 65.

7. Brett, "Consort Song," 80.

8. John Stevens, "Shakespeare and the Music of the Elizabethan Stage: An Introductory Essay," in *Shakespeare in Music*, ed. Phyllis Hartnoll (New York: Macmillan and Co., 1966), p. 8.

9. E. g., Spink, "English Cavalier Songs," 65; Nigel Fortune, "Solo Song and Cantata," *New Oxford History of Music*, Vol. IV, ed. Gerald Abraham (London: Oxford Univ. Press, 1968), belittles Italian influence (p. 211) but goes on to show some good instances of it in the lute songs.

10. D. P. Walker's by now classic article, "Musical Humanism in the sixteenth and Early seventeenth Centuries," *The Music Review*, II (1941), 1-13, 111-21, 220-27, 288-308; and III (1942), 55-71, surveys sixteenth-century beliefs about ancient music and their sources,

both from Classical writings and from the conjectures of sixteenth-century theorists. Walker cites three primary means through which the humanists thought they could achieve the effects attributed to Greek music: use of the Greek modes; use of the Greek *genera*, in particular the chromatic and the enharmonic; and "subjection of music to text." Walker virtually dismisses the first two as unaccomplished and impossible of accomplishment by the humanist composers, and, in fact, most of what I have to say concerns the last as well. It should be pointed out, however, that the relationship of mode and mood, unstable as the concepts were, remained an important element in the theoretical establishment of "affetti" well into the seventeenth century.

11. See Walker, "Musical Humanism" (1941), 9.

12. The exact meaning of the term *musica reservata* has been disputed. Henry Coats and Gerald Abraham say *"Musica reservata* most probably means 'music closely expressing the text.'" *(New Oxford History of Music,* Vol. IV, p. 348.) They list other references for this and other opinions about the meaning of the term.

13. Jerome Mazzaro, in his otherwise excellent book on the changes taking place in the English lyric in this period *(Transformations in the Renaissance English Lyric* [Ithaca: Cornell Univ. Press, 1970]), seems to confuse these two positions when he equates the rhetoric of music with word-painting (pp. 111ff., and especially p. 132), and links the humanist movement generally with composers of madrigals, both English and Italian, rather than with composers of solo songs (e.g., p. 126). In whatever measure the English "failed to develop [musical rhetoric] as an avenue for full self-expressiveness" (p. 133), the difficulty lay, not in an inability to use word-painting, but in the problem of finding a suitable rhetorical style of declamation.

14. E.g., Giovanni de' Bardi, in his Discourse on *Ancient Music and Good Singing:* "In composing, then, you will make it your chief aim to arrange the verse well and to declaim the words as intelligibly as you can, not letting yourself be led astray by the counterpoint . . . for you will consider it self-evident that, just as the soul is nobler than the body, so the words are nobler than the counterpoint." (Trans. in Oliver Strunk, *Source Readings in Music History* [New York: W. W. Norton, 1950], p. 295.)

15. E. g., Giulio Caccini, in the Preface to *Nuove Musiche:* "For these most knowledgeable gentlemen [members of the Camerata] convinced me, not to esteem that sort of music which, preventing any clear understanding of the words, shatters both their form and content, now lengthening and now shortening syllables to accommodate the counterpoint (a laceration of the poetry!), but rather to conform to that manner so lauded by Plato and other philosophers (who declared that music is naught but speech, with rhythm and tone coming after; not vice versa) with the aim that it enter into the minds of men and have those wonderful effects admired by the great writers" (trans. in *Le Nuove Musiche,* ed. H. Wiley Hitchcock [Madison, Wis.: A-R Editions, 1970], p. 44); and Claudio Monteverdi, with the phrase that has become the defining motto for later scholarship on Italian monody: "By Second Practice . . . he understands the one that turns on the perfection of the melody, that is, the one that considers harmony not commanding, but commanded, and makes the words the mistress of the harmony." (Foreword, *Il quinto libro de' madrigali,* trans. in Strunk, *Source Readings,* p. 409.)

16. The dramatic portrayal was also considered to be a part of the heritage from ancient Greece, as evidenced by Vincenzo Galilei: "When the ancient musician sang any poem whatever, he first considered very diligently the character of the person speaking: his age, his sex, with whom he was speaking, and the effect he sought to produce by this means; and these conceptions, previously clothed by the poet in chosen words suited to such a need, the musician then expressed in the tone and with the accents and gestures, the quantity and quality of sound, and the rhythm appropriate to that action and to such a person." *(Dialogo*

della musica antica e della moderna, trans. in Strunk, *Source Readings,* p. 319.) This dramatic goal is good evidence in support of John Hollander's suggestion that an essential feature
of the changing musical style was a shift from music for the performer's pleasure to music
for the audience. (John Hollander, *The Untuning of the Sky* [Princeton, N. J.: Princeton
Univ. Press, 1961; repr. New York: W. W. Norton, 1970], pp. 182 and 226ff.)

17. Caccini, *Nuove Musiche,* p. 46.

18. *Ibid.*

19. Strunk, *Source Readings,* pp. 364-65.

20. Modern edition in Claudio Monteverdi, *Arie, canzonette e recitativi,* ed. G. Francesco
Malipiero (Milan: Ricordi, 1953; repr. 1972), pp. 7ff.

21. It might be noted in passing here that melodically this convention is very close to
that associated with chant and with psalmody.

22. Jacopo Peri, *Euridici.* See, for example, the excerpt in *Historical Anthology of Music,*
ed. Archibald T. Davison and Willi Apel (Cambridge, Mass.: Harvard Univ. Press, 1966), Vol.
II, p. 1.

23. Emslie, "Nicholas Lanier," 21.

24. Whether the half note or the whole note is felt to be the beat will depend to some extent on the tempo of performance; and if, as in English, the poetic meter is accentual, its
unit of measurement will also be a mitigating factor in the perception of the unit of musical
measurement. Here, of course, poetic meter—being syllabic—does not appreciably affect the
listener's perception of a tactus.

25. See Thurston Dart, "Preface," John Coprario, *The Songs of Mourning; The English
Lute-Songs,* Series I, Vol. 17, ed. Gerald Hendrie and Thurston Dart (London: Stainer and
Bell, Ltd., 1959), p. ii.

26. This rhythmic and melodic "festooning" is apparent in other songs of Coperario's set
as well:

Example a.

John Coprario, "Fortune and Glory." From *Songs of Mourning* (1613); *The English
Lute-Songs,* Series I, Vol. 17, p. 25. Transcribed and ed. Gerald Hendrie and Thurston Dart, 1959. Reproduced by permission of Stainer and Bell, Ltd. and Galaxy Music Corp.

Example b.

gun   had been clos'd up by   his   re- li - gious Son!

John Coprario, "O poor distracted world." From *Songs of Mourning* (1613); *The English Lute-Songs*, Series I, Vol. 17, p. 35. Transcribed and ed. Gerald Hendrie and Thurston Dart, 1959. Reproduced by permission of Stainer and Bell, Ltd. and Galaxy Music Corp.

27. Declamation is somewhat better served by performance in four beats instead of the two that the composer's ₵ indicates.

28. Dowland's place in the declamatory development in English song may be more clearly seen in what I have called the "pathetic airs." See Chapter 6.

29. Spink, "English Cavalier Songs" 64.

30. Emslie, "Nicholas Lanier," 21-22.

31. Emslie, "Nicholas Lanier," 22.

32. Emslie, "Nicholas Lanier," 21.

33. See Spink, pp. 193-94.

34. Emslie, "Nicholas Lanier," 17.

35. Nicholas Lanier, *Hero and Leander*, in *English Songs*, ed. Ian Spink, pp. 12-21.

36. Douglas Bush says of Marlowe's *Hero and Leander*: "It was immensely admired before and after its formal publication, and was enthusiastically quoted and plagiarized for two generations." *Mythology and the Renaissance Tradition in English Poetry*, rev. edition (New York: W. W. Norton, 1963), p. 121.

37. Andrew Sabol has suggested to me the possibility that Lanier wrote this text himself.

38. This principle theoretically was demanded by the style and was spelled out in detail by Samuel Butler: "As the ditty is distinguished with points (period, colon, semicolon, and comma), so is the harmony, answering unto it, with pauses, and cadences. Semibrief rests, one or more, answer to a period or to a colon: which also is of perfect sense. Minim and crochet rests to semicolons, commas, breathings, and signs. So like wise, primary cadences perfect, which close the harmony, answer fitly to periods ending the ditty; or some principle part of it: and secondary, to colons or interrogations. But improper, and imperfect cadences answer to points of imperfect sense (commas and semicolons). These directions being observed (with discretion) in the harmony, help not a little to the manifesting and understanding of the ditty." (*The Principles of Musik in Singing and Setting* [1636], introduced by Gilbert Reaney [New York: Da Capo Press, facsimile 1970], p. 97.) I have modernized spelling and punctuation.

39. William Cartwright, *Ariadne Deserted*, quoted from the setting by Henry Lawes, *Ayres and Dialogues . . . by Henry Lawes* (London: John Playford, 1653), pp. 1-7.

40. Pamela J. Willetts thinks differently on this matter: "Lawes attempts a detailed setting of the changing thought of his text and his music shifts frequently from major to minor tonality." *The Henry Lawes Manuscript* (London: British Museum, 1969), p. 8.

41. That this feature of Lawes' settings (his rhythmic representation of iambic accentual patterns in dotted rhythms) is a primary factor in his reputation with poets may be seen in the wording of the accolades to his music, from Milton's "committing short and long," to these lines by Charles Colman:

'Tis Thou hast honour'd Musick, done her right,
Fitted her for a strong and useful Flight;
Shee droop'd and flaggd before, as Hawks complain
Of the sick Feathers in their Wing and Train:
But thou hast imp'd the Wings She had before.
Musick does owe Thee much, the Poet more;
Thou lift'st him up, and dost new Nature bring,
Thou giv'st his noblest Verse both *Feet* and *Wing.*

Select Ayres and Dialogues, The Second Book (London: John Playford, 1669; facsimile ed., Ridgewood, N.J., Gregg Press, Inc., 1966), [p. A4].

42. Eric Ford Hart's "Introduction to Henry Lawes," *Music and Letters,* XXXII (1951), 217-344, is in general agreement with my point on Lawes' representation of rhyme scheme, as well as on various other technical features of Lawes' style pointed out in this study.

43. R. J. McGrady, "Henry Lawes and the Concept of 'Just Note and Accent,'" *Music and Letters,* L (1969), 91.

44. Among the few who have written about Lawes in any detail, there seems to be almost willful disagreement as to the relevance of the bar line. See Willetts, *Henry Lawes Manuscript,* p. 13 ("The barline does not have any accentual significance for Lawes"). My feeling is that musical meter was unquestionably at least available to the composer of solo song; the very strong and regular meters of the dance songs is surely sufficient evidence of this. Although the bar line did not at first imply this meter, it gradually came to be placed coincident with the meter, and I believe that Lawes used this possible significance, even if he did not always feel constrained by it.

Chapter 6: Pathetic Airs

1. Most of the important English treatises are available in *Elizabethan Critical Essays,* 2 vols., ed. G. Gregory Smith (London: Oxford Univ. Press, 1904; repr. 1967).

2. Theories of rhetoric in Renaissance England are well described in Miriam Joseph, C.S.C., *Shakespeare's Use of the Arts of Language* (New York: Columbia Univ. Press, 1947).

3. A third, generally pejorative definition, not current in the Renaissance but often implied by the word "rhetoric" in modern usage, seems to be most clearly related to the part of Classical rhetoric dealing with delivery. The devices of the orator who is able to sway the emotions of large groups of people through the projection of some kind of personal magnetism, rather than through the demonstration of truth in what he says, would fall into this concept of rhetoric.

4. I will use the terms "ornament" and "embellishment" in this sense with reference to both music and poetry throughout this chapter. I do not, unless otherwise specified, mean "ornament" in the sense of the ornamentation or division common in the music of the period.

5. Marcus Tullius Cicero, *Institutio oratoria,* tr. J. S. Watson [Bohn's Classical Library], II, p. 146; quoted from Joseph, *Shakespeare's Use of the Arts of Language,* p. 32.

6. George Puttenham, *The Arte of English Poesie;* quoted from Smith, ed., *Elizabethan Critical Essays,* pp. 159-61.

7. Puttenham, *Arte of English Poesie,* pp. 160-61.

8. Puttenham, *Arte of English Poesie,* p. 165.

9. Joseph, *Shakespeare's Use of the Arts of Language,* p. 37.

10. Some Renaissance rhetoricians did, however, attempt to relate various musical procedures and devices to the figures of speech. See Joachim Burmeister, *Musica Poetica: De-*

finitibus et Divisionibus breviter delineata . . . (Rostock: 1606); Henry Peachum, *Garden of Eloquence* (London: 1593); Francis Bacon, *The Advancement of Learning* (London: 1605); Jan Albert Ban, *Dissertatio Epistolica De Musica Natura* (Leyden: 1637).

11. To this extent Jerome Mazaro is no doubt on the right track in trying to relate the devices of word-painting to a rhetoric that may be supplied through music (*Transformations in the Renaissance English Lyric* [Ithaca, N.Y.: Cornell Univ. Press, 1970], Chapter IV, *passim*), and I shall follow him in correlating word-painting with certain kinds of rhetorical figures. But Mazzaro's scope is too limited to be very useful, since he does not seem to think there are any other possibilities. In the same way, Eric Ford Hart, who thinks Henry Lawes' declamatory songs are ultimately "rhetorical" statements, is limited by his understanding of rhetoric as "the traditional methods of the orator." (Eric Ford Hart, "Introduction to Henry Lawes,"*Music and Letters*, XXXII [1951], 337.) Hart's rhetoric of music is thus restricted to the performative interpretation of grammar and punctuation, perhaps a more workable viewpoint than Mazzaro's and more relevant to midseventeenth-century song, but leaving out the more genuinely musical expressiveness that is the strength of Mazzaro's thesis.

12. Though perhaps not to the singer's perception. See remarks on this aspect of the madrigal in the Prologue to Part II.

13. Joseph, *Shakespeare's Use of the Arts of Language*, p. 128.

14. The technique has great implications for the symbolic use of music that would reach its apex in the work of Wagner, although at this early stage its success is dependent on the agreed-upon meaning of the figure.

15. Joseph, *Shakespeare's Use of the Arts of Language*, p. 116.

16. *Ibid.*, p. 149.

17. John Danyel, "Can doleful notes," *Songs for the Lute, Viol, and Voice* (1606); *The English Lute-Songs*, Second Series, Vol. 8, ed. Edmund H. Fellowes, rev. Thurston Dart and David Scott (London: Stainer and Bell, Ltd., 1970), pp. 36-43. For discussion of this poem, see John Hollander, *The Untuning of the Sky* (Princeton, N.J.: Princeton Univ. Press, 1961; repr. New York: W. W. Norton, 1970), pp. 188-89.

18. The dissonance on "jarring" in Coperario's setting should, however, be noted as an example of word-painting.. It might also be noted that the one subtlety of Coperario's handling of this line—the simultaneous singing of "My music" and "hellish" in the second measure of the Example—is not available to Dowland since "In darkness" is not one of the airs he published as a part song.

19. Joseph, *Shakepeare's Use of the Arts of Language*, p. 55.

20. Mazzaro, *Transformations*, p. 150.

21. Interestingly, Dowland's textual repetition in this line seems to supply a missing term in the argument. The lines read:

> Thou canst not die, and therefore living tell me
> Where is thy seat? why doth this age expel thee?

But the reasoning goes something like this:

> You cannot die;
> Therefore you are alive;
> Since you are alive, tell me
> Where is the locus of your existence, etc.

hinging on the dual use of "therefore" which Dowland very neatly supplied in both contexts through the repetition.

22. See p. 217 above.

23. A sort of back-handed support for this correlation between musical and poetic uses

of language is that occasionally, when images of "pathetic" words common in Elizabethan song verse do appear in the poetry set by continuo composers, they are treated with the old musical conventions, as is "moaning" in Henry Lawes' "Come, sad Turtle":

Example a.

Henry Lawes, "Come, sad Turtle." From *Select Ayres and Dialogues, The Second Book*, p. 35. London: John Playford, 1669. Facsimile ed. Ridgewood, N.J.: Gregg Press, Inc., 1966.

and on a slightly larger scale, the pictorially dropping tears in Robert Johnson's otherwise declamatory setting of "Woods, Rocks, and Mountains":

Example b.

Robert Johnson, "Woods, Rocks, and Mountains." From Additional MS 11608, ff. 15v-16. Reprinted with permission of The British Library, Department of Manuscripts. The manuscript is usually dated about 1650.

24. For discussion of this change in the function of the persona, see Mazzaro, *Transformations*, pp. 16-17 and *passim*.

25. Charles Butler, *The Principles of Musik in Singing and Setting* (London: John Haviland, for the Author, 1636; repr. New York: Da Capo Press, 1970), p. 2. The italics and brackets are Butler's.

26. The declamatory rhythms are slightly different in the William Lawes autograph song book (British Library Add. MS 31432); in particular the rests after "Amarilis" and after "Breast" are lacking and the rhythmic values altered accordingly, thus further emphasizing the phrasing of the text through musical phrasing.

27. Sir John Suckling, "No, no fair heretic," quoted from the setting by Henry Lawes, *The Treasury of Musick* (London: John Playford, 1669; facsimile ed., Ridgewood, N.J.: Gregg Press, 1966), p. 46.

28. The shift to triple meter for the final couplet is a standard feature of a significant

group of songs, referred to by Murray Lefkowitz (*William Lawes* [London: Routledge and Kegan Paul, 1960], p. 168) as "bipartite 'recitative-ballad' form." Lefkowitz has pointed out the coincidence of this musical structure with "a change in mood or emphasis of the poem, separating the more continous thought from general or moral specualtion"; Ian Spink remarks that the concluding section of such songs (sometimes set as a Chorus) "sets the final verse or couplet as a sort of peroration, which was probably the intention of the poet in writing it." ("English Cavalier Songs, 1620-1660," *Proceedings of the Royal Musical Association,* LXXXVI [1960], 75.) In that they combine the techniques and conventions associated with more than one attitude toward the text (the duple meter declamatory style for the particular and the triple meter tuneful style for the general or conventional), these songs form an interesting hybrid style, playing upon more than one set of expectations in the listener.

29. The song appears in editions published by John Playford in 1652, 1653, 1659, and 1669. See Pamela J. Willetts, *The Henry Lawes Manuscript* (London: British Museum, 1969), pp. 50-51.

30. There is a figure of word-painting implied by Lawes' changes too: the manuscript version adds falling and rising melodic motives to the words "down" and "up," and the equivocal aspect of "held . . . up *too* high" is represented in the return to middle register for "high." This same gesture was used by Thomas Morley in 1600:

Footnote 30.

but not to mount,   but not to mount,   but not to mount too high.

Thomas Morley, "Love wing'd my hopes." From *The First Book of Ayres* (1600); *The English Lute-Songs,* Series I, Vol. 16, p. 24. Ed. Edmund H. Fellowes. Rev. Thurston Dart, 1966. Reproduced by permission of Stainer and Bell, Ltd. and Galaxy Music Corp.

Bibliography

Bibliography

I. *Musical Sources for Works Cited.* For a more complete list of the song-books and manuscript sources for seventeenth-century English song, the reader is referred to the Bibliography in Ian Spink, *English Song, Dowland to Purcell.*

Bartlet, John. *A Booke of Ayres* (1606). Edited by Edmund H. Fellowes. *The English School of Lutenist Song Writers.* Second Series. London, Stainer and Bell, Ltd., 1925.

Brett, Philip, ed. *Consort Songs. Musica Britannica*, Vol. XXII. London: Stainer and Bell, Ltd., 1967.

British Library. MS Additional 11608.

_____. MS Additional 31432. William Lawes Autograph.

_____. MS Additional 53723. Henry Lawes Autograph.

Caccini, Giulio. *Le Nuove musiche* (1602). Edited by H. Wiley Hitchcock. Madison, Wis.: A-R Editions, 1970.

Campion, Thomas. *The Songs from Rosseter's Book of Airs* (1601). Edited by Edmund H. Fellowes. Revised by Thurston Dart. *The English Lute-Songs.* Series I, Vol. 4/13. London: Stainer and Bell, Ltd., 1969.

_____. *Third Booke of Ayres* (c. 1617). Edited by Edmund H. Fellowes. Revised by Thurston Dart. *The English Lute-Songs.* Series II, Vol. 10, London: Stainer and Bell, Ltd., 1969.

_____. *The Works of Thomas Campion.* Edited by Walter R. Davis. New York: Doubleday and Co., Inc., 1967, and Faber and Faber, Ltd., 1967.

Coprario, John. *Funeral Teares* (1606); *Songs of Mourning* (1613); *The Masque of Squires* (1614). Edited by Gerald Hendrie and Thurston Dart. *The English Lute-Songs.* Series I, Vol. 17. London: Stainer and Bell, Ltd., 1959.

Corkine, William. *Second Booke of Ayres* (1612). Edited by Edmund H. Fellowes. *The English School of Lutenist Song Writers.* Second Series. London: Stainer and Bell, Ltd., 1970.

Danyel, John. *Songs for the Lute, Viol and Voice* (1606). Edited by Edmund H. Fellowes. Revised by Thurston Dart and David Scott. *The English Lute-Songs.* Second Series, Vol. 8. London: Stainer and Bell, Ltd., 1970.

Davison, Archibald T., and Apel, Willi, eds. *Historical Anthology of Music.* Two volumes. Cambridge, Mass.: Harvard Univ. Press, 1966.

Dowland, John. *The First Book of Ayres* (1597). Edited by Edmund H. Fellowes. Revised by Thurston Dart. *The English Lute-Songs.* Series I, Vol. 1/2. London: Stainer and Bell, Ltd., 1965.

_____. *Second Book of Songs* (1600). Edited by Edmund H. Fellowes. Revised by Thurston Dart. *The English Lute-Songs.* Series I, Vol. 5/6. London: Stainer and Bell, Ltd., 1969.

_____. *The Third Booke of Songs* (1603). Edited by Edmund H. Fellowes. Revised by Thurston Dart and David Scott. *The English Lute-Songs.* Series I, Vol. 10/11. London: Stainer and Bell, Ltd., 1970.

_____. *A Pilgrimes Solace* (1612). Edited by Edmund H. Fellowes. Revised by Thurston Dart. *The English Lute-Songs.* Series I, Vol. 12/14. London: Stainer and Bell, Ltd., 1969.

Dowland, Robert. *A Musicall Banquet* (1610). Edited by Peter Stroud. *The English Lute-Songs.* Second Series, Vol. 20. London: Stainer and Bell, Ltd., 1968.

Expert, M. Henry, ed. *La Fleur des musiciens de P. de Ronsard.* New York: Broude Brothers, Ltd., 1965.

Ferrabosco, Alfonso, II. *Manuscript Songs.* Edited by Ian Spink. *The English Lute-Songs.* Second Series, Vol. 19. London: Stainer and Bell, Ltd., 1966.

Fuller Maitland, J. A., and Squire, W. Barclay, eds. *The Fitzwilliam Virginal Book.* Two volumes. New York: Dover Publications, Inc., 1963. First published 1899.

le Jeune, Claude. *Le Printemps (Ier Fascicule)* (1603). Edited by M. Henry Expert. *Les Maîtres musiciens de la renaissance française.* Vol. XII. New York: Broude Brothers, Ltd., n.d.

Jones, Robert. *First Booke of Songes and Ayres* (1600). Edited by Edmund H. Fellowes. Revised by Thurston Dart. *The English Lute-Songs.* Second Series, Vol. 4. London: Stainer and Bell, Ltd., 1959.

Lawes, Henry. *Ayres and Dialogues, For One, Two, and Three Voyces.* London: John Playford, 1653.

_____. *Select Ayres and Dialogues To Sing to the Theorbo-Lute or Basse Viol. The Second Book.* London: John Playford, 1669. Facsimile edition, Ridgewood, N.J.: Gregg Press Inc., 1966.

_____. *Select Ayres and Dialogues To Sing to the Theorbo-Lute or Basse Viol. The Third Book.* London: John Playford, 1669. Facsimile edition, Ridgewood, N.J.: Gregg Press Inc., 1966.

_____, *The Treasury of Musick Containing Ayres and Dialogues, Book I.* London: John Playford, 1669. Facsimile edition, Ridgewood, N.J.: Gregg Press Inc., 1966.

Mauduit, Jacques. *Chansonnettes mesurées de Ian-Antoine de Baïf* (1586). Edited by M. Henry Expert. *Les Maîtres musiciens de la renaissance francaise.* Vol. X. New York: Broude Brothers, Ltd., n.d.

Monteverdi, Claudio. "A voce sola." *Arie, Canzonette e Recitativi.* Edited by G. Francesco Malipiero. Milan: Ricordi, 1953. Repr. 1972.

Morley, Thomas. *The First Booke of Ayres* (1600). Edited by Edmund H. Fellowes. Revised by Thurston Dart. *The English Lute-Songs.* Series I, Vol. 16. London: Stainer and Bell, Ltd., 1966.

New York Public Library. MS Drexel 4041.

_____. MS Drexel 4257.

Oxford Bodleian Library. MS Don. c. 57.

Pilkington, Francis. *The First Booke of Songs* (1605). Edited by Edmund H. Fellowes. Revised by Thurston Dart and David Scott. *The English Lute-Songs.* Series I, Vol. 7/15. London: Stainer and Bell, Ltd., 1971.

Sabol, Andrew J., ed. *Four Hundred Songs and Dances from the Stuart Masque.* Providence, R.I.: Brown Univ. Press, 1978.

Spink, Ian, ed. *English Songs, 1625-1660. Musica Britannica.* Vol. XXXIII. London: Stainer and Bell, Ltd., 1971.

Verchaly, André, ed. *Airs de cour pour voix et luth (1603-1643).* Paris: Société Française de Musicologie, 1961.

II. Books and Periodicals: Works Cited or Used in Preparation of this Study.

Anthony, James R. *French Baroque Music from Beaujoyeulx to Rameau.* New York: W. W. Norton, 1974.

Arbeau, Thoinot. *Orchesography.* Translated by Mary Stewart Evans. Introduction and Notes by Julia Sutton. New York: Dover Publications, Inc., 1967.

Arthos, John. *On a Masque Presented at Ludlow-Castle, by John Milton.* Ann Arbor, Mich.: Univ. of Michigan Press, 1954.

Attridge, Derek. *Well-Weighed Syllables: Elizabethan Verse in Classical Metres.* Cambridge: Cambridge Univ. Press, 1975.

Ault, Norman, ed. *Elizabethan Lyrics from the Original Texts.* New York: Capricorn Books, 1960. First printed New York: 1949.

Beardsley, Monroe C. "Verse and Music." *Versification: Major Language Types.* Edited by W. K. Wimsatt. New York: New York Univ. Press, 1972. Pp. 238-52.

Brett, Philip. "The English Consort Song, 1570-1625." *Proceedings of the Royal Musical Association,* LXXXVIII (1962), 73-88.

_____. "Word-Setting in the Songs of Byrd." *Proceedings of the Royal Musical Association,* XCVIII (1972), 47-64.

Bush, Douglas. *Mythology and the Renaissance Tradition in English Poetry.* Revised edition. New York: W. W. Norton, 1963.

Butler, Samuel. *The Principles of Musik in Singing and Setting.* London: John Haviland, for the Author, 1636. Facsimile edition, introduced by Gilbert Reany. New York: Da Capo Press, 1970.

Caccini, Giulio. "To the Readers." *Le Nuove musiche* (1602). Translated and edited by H. Wiley Hitchcock. Madison, Wis.: A-R Editions, Inc., 1970.

Campion, Thomas. *The Works of Thomas Campion.* Edited by Walter R. Davis. New York: Doubleday and Co., Inc., 1967.

Carew, Thomas. *The Poems of Thomas Carew.* Edited by Rhodes Dunlap. Oxford: Clarendon Press, 1949.

Chambers, E. K. *The Elizabethan Stage.* Four volumes. London: Oxford Univ. Press, 1967. First printed London: 1923.

Cicero, Marcus Tullius. *Institutio oratoria.* Translated by J. S. Watson. [Bohn's Classical Library], Vol. II, p. 146. Quoted from Sister Miriam Joseph, C.S.C. *Shakespeare's Use of the Arts of Language.* New York: Columbia Univ. Press, 1947.

Cooper, Grosvenor, and Meyer, Leonard. *The Rhythmic Structure of Music.* Chicago: Univ. of Chicago Press, 1960.

Crum, Margaret. *First-Line Index of English Poetry, 1500-1800, in Manuscripts of the Bodleian Library.* London: Oxford Univ. Press, 1969.

_____. "A Manuscript of John Wilson's Songs." *The Library,* 5th Series, X (1955), 55-57.

_____. "Notes on the Texts of William Lawes' Songs in B. M. MS Add. 31432." *The Library,* 5th Series, IX (1954), 122.

Crystal, David. *Prosodic Systems and Intonation in English.* Cambridge: Cambridge Univ. Press, 1969.

Cutts, John P. "A Bodleian Song Book MS Don. c. 57." *Music and Letters,* XXXIV (1953), 192-212.

_____. "British Museum Additional MS 31432, William Lawes's Writing for Theatre and Court." *The Library,* 5th Series, VII (1952), 231.

_____. "Early Seventeenth-Century Lyrics at St. Michael's College." *Music and Letters,* XXXVII (1956), 221-33.

_____. "Elizabeth Davenant Her Booke, 1624." *Review of English Studies,* X (1959), 26-37.

_____. "Jacobean Masque and Stage Music." *Music and Letters,* XXXV (1954), 185-200.

_____."Robert Johnson: King's Musician in His Majesty's Public Entertainment." *Music and Letters,* XXXVI (1955), 110-25.

_____. ed. *Seventeenth Century Songs and Lyrics, Collected and Edited from the Original Music Manuscripts.* Columbia, Mo.: Univ. of Missouri Press, 1959.

_____. "The Strange Fortunes of Two Excellent Princes and The Arbor of Amorous Devises." *Renaissance News,* XV (1962), 11.

_____. "Two Jacobean Theatre Songs." *Music and Letters,* XXXIII (1952), 333-34.

Dart, Thurston. "Rôle de la danse dans l' 'ayre' anglais." *Musique et poésie aux XVIᵉ siècle.* Paris: Centre National de la Recherche Scientifique, 1954. Pp. 203-9.

Davis, Walter. "Melodic and Poetic Structure: The Examples of Campion and Dowland." *Criticism,* IV (1962), 89-107.

Diekhoff, John S., ed. *A Maske at Ludlow: Essays on Milton's Comus.* With the Bridgewater version of Comus. Cleveland: Case Western Reserve Univ. Press, 1968.

Doughtie, Edward, ed. *Lyrics from English Airs, 1596-1622.* Cambridge, Mass.: Harvard Univ. Press, 1970.

Duckles, Vincent. "The 'Curious' Art of John Wilson (1595-1674): An Introduction to His Songs and Lute Music." *Journal of the American Musicological Society,* VII (1954), 93-112.

_____. "The Gamble Manuscript as a Source of *Continuo* Song in England." *Journal of the American Musicological Society,* I (1948), 23-40.

_____. "Jacobean Theater Songs." *Music and Letters,* XXXIV (1953), 88-89.

_____, and Zimmerman, Franklin. *Words to Music: Papers on English Seventeenth-Century Song.* Clark Library Seminar. Los Angeles: Univ. of California Press, 1967.

Emslie, McDonald. "Nicholas Lanier's Innovations in English Song." *Music and Letters,* XLI (1960), 13-27.

Evans, Willa McClung. *Ben Jonson and Elizabethan Music.* New York: Da Capo Press, 1965. First printed n. p.: 1929.

_____. *Henry Lawes, Musician and Friend of Poets.* New York: Kraus Reprint Corp., 1966. First printed New York: 1941.

Fabry, Frank J. "Sidney's Poetry and Italian Song-Form." *English Literary Renaissance,* III (1973), 232-48.

Finney, Gretchen Ludke. *Musical Backgrounds for English Literature: 1580-1650.* New Brunswick, N.J.: Rutgers Univ. Press, 1962.

Ford, Wyn K. *Music in England Before 1800: A Select Bibliography.* London: The Library Association, 1967.

Gibbon, John Murray. *Melody and the Lyric from Chaucer to the Cavaliers.* New York: Haskell House, 1964. First printed London: [1930].

Greer, David. "The Part-Songs of the English Lutenists." *Proceedings of the Royal Musical Association,* XCIV (1967-68), 97-110.

Harding, D. W. *Words into Rhythm.* Cambridge: Cambridge Univ. Press, 1976.

Hart, Eric Ford. "Caroline Lyrics and Contemporary Song-Books." *The Library,* 5th Series, VIII (1953), 89-110.

_____. "An Introduction to Henry Lawes." *Music and Letters,* XXXII (1951), 217-25 and 328-44.

Hendrickson, G. L. "Elizabethan Quantitative Hexameters." *Philological Quarterly,* XXVIII (1949), 237-60.

Hollander, John. "Donne and the Limits of Lyric." *John Donne: Essays in Celebration.* Edited by A. J. Smith. London: Methuen, 1972. Pp. 259-72. Reprinted in John Hollander. *Vision and Resonance.* New York: Oxford Univ. Press, 1975.

_____. "'Sense Variously Drawn Out': Some Observations on English Enjambment." *Literary Theory and Structure: Essays in Honor of William K. Wimsatt.* Edited by Frank Brady, John Palmer and Martin Price. New Haven: Yale Univ. Press, 1973. Pp. 201-25. Reprinted in John Hollander, *Vision and Resonance.* New York: Oxford Univ. Press, 1975.

_____. *The Untuning of the Sky.* New York: W. W. Norton, 1970. First printed Princeton, N.J.: 1961.

Ing, Catherine. *Elizabethan Lyrics.* New York: Barnes and Noble, 1969. First printed London: 1951.

Irwin, John T. "Thomas Campion and the Musical Emblem." *Studies in English Literature,* X (1970), 121-41.

Johnson, Paula. *Form and Transformation in Music and Poetry of the English Renaissance.* New Haven: Yale Univ. Press, 1972.

Joiner, Mary. "British Museum Add. MS 15117: A Commentary, Index and Bibliography." *Royal Musical Association Research Chronicle,* VII (1967), 51-109.

Joseph, Sister Miriam, C.S.C. *Shakespeare's Use of the Arts of Language.* New York: Columbia Univ. Press, 1947.

Kastendieck, Miles Merwin. *England's Musical Poet: Thomas Campion.* New York: Russell and Russell, 1963. First printed New York: 1938.

Kerman, Joseph. *The Elizabethan Madrigal.* New York: American Musicological Society, 1962.

Lebègue, Raymond. "Ronsard et la musique." *Musique et poésie au XVIᵉ siècle.* Paris: Centre National de la Recherche Scientifique, 1954. Pp. 105-19.

Lefkowitz, Murray. "New Facts Concerning William Lawes and the Caroline Masque." *Music and Letters,* XL (1959), 324-33.

_____. *William Lawes.* New York: Dover Publications, 1960.

Levy, Kenneth Jay. "Vaudeville, vers mesurés et airs de cour." *Musique et poésie au XVIᵉ siècle.* Paris: Centre National de la Recherche Scientifique, 1954. Pp. 185-201.

Lowbury, Edward; Salter, Timothy; and Young, Alison. *Thomas Campion: Poet, Composer, Physician.* London: Chatto and Windus, 1970.

Mazzaro, Jerome. *Transformations in the Renaissance English Lyric.* Ithaca, N.Y.: Cornell Univ. Press, 1970.

McGrady, R. J. "Henry Lawes and the concept of 'just note and accent.'" *Music and Letters,* L (1969), 86-102.

Mellers, Wilfrid. *Harmonious Meeting.* London: Dennis Dobson, 1963.

_____. "Words and Music in Elizabethan England." *The Age of Shakespeare.* Edited by Boris Ford. *Pelican Guide to English Literature,* No. 2. Revised edition. Baltimore: Penguin Books, Ltd., 1962.

Miner, Earl. *The Cavalier Mode from Jonson to Cotton.* Princeton, N.J.: Princeton Univ. Press, 1971.

_____. *The Metaphysical Mode from Donne to Cowley.* Princeton, N.J.: Princeton Univ. Press, 1969.

Ostriker, Alicia. "Song and Speech in the Metrics of George Herbert." *Publications of the Modern Language Association,* LXXX (1965), 62-68.

Pattison, Bruce. *Music and Poetry of the English Renaissance.* Second edition. London: Methuen, 1970. First printed London: 1948.

Phillips, James E. "Poetry and Music in the Seventeenth Century." *Music and Literature.* Clark Library Seminar Papers on Seventeenth and Eighteenth Century Literature. Los Angeles: Univ. of California Press, 1953. Pp. 1-21.

Playford, John. "To all UNDERSTANDERS and LOVERS of Vocal MUSICK." *Select*

Ayres and Dialogues. The Second Book. London: John Playford, 1669. Facsimile edition, Ridgewood, N.J.: Gregg Press Inc., 1966.

Poulton, Diana. *John Dowland.* London: Faber and Faber, 1972.

Preminger, Alex; Warnke, Frank J.; and Hardison, O.B., Jr. *Princeton Encyclopedia of Poetry and Poetics.* Princeton, N. J.: Princeton Univ. Press, 1965.

Puttenham, George. *The Arte of English Poesie. Elizabethan Critical Essays.* Vol. II. Edited by G. Gregory Smith. London: Oxford Univ. Press, 1967. First printed London: 1904.

Raynor, Henry. "Framed to the Life of the Words." *Music Review,* XIX (1958), 261-72.

Sachs, Curt. *Rhythm and Tempo.* New York: W. W. Norton, 1953.

Scholes, Percy. *The Puritans and Music in England and New England.* London: Oxford Univ. Press, 1969. First printed London: 1934.

Sebeok, Thomas A., ed. *Style in Language.* New York: Wiley, 1960.

Sidney, Philip. *The Poems of Sir Philip Sidney.* Edited by W. A. Ringler. London: Oxford Univ. Press, 1962.

Smith, Hallett. *Elizabethan Poetry.* Cambridge, Mass.: Harvard Univ. Press, 1966.

Spink, Ian. "English Cavalier Songs, 1620-1660." *Proceedings of the Royal Musical Association,* LXXXVI (1960), 61-78.

_____. *English Song: Dowland to Purcell.* London: B. T. Batsford, Ltd., 1974.

_____. "Sources of English Song, 1620-1660: A Survey." *Miscellanea Musicologica,* (1966), 117-36.

Stevens, John. *Music and Poetry in the Early Tudor Court.* Cambridge: Cambridge Univ. Press, 1961; repr. 1979.

_____. "Shakespeare and the Music of the Elizabethan Stage: An Introductory Essay." *Shakespeare in Music.* Edited by Phyllis Hartnoll. New York: Macmillan and Co., Ltd., 1966.

Strauss, Richard, and Rolland, Romain. *Correspondence.* Edited by Rollo Myers. Berkeley and Los Angeles: Univ. of California Press, 1968.

Strunk, Oliver. *Source Readings in Music History.* New York: W. W. Norton, 1950.

Verchaly, André. "Introduction." *Airs de cour pour voix et luth.* Edited by André Verchaly. Paris: Publications de la Société Française de Musicologie, 1961.

_____. "Poésie et air de cour en France jusqu'à 1620." *Musique et poésie au XVIe siécle.* Paris: Centre National de la Recherche Scientifique, 1954. Pp. 211-24.

Walker, D. P. "Le chant orphique de Marsile Ficin." *Musique et poésie au XVIe siècle.* Paris: Centre National de la Recherche Scientifique, 1954. Pp. 17-34.

_____. "The Influence of *musique mesurée à l'antique*, particularly on the *airs de cour* of the Early Seventeenth Century." *Musica Disciplina,* II (1948), 141-163.

_____. "Musical Humanism in the Sixteenth and Early Seventeenth Centuries." *Music Review,* II (1941), 1-13, 111-21, 220-27, 288-308; III (1942), 55-71.

_____. "Some Aspects and Problems of *musique mesurée à l'antique.*" *Musica Disciplina,* IV (1950), 163-86.

Warlock, Peter (Philip Heseltine). *The English Ayre.* Westport, Conn.: Greenwood Press, 1970. First printed London: 1926.

Willetts, Pamela J. *The Henry Lawes Manuscript.* London: British Museum, 1969.

Yates, Frances A. *The French Academies of the Sixteenth Century.* Studies of the Warburg Institute, London. Nendeln, Liechtenstein: Kraus Reprints, 1968. First printed London: 1947.

Index

Index

When titles or first lines are listed under names of persons, the names refer to composers unless otherwise noted; the exception is Thomas Campion who is both poet and composer. For Campion's poems set by others, and for song texts whose musical settings are not referred to in the text, the composer's name is added in parentheses.

Jones, Robert, 107, 129
— "When love on time," 110-11
Jonson, Ben, 16, 186, 221, 240
— (poet), "Nay, nay, you must not stay" (*Oberon*), 186-87

"Lacrimae" (also spelled "Lachrymae"). *See* "Flow my tears"
Lament, 171-75 and Chapter 5 *passim*; "Ah, alas, you salt sea gods!" (Farrant), 172, 174-75, 193; *Ariadne Deserted* (Henry Lawes), 172-73, 201-09; *Hero and Leander* (Lanier), 172-73, 189-201; *Lamento d'Arriana* (Monteverdi), 172-73, 178, 179, 180-81
Lanier, Nicholas: syntax, musical setting of, 54, 188, 195, 198-200; textual rhythm, setting of, 187, 190, 198; influence of Italian style on, 189-90; 198, 200-201; musical rhetoric in, 196-201; attitude toward musical setting of, 200-01, 255; mentioned, 7
— "Bring away this sacred tree." *See* "Weep no more my wearied eyes"
— *Hero and Leander*, 172-73, 189-201
— "Unwilling Parting," 54
— "Weep no more my wearied eyes," 186, 187-89
Lawes, Henry: praised by poets, x, 7, 128, 256, 273-74n*41*; textual rhythm, musical setting of, 43, 46-48, 104, 166, 205-08; syntax, setting of, 54, 58-60, 208, 209, 248-50; thematic poetic structure, setting of, 62-63, 210-12; evidence of French style in, 93, 106; attitude toward musical setting of, 104-05, 116, 204-08, 248, 255; sound in poetry, setting of, 105, 206-07; versification, setting of, 116, 208, 209; accentual meter, setting of, 124, 152-61, 167-69, 206; dance in songs of, 151-61; evidence of Italian style in, 205; musical rhetoric in, 205, 208, 224, 248; stanzas, setting of, 248-50; mentioned, 127, 131-32, 146, 148, 172 and *passim*
— "A strife betwixt two CUPIDS," 156-58
— "A Willow Garland," 124, 154
— "Amidst the Mirtles," 154
— *Ariadne Deserted*, 172-73, 201-09
— "Beauty and love," 168-69

— "Break heart in twain," 63-64, 210-13, 263n*11*
— "Come, sad Turtle," 276n*23*
— "Hee that loves a Rosie cheeke," 62
— "I do confess," 152-54, 155-56
— "I Love thee for thy Fickleness," 152-53, 155-56
— "If I freely may discover," 104-05
— "Love thee! Good sooth, not I," 43
— "More than most fayre," 243-45
— "No, no, fair heretic," 46-48, 248-50, 277n*30*
— "O sweet woods," 265-66n*14*
— "On a Bleeding Lover," 155-56
— "Out upon it, I have lov'd," 167
— "Sufferance," 158-60
— "The Chyldish God of Love," 224-25, 243, 245
— "Though Cupid be a God," 268-69n*7*
— "Weep not, my dear," 58-60, 263n*5*, 263n*12*
— "When thou, poor excommunicate," 54, 56, 209-10
— "Whither are all her false oathes blown?" 105, 267n*37*
Lawes, William: accentual meter, musical setting of, 34-35; syntax, setting of, 34-35, 243, 244-46; versification, setting of, 55-57; musical rhetoric in, 224; mentioned, 7
— "Amarillis, tear thy hair," 243-44, 276n*26*
— "Gather ye rosebuds," 34-35
— "God of winds," 55-56, 224
— "He that will not love," 57-58
— "To whom shall I complain," 244-46
le Jeune, Claude, 97, 106
— "Voicy le verd et beau May," 89-90
Le Nouve Musiche (Giulio Caccini), 177
"Lettera amorosa," 178-82
"Look mistress mine," 226-27
"Love stood amazed," 40-41, 46, 262n*27*
"Love thee! Good sooth, not I," 43
"Love wing'd my hopes," 277n*30*
Lovelace, Richard, 16
— (poet), "The Chyldish God of Love," 225, 243, 245
"Love's Drollery." *See* "I Love thee for thy Fickleness"
Lute song: characteristics of, 75, 78-80; development of, 77-81, 93, 129-32;

Elise Bickford Jorgens received her Ph.D. in music at the City University of New York where, in 1976-77, she held an Andrew Mellon Postdoctoral Fellowship in the Humanities. She has lectured in both music and literature, and is now assistant professor of English at Western Michigan University.